KEY IDEAS in SOCIOLOGY

Martin Slattery

Published in 2003 by:
Nelson Thornes Ltd
Delta Place
27 Bath Road
CHELTENHAM
GL53 7TH
United Kingdom

03 04 05 06 07 / 10 9 8 7 6 5 4 3 2 1

A catalogue record for this book is available from the British Library

ISBN 0 7487 6565 4

Page make-up by Florence Production Ltd

Printed and bound in Spain by GraphyCems

Contents

The Classical: The Founding Fathers and their Contemporaries

Modern

Post-modern/Late Modern

An Introduction
and a Welcome

Key Ideas in Sociology was originally published in 1991 as an introduction to the great sociological ideas of the nineteenth and twentieth centuries. It was based on the *Key Ideas* series published by the current affairs magazine *New Society*, and it was aimed at students taking A-level or introductory courses in sociology and related social science courses.

It has now been completely rewritten and restructured to bring it up to date with current developments in social thinking as we leave the twentieth century and enter the twenty-first.

The focus of the book is on the key ideas that have – and are – driving sociology and social thinking forward as a means to understanding, interpreting and, in some cases, changing the world we live in

The book is organised into three main sections or periods – not because sociological ideas fall neatly into categories or specific periods of history; they certainly don't – but because such a division will help readers new to the subject gain some sense of its origins, its development, before and after the Second World War, and the way it is developing today as we enter the new millennium. Sociology has developed enormously over the past 150 years and its ideas have had a major impact on the development of society and on the thinking of ordinary people as well as on academics and even politicians. It has had much to say about the past. It has had even more to say about the future; about the state of society today, tomorrow and beyond. It is this desire to change society, to improve it and the lives of its inhabitants that still drives this subject, motivates its members and inspires its key thinkers. An historical perspective, a sense of history, is therefore critical if readers are to gain a real understanding of the key ideas of any period, what inspired them and why they have had the impact they have had. An introductory chapter is therefore included providing a brief overview of the historical development of sociological thinking and how the ideas in this book fit together.

As explained at the beginning, this is not a comprehensive guide to sociological theory, nor is it a textbook. It is simply an introduction – a starting point for students on A-level and introductory courses. To progress, readers need to read further and each section includes examples of suggested and further reading, including the publications of the key thinkers themselves.

Finally, sociology is not only about ideas, it is about debating ideas. Debate – often quite heated, even highly political – is at the heart of sociological thinking. It is the very lifeblood of this discipline and without debate the subject would shrivel up and die. Every one of the key ideas in this book has been the subject of intense, and at times quite bitter, debate. These, though, are the ideas that have stood the test of time, have contributed most to the development of the subject and to the development of society. These are the key ideas that have focused most on the key questions in sociology:

- the nature of society and the laws that govern it;
- the nature of history and the future of society;
- the nature of man and his relationship with the society in which he lives.

At the heart of sociology is the debate about man and society, about whether men and women make their own society and control their own destiny or whether society is something above and beyond its members, a supernatural entity with a mind and a destiny of its own and within which we are all subjects, pawns in a giant game of historical development governed not by man but by its own laws of destiny and development.

This sociological 'chicken and egg', this conundrum over the nature of man and the nature of society underpins all sociological thinking and is the primary basis for dividing sociologists into different perspectives, schools of thought or even opposing camps, be they Marxists and functionalists, post-industrialists or post-modernists. This is the nature and the nurture of sociology and out of this debate ideas move forward – or die out. This is the great strength of sociology, its great challenge as a subject and as a discipline if it is to continue to contribute to social thinking, social develop-ment and to the sociological imagination that has made this subject so popular and engaging over the past 50 years. Each section, therefore, includes a cross-reference to the other key ideas involved in a particular debate or discussion.

To sum up, this book is organised as follows:

- An introductory overview of key ideas in sociology in the nineteenth, twentieth and twenty-first centuries.
- A selection of the key ideas in sociology divided into three key periods:
  - the classical period of the founding fathers;
  - the modern period of the twentieth century pre and post World War II;
  - the post-modern or late modern period of the late twentieth century and the beginning of the twenty-first.
- An explanation and discussion of each idea divided into:
  - an outline of the key idea;
  - a review of the idea in action and the debate it inspired;
  - a cross-reference to other related key ideas;
  - suggested and further reading: the suggested reading is for keen and committed A-level students. The further reading is intended more for A-level teachers as background material and for undergraduate students on introductory degree courses.
- A bibliography of all the books cited.

I hope that this introduction is helpful. I hope that alongside your textbooks it offers an accessible and readable guide to the key ideas in sociology; ideas that have inspired great debate within the discipline; ideas that even today inform discussion across the social sciences; ideas that I hope will inspire you to think about and debate the great issues of our time. Maybe one day you, too, will have a great idea that will inspire others to think and even to act to improve and change the world we live in. That is the heart of the sociological challenge. That is what inspires the subject and that is what I hope will inspire you too.

Happy reading.

Dedication

I wish to dedicate this edition of *Key Ideas in Sociology* to my son, daughter and grandson, Ben, Rachel and Owen. I love them very much and I am very proud of them.

Acknowledgements

This is the second version of *Key Ideas in Sociology*. This time I would like to thank Rick Jackman of Nelson Thornes for his enthusiasm and encouragement in updating and extending this book, and his associate editors, Tracy and Elaine, for sorting out the detail.

My special thanks, however, go to Jacqueline, without whose loving support and encouragement this project would not have been completed.

Martin Slattery

The author and publishers would like to thank the following for permission to reproduce photographs:

Photo credits

- Bettman/Corbis (p.56, 72)
- Hulton Archive/Getty images (p.109)
- Hulton-Deutsch Collection/Corbis (p.67)
- Illustrated London News v2 (NT) (p.15)
- Mary Evans/Explorer/Lausat (p.165)
- Mary Evans Picture Library (p.39)
- Nigel Stead © London School of Economics (p.215)

A Brief History

Classical sociology: its origins and early years

THOUGH the history of social thought can be traced back to the earliest of civilisations – to the Greeks, Romans and Chinese – the history of sociological ideas as a distinct academic discipline is quite short – barely spanning the 150 years since Auguste Comte first coined the term 'sociology' (or, as he initially called it, social physics). Sociology as a subject emerged from the great ideas of its three founding fathers – Emile Durkheim, Max Weber and Karl Marx. The grand theories of this 'holy trinity' have laid the foundation for sociological thought and research ever since. They sought to discover the inner workings of society at large. They tried to explain what society is, what the relationship between society and the individual is, and what the dominant forces on social and historical change are.

- All three saw society as an entity in its own right.
- All three saw economic, political and ideological factors as crucial to social order and social change, though they differed radically in their interpretations of which factor(s) was the most important.
- All three sought to unravel that most complex of issues, the relationship between man and society – is society more than the sum of its members? Does it have a reality of its own and the ability to control the lives and destinies of those living within its structure? Or, is man a free agent, capable of controlling society and of determining his own future?

They identified the key issues for sociological analysis – issues such as social order and change, power and social control, inequality and social stratification – and laid down the foundations for sociology as a scientific discipline.

Durkheim, Weber and Marx, however, were not simply academics or armchair theorists. They honestly, and in Marx's case at least, passionately, believed that social analysis could change the world, that a science of society was not just a philosophical enterprise, but had the potential to improve society in the future. They, like many sociologists since, were inspired by the times they lived in. The eighteenth and nineteenth centuries in Western Europe experienced some of the great social, economic and political upheavals in human history; upheavals that were to change the face of Western society as three great 'revolutions' broke forth almost simultaneously – the economic, the political and the ideological:

- The great Agrarian, Industrial and Urban Revolutions of the seventeenth, eighteenth and nineteenth centuries which transformed Britain and then Europe and America from rural agricultural societies into advanced industrial economies based on urban structures and modern capitalism.
- The great political revolutions of the late eighteenth and nineteenth centuries which began with the French Revolution, swept away the old feudal power

structures and unleashed the forces of democracy, equality and freedom, and the ideologies of liberalism and socialism.

- The great Intellectual Revolution of the seventeenth and eighteenth centuries, the Enlightenment, the Age of Reason and the great Scientific Revolution which transformed Western ways of thinking, overthrew the dominance of religion and introduced 'science' as we know it today as a way of analysing, organising and controlling the world about us.

While today we are used to rapid change and accept it as part of modern life, to the men and women of the eighteenth and nineteenth centuries life was in turmoil and society seemed to be in the grip of forces beyond man's control. Traditional life, the very moral fabric and community spirit of the old order was being overturned and all the future seemed to offer was chaos and anarchy. It was against this background that the grand theories of Durkheim, Weber and Marx must be understood and appreciated. They had no modern computers, no specialist research teams, nothing but brilliant minds and profound social insight. Their true legacy is the fact that, even today, 100 years later, all three are major schools of thought within sociology; all three still inspire intense debate and detailed research.

This book can only offer a taste of their ideas and the key thinkers that followed, but it does highlight some of their chief concerns and the context within which their ideas evolved.

Durkheim's concept of social solidarity and Marx and Engels' theory of historical materialism were both major attempts to explain social order and change, and yet sought to capture the sense of anomie and alienation felt by individuals caught up in forces beyond their control. Though Weber also saw industrialisation as progressive, he too feared that modern man would soon be trapped in an 'iron cage', one created not by the underlying economic or social forces within society, but by its inner logic of thought and organisation, the techno-rationality that infused both the protestant ethic as the spirit of capitalism and bureaucracy as the major form of organisation in advanced societies.

Emile Durkheim legitimised sociology and established it as a respectable academic discipline. Building on the ideas of Auguste Comte, his focus was on social order and social evolution, on adaptation through reform, amid the collapse of traditional society and the growth of political and social conflict at the turn of the century. His focus on the underlying structures of society, on social facts and common morality (the collective conscience) laid the foundations for functional analysis and scientific sociology as we know it.

While Durkheim focused on *social order*, Karl Marx and his collaborator Friedrich Engels focused on social conflict. They even advocated political conflict and proclaimed *social revolution* as the underlying force in history and as the means to progressing from class-based societies to the classlessness of the communist utopia of the future. Drawing on the philosophical ideas of G.W.F. Hegel, the dominant force in German thought in the late nineteenth century, Marx turned Hegel on 'his head' using his own methodology – the dialectic – to develop a scientific theory of historical materialism which on the one hand sought to explain history and on the other presented a revolutionary plan for liberating the human spirit by transforming the social structure. Marx (1965) saw intellectual analysis not as a separate and distinct activity but as a prelude to action: *'The philosophers have only interpreted the world . . . the point however is to change it'*.

In particular, Marx focused his analysis on nineteenth-century capitalism within which he perceived all the ills of society – and the seeds of a future utopia. Capitalism and its underlying dynamic – the insatiable search for private profit – created a class-based society of intense inequality, exploitation and oppression. Beneath the surface, beneath the inherent contradictions and horrors of capitalism lay the basis for a class struggle that would eventually explode and propel society through revolution onto socialism and eventually communism. Marx's role, he believed, was to analyse *capitalism* and to prepare the proletariat, the vanguard of the Revolution, for their future role in making history, their history. While his contemporaries feared social change, Marx welcomed it. While his contemporaries worked in the lofty towers of university life, Marx lived on the streets hounded by the authorities across Europe and forced into exile finding final refuge and a little comfort in his last years in London. Marx was not a sociologist, more an economist, but the impact of his ideas on the twentieth-century world and on socio-logical thought has been immense. Societies and governments across Europe, Africa and Asia have been transformed in his name and even today, even after the collapse of the Berlin Wall and the Soviet Union, his ideas continue to inform post-modern sociology and socialist thinking.

While Durkheim heralded and became the founding father of French sociology, Max Weber emerged as the dominant figure in German sociological thought. Ironically, much of Weber's work was a 'debate with Marx' – not an outright rejection of his theories but a challenge and a revision, an attempt to restore the power of *ideas* to their place in history and an attempt to identify and analyse how far rationality, the spirit of reason, infused and informed modern capitalism and modern organisation as both a progressive and a regressive influence. Hence his claim that the ethic of Protestantism was as powerful an influence on the development of Western capitalism as the economic factors Marx proclaimed; hence Weber's analysis of bureaucracy as the embodiment of rational thought, planning and control in modern society, be it capitalist or socialist. While Weber saw rationality as the dominant force in developing modern society, he feared that it would crush individuality, spontaneity and creativity in the interests of efficiency and speed and so put modern man into 'an iron cage' from which there would be little escape. He, unlike Marx, foresaw the inherent dangers of the planned economies and authoritarian states that were likely to emerge under state socialism.

Though much of Weber's theory is underpinned by a conflict perspective, he was at heart a liberal – albeit a critical one – and so much more acceptable to the academic establishment and to the German authorities than his revolutionary counterpart. While Marx founded the Communist League, Weber founded – with his colleague Georg Simmel – the German Sociological Society (1910) and produced the wealth of middle-range theories and the wealth of insights that have informed European, British and even American sociology ever since.

These three great thinkers were not, however, the only important social theorists of the late nineteenth and early twentieth centuries. They simply laid the foundations of three of the major theoretical perspectives within modern sociology. Many other social theorists provided crucial insights and laid the foundations for what have become key themes within the sociological tradition.

- Auguste Comte founded positivism and the idea that sociology could and should be a science.

- Ferdinand Tönnies evoked the concepts *of gemeinschaft–gesellschaft* to express his fears about the 'loss of community in industrial society' and so founded the sociological tradition of community studies, which evolved into present-day urban sociology.

- Robert Michels, alongside colleagues such as Mosca and Pareto, established the sociology of power, especially of elite power, as a central focus of modern sociology.

- George Herbert Mead laid the foundations of symbolic interactionism.

- F.W. Taylor, though a businessman rather than an academic, preached the virtues of scientific management, an idea that has become a key concept and source of much debate in industrial sociology.

All these classical thinkers took, as the focus of their analyses, issues of central concern to Western society at the turn of the century – society at large, the individual in modern society, the causes and effects of social change. All helped to establish and spread the new discipline of sociology, though more among fellow academics than society at large. It is interesting to note the preponderance of European, especially German, thinkers in this age of grand theory. American and especially British sociology has always been more empirical and practical, more directed to factual evidence and social policy than abstract theory. In contrast to the grand theory developing within European sociology, British sociology, for example, was founded on a more insular, empirical and pragmatic tradition with a focus on highly detailed sociological studies, scientifically based rather than theoretical in nature and driven by the desire to reform society rather than transform it. Grand theorists like Herbert Spencer, for example, provoked greater interest abroad and in America than in Victorian Britain – though his idea of social Darwinism was later of some influence on the New Right ideas of the Conservative governments of the 1980s and 1990s.

Modern sociology: the twentieth century

IN the twentieth century, sociological thought became more professional and technical, more specifically academic, specialist and university based. While brilliant individuals like Durkheim, Marx and Weber, with encyclopaedic knowledge and an enormous breadth of vision and sociological insight, do still exist and occasionally come to the fore, modern sociology is primarily an academic profession conducted in universities and divided into specialist sub-disciplines concentrating on such 'sociologies' as education, development, deviance and so on. While some continue to develop abstract theory, others using modern computer techniques and quantitative analysis have opened up whole areas of social life to surveys and other forms of empirical research. Schools of sociology and research programmes characterise modern sociology more than outstanding individual thinkers.

Similarly, the grand theories of the founding fathers which sought to take in and explain every aspect of modern society have tended to give way to what Robert Merton has called 'theories of the middle-range' – more limited concepts or theoretical explanations of one particular area or topic in sociology. Examples of this approach include Basil Bernstein's idea of linguistic codes in education and Howard Becker's theory of labelling in the study of deviance. Equally, the Chicago School in America and the Frankfurt School in Germany exemplified the team approach, an approach whereby 'schools' of sociologists using a common theoretical framework have sought to analyse and explain a wide range of contemporary social issues.

The great exception to this decline of grand theory in the modern period was Talcott Parsons' idea of structural functionalism. As its title so clearly shows, this was a highly technical and very abstract theory of social order and change. Though inspired by such European thinkers as Simmel, Weber and, especially, Durkheim, Parsons' schema reflected the emergence of American sociology on to the Western scene and, like much else American in this period, dominated Anglo-American sociology to the point that most sociology in the 1940s and 1950s was structural-functionalist in perspective. The rise of 'new', more radical sociologies in the 1960s was in part inspired by a desire to throw off the theoretical 'shackles' of structural functionalism and to revive sociology by turning back to the great ideas of Marx and Weber.

Just as the nineteenth century was an age of revolution, so the twentieth century, too, experienced major economic, political and social upheavals – two world wars, the Russian and Chinese Revolutions and the spread and collapse of communism; Germany, Italy, Spain and the rise of fascism; Hitler, Stalin and the growth of the totalitarian state; the Cold War and the Nuclear Arms Race; the Great Crash and the economic depressions of the 1930s and 1970s; the collapse of the great European empires; the spread of nationalism and emergence of Third World nations into world politics and the world economy; and the globalisation of world markets, world politics and world communication. Issues like these have inspired and informed many sociological theories such as A. Gunder Frank's concern with the relationship of dependency that exists between First and Third World nations, and C.W. Mills' concern about the power of the modern state. Underlying many of these ideas is a concern, even fear, for the individual in modern mass society – a fear that he is oppressed, alienated and manipulated – a fear epitomised by the Frankfurt School's 'critical theory' and by the Chicago School's studies of the inner cities as it sought to plot the plight of urban man. Similarly, many of the ideas of the 1960s were directly inspired by, and also acted as inspirations for revolution, revolutions such as those by students in Britain, America and Europe in the 1960s – revolutions which reflected a growing concern about civil rights and the rights and freedoms of 'minority and oppressed' groups. Blacks, women and gays became the new 'underclasses' which have replaced or joined the working class as the basis of the new theories of radical change or social reform, theories such as Ralf Dahrendorf's 'notion of conflict' and feminists' 'theory of patriarchy'.

The best way, however, to view much modern sociology is as a debate – a debate either with contemporary theorists or with the founding fathers, a debate about how sociology generally, or about how particular sub-disciplines within sociology should progress and develop. For example, while Western sociology in general, and Anglo-American sociology in particular, in the 1930s and immediate post-war years, reflected the dominance of structural functionalism, the late 1960s and early 1970s saw a theoretical revolution which affected and infected sociology everywhere. Younger, more radical sociologists threw off the conservative mantle of structural functionalism in search of more exciting theories which could explain more clearly the growth of violence, conflict and group struggle in Western society as student revolution, black power, women's rights and environmental groups poured on to the streets in protest. Some turned to the conflict-based ideas of Marx and Weber, others used phenomenology in its various forms (symbolic interactionism, ethnomethodology) to challenge the sociological establishment and the dominance of functionalism and positivism. Hence the emergence of labelling theory, the sociology of development, urban sociology, neo-Marxism and neo-Weberian ideas. Hence the renewed debate about sociology as a science and a renewed focus in theory and research on the individual, small groups and personal relationships. This challenge, however, was not just of new against old, but also female against male as the feminist assault on the male establishment grew in force and numbers. Just as sociologists never refer to 'founding mothers', so feminists highlighted the invisibility of half the human race from virtually all sociological perspectives. It was simply taken for granted that male sociologists were capable of representing women as well as their own sex. Feminists forced the issues of gender and patriarchy on to the sociological agenda and established 'women's studies' as an accepted sub-discipline within sociology and even as a discipline in its own right. How far male sociologists have incorporated gender issues into their analyses is still highly debatable. A similar 'revolution' in male thinking has yet to occur.

These debates raged across the whole of sociology and within particular sub-disciplines. Hence, for example, the secularisation debate between Bryan Wilson and David Martin in the field of religion, the Rostow–Frank debate on development in the Third World and T.S. Kuhn's critique of traditional views of science and knowledge. What is significant throughout all these discussions is the extent to which, in this search for new ideas, younger sociologists turned again to the founding fathers for inspiration. Durkheim, Weber and, in particular, Marx again became the centre of sociological thought and debate. No one theoretical perspective dominated in the way structural functionalism did in the period 1930 to 1960, but Marxist ideas proliferated in the 1970s and early 1980s and continued to be highly influential, right up until the collapse of the Berlin Wall in 1989 and the implosion of communist regimes of Eastern Europe in the 1990s. Marxism was never restricted solely to sociological thought. It influenced thinking throughout the social sciences, humanities, and even extended into such fields as literature, art and science. Equally, it was never a single creed with only one orthodoxy, but always the subject of intense, often bitter, debate and re-interpretation. Even in his own time Marx had to disclaim the way some of his followers interpreted his ideas, even to the point of declaring, 'As for me, I am not a Marxist'. The incomplete and very complex nature of his writings, their popularisation by Friedrich Engels and the ever-changing nature of the real world have all added fuel to the argument about the validity of Marx's theory which is as strong today as ever it was 100 years ago. While much of nineteenth-century sociology developed as a 'debate with Marx', early Marxism after Marx's death was a debate on his behalf, a debate that sought to develop his thesis further, notably on the economic laws underlying history and on the role of the individual in progressing the revolution. Marx's legacy to the twentieth century has been the essential and apparent contradiction between the economic determinism in his later writings and his earlier Humanist period during which he focused on the individual and on man's consciousness and capacity for change. While orthodox Marxists, led by Engels, proclaimed the inevitability of the collapse of capitalism, the Hegelian Marxists sought to restore the revolutionary potential of the individual to make his own history. This tradition of twentieth-century Marxism – humanism – can be traced back to the work of Georg Lukacs, and it exploded – largely in response to the inflexible arrogance of orthodox Marxism and to the disasters of socialist revolutions in Russia and Eastern Europe – through critical theory and the work of the Frankfurt School of the 1920s and 30s, a school of thought composed of theorists forced to flee Nazi Germany and to seek refuge in the very heartland of Western capitalism, the United States of America. Follow the ideas of the Frankfurt School and those of Antonio Gramsci, Louis Althusser, Harry Braverman and Jürgen Habermas – and you will get some idea of the ebb and flow of modern Marxism as current events have challenged and contradicted the original ideas of its author and authority, Karl Marx; most notably the fact that the modern working class, far from rising up in revolution and over-throwing the capitalist state, has now virtually disappeared from the sociological scene altogether – or so it appears.

While sociology as an academic tradition and as a blueprint for social change and even revolution was born in Europe, it grew up and enjoyed its adolescence in America in the 1920s, 30s and 60s. At a time when Europe was submerged beneath world war, mass unemployment and the rise of fascism, America continued to enjoy the fruits and freedoms of capitalism and remained the land of the free in the face of the 'iron fists' of fascism and communism that dominated Europe and Asia at that time.

In contrast to the conservative ideology that pervaded European sociology at the turn of the century, American sociology grew up in the political environment of liberalism and individualism. America was already the 'Land of the Free', the 'Land of Plenty'. Men and women fled from the constraints and class oppression and poverty of Europe to join the American Dream and the opportunities for individual fulfilment offered by American capitalism and democracy. There was no need for social revolution, merely reform; there was no need to change capitalism for socialism, only the need to maintain competition and the rights of the individual (or at least those of white men). The challenge for America in the 1920s was not historical change but one of maintaining order amid individualism, of maintaining American capitalism in the face of its inherent ills and evils. Hence the attractiveness to American sociology of:

- Herbert Spencer and evolutionary sociology; its 'scientific' claims to justifying the survival of the fittest and its underlying belief in moral as well as social progress appealed greatly to American Puritanism and to Americans' sense of being a chosen people. Spencer's ideas of social Darwinism influenced theorists like William Sumner and C.H. Cooley, but with the advent of two world wars and a mass depression, ideas of *inevitable* and everlasting social progress seemed unsustainable even in America.

- Georg Simmel and his perceptions on urban life and urban man provoked and stimulated the Chicago School of the 1900s under its founder Albion Small, and later informed the work of Robert Park and his associates in their studies of urban America in the 1920s and 1930s. George Herbert Mead (1863–1931) and the theory of symbolic interactionism was the other main tradition to emerge out of the 'Chicago' period, drawing on the one hand on Simmel's interest in interaction and on the other on Mead's insights into consciousness. It was, however, the writings of Herbert Blumer (1900–87) and his colleagues that encouraged and enabled symbolic interactionism to flourish and to spread in the 1960s and 1970s.

- Durkheim and Weber stimulated the ideas of Talcott Parsons and so underpinned the development of structural functionalism in the 1930s. Parsons introduced the European founding fathers to American sociology as the basis for a theory of social action and social system; a theory that dominated the whole of Western sociology until its downfall in the late 1960s.

- Karl Marx: while Talcott Parsons rejected Marx in favour of the more evolutionary and liberal theories of Durkheim and Weber, the Frankfurt School of Critical Theory sought to rejuvenate and revive Marxist theory after the horrors of Nazism and Soviet socialism – even if they had to flee from Nazi Germany to capitalist America and Columbia University to do so. Thus, ironically, a key powerhouse of Marxian theory moved to the very centre of western capitalism to escape the dictatorships of Eastern Communism. The humanism of critical theory, the liberalism adopted from Max Weber and the adoption of a highly academic approach using social scientific methodology made the Frankfurt theorists more acceptable to American establishment; less of a radical threat even in the years of McCarthyism and its communist purges. Marxism equally informed C.W. Mills' radical critique of post-war American society; his claim that right at the heart of American democracy lay a power elite, an industrial military complex every bit as powerful and unaccountable as the communist dictatorships America was fighting in the Cold War and in Eastern Europe and Asia. Such left-wing ideas, however, never had a major or lasting influence on American sociology or on American society at large. While American universities seethed with unrest in the 1960s and 70s, they seethed over civil rights not class welfare.

The post-war era, and in particular the 1960s and 1970s, saw a radical change in modern sociology, a revolution in sociological thought that reflected the revolution on the streets of Western society. After the stability of the post-war period, Europe and America exploded into violence as the growing demands and expectations of consumers and the frustrations and anger of the exploited and oppressed reached breaking point. Capitalism itself was under pressure to provide for the masses, while governments throughout the Western world faced protest on the streets from those demanding their rights and their equality in a democratic society – the unions and the working class, women's lib and women's rights, black power and gay rights. And at the forefront of such protests was a new generation of students, young radicals prepared to take to the streets and to face the police and army on behalf of minorities and the oppressed and in protest against the Vietnam War.

Western societies and American cities were almost literally exploding in an orgy of protest, confrontation and revolution. Contemporary sociology, and structural functionalism in particular, could not explain such fundamental conflicts over rights and opportunities, so Western sociology turned to more radical, conflict-based theories – to theories such as neo-Marxism and neo-feminism and to interpretative sociology, to theories and ideas that sought to explain social conflict and to look at society from the individual's perspective, from the perspective of everyday life. Structural functionalism and the ideas of social consensus could not withstand such pressure and so they gave way in the 1970s and 1980s to newer, more radical ideas, notably:

- Marxism and neo-Marxism within the works of writers such as Louis Althusser, Manuel Castells, Nico Poulanzas, Antoni Gramsci and the critical theorists of both the original Frankfurt School and the second generation led by Jürgen Habermas. The fall of the Berlin Wall and the collapse of the Soviet Union in the 1990s, however, in turn took the ground from under the feet of neo-Marxist writers and led some to accept defeat (e.g. Aronson 1995) and forced others to re-evaluate the relevance of Marxist ideas in a post-modern world.
- Feminism and feminist theory. What started as a liberal movement fighting for equal rights grew in the 1960s and 70s into more radical, even revolutionary, critiques, not only of patriarchy within society at large but of the masculine bias inherent within traditional sociology, and the sociological establishment. Feminism is today an international movement, women's studies a whole new academic discipline, and feminist theory a new intellectual and academic paradigm. What began as a 'minority movement' is now a mainstream study.
- Phenomenology and its theoretical framework of interpretative sociology; its focus on the world of everyday life and conscious interaction. A major offshoot of this

perspective was Harold Garfinkel's work on ethnomethodology and its fundamental challenge to positivist sociology about the use and appropriateness of scientific method in sociological study.

Post-modern sociology: the late twentieth century and the new millennium

THE modern era of sociology, the period prior to and shortly after the Second World
War, was a period rich in debate and sociological development, but equally one in
which the classical ideas of the founding fathers were severely tested by contemporary
events. The ideas of Karl Marx in particular, so powerful and prominent throughout
the twentieth century, were left in a heap with the collapse of the Berlin Wall and the
implosion of East European communism. Instead of capitalism collapsing, it was
communism which collapsed, and a whole new world, a post-modern world in which
capitalism is as all powerful and all pervasive in the Third World as it is in the First,
seemed to be emerging. Newer sociologies, post-modern sociologies, have entered the
sociological arena to explain and debate the global and post-modern society in which
we now apparently live.

The term *post-modern* is a strange one to anyone new to sociology. The prefix 'post'
seems to imply something beyond modern, yet what can be beyond today except the
future? This is part of the thinking behind this term. It is a concern about future society,
its shape and structure and its implications for the individual. It is, however, more than
that for the sociologists who use it. It is a deliberate attempt to formally state that
society today – and in the future – is distinctly different from society in the past.
Society today in the view of post-modern thinkers is a distinctly different society in
nature and in structure to anything that has gone before. It is not merely the next stage
of social, industrial or historical development; it is a new type of society, a new form
of social structure that requires a completely new sociological perspective or paradigm
to understand it. Sociologists of this persuasion include the French writers Jean
Baudrillard and Jean François Lyotard and the post-structuralist philosopher Michel
Foucault.

Inevitably not all sociologists agree with this stance and many fundamentally oppose
it, rejecting the term post-modern and the assumptions behind it. They argue instead
that society is still evolving, that present day and future society *do* reflect much of the
past and that both modern and especially classical sociological thinking still have much
to offer contemporary sociology. Anthony Giddens, from a liberal perspective, for
example, and Jürgen Habermas, from a Marxist framework, still base their ideas and
their theories on the optimism and the faith in reason and rationality that dates back
to the Age of Enlightenment of the eighteenth century. Giddens uses the term *late
modernity* in contrast to post-modernity to emphasise the continuity of the present
with the past. He rejects the notion of a fundamental break in sociological development while fully recognising that we now live in a new era, a global era and a world
society. Though post-modernists tend to have a very pessimistic view about the future
and paint a very gloomy picture of the twenty-first century, Giddens and Habermas,
whatever their misgivings about the present, hope and believe that common sense and
reason will prevail and so enable man to regain control of the world he has created,
before this 'juggernaut' as Giddens describes it, gets completely out of control and
destroys us all.

This debate about the nature of contemporary and future society – whether it is post-
modern or late modern – is at the heart of sociology today as today's key thinkers seek

either to bring the great ideas of the past up to date and apply them to contemporary society; or seek to break with them altogether in the search for a new post-modern/post-structuralist paradigm or theoretical framework.

The post-modern section of this book seeks to reflect this debate by making extensive use of the term 'post', be it post-modern, post-structuralist, post-industrial or post-Fordism. The key topics of contemporary debate nevertheless remain the same, namely:

- the nature and structure of society;
- the nature and relationship between the individual and society;
- the nature and structure of the modern state and its relationship with society and the individual.

These three key themes are as well reflected in post-modern sociology as in the past. They are as essential to the key ideas included in this section of the book as they were to the ideas of the classical and modern eras. They inform the post-modern debates as much as debates in the past, debates such as:

- The nature of post-industrial society and the key characteristics of industrial life today. This debate originated with the ideas of Daniel Bell in the 1960s and 70s about the future of industrial society and this has been a key theme in the post-Fordist debate on the nature of modern industrial organisations.
- The nature of the world economy and world society. Here the ideas of Anthony Giddens on globalisation, Manuel Castells on informational society and Ulrich Beck on risk society have led the way in seeking to analyse and understand the nature and the implications of global capitalism and the global world with the development of a world economy and the communications revolution inspired by the Internet. We are moving as citizens, consumers and individuals into a *world* society, a world of great opportunity, with the potential to create a global community that is fairer and more peaceful; it is equally a world of intense risk (Beck), a potential 'juggernaut' (Giddens) that could run out of control if the issues underlying world terrorism, world poverty and global warming are not addressed. We have the technology, as Manuel Castells clearly reminds us, but do we have the will and the will power to regain control of the future?
- The nature of culture in modern society and its impact on the individual. Culture appears to be a much more powerful feature in society today, given the power of the media, the growth of consumerism and the age of leisure. Stuart Hall and his colleagues at Birmingham University led the way in the 1970s in establishing cultural studies as a force in post-war sociology and in establishing this field of study as an independent discipline in its own right. Their writing raised the profile of culture as a force in society and their analysis of youth culture, class culture and minority lifestyles reflected the fundamental changes occurring in post-modern society.

The individual, his or her identity and the culture of modern society has developed as a key theme in contemporary sociology and particularly in post-modern writings. We live in a much more individualistic society, a society where class and a sense of community no longer seem evident; where consumerism, materialism and lifestyle seem to be the primary considerations in life. Jean Baudrillard and Jean François Lyotard laid the foundations for the post-modern view that society today is no longer 'real'. It is a virtual reality, offering man a material utopia but one that is devoid of any real content or creative culture, soul or sense of spirit. The individual is portrayed as a cultural zombie, helpless, seduced and manipulated and incapable of independent action. Such writers paint a very grim and bleak picture of the future and one that gets even worse when reading the ideas of Michel Foucault and his post-structural analysis of the way 'Big Brother' is all around and all powerful. In contrast, Anthony Giddens' notion of structuration is almost light relief and his attempt to plot the relationship between the 'actions' of the individual and the structure of society is both liberating and refreshing in an age when apathy, alienation and isolation seem rife.

- The nature of power and the role of the modern state equally remain critical themes in sociological analysis and here the influence of Marx and Weber continue to inform and infuse sociological debate. Jürgen Habermas's study of legitimation is but one element in his project to comprehensively analyse modern society. It provides profound insights, nevertheless, into the way modern governments seek to maintain and legitimise their power amid the inevitable crises that modern capitalism creates. Giddens, in contrast, and from a more liberal, Weberian position, has sought to provide the New Labour government in Britain with a 'Third Way', a middle ground for combining socialist and democratic ideals in a capitalist world. Nicos Poulantzas' notion of relative autonomy, and particularly the ideas of Louis Althusser, have been attempts to revive and revitalise modern Marxism in analysing the state in capitalist societies and in rescuing Marxism as a theoretical and political force after the atrocities of Soviet socialism made it seem morally bankrupt and politically unacceptable.

Thus these three key themes remain as central to sociology today as they were in the past and although the founding fathers are no longer so influential, the discipline has sought to respond to the changing nature of society today and to the way global capitalism and its underlying ethics are influencing and promoting individualism, consumerism and a huge variety of lifestyles. Class and community no longer seem to be the key characteristics of society today. Human rights and equal opportunity do, and such ideological forces may in the future shift the balance of power away from the state and back to the individual. Certainly the feminist movement has not only championed the liberation of minority rights but has itself now become more focused on the lives, ambitions and lifestyles of women at large. Those, however, who believed that the gender war had been won, received a severe chastising recently from one of its founding sisters, Germaine Greer, in her recent publication *The Whole Woman* (2000).

Sociology today, therefore, is for many at a crossroads. Some have rejected altogether the agendas and frameworks of thought proposed by the founding fathers. Others have continued to use such key ideas but have adapted and amended them in proposing new ways of interpreting the world before us. The founding fathers no longer dominate sociological thinking. For many, Marxism and structural functionalism are dead and have no future. For others, the society before us, the world we are about to inherit and inhabit, is so different to that in the past that the ideas of the past no longer have any relevance or application. As Thomas Kuhn (1962) would say, there is no dominant paradigm in sociology today. It is yet again in a state of revision and revolution.

Nevertheless, as we enter the twenty-first century, as we enter the new millennium, sociology is as rich and varied as ever before. Its primary characteristics remain diversity and, beneath the surface, division; a division that may soon emerge as a battle between modernists seeking to maintain the sociological traditions and methodologies of the past and to apply them to the new post-industrial era, and post-modernists whose view of the world is so fundamentally different that only a new sociology will do. In between, the pressures to reflect and represent all spectrums of social experience within a multicultural sociology have led some to celebrate its rich diversity, others to despair of it ever achieving intellectual coherence and continuity. Whatever the outcome, as this book hopefully reflects, sociology continues to provoke and challenge, stir and stimulate thinking about the past and the future and the risks and uncertainties before us. Whether sociology can illuminate the twenty-first century in the way that the founding fathers illuminated our understanding of the twentieth century, remains to be seen. Such intellectual giants are a hard act to follow and the risks and uncertainties before us in the age of the Internet, biotechnology and genetic engineering desperately needs a new guiding light, a new Holy Trinity capable of not only understanding the underlying forces of post-industrial society but of identifying the new moral order needed to support its progress and survival. The alternative – as all three founding fathers feared at the turn of the twentieth century – is chaos and anarchy, division and conflict, anomie and alienation in a moral vacuum, a virtual reality where man's ever material need – and want – can be met, but where his spiritual and moral needs remain vacant and unfulfilled. We may have the means to a perfect life but is materialism enough? The individual may be God but has individualism and privatisation got to the point where all else has collapsed or is under such threat that it can no longer fulfil its social functions and hold society together – the family, the church, the education system, the government are all victims of society's disillusion with authority. Only the media seems to reign supreme and at what price? The founding fathers put moral values at the heart of their analyses. Are we today, however, a 'heartless' society, a society without a common sense of values and humanity to guide, inform and inspire us?

The challenge for sociology today is as great, if not greater than that facing the founding fathers of twentieth-century sociology. Who will lead us into the twenty-first century or has sociology also lost its way and diversified to such a point that it has little more to say? There are signs of a return to grand theory, but will it be grand enough and accessible enough to have the power and inspiration of a Marx, Weber or Durkheim? What will be the key ideas of the twenty-first century? Who will star in the next edition of this book?

This, then, is a very brief overview of the key ideas in sociology and in particular of the key ideas covered in this book. It is incomplete and sketchy and any serious appreciation of the value and excitement of theoretical ideas can only come by follow-up reading using the references below. Social theory, however, is never easy, and often made all the more difficult by the abstract language in which it is written. It does require real effort, imagination and careful thought if you are really to get to grips with it. Make that effort, read as much as you can and you will find it extremely rewarding. It will help make sense of sociology in general, but, more important, help you to understand the society in which you live. These key ideas are just a start. Hopefully they will inspire you to read further and deeper in a field of fascinating insights and ideas. Maybe they will change the way you think. Maybe they will change your life.

Suggested reading

THE following texts offer valuable and up-to-date reviews of sociological theory that are reasonably accessible to the advanced A-level student and well worth reading:

CUFF, E.C., SHARROCK, W.W. AND FRANCIS, D.W. (1998) *Perspectives in Sociology*, 4th edition, Routledge, London – an update of a traditional A-level introduction to sociological theory.

HAMILTON, P. (ED.) Key Sociologists and Key Ideas series, Tavistock, London – a short, very readable and accessible series.

O'DONNELL, M. (2001) *Classical and Contemporary Sociology: Theory and Issues*, Hodder & Stoughton, London – highly recommended from a leading A-level textbook writer.

PAMPEL, F.C. (2000) *Sociological Lives and Ideas: An Introduction to the Classical Theorists*, Macmillan, Basingstoke – a valuable and quite readable background text to Marx, Durkheim, Weber, Simmel and George Herbert Mead, setting out their key ideas in the context of their times and their personal influences. Worth dipping into.

RITZER, G. (1996) *Sociological Theory*, McGraw Hill, New York, 4th edition – a very thorough and comprehensive review of sociological theory from classical to modern times by an authority in this field. This is not a text for the faint hearted and is probably more for school or college libraries and for updating teachers in this field.

STONES, R. (ED.) (1998) *Key Sociological Thinkers*, Macmillan, Basingstoke – an ambitious overview of 21 of the most influential thinkers in sociology from Marx and Durkheim to Foucault and Giddens, with a chapter on each key thinker written by a leading figure in this field today. Valuable background or library text that can be dipped into chapter by chapter.

Further reading

THE following texts are much more advanced reviews and more suited to A-level teachers and/or undergraduate students than to students studying A-level.

ANDERSEN, H. AND KASPERSEN L.B. (EDS.) (2000) *Classical and Modern Social Theory*, Blackwell, Oxford.

CALLINICOS, A. (1999) *Social Theory: A Historical Introduction*, Polity Press, Cambridge.

ELLIOTT, A. AND TURNER, B.S. (EDS.) (2001) *Profiles in Contemporary Social Theory*, Sage, London.

MAY, T. (1996) *Situating Social Theory*, Oxford University Press, Oxford.

MILES, S. (2001) *Social Theory in the Real World*, Sage, London.

SEIDMAN, S. AND ALEXANDER, J.C. (EDS.) (2001) *The New Social Theory Reader: Contemporary Debates*, Routledge, London.

SWINGLEWOOD, A. (2000) *A Short History of Sociological Thought*, 3rd edition, Macmillan, Basingstoke.

Finally, 'surf' the Internet. Search out the latest ideas and critiques of your favourite thinkers, incorporate them into your notes and into your own thinking. Then join in the debate yourself with the thinkers of today about the 'Key Ideas' of tomorrow. Happy hunting.

Alienation

Karl Marx

HAVE YOU EVER FELT 'ALIEN' OR 'ALIENATED'? HAVE YOU EVER FELT THAT EVERYONE IS against you, that you are a stranger in your own home, a foreigner in your own land, that no-one understands you and that you feel isolated, rejected and divorced from the people around you, whether they be your parents, your family, your friends, or just the people in your local community or town? You feel that you no longer belong and you feel a deep and profound sense of anger and frustration. Pretty strong feelings, no doubt, that on the one hand make you feel inadequate, inferior and unwanted; and on the other hand make you feel passionately angry, resentful and determined to prove people wrong and to re-establish your rightful place in your group, society or community. Such feelings, such passions inspire either fatalism, an acceptance of alienation, of inferiority and of being displaced, 'homeless' even; or a fervent, passionate, even radical determination to change the situation, to change the world and make it more friendly, humane and inviting.

From a sociological and political point of view you can see in these words, the seeds of a radical, even revolutionary theory of how the world is – because people just accept it – and one of how the world could be if people were inspired to rise up and seek to change it, to make it a more human, friendly and just place. This indeed was the inspiration for Karl Marx as a young radical living in a period of immense and intense change, the Age of Revolution that swept across Europe in the eighteenth and nineteenth centuries:

- the political revolutions in America, France and Europe;
- the economic revolutions that transformed Western societies from rural and agrarian communities to urban and industrial powerhouses;
- the scientific and intellectual revolution that not only inspired completely new ideas about the universe and about nature but also led to the development of modern science and the revolutionary ideas of the Enlightenment about the rights of man and the nature of society;

- the nationalist movements that swept across Europe and led to the unification of Germany, Italy and many other principalities and territories.

The range and depth of social change during this time was enormous and quite awesome. No-one seemed to be in control and so inevitably for most ordinary people there was an intense, uncontrollable feeling of helplessness, of being displaced, of being swept away by forces beyond their control, away from the homes and rural communities they belonged to, into the new and frightening world of the industrial factory and the urban city. How could all this change be explained? How could it be brought under control, and how could it be made less alienating, more welcoming, more humane?

Explaining this avalanche, this tidal wave of change, was the task that the young Karl Marx set himself in developing his initial ideas about capitalism and the capitalist revolution; changing this world for a better one, for a communist one, was the task that the older, more mature Marx set about in his later, more theoretical and scientific analyses and his call for a communist revolution.

As a Jew, born and brought up in Germany, Marx himself felt alienated, something of an alien or foreigner in his own country. As a radical writer and revolutionary activist forced to flee from Germany and then Paris, living in poverty with his family in London, he made himself homeless and an alien, unwanted in his homeland in the Rhineland and feared throughout Western Europe for his revolutionary activities. The 'Red Doctor' was refused citizenship even at one time by the British government and died in London in 1853. He may have died alone and in poverty, but as his colleague Friedrich Engels predicted at his graveside, 'His name will endure through the ages and so will his work'. Born in an age of revolution,

Karl Marx

Marx's ideas swept across Europe in the late nineteenth century and dominated the political history of the twentieth century. They inspired the communist revolutions in Russia and Eastern Europe, China and Asia, Africa and South America, and laid the basis for the communist-capitalist confrontations of the Cold War that followed World War II. No writer has inspired such radical change, no writer has inspired such passion and hatred, no writer has influenced the history of modern man as greatly as Karl Marx.

Karl Marx's key work, *Das Kapital* (1970), was a 'scientific' study of capitalism as an economic system and mode of production. His study of alienation was in contrast a study of the social, psychological and personal effects of capitalism on people's feelings and self-image. For Marx, capitalism is not only an unjust and inefficient system of economic production, it is an immoral and exploitative one, one that denies man his true nature, separates him from the products of his own labour and sets man against man in an economic 'jungle'. For Marx the essence of human nature, what distinguishes man from the animals, is his consciousness, his imagination, his ability to control his own environment. This power is most clearly expressed in the productive process where, by working together, men transform nature – felling trees to make houses, clearing forests to make roads. However, whenever this form of self-expression and social co-operation is in any way limited or thwarted, then alienation will occur.

In the *Paris Manuscripts* of 1844 (quoted in Bottomore and Rubel 1961) Marx outlined four key forms of alienation:

- When the worker has lost control of the end product. What he has produced, be it a table or chair, is no longer his but owned by his employer.
- When, through the extensive division of labour in modern factories, the worker no longer feels involved in the production process. He is merely 'a cog in the wheel', motivated not by the intrinsic satisfaction of work but only by the extrinsic one of the wage at the end of the week.
- When relationships between workers are not those of colleagues but of rivals, competitors for jobs, bonuses and promotion; and those between employer and worker are not the relationships of equals but of master and slave, as employers seek to maximise the profits from their workforce.
- Whenever the individual is denied the true essence of his human nature – self-expression through work. His work no longer feels part of him, nor represents his true talents. It is no longer a source of pride and achievement.

In Marx's own words: *'In what does this alienation of labour consist? First, that the work is external to the worker, that it is not a part of his nature, that consequently he does not fulfil himself in his work but denies himself, has a feeling of misery, not of well-being, does not develop freely a physical and mental energy, but is physically exhausted and mentally debased. The worker therefore feels himself at home only during his leisure, whereas at work he feels himself homeless. His work is not voluntary but imposed, forced labour. It is not the satisfaction of a need, but only a means for satisfying other needs. Its alien character is clearly shown by the fact that as soon as there is no physical or other compulsion it is avoided like the plague. Finally, the alienated character of work for the worker appears in the fact that it is not his work but for someone else, that in work he does not belong to himself but to another person'* (Bottomore and Rubel 1961).

Workers are therefore alienated from their work, from the products of their labour, from other workers and ultimately from their true selves. As Friedrich Engels argued, *'Nothing is more terrible than being constrained to do alone one thing every day from morning to night against one's will'* (quoted in Ritzer 1996: 59). Work becomes torture and so men turn elsewhere for release and a sense of control. They turn to drink and depression or to consumerism and a privatised lifestyle.

Although in Marx's analysis of history all previous economic systems involved a class structure and exploitative relationships and so generated a sense of alienation, capitalism does so more markedly – not only because exploitation is at its highest in such societies but because its 'market forces' lead to men being treated not as individuals but merely as another commodity of production to be used or discarded as the need arises. Only in a classless society, where the means of production are communally owned, will, Marx predicted, alienation be eliminated forever. Amid the abundance of modern mass production, 'communist' man would no longer work simply to survive, no longer specialise in one form of production or career but be free to express all his talents all of the time – to fish in the morning, hunt in the afternoon and criticise in the evening. All social divisions be they gender, or of race, town or country, brain or brawn, will, he predicted, disappear amid a society of equal individuals and communal care.

While man creates the social world through his own activity, the capitalist world is a world that people experience as alien and oppressive, a world in which relationships are experienced not personally but as things. '*Political economy does not deal with the proletarian as a human being but "as a draught horse, as a beast whose needs are strictly limited to bodily needs"*.' (Marx 1963). Although for Marx the proletariat is the most alienated social class in capitalist society, in his view even capitalists in their search for profit inhabit an alienated world. Even among the rich and wealthy, work and relationships are dehumanised and instead of work being an expression of human creativity, it is a denial of man's potential and an obstacle to building a truly human community. Man and his work in capitalist societies are fragmented by the division of labour and the division of ownership. Capitalist society is by definition built on alienated labour as the capitalist seeks to exploit the working class, extracting the surplus value of work from the proletariat as profit and as capital. Workers are alienated from the very fruits of their own labour. Work is no longer a means in itself but simply a means to survival.

In his later writings, Marx developed a more deterministic approach which portrayed man in a more passive mode. In *Gründrisse* (1973), for example, Marx wrote that '*social wealth confronts labour in more powerful proportions as an alien and dominant power . . . a monstrous objective power which created through social labour belongs not to the worker but . . . to capital*'. As capital accumulation grows, so labour becomes an ever-cheaper commodity, devalued and dehumanised – despite the appearance of men freely entering contractual agreements. So, argues Swinglewood (2000), alienation does not disappear from Marx's later works such as *Gründrisse*; it changes expression and becomes a more theoretical concept.

In Marx's view, therefore, while human history has seen a progressive increase in man's control over nature, this has been paralleled ironically by a corresponding increase in alienation, particularly in capitalist societies. People no longer recognise themselves in their own work, in their own society. They feel strangers at work, isolated and powerless in society and frustrated with having no outlet for their talents and ambitions. The world around them – even the products of their own work – becomes objectified. They feel powerless against the impersonal forces at work and in society at large and the products they produce are commodities to be sold at a price in the market place, not an expression of their own skills and creativity. Workers are prisoners of market forces over which they have no control. They have to sell their labour to survive and they have no control over supply, demand or price. In Marx's view, however, market forces are not natural or external forces with a life of their own; rather they are controlled by the capitalist class, by big business and the global corporations who own the means of production and seek to exploit labour as the primary means of capital accumulation and profit.

For Marx the result of wage labour and alienation is that man is degraded, dehumanised and 'no longer feels himself to be anything but an animal'. What distinguishes man from animals, work and the free conscious act of creativity disappears, and so man loses his 'species being', his distinct human qualities. Moreover the isolation and alienation of wage labour equally alienates men and women from each other and so destroys man's social being too, his sense of community and well-being as the distress and poverty of capitalist working life drives man into isolation and loneliness.

Thus, argued Marx, capitalism is an inverted world with those with the least talent at the top exploiting and living off the labours of others. Such power and control is hidden behind the illusion of market forces. It was Marx's aim to reveal such distortion and to set out a programme by which man might emancipate himself from the slavery of capitalist society and be reunited as a full human being – free, dignified and fulfilled within an egalitarian and co-operative communist community.

Marx believed passionately in the power and potential of human beings. This belief was his primary motivation for analysing why man is so unfulfilled in present day capitalist society and how communist or classless society would free man, his spirit and his talents. Man differs from animals essentially in his consciousness and in particular, his self-consciousness, which arises from human action and interaction in a social context. What specifically distinguishes man from animals is his ability to consciously control, plan and pace his activity, his creative intelligence. Each historical epoch encourages or restricts such creative potential and class societies in particular suppress talent, consciousness and motivation. In comparing primitive society to capitalism, Marx argued that *'The ancients provide a narrow satisfaction whereas the modern world leaves us unsatisfied, or where it appears to be satisfied with itself, it is vulgar and mean'* (Ritzer 1996: 53). Capitalism has unleashed man's ability to produce unparalleled abundance in terms of material goods but it will take communism to bring out man's full talents and ambitions, his 'species power' as a distinct and unique human being in both work and leisure.

Marx equally believed in man's inherent sociability; *'Man is in the most literal sense of the word a "zoon politikon", not only a social animal but an animal which can develop into an individual only in society'* (Ritzer 1996: 55).

While class-based societies like capitalism distort man's consciousness and exploit and suppress his talents in the interests of profits and privilege, classless societies will free man as a fully conscious and highly co-operative productive being in the truest sense of the word.

For Marx, not only does the capitalist mode of production turn people's work, the fruits of their labour into a thing, a commodity, an object outside of their control, but it generates a 'fetishism of commodities', an obsession with owning things and with 'reification', the belief that society is a thing above and beyond the individual over which man has no control. Such reification may begin in the workplace and the market place with the apparently all embracing and impersonal power of the modern organisation and the vast powers of market forces, but it can be equally applied to our view of religion and the modern state. All property, and in particular the means of production, are privately owned. 'Private property is thus the product of alienated labour'.

The Idea in Action

THE CONCEPT OF ALIENATION IS A POWERFUL IDEA THAT INSPIRES PASSIONATE ANGER whenever people are treated inhumanely, displaced or denigrated. The word itself is innately ugly, unfriendly and threatening enough to inspire film producers and screen writers as well as radical thinkers. As used by Marx, however, as a concept to explain the inhuman and exploitative nature of capitalism, alienation is an inspirational idea that arouses passionate indignation and revolutionary fervour. Hence its sociological and political power, hence its power in lifting Marx's analysis of capitalism from simply being an intellectual exercise to being a work of revolution and profound passion.

For Marx the concept of alienation therefore had two distinct but interrelated meanings:

- it is a subjective feeling, a sense of powerlessness and isolation;
- it is a structural analysis of economic systems that deprive men of both the fruits of their labour and control over their work.

Much written since, however, has separated these two interrelated ideas and so distorted much of the meaning and power of alienation as a theoretical concept and as a motivating force for changing modern methods of work and working practice.

- In the 1950s and 1960s American social scientist, M. Seeman (1959) broke down the concept of alienation into five psychological components (isolation, meaninglessness, powerlessness, normlessness and self-estrangement) and Robert Blauner (1964) linked four of these to different types of work structure, arguing that assembly-line work is especially alienating and craft work the most creative. Blauner believed that automation would remove alienation from modern work because it would put the worker in control of the machinery – a thesis totally rejected by Marxists such as Harry Braverman (1974), who argues that not only does automation not alter the relations of production (the bosses are still in control) but it is a means to increased exploitation since workers are 'deskilled' and eventually replaced by such machinery (see Deskilling, p. 98).

- Other writers have applied the term alienation to a whole range of modern malaises – the feeling of discontent, isolation, powerlessness and impersonality felt by many groups in today's mass society (the young, minority groups, women); their sense of isolation, frustration and rejection, their need to change things for the better, for ordinary people. The term alienation has been used to explain the high rates of strikes and absenteeism in today's giant factories. Marx himself applied it to religion. Like the young Hegelian, Ludwig Feuerbach, Marx equally saw religion as a form of alienation as man gives up his own creative spirit and ability to control life for a belief in a supernatural being who apparently controls him. God didn't create man, argued Feuerbach, man created God and then gave him total power over mankind. Man has objectified himself and made himself into an object. For Marx, religion was a form of false consciousness, a form of alienation.

- The concept of alienation has also been a major source of dispute between rival schools of Marxists, with humanists seeing it as a central theme in Marx's work (particularly with the post-war publication of *Gründrisse*) and structuralists like Louis Althusser, arguing that Marx rejected this term altogether in his more mature works, in favour of exploitation of a more scientific or structural analysis of capitalism. The Frankfurt School and its critical theory on the other hand revived the concept of alienation and used it to develop a more humanist, less deterministic Marxism, focusing on individual consciousness and the power of ideology and culture in developing a more flexible critique of Western capitalism, Eastern socialism and the rise of the authoritarian state. Herbert Marcuse (1964), for example, blended it with the psychology of Sigmund Freud and inspired a generation of American hippies and radicals in the 1960s to rise up and criticise capitalist America.

- It is difficult to judge whether the sense of alienation is less in 'socialist' than capitalist societies since such a subjective feeling is almost impossible to measure. Certainly the workers in the Eastern bloc countries do not seem to feel in control, if the rise of solidarity in Poland, the destruction of the Berlin Wall and the revolutions of 1989–90 in Eastern Europe are anything to go by. Possibly the Chinese communes, Yugoslav factories and some small-scale experiments such as Kibbutzim have had greater success.

Thus, while the concept of alienation has been used in a wide variety of social sciences, many sociologists feel that it has lost all real meaning and is now of little analytical value. Nevertheless, when used as Marx originally intended – as an analysis of work, of human nature and of the subjective effect of class exploitation – it still wields considerable moral, if not sociological force. It inspired a century of revolution and it changed many parts of the world forever.

 **See Also**

- **ANOMIE** (p. 22) as Durkheim's explanation of this industrial malaise.
- **CRITICAL THEORY** (p. 84), as an attempt to expand this idea of early Marx into a humanist and post-war school of Marxist thinking.
- **HISTORICAL MATERIALISM** (p. 43), as an overview of Marx and Engels' general theory of historical and economic development.
- **SIMULATIONS** (p. 260), as a post-modern perspective on alienation.

Suggested Reading

CAREW HUNT, R.N. (1950) *The Theory and Practice of Communism,* Penguin, Harmondsworth.

MCCLELLAN, D. (1975) *Marx,* Fontana, London.

PAMPEL, F.C. (2000) KARL MARX, Ch. 1 in Pampel F.C., *Sociological Lives and Ideas: An Introduction to the Classical Theorists*, Macmillan, Basingstoke.

RUIS (1986) *Marx for Beginners,* Unwin Paperbacks, London.

WORSLEY, P. (1982) *Marx and Marxism,* Tavistock, London.

Further Reading

BOTTOMORE, T.B. AND RUBEL, M. (EDS.) (1961) *Karl Marx: Selected Writings,* Penguin, Harmondsworth.

CALLINICOS, A. (1983) *The Revolutionary Ideas of Karl Marx,* Pluto Press, London.

JESSOP, B. (1998) Karl Marx, Ch. 1 in Stones, R. (ed.), *Key Sociological Thinkers*, Macmillan, Basingstoke.

MANSON, P. (2000) Karl Marx, Ch. 2 Part I in Andersen, H. and Kaspersen, L.B. (eds.), *Classical and Modern Social Theory*, Blackwell, Oxford.

MARX, K. (1965) *The German Ideology,* Lawrence & Wishart, London.

MARX, K. (1968) 'The Communist Manifesto', in *Selected Works,* Lawrence & Wishart, London.

MARX, K. AND ENGELS, F. (1956) *The Holy Family,* Foreign Languages Publishers, Moscow.

SEEMAN, M. (1959) 'On the Meaning of Alienation', *American Sociological Review*, 33, 46–62.

Anomie

Emile Durkheim

![The Idea]

WHILE KARL MARX DEVELOPED THE THEORY OF ALIENATION TO EXPLAIN THAT SENSE of isolation and rejection, powerlessness and frustration felt by many in today's mass society, the French sociologist and educationalist, Emile Durkheim, developed the idea of anomie – a word that looks like and sounds like 'anonymous' – unknown, unseen, invisible; a word that reflects the anonymity many individuals feel amid the masses today of modern urban society. Writing from a very different point of view to Marx – from a positivist perspective – Durkheim developed a functionalist theory of society, a theory that society is not merely the sum of its parts, a theory that society is not simply a collection of independent individuals. Rather, society is a thing in its own right, an entity in itself. It functions like any other natural organism as a system of independent parts – the economy, the family, the government and so on – held together not by a central nervous system but by a central value system, a set of social guidelines called norms, based on an underlying moral consensus, or collective consciousness. Such norms not only give society a basic framework and source of stability but are crucial in controlling and directing its individual members. In Durkheim's view, man's appetites are unlimited, insatiable, and if any form of social order or civilisation is to exist, such desires must be controlled. Simply for their own personal well-being, the individual needs to keep his ambitions in check, needs moral guidelines, or else he or she will end up frustrated, isolated and rootless. Thus, in Durkheim's view, there is always going to be an underlying conflict or tension between the individual's aspirations and society's needs for order and control.

An absence of norms or a fundamental conflict over society's basic values Durkheim called *anomie*, and he particularly feared that such a social 'sickness' would occur during periods of social upheaval or transition. In small-scale traditional societies, where relationships are personal and there is a limited division of labour, it is fairly easy for a general consensus as to the values and norms of society and of the rights and privileges of individual members to be established and upheld – especially if backed by the moral authority and sanctions of religion. Everyone knows their place and aspires no higher. However, in the transition from the mechanical solidarity of such societies to the organic solidarity of industrial ones, where there is an extensive division of labour and where relationships are often highly impersonal, a breakdown in social consensus and so of social controls over the individual is highly possible. Just such a situation faced Durkheim and his contemporaries in the late nineteenth century as both political revolutions and industrialisation swept across Europe, destroying not only traditional communities but the very moral fabric of society. The new industrial division of labour seemed to be out-stripping existing moral values. Without the discipline of traditional social norms, Durkheim feared that individual ambitions would rise sky-high and so be very frustrated if the new social order was unable to fulfil its apparent promises. As people in the nineteenth century left their traditional roots in the village, their family and friends, for the bright lights and high wages of the new industrial cities, many soon found themselves disillusioned, isolated and friendless, creating in Durkheim's view an enormous potential for social disorder; as evidenced in the rampages of 'the mob' in many European cities at this time.

Anomie literally means normlessness. It arises when social controls are weak, when moral and political constraints collapse and is particularly prevalent during periods of rapid social change, such as industrialisation and urbanisation, when traditional norms and values are disrupted and uprooted. People become restless and dissatisfied and a new moral consensus about what people can reasonably expect from life is needed. Industrialisation and consumerism accentuate this process, encouraging specialisation and self-interest.

Anomie is thus a state of deregulation, a breakdown of social controls and social order unleashing unrestrained individualism. Passions and desires multiply amid the consumerism of modern capitalism and traditional disciplines and restraints no longer hold sway. Men are no longer content with their lot, no longer modest in their ambitions. Durkheim mistrusted popular democracy and feared its consequences. Individuals can only achieve security, happiness and some degree of freedom if they subject themselves to a moral order and to some form of supra-individual force. Social order and individual happiness depends on a high degree of social integration.

Durkheim, however, was not as pessimistic as fellow writers such as Ferdinand Tönnies. Beneath the social upheavals and demand for individual rights and liberties in the late nineteenth century, he perceived the potential for a new social order based on the morality and ethics of the new professional guilds and associations.

Durkheim saw the solution or cure to anomie in the development of occupational associations capable of

- reintegrating individuals into social groups and collective values;
- establishing a new consensus about the rewards people could reasonably expect.

Such associations would seek to work with the state and so establish a new civic and industrial moral order and consensus based on a vision and commitment to society at large to re-establish 'society within the individual'.

However, he recognised that within the organic solidarity of modern society, anomie is likely to be an underlying pathology, a social sickness generated by the loosening of traditional ties and values and the rise of individualism over communal or social responsibilities. Nevertheless, and despite the growth of 'the cult of the individual', Durkheim put his faith in social reform and evolutionary change rather than the revolutionary doctrines of contemporaries such as Marx and Engels.

A normal healthy society is in harmony; an unhealthy or sick society lacks a strong moral consensus as to right and wrong and so is likely to collapse into anarchy and destruction. Pessimistic about restraining man's insatiable passions and egotism, Durkheim looked to external forces and to the moral superiority of society's leaders and to professional associations to impose their authority and their values, to generate a new 'moral consensus' and to re-establish social controls.

The concept of anomie, therefore, as Anthony Giddens argues (1978), is not only an analysis of social disorder but an explanation of individual behaviour. The classic example of this is Durkheim's analysis of suicide and in particular of 'anomic' suicide, the type of suicide that occurs during periods of social instability such as economic booms and slumps. Those at the top of their profession, particularly in such fields as business and commerce, argued Durkheim, are particularly prone to anomic suicide because they are the ones with the greatest personal ambitions, the ones least restrained by traditional morality and social controls and the ones for whom personal failure is particularly devastating. Thus, while the suicide rate in America generally shot up after the 1929 Wall Street crash, it was businessmen and financiers who were most likely to throw themselves out of skyscraper windows.

The Idea in Action

THE CONCEPT OF ANOMIE HAS BEEN ADAPTED AND REINTERPRETED IN A VARIETY OF ways. Some have used it to explain juvenile delinquency, the growth of crime and social unrest in advanced industrial societies and even the riots in America in the 1960s and Britain in the 1980s, arguing either in terms of inadequate socialisation, of parents failing to bring up their children properly or of the need for stricter social controls and for a stronger emphasis on traditional moral values via the family and the church. Others have used it to explain the collapse of social consensus and order in societies such as Northern Ireland and the Middle East.

The American sociologist, Robert Merton, applied the notion of anomie to try and explain crime rates and social deviance in the USA. He used the idea of norm conflict as the basis of the high rate of crime, deviancy and unrest in modern America. According to his analysis, there is a lack of fit between the unlimited ambitions of the American Dream into which all young people in America are socialised, and the limited opportunities available for achieving such wealth and fame. Not everyone can become a millionaire or president and for some groups like the Blacks the opportunities to rise are virtually non-existent. So how do people adapt to such failure? Merton outlined five forms of adaptation, four of which involved some form of deviance. While a few reach the top legitimately by conforming – by promotion, luck or skill – others succeed by illegitimate means through crime. The rest adapt to failure by withdrawing into drugs, retreating to alternative societies such as communes or even rebelling against the whole idea of such materialism and competition by joining urban guerilla groups such as the Black Panthers or Minutemen. In the 1960s a whole range of programmes of 'positive discrimination', particularly the massive Headstart Programme, were instituted to try to increase opportunities for deprived groups especially young Blacks and to socialise them into 'normal' social values, to overcome their 'culture of poverty' and draw them into mainstream society. However, this approach had limited success and, as its critics argued, it left the basic inequalities of American society unaltered.

The concept of anomie, however, has further suffered from the more general critique of the whole functionalist model, in particular the idea that societies rest on an underlying consensus and that all age groups in society accept the same norms and values. Moreover, Durkheim's idea that the ethics of professions such as doctors, accountants and lawyers could provide the moral basis for industrial societies, is accepted by few writers today.

Nevertheless the concept of anomie has highlighted a key social problem for advanced industrial societies, that of rapid social change, and stressed the importance of moral guidelines for the well-being of both society at large and the individual in particular. When morality breaks down, when people lose any sense of social solidarity, any sense of values, any sense of belonging and of being part of something greater than themselves, then society itself collapses, chaos ensues and everyone feels helpless, lost and alone.

 **See Also**

- **ALIENATION** (p. 14), as Karl Marx's theory of this modern malaise.
- **SOCIAL SOLIDARITY** (p. 72), as the background theory to this idea.

Suggested Reading

GIDDENS, A. (1978) *Durkheim*, Fontana, Glasgow.

THOMPSON, K. (1982) *Emile Durkheim*, Tavistock, London.

PAMPEL, F.C. (2000) Emile Durkheim and the Problem of Social Order, Ch. 2 in Pampel, F.C., *Sociological Lives and Ideas: An Introduction to the Classical Theorists*, Macmillan, Basingstoke.

The above offer concise, readable and authoritative outlines of Durkheim's life, work and ideas.

Further Reading

DURKHEIM, E. (1951) *Suicide: A Study in Sociology* [1897], Free Press, Glencoe.

DURKHEIM, E. (1954) *The Elementary Forms of Religious Life* [1912], Allen & Unwin, London.

DURKHEIM, E. (1958) *The Rules of Sociological Method* [1895], Free Press, Glencoe.

GUNERIUSSEN, W. (2000) Emile Durkheim, Ch. 5, Part I in Andersen, H. and Kaspersen, L.B. (eds.), *Classical and Modern Social Theory*, Blackwell, Oxford.

LUKES, S. (1972) *Emile Durkheim: His Life and Work,* Allen & Unwin, London.

POPE, W. (1998) Emile Durkheim, Ch. 3 in Stones, R. (ed.), *Key Sociological Thinkers*, Macmillan, Basingstoke.

Bureaucracy

Max Weber

M AX WEBER'S STUDY OF BUREAUCRACY IS GENERALLY CONSIDERED A SOCIOLOGICAL classic and it has formed the foundation of studies of modern organisations ever since. Writing at the turn of the century, Weber (1864–1920) sought to identify the key features of modern industrial society and to try and capture the underlying spirit and dynamic of Western capitalism. Weber's classic study of an ideal type bureaucracy therefore embodied three of his key themes concerning the nature of advanced industrial societies and the nature of sociological research.

- His belief that the prime feature of capitalist, and communist, industrial societies is the trend towards rationalisation, towards logical, rational and calculating modes of thought, action and planning. Bureaucratisation is a classic example of this trend towards institutionalised power, towards an organisational society. As the American sociologist Amitai Etzioni (1964) has noted, *'We are born in organisations, educated by organisations and most of us spend much of our lives working for organisations. We spend much of our leisure time paying, playing and praying in organisations. Most of us will die in an organisation, and, when the time comes for burial, the largest organisation of all – the state – must grant official permission'.*

For Weber capitalism and bureaucracy were the 'two great rationalizing forces'.

- His view that the basis of power in modern society is rational – legal authority, rule by laws and regulations rather than rule by men; power legitimised by consent and authorised by office – rather than by tradition or personal charisma. Bureaucracy is a classic example of such rule by regulation, such impersonal and impartial power. Bureaucrats act without prejudice or passion, applying the rules to all, irrespective of differences in social rank or background, while they themselves are subject to a higher authority, the will of the people as executed by the government of the day. The power of modern-day officials rests not in themselves but in the posts they hold, be it as a civil servant, judge or policeman. While in office they have the authority to issue orders, but only within limits, and only to their subordinates. In office the ideal official is a faithful servant, obediently executing orders and rules from above; out of office he is powerless.

- His attempt to use ideal-types, model examples of key characteristics of various social, political and economic institutions, as a basis of sociological analysis and comparison.

Weber (1949) defined bureaucracy as '*a hierarchical organisational structure designed rationally to co-ordinate the work of many individuals in the pursuit of large-scale administrative tasks and organisational goals*'. Though he argued that many private, capitalist organisations were becoming bureaucratic in character, the main focus of his analysis at this time was on public institutions, in particular state bureaucracies. He identified the following as the key features of an ideal type or pure form of bureaucracy:

- A specialised division of administrative labour. Complex tasks are broken down into manageable parts, with each official specialising in a particular area, be it education, finance or housing. Within each department, every official has a clearly defined sphere of responsibility.

- A hierarchy of offices and authority whereby every lower office is under the control and supervision of a higher one in a hierarchical chain of command.

- Rule by regulations whereby all the operations of the bureaucracy are governed by '*a consistent system of abstract rules*' and '*the application of these rules to particular cases*' (Weber 1948). Such rules both direct officials' actions and clearly define the limits of their power. They impose strict discipline and central control. They leave little room for personal initiative or discretion.

- Formal impersonality is the governing characteristic of all bureaucratic action. The ideal official performs his duties without regard for persons or for his own feelings, but solely according to the rules.

- Appointment on the basis of merit becomes the sole criterion for selecting and promoting officials. '*Bureaucratic administration means, fundamentally, the exercise of control on the basis of knowledge. This is the feature of it which makes it specifically rational*' (Weber 1948).

- A strict separation of private and official income and life. '*Bureaucracy segregates official activity as something distinct from the sphere of private life*' (Weber 1948).

These features, argued Weber, distinguished modern bureaucratic organisation from previous forms of administration where corruption, nepotism and personal favour all abounded, producing gross inefficiency. Modern industrial societies, whether capitalist or communist, require highly efficient organisational structures to function properly. Bureaucracy, in his view, is the most efficient and technically superior form of organisation, precisely because it relies on rules, not men, on a hierarchy of offices, not on a network of personal relationships. In fact, the more formal and impersonal the bureaucracy, the more efficient it will be, because then, even if all the present incumbents were replaced by an entirely new set of officials, the system would continue to function as before. As Frank Parkin (1982) has commented, '*On Weber's account, the behaviour of bureaucrats is fashioned by the internal logic of the administrative machine, not by the subjective meanings and perceptions of the actors. Personal motives and subjective meanings appear to be no more relevant to the conduct of Weber's typical bureaucrat than they are to the conduct of Marx's typical capitalist*'.

Weber's analysis of bureaucracy arose not only from his study of rationalisation but also his analysis of power and authority. While in the past authority rested on tradition or personality (charisma), modern authority in Weber's view rests on rationality, on the power of the law to bestow power impartially and by agreed rules to specified individuals or officeholders. Weber saw bureaucracy as the 'purest' form of legal authority and he constructed an 'ideal type' bureaucracy to depict its primary features. Weber saw bureaucracy as the purest and most efficient form of legal authority, administration and political control because it is so much more predictable, disciplined and reliable than traditional forms of organisation.

Weber's fascination with power and authority, the state and bureaucracy reflected partly his lifelong study of rationalisation, partly his father's occupation and attitude of mind. It equally reflected his own political orientation, his belief in a strong nation state capable of leading and organising modern society. He believed in liberal democracy but rejected totally the notion of direct democracy or will of the people: *'All ideas aiming at abolishing the dominance of men over men are "utopian"'* (Mommsen 1974). Like Robert Michels he saw modern mass political parties as inevitably bureaucratic. He distrusted the masses despite his fears for the individual being dehumanised within a 'new iron cage of serfdom'. Bureaucracy is part of the process of domination in modern society. Modern society cannot hope to escape it, save perhaps through charismatic leadership.

The Idea in Action

TODAY WE ALL LIVE WITH, ARE SERVED BY AND POSSIBLY WORK FOR ORGANISATIONS organised in the bureaucratic fashion outlined by Max Weber. Bureaucracy is a key feature of modern society as all organisations, both public and private, seek to serve the public efficiently and effectively. Some of the largest bureaucracies are in the public sector – the Civil Service, the Health and Education services, the Armed Forces and even the Church – but even the private sector is highly bureaucratised as it seeks to serve the consumer needs of the mass of the public and to cut costs sufficiently to make profits. Bureaucracy is a fact of modern life, a necessary feature in organising mass society, whether capitalist or centrally planned. Weber's ideal type was designed to identify and draw together the key features of modern bureaucracy. It has, however, often been taken as an 'ideal' or model of organisational efficiency and so provoked an extensive debate about whether in real life bureaucracies are either as efficient or democratic as Weber appeared to claim they are.

Bureaucratic efficiency

IN contrast to Weber's claim that bureaucracy is technically the most superior form of organisation, a wide variety of writers have pointed out its administrative weaknesses. Robert Merton (1957) pointed out the features of bureaucracy he considered to be 'dysfunctional' which may even prevent the achievement of organisational goals, in particular the inefficiencies created by bureaucrats' slavish adherence to rules and regulations, their conservatism, fear of change and their cold, impersonal treatment of their clients. Many people have complained of being tied up in 'red tape', of being ignored by faceless bureaucrats. Bureaucracies are notorious for their inability to respond quickly to new circumstances, new initiatives.

Bradley and Wilkie (1974) cite a classic example of bureaucratic paralysis: 'The story has been told of a Soviet citizen taking a rifle into Red Square and firing a number of shots at President Mikoyan's car. Red Square at that time was saturated with security guards, but they did not dare act immediately without orders because they could not be sure that the attempted assassination was not sanctioned by an even higher authority than Mikoyan. The guards were effectively paralysed until higher "clearance" was obtained to shoot the offender'.

Peter Blau (1963) showed in his studies of both a federal law enforcement agency and an American employment agency how the 'informal' techniques adopted by employees were far more efficient than those laid down in the official rule book. Michel Crozier (1964) took this analysis further by showing how employees often ignore and bend the rules, pay lip-service to them, but in practice withhold or distort information so that their superiors do not know exactly what is going on. In an attempt to reassert control, senior managers create more rules, but in so doing only increase inefficiency and misinformation.

Alvin Gouldner's (1954) study of a gypsum mine and Burns and Stalker's (1966) study of electronics firms, showed that although a bureaucratic system of organisation is ideal when conditions are highly stable and predictable, a much more 'organic' structure is required in more fluid and unpredictable situations. Bureaucratic structures are totally unsuited to responding quickly to the dangers of work down a mine or the ever-changing circumstances of new technologies and new markets.

Democratic accountability

WHILE extolling the technical virtues of bureaucracy, Weber was well aware of the power of officialdom, well aware that such institutionalised power could enslave not only its employees, but become a threat to democracy itself. He foresaw the danger of hierarchical control crushing individual initiative and creativity, of creating 'specialists without spirit', trapped in an iron cage of rules and regulations, helplessly dependent on orders from above. Equally, Weber recognised that, while modern democracies require bureaucracies to function effectively, there is the inherent danger of the civil servant coming to rule his elected political master: 'The political master always finds himself, vis-à-vis the trained official, in the position of a dilettante facing the expert.' Through their expert knowledge, secrecy and traditional anonymity, civil servants have power without responsibility. They are continually in office; politicians simply come and go. Weber saw the key to this dilemma as being control of the civil service by Parliament and regular accountability. Other writers have been less optimistic, most notably Robert Michels in his thesis about the iron law of oligarchy (see p. 52). A wide variety of studies of modern government have highlighted the power of officials to the point where many have claimed that the British Civil Service is a form of 'ruling class' (Brian Sedgemore, Tony Benn, Crowther-Hunt Report 1980). The various techniques used by officials to keep ministers in their place are outlined in amusing detail in the Crossman Diaries (1977) and in the television series Yes, Minister and Yes, Prime Minister.

Marxist writers go even further, arguing that the whole of the capitalist state – Parliament, government and civil service combined – is an instrument of class control;

as Lenin put it, 'an organ for the oppression of one class by another'. Though Marx, Engels and Lenin were primarily concerned with state bureaucracies, modern Marxists like Harry Braverman (see p. 98) have argued that all forms of bureaucratic structure, whether public or private, are essentially systems of control by which the bourgeoisie keep the proletariat in their place. Claims of technical efficiency are merely ideological myths to justify such oppression and exploitation.

Ironically, it is in communist societies that the bureaucratic model of centralised planning and control has reached its height, spreading its tentacles into every corner and producing a society in which the party bureaucrats and bureaucratic mentality are supreme. As Alfred Meyer (1965) has argued, *'The USSR is best understood as a large, complex bureaucracy.'* Milovan Djilas (1957) went further, arguing that the bureaucrats of the Communist Party use their powers and privilege to exploit the masses and promote their own interests and oligarchical rule. Mao Tse-Tung's attempt during his Cultural Revolution to restore 'power to the people' by giving the masses control of China's all-embracing administrative structure, met with some temporary success until his death. Gorbachev's *glasnost,* however, achieved more permanent success in stirring the Russian empire out of its bureaucratic inertia in the 1970s.

Thus, in reality, bureaucracy has proved far from the model of efficient planning and democratic organisation portrayed by Weber. Rather, his own very worst fears seem to have been realised the more bureaucratic the organisation or society. As Frank Parkin (1982) pointed out, it is *'the dictatorship of the officials, not of the proletariat, that is marching on'.* As Weber feared, the bureaucratic lust for order and routine has tended to crush individual initiative and it is interesting to note the variety of attempts now being made by modern governments, both capitalist and communist, from Gorbachev to Thatcher, to break the power of bureaucracy and free the spirit of enterprise and individual freedom. In fact, Weber's ideal bureaucrat, untainted by human emotions, would actually emerge as little more than a mindless robot. It is somewhat ironic, therefore, that a social theorist like Weber, who put social action, individualism and subjectivity (*verstehen*) at the forefront of his sociological analysis, should have produced an ideal type that so thoroughly eliminated such vital elements of social behaviour. While Weber provided an ideal type bureaucracy, he did not, despite his theory of social action, offer a social psychology of the ideal bureaucrat, nor of how individuals behave within bureaucracies in either conforming to or resisting its rules and regulations and yet it is the behaviour of officials within large scale bureaucracies that has led to so much criticism and fear. How do we humanise and sensitise bureaucracy and make bureaucrats the servants of society, not the masters?

Weber was well aware of all these weaknesses. He tried to portray bureaucracy positively despite the failings he was aware of. *'From a purely technical point of view, a bureaucracy is capable of attaining the highest degree of efficiency, and is in this sense formally the most rational known means of exercising authority over human beings. It is superior to any other form in precision, in stability, in the stringency of its discipline, and in its reliability. It thus makes possible a particularly high degree of calculability of results for the heads of the organization and for those acting in relation to it. It is finally superior both in intensive efficiency and in the scope of its operations and is formally capable of application to all kinds of administrative tasks* (Weber 1968: 223).

However, while portraying bureaucracy positively and as the most superior form of organisation, Weber equally saw it as the epitome of his disenchantment with rationality and his fear for the loss of individual freedom in a bureaucratic society: *'The passion for bureaucratization drives us to despair'*. He predicted that *'the future belongs to bureaucratization'* and it was a future he feared and he saw no alternative, not even in the socialist utopia proposed by Marx. In fact he correctly foresaw socialism as being even more bureaucratic because all its leaders would be bureaucrats and because socialist societies would be centrally planned. In contrast, businessmen, even politicians in capitalist societies, are not bureaucrats by occupation and the competitive nature of market forces at least encourages initiative and enterprise. Hence Weber's preference and hope that capitalism offered a better prospect for individual freedom and creative leadership. Ultimately, however, Weber saw the march and domination of bureaucratisation as both relentless and all pervasive – the only hopes, the only sources of countervailing power being the rise of visionary and charismatic leaders and the power and independence of the professions (the intellectuals, the scientists and the politicians), but even they represent but a feeble hope against the overwhelming power of bureaucratisation; even they too are as subject to rationalisation, to the power of bureaucracy as the rest of society. Weber expressed his fears and concerns about mindless bureaucracy as follows: *'So much more terrible is the idea that the world should be filled with nothing but those cogs who cling to a little post and strive for a somewhat greater one . . . [It's] as though we knowingly and willingly were supposed to become men who need order and nothing but order, who become nervous and cowardly if this order shakes for a moment'* (Mitzman 1969: 177–78).

Ultimately Weber's vision of the future is therefore highly pessimistic, even fatalistic. Despite his belief in the individual and in charisma, he portrays bureaucratisation as inevitable, the masses as passive and the outcomes oppressive. The spirit of creativity and enterprise and the dynamism he portrayed in his study of the Protestant Ethic, the social action approach he cried out for, seem to have been extinguished within the 'Iron Cage'. Future society, according to Weber, seems to be as soulless and disenchanted as the bureaucracies themselves.

Throughout Weber's work is the underlying tension and conflict between the power of rationalisation and the freedom of the individual, the need in advanced industrial societies for creativity and entrepreneurship and the crushing power of the state and bureaucracy over its citizens. Weber was disenchanted with the power of rationalisation and longed for charismatic leaders to rise up and rouse the masses from the stupor of mass democracy, to lead the people to freedom, yet he remained critical of such movements as socialism and nationalism in achieving this, whatever the motives and charisma of their leaders.

More modern writers, however, are less pessimistic. As we enter the twenty-first century, bureaucracy may seem less inevitable and less powerful. It can be challenged and constrained. Ray and Reed (1994), for example, believe that people today are less and less willing to accept the authority and legitimacy of bureaucracy and even that of the state and that through democratic – and undemocratic means – mass protest and modern elections do give some power to the people. Modern writers believe that bureaucratic organisations are no longer the dominant form of institution in post-industrial society. Rather, modern organisations are far more flexible and decentralised, giving far more power and authority to the individual worker or team (Clegg 1992).

Nevertheless, whatever its weaknesses, possibly even because of them, Weber's model of an ideal type bureaucracy has proved to be a major contribution both to our understanding of modern organisations and modern government, and to the underlying spirit of advanced industrial societies.

 See Also

- THE IRON LAW OF OLIGARCHY (p. 52).
- DISCOURSE (p. 208), as a post-modern view of the power of the modern state.

Suggested Reading

MACRAE, D. (1974) *Weber,* Fontana, London.

PAMPEL, F.C. (2000) Max Weber and the Spread of Rationality, Ch. 3 in Pampel, F.C., *Sociological Ideas and Lives: An Introduction to the Classical Theorists,* Macmillan, Basingstoke.

PARKIN, F. (1982) *Max Weber,* Tavistock, London.

These are brief but readable overviews of Weber's life and work.

Further Reading

ETZIONI, A. (1964) *Modern Organizations,* Prentice-Hall, Englewood Cliffs, NJ.

KELLNER, P. AND CROWTHER-HUNT, LORD (1980) *The Civil Servants: An Inquiry into Britain's Ruling Class,* Macdonald, London.

PONTING, C. (1986) *Whitehall: Tragedy and Farce: The Inside Story of How Whitehall Really Works,* Sphere Books, London.

SCAFF, L.A. (1998) *Max Weber,* Ch. 2 in Stones, R. (ed.), *Key Sociological Thinkers,* Macmillan, Basingstoke.

Formal Sociology

George Simmel

The Idea

THE IDEA OF FORMAL SOCIOLOGY, OF TRYING TO MAKE SOCIOLOGY MORE ANALYTICAL, scientific and academically formal in a way that compares with mathematicians and linguists, dates back to the writings of the German philosopher George Simmel (1858–1918). Although he has been overshadowed by such contemporary 'giants' in sociology as Marx and Weber, Georg Simmel has rightly been acclaimed recently as one of the founding fathers of sociology. In contrast to traditional sociology, which has tended to operate at the macro level, trying to produce such grand theories of social order and change as functionalism and Marxism, Simmel sought to produce a 'pure' sociology, one that captured the feelings, the spirit, the minutiae of everyday life and relationships, a sociology of knowledge that could interpret reality in terms of the underlying 'form' and content of sociological life. In contrast to other leading sociologists of his time, Simmel's sociology is highly individualistic, subtle and philosophical. The key focus of his attention was the individual in modern mass society, struggling to survive and express himself within the 'iron cage' of modern bureaucracy, materialism, urbanisation and technology. In particular, he was both fascinated and depressed by life in pre-war Berlin, *'a metropolis, a world city and epitome of the modern spirit'* (Simmel 1971); a whirl of social life and activity in a city where most people were ironically strangers.

The essence of Simmel's approach to sociology – the key contrast with the grand schemes of contemporaries such as Weber and Marx – was the view that *'society exists only in the minds of individuals who participate in relationships with others'* (Pampel 2000: 137). Groups and societies do not exist as objects above and beyond individuals; they exist only when individuals work together for 'agreed' purposes. Hence his focus on social interaction and social relationships, on the minutiae of everyday social life that underpins the great social institutions of the social system and the ways in which individuals interpret and re-interpret social activity.

The role of sociology, argued Simmel, is to understand and make explicit the common forms of social interaction, the form and content of social life and order in the same way as grammarians study the form and structures of language, and mathematicians the form and shape of physical objects.

Georg Simmel's approach to sociological analysis, his attempt to construct a unified and comprehensive social theory was called *formal sociology*. Like other founding fathers, he too sought to establish sociology as a separate academic discipline, as a science even. However, in contrast to the positivist approach adopted by Auguste Comte and others, Simmel's analysis focused as much on social interaction and individual interpretation as on discovering general laws of human behaviour.

Simmel's analysis starts from three key observations:

1. Individuals are motivated by a wide variety of forces which range from self-interest to compassion, and that the study of such phenomena forms the subject matter of psychology.
2. The individual does not explain him/herself solely by reference to self, but in relation to others. The study of groups, their interrelationships and internal dynamics, forms the subject matter of social psychology.
3. Human activities develop in *forms,* within social structures such as the family, school and church, or according to general forms of behaviour such as imitation, competition and social hierarchy. The study of social forms, the study of the recurring and universal forms of social interaction, argued Simmel, constitutes the subject matter of sociology.

Simmel went on to distinguish further between the *form* and the *content* of social life. While forms of social interaction refer to stable, patterned aspects of social life, identifiable within very varied situations (the state, trade union or family), content refers to variable aspects of social interaction such as the interests and ambitions of the individuals involved in a particular situation. The aim of formal sociology was to analyse *forms* of social interaction by extracting them from their social context, and so produce sociological laws capable of describing the regularities which occur in various types of social organisation, despite considerable variations in context. Thus, for example, despite their very different social and historical contexts, the relationship between an artisan and a lord in eighteenth-century England is essentially the same as that between a peasant and landlord in twentieth-century South America, namely one of patronage.

Simmel's approach to sociology therefore operated at four levels:

- the microcosm of the psychological components of social life;
- the sociological components of interpersonal relationships;
- the structure of the social and cultural spirit of modern times;
- the metaphysical principles of modern life.

Simmel extended this analysis by using both geometrical analogies and social types.

Geometrical analogies

USING geometry as the basis of many of his analogies, he sought to develop 'a geometry of social life'. He argued, for example, that social situations vary in terms of their nature and type according to the number of people involved. A social situation involving two or three people is fundamentally different from one involving a hundred people. Equally, though, a social situation involving two or three people is at heart the same in terms of form and relationship as that between two or three nations. Number not only acts as a determinant of group organisation, but affects the likelihood and form of social conflict – compare, for example, a political debate between ten or so people and a mass rally in which genuine debate is impossible. It further determines the nature of relationships. While one person alone exists in solitude, and a couple may form relationships of profound intimacy, equality and depth, a threesome introduces new divisions which may lead to alliances of two against one. Marriage is a classic example of the way number fundamentally alters the nature of even this most intimate of relationships. Within monogamy, a married couple have only each other to consider and so are usually extremely close, until the arrival of a third person, their first child, alters this dyadic relationship fundamentally. Similarly, though polygamy is as much a form of marriage as monogamy, its content, its relationships are fundamentally different. Simmel was especially interested in the triadic form, or the way that the third person can significantly alter a relationship between two individuals, groups or countries by playing a variety of roles: ally, referee or rascal!

The key point of all this numerical analysis was to illustrate Simmel's belief that specific and relatively autonomous *forms* exist independently of their social context; that whatever the social or historical situation, a triad of people, groups or nations produce similar types of behaviour. In a sense, therefore, Simmel was arguing for formal sociology to be considered as a geometry of social forms.

Social types

SIMMEL highlighted the way certain social types occur and recur throughout history and in a multitude of social situations, yet nevertheless represent essentially the same form and produce the same reaction. The stranger and the adventurer are two such social types, labelled and reacted to in much the same way, whether they are found in tribal Africa or modern Europe.

Simmel, therefore, sought to extract from their social context such key concepts as conflict, differentiation and power, and analyse them scientifically, just as a chemist analyses compounds or a physicist atoms. Social content, he argued, is crucial to socio-logical interpretation, but a clear distinction between form and content must always be maintained if a science of sociology is to be established. Individual motives, passions, feelings and ambitions are crucial, but only become concrete, only materi-alise, within specific relationships, within specific social forms. Daily life itself involves a succession of social forms – work, meals, social activities. Without forms there is no society. *'In every known society there exists a great variety of forms which bind us together, that is, socialise us . . . if one imagines an absence of all forms, society would not exist'*, argued Simmel (Frisby 1984). Sociology, therefore, is the science which abstractly analyses social forms on the understanding that these do not merely make society, they are society.

This emphasis on scientific abstraction, however, did not lead Simmel to reify society, to see society as a 'form' above and beyond its members. Rather, society is a man-made creation, since 'it exists only where many individuals interact'.

'If society is merely a . . . constellation of individuals who are the actual realities, then the latter and their behaviour also constitutes the real object of science and the concept of

society evaporates . . . What palpably exists is indeed only individual human beings and their circumstances and activities: therefore, the task can only be to understand them, whereas the essence of society, that emerges purely through an ideal synthesis and is never to be grasped, should not form the object of reflection that is directed towards the investigation of reality' (Frisby 1984).

At heart, therefore, Simmel's formal sociology was an attempt to combine philosophical analysis and social psychology as a basis for explaining both the form and content of social life. Using Immanuel Kant's philosophy of knowledge, Simmel's notion of forms was based on the view that knowledge is not based simply on observing and categorising a real and objective external reality but rather it is a subjective experience by which individuals and groups seek to interpret and make sense of the world about them by developing a common and agreed conceptual framework of *forms* or categories of social action and social life. Social institutions like the family and the law, and social concepts such as love and alienation, do not exist above and beyond the meaning people give them. There is, therefore, no such thing as society above and beyond the everyday life and social interactions of groups of individuals living in a particular culture or environment. *'The concept of form enabled Simmel to analyse institutions and social processes objectively while retaining the notion of the active human subject . . . Without forms there is no society. It is only through what Simmel called the "great forms" that the complex reality of human society is rendered intelligible'* (Swinglewood 2000: 84).

The Idea in Action

THROUGH FORMAL SOCIOLOGY, GEORG SIMMEL HAS BEEN CLOSELY ASSOCIATED WITH social psychology and symbolic interactionism. He has been strongly identified with the study of small group dynamics and relationships. While the ability to capture the subtleties and intimacies of social relationships in an essay form was a key characteristic of his work, Simmel also wrote extensively about social structures, social differentiation, religion, money and the nature of sociology. His contribution to sociology was as much philosophical as psychological. Simmel used formal sociology as the basis of his sociological analysis, as the means for promoting sociology's claim to being a science and as a means of distinguishing it from other social sciences. However, he failed to develop this insight into a comprehensive and systematic sociological theory capable of analysing society at large. Rather, he felt that sociology was too young a discipline, at too early a stage in its development to embark on grand theory. In fact, by 1913 his interest in sociology was on the wane. Attempts have been made since to revive, refine and develop his work, the most notable being that by Leopold von Wiese, but with limited success. The fragmentary, diverse and fleeting nature of Simmel's insights, his use of images rather than empirical evidence, the very style of his essays, have made his work both highly personal and almost impossible to replicate. His ability to focus on the minutiae of daily life, on the intimacy of social relationships, rather than on the grand topics of sociology – the state, class, wealth – were both his strength and his weakness; were the reason why his impact on modern sociology has been both limited and indirect. The richness and diversity of his social analysis, which extended from women's rights to the modern Metropolis, from Goethe to Rembrandt, and his fleeting insights have often left his readers as much frustrated as enlightened. *'It is the microsociological character of Simmel's work that may always give him an edge in timeliness over the other pioneers. He did not disdain the small and the intimate elements of human association, nor did he ever lose sight of the primacy of human beings, of concrete individuals, in his analysis of institutions'* (Nisbet 1966: 480).

Georg Simmel's approach was highly original and individual, a clear alternative to the positivist perspective of Comte, Spencer and Durkheim that was to dominate and drive modern sociology right up until the 1960s. As many reviewers have commented, Simmel's work deserves re-reading, revival and re-appreciation. As Bryan Turner (1985) has commented, *'Simmel laid the foundations for the discipline of sociology long before Max Weber turned to the problem of sociology as a special discipline.'* Simmel's focus on micro-sociology and his enthusiasm for 'sociological imaginations' rather than sociological experiments informed and inspired the development of phenomenology (see p. 165) and its various offshoots, such as symbolic interactionism and ethnomethodology, the Chicago School of Sociology and studies of urban life in America in the 1920s and 30s. Marginalised and overshadowed in his own time, Georg Simmel has however had a profound influence on modern sociology and even enjoyed a renaissance recently among academics following the publication of his biography by David Frisby in 1984. As Henrik Ørnstrup concluded (2000) *'Today Simmel is considered one of the founding fathers of modern sociology along with his contemporaries Max Weber and Ferdinand Tönnies'.*

 **See Also**

- POSITIVISM (p. 56) for a contrasting view of sociology and society.
- POST-MODERNISM (p. 245) and the revival of some of Simmel's ideas.

Suggested Reading

FRISBY, D. (1984) *Georg Simmel,* Tavistock, London.

PAMPEL, F.C. (2000) Georg Simmel and Forms of Social Interaction, Ch. 4 in Pampel, F.C., *Sociological Lives and Ideas: An Introduction to Classical Theorists,* Macmillan, Basingstoke.

Further Reading

FRISBY, D. (ED.) (1994) *Georg Simmel: Critical Assessments,* Routledge, London.

TURNER, B.S. (1985) 'Georg Simmel' in *Thinkers of the Twentieth Century,* Firethorn Press, London.

WATIER, P. (1998) Georg Simmel, Ch. 5 in Stones, R. (ed.), *Key Sociological Thinkers,* Macmillan, Basingstoke.

Gemeinschaft–Gesellschaft

Ferdinand Tönnies

The Idea

THE CONCEPT OF *GEMEINSCHAFT–GESELLSCHAFT* – THE IDEA OF COMPARING AND contrasting the old traditional and agrarian way of life with the new modern and urban one in terms of ideal types and in terms of their different and contrasting social relationships and lifestyles – dates back to the writings of Ferdinand Tönnies, one of the founding fathers of the sociology of community.

Writing in the late 1880s, Tönnies, like his contemporaries around him – Weber, Durkheim and Georg Simmel – sought to make sense of the massive social, economic and political changes sweeping across Europe and America, most notably industrialisation, urbanisation and the fundamental breaks with the past he saw all around him. In his major work, *Gemeinschaft–Gesellschaft*, Tönnies sought to capture the key differences between the societies of the past and the industrial age Europe was entering, in particular the nature and extent of change in social relationships.

Ferdinand Tönnies

The term *gemeinschaft* is usually translated as 'community', a term that evokes romantic memories of a bygone age of harmony and stability. Tönnies, however, used the term more specifically to refer to human relationships that are highly personal, intimate and enduring, those where a person's involvement is considerable if not total, as in the family, with real friends or a close-knit group. He strongly linked such communal ties with traditional village communities where there was a stable social order in which everyone knew their place, where status was ascribed, mobility, be it social or geographical, limited, and the whole way of life governed by a homogeneous culture, a strict set of values and morals based on organised religion and reinforced by the two key social controls: the family and the church. In such small-scale societies, everyone knew everyone else and were interrelated by blood or marriage. Tied to the land, kin and the rhythms of nature, few moved outside their own territory. Relationships seemed to be more natural, organic and emotional. They seemed to have more meaning than today.

The term *gesellschaft* in contrast is usually translated as 'society' or 'association'. Tönnies used it to refer to everything opposite of *gemeinschaft,* in particular the apparently impersonal, superficial and transitory relationships of modern urban life. Commerce and industry require a more calculating, rational and self-interested approach to one's dealings with others. We make contracts or agreements rather than getting to know people. Our business, and even our everyday relationships are mainly a means to an end, to getting something from others. So they are fairly specific and limited. We talk to the shop assistant or bank clerk merely as a means to buying something. He or she is not a colleague or friend. There is no time or place for sentiment or emotion in modern industrial life. The whole pace of life is much faster, more dynamic, competitive and large-scale as we strive towards economic progress, a higher standard of living and greater social status. Instead of one culture, there is a multitude of different ways of life with few social sanctions.

Tönnies' typology is often depicted as contrasting roles and relationships in the city with those in the village – the friendly village bobby with the urban 'cop', jovial Farmer Giles with the faceless bureaucrat, the tranquillity of the countryside with the urban 'rat race'. He also used it to compare the difference in the type and quality of relationship between, for example, a friend and an acquaintance, a family business and a modern corporation, the warmth of personal relationships compared to the coldness and ruthlessness of business ones. Similarly Tönnies seems to have been deeply pessimistic, seems to have been arguing that industrialisation was destroying any sense of community and with it the broader basis of civilisation. Yet he also used these twin terms as part of a sociological analysis of organisations, culture and human 'will', intended to form the basis of an analysis of man's social evolution from primitive agrarian communism through industrial capitalism to a new socialist order in the future in which *gemeinschaft* would re-emerge. Here Tönnies made a distinction between 'natural will' (*wesenwille*) including habitual as well as instinctive or traditional ways of acting, with rational will (*kurville*). Like Durkheim and Weber he saw modern urban society as a reflection of underlying social structures and lifestyles. He could not help mourning the loss of the past, the loss of traditional human relationships and ways of relating to one another, though he recognised the inevitability of change, even if he did not like it.

Tönnies never finished this grand scheme, this grand typology. He never tied these two terms to any particular locality, never said that rural societies create a sense of community and urban ones destroy it, though he did strongly imply this. Rather he argued that *gemeinschaft* and *gesellschaft* were two pure or ideal types. In reality there would always be a mixture of both – some *gemeinschaft* in the city; some *gesellschaft* in the village. Nor did he say that industrialisation caused the collapse of community, but rather argued that the decline of *gemeinschaft* created the conditions, the rationalism, calculative habits and contractual relationships necessary for industrial capitalism to flourish. He even used these concepts to analyse deviancy, arguing, for example, that as *gemeinschaft* declined, so crime and suicide increased.

In later works, Tönnies went on to distinguish between typical rural and urban criminals; between the 'malefactors' (e.g. arsonists and thugs) of village communities and the 'crooks' found in towns and cities, the thieves, burglars and swindlers of urban environments; spontaneous and passionate crime compared to the more calculating, premeditated and ruthless criminality of urban society.

Tönnies foresaw within *gesellschaft* and within modern society the growth of class consciousness and class conflict. A new culture, a new way of life based on reinstating the ideas and ideals of *gemeinschaft* needed to be fostered and developed. He therefore supported socialism and social reform and bitterly opposed national socialism and '*Volksgemeinschaft*', the Nazi version of his ideas.

The Idea in Action

THE DUAL CONCEPT OF *GEMEINSCHAFT–GESELLSCHAFT* EARNED TÖNNIES A PLACE IN THE sociological history books as the founding father of community studies and urban sociology. Though his book was not widely read until the 1930s, it (and the works of Durkheim and Simmel) inspired a mass of studies of every type of society, every aspect of community life, and strongly influenced the urban studies of the famous Chicago School in America in the 1900s. Such social scientists developed the theory of the rural–urban continuum with Robert Redfield (1930) and Louis Wirth (1938), in particular, comparing the peasant and urban ways of life as '*two poles in reference to which one or other of all human settlements tend to arrange themselves*'. In other words, *where* you lived determined *how* you lived. However, such a 'search for community' was not limited to academics. It inspired such diverse movements as the 'hippie' communes of the 1960s, the new towns and garden cities so beloved by town planners in the 1970s and the commuter villages of the urban middle class that have grown up ever since.

As already explained, however, Tönnies' analysis of community was somewhat more subtle and complex than that above. By tying it to a particular locality, the community studies tradition produced a narrow, even distorted version of *gemeinschaft–gesellschaft* and once studies started to show the existence of tight-knit communities *within* the city (as in Young and Wilmott's study of Bethnal Green (1962), or of 'class conflict' in the country (as in Ray Pahl's study of commuter villages, 1965) then the theory of a rural–urban continuum was doomed. Raymond Williams' (1973) analysis of the traditional community as simply the 'mutuality of the oppressed', as the reaction of medieval peasants to their harsh way of life and the cruelty and oppression of the gentry, further destroyed this myth. Finally, there was nothing in even the original version of *gemeinschaft–gesellschaft* that could explain the race riots that exploded in American cities in the 1960s; and so younger, more radical, urban sociologists turned to the theories of Marx and Weber to illuminate the influence of power and class conflict in determining the shape of the modern city and the behaviour of its inhabitants.

Today Tönnies has been consigned to the sociological history books rather than inspiring modern sociology in the way Durkheim, Marx and Weber continue to do. However, so long as the 'quest for community' and the romantic images of rural life continue to inspire people, so the concepts of *gemeinschaft–gesellschaft* will live on and continue to inform sociological debate and ideals of a better, more community-based lifestyle.

 See Also

- **URBANISM** (p. 201), as developments of this thesis and as applied to America in the 1920s and 1930s.

Suggested Reading

SLATTERY, M. (1985) *Urban Sociology,* Causeway Press, Ormskirk.

Further Reading

FALK, J. (2000) Ferdinand Tönnies, in Andersen, H. and Kasperson, B.K. (eds), *Classical and Modern Social Theory*, Blackwell, Oxford.

TÖNNIES, F. (1951) *Community and Society* [1887], Harper Row, New York.

YOUNG, M. AND WILMOTT, P. (1962) *Family and Kinship in East London,* Penguin, Harmondsworth.

Historical Materialism

Karl Marx

![The Idea]

HISTORICAL MATERIALISM IS ONE OF THE GREATEST AND MOST INFLUENTIAL IDEAS within the social sciences and within world history. It formed the basis of the Marxist theory of economic, political and social development, which in turn underpinned the spread of communism throughout Eastern Europe and South-East Asia during the course of the twentieth century. It is a complex idea, a profound and rigorous theory of historical and social development. It derives from the ideas and writings of Karl Marx and his co-author Friedrich Engels, and it clearly reflects in its sweep and in its monumental attempt not only to predict the future but also to make it happen, the life and times of the men who wrote it. Marx, a radical journalist, and Engels, a socialist businessman, lived, worked and campaigned for change during one of the greatest periods of revolutionary turmoil in human history, the nineteenth century; a period that embraced the political revolutions that swept France and the rest of Western Europe, the economic transformations brought about by the Agrarian and Industrial Revolution and the intellectual outpourings created by the Scientific Revolution. Revolution was everywhere and Marx and Engels led the way in promoting a new version of history, a new vision of society, a new utopia – communism.

The term 'historical materialism' reflects the basic thesis of Marx's view of history, namely that it is economic forces, not political leaders, who have been the driving force behind historical change; it is the economic or material base of society, not the political superstructure that determines social life and human development. Traditionally, history is seen as the progressive unfolding of man's social and economic development propelled forward by the political actions of certain key historical figures – Julius Caesar, Napoleon, Nelson – and certain outstanding kings and queens. Historical materialism similarly sees history as progressive but rejects the idea that it is the actions of individuals, however powerful, that is the key dynamic. Rather, for Marxists the key dynamism is economic development. As Engels summed it up (*Socialism: Utopian and Scientific*) historical materialism '*designate[s] that view of the course of history which seeks the ultimate cause and the great moving power of all important historic events in the economic development of society, in the changes in the modes of production and exchange, in the consequent division of society into distinct classes, and in the struggle of these classes against one another'.*

Historical materialism, therefore, is a theory of historical development through economic or material forces rather than political or social ones.'

The term 'materialist' is a philosophical concept that sees the *external* world as real, governed by its own laws of cause and effect and independent of human consciousness. This perspective contrasts with idealism which sees the external world, both natural and social, as ultimately determined by men's ideas and consciousness of it. The philosophical debate between these two views was at its height in mid-nineteenth-century Germany, with the great German philosopher Hegel proclaiming that ideas were the dominant force in history, that history was simply the progressive unfolding of reason. Marx 'stood Hegel on his head', declaring that it was not ideas that determined historical development but the economic facts of life, not least man's need to produce food, shelter and water.

'The simple fact [is] that human beings must have food, drink, clothing and shelter first of all, before they can interest themselves in politics, science, art, religion and the like. This implies that the production of the immediate material means of subsistence, and consequently the degree of economic development of a given people or epoch, form the foundation upon which the state institutions, the legal conceptions, the art, and even religious ideas are built up. It implies that these latter must be explained out of the former, whereas the former have usually been explained as issuing from the latter' (Engels' speech at the graveside of Karl Marx, 17 March 1883).

'It is not the consciousness of men that determines their being, but, on the contrary, their being that determines their consciousness' (Karl Marx, Preface to *A Critique of Political Economy*, 1971 [1859])

Historical materialism, therefore, is a theory of social structure and social change based on the following key concepts:

- That society is a totality based on two key structures:
  - an economic substructure concerned with the production and distribution of goods and services;
  - a social, political and ideological superstructure comprising such key social institutions as the state, the law and the family.
- That the economic substructure forms the basic foundation of society. It determines not only the production of goods and services but all other major social institutions in the superstructure – even a society's way of life, form of government and the way it thinks. It can be broken down into two key elements:
  - the forces of production – the methods and tools of production including labour and machinery;
  - the relations of production that exist between the owners of the means of production and the workers. These will vary from one mode of production to another. Under feudalism they were those of master and serf; under capitalism, bourgeoisie and proletariat.

- That a mode of production refers to the economic system prevailing at any particular point in historical time. Thus, in the Middle Ages, feudalism was predominant, based on land as the chief means of production. In capitalist society industry and trade predominate. Besides socialism, Marx identified four major modes of production (MOP): Asiatic, Ancient, Feudalism, Capitalism. Each MOP is a progressive step forward in man's march forward towards socialism.

The key dynamic for social change in the theory of historical materialism is the dialectic, the notion that progressive change comes about not through evolution but through revolution and conflict. Within Marxist theory there are two key sources of dialectic materialism:

1. The underlying contradictions within the economic substructure resulting in a growing conflict and mismatch between the forces and relations of production as new economic methods start to outgrow their social and legal structure as, for example, when industry and commerce began to outgrow feudalism.
2. The growth of class conflict as the owners of the means of production begin to increase their exploitation of the workforce in order to maintain their privilege and profits. Social classes for Marxists arise simply from the ownership and non-ownership of the means of production, a relationship which at heart is antagonistic due to its exploitative nature and unequal distribution of wealth, be it between feudal lords and serfs or capitalists and workers.

For Marx and Engels (1948) 'the class struggle' was the heart of historical materialism, the dynamic of social change: 'the history of all hitherto existing society is the history of class struggle'. And though immediately destructive, ultimately such conflict is progressive: 'no antagonism, no progress', claimed Marx.

Marx used the 'guiding threads' of historical materialism to outline in detail his analysis of his contemporary mode of production, *capitalism*.

Capitalism

THE key *forces of production* in capitalist society are industry and commerce, the factory and the mill; the key *relations of production* are those of bourgeoisie and proletariat – the bosses and the workers. While the forces of production are governed by the market forces of supply and demand and by the capitalist search for continuous profit and investment, the binding tie of the capitalist–worker relation of production is the impersonal and solely self-interested one of the 'cash nexus'; that is, the capitalist employs the worker solely as a means to making profit and so will exploit or discard him as the need arises. The capitalist superstructure serves and legitimises this substructure with the family and education system producing healthy and disciplined workers, while the state, legal system and media ensure both physical and ideological control of the masses, ensuring that through materialism and exclusion of alternative ideas the working class is kept in a state of 'false consciousness'.

However, like all antagonistic modes of production, capitalism contains the 'seeds of its own destruction' due to its own inherent contradictions. The very heart of capitalism is competition in pursuit of profits. Ultimately, however, such competition and cost cutting will lead to a collapse in the bourgeois class, as more and more of its members 'go to the wall', and to a growth in the size, unity and class consciousness of the working class reduced to subsistence wages and threatened by mass unemployment. This, in turn, will create and exacerbate capitalism's periodic crises of boom and slump and increase class antagonisms and polarisation to the point where the workers will unite, throw off their chains, seize control of the state and means of production and so inaugurate the final MOP of socialism – communism. Here, class conflict, inequality and false consciousness will no longer exist because the means of production will be communally owned by all the people. Man will at last be free from exploitation and alienation, free *'to hunt in the morning, fish in the afternoon . . . and criticise after dinner'* (Marx 1965).

Thus, while in Marx and Engels' view the capitalist mode of production is evil and exploitative and produces 'its own gravediggers', it also creates the economic forces of production necessary for material abundance, necessary for freedom from want and hardship, allowing man time to think, reflect and philosophise in a communist society based on the principle of 'from each according to his ability, to each according to his need'.

The Idea in Action

HISTORICAL MATERIALISM WAS THEREFORE DESIGNED NOT ONLY AS AN ACADEMIC theory but a programme of action, a 'guiding thread' for revolutionaries as well as for social theorists and historians. Engels converted it into a guiding light for socialists throughout the world declaring it to be not just an historical interpretation but a scientific law. As Engels proclaimed at Marx's graveside: *'Just as Darwin discovered the law of development of organic nature, so Marx discovered the law of development of human history.'*

Its radical analysis of historical exploitation, oppression and inequality and its vision of a utopian future inspired communist revolutions throughout the world and a crude version of historical materialism became the 'Bible' of the Soviet Revolution in Russia and Eastern Europe. As Marx so boldly proclaimed: *'The philosophers have only interpreted the world – the point however is to change it.'*

The theory of historical materialism, however, has also been the subject of intense criticism and debate both within Marxism and from without.

Economic determinism

THE key controversy, one that still inspires heated debates, is the underlying element of economic determinism within historical materialism. According to cruder versions of this theory:

- The economic substructure determines all else. Political, social and ideological factors are all subordinate to economic ones and have no independent causal influence on history. All social conflicts, institutions and behaviour can be explained in terms of the economic stage of development.
- Modes of production are clearly defined stages of economic development and all societies must follow the same pathway to socialism.

Many sociologists and historians would totally reject such a deterministic and simplistic analysis, arguing that political and social forces have as much influence on social change as economic ones. Max Weber, in particular, led this critique using his concept of the *Protestant ethic* (see p. 61) to highlight the importance of cultural factors in that most crucial of social changes, the Industrial Revolution. Detailed historical analyses of past and present societies have shown that a division of history into four or five modes of production is too simple, while present-day 'communist' societies such as Russia and China are clear evidence of the way industrial advance can be achieved without going through *laissez-faire* capitalism first. Within Marxism itself the dictates of orthodox Marxism and the inhumanities committed in the name of historical materialism led to a radical reassessment of economism. Some, like the Frankfurt School (see p. 84), turned back to the early Marx for a more humanistic and flexible interpretation. Others like Louis Althusser and structural Marxists (see p. 265) sought to make it more scientific. However, both schools of Marxist thought gave far greater emphasis to political and especially ideological factors in late capitalism.

The source of this controversy is partly Marx, partly Engels and partly the fact that Marx's work was never completed and was being continually revised. Marx's own style, his dogmatism and claims to scientific certainty, all aided this impression of economic determinism. For example, while declaring that '*men make their own history*' he went on to say that '*they do not make it under conditions chosen by themselves*'.

However, both Marx and Engels publicly denied economic determinacy in their theory of historical materialism. Engels claimed that it was only a 'guide to study' and attacked crude interpretations that were evolving even in his own time.

'*According to the materialist conception of history, the ultimately determining element in history is the production and reproduction of real life. More than this neither Marx nor I have ever asserted.*

... If someone twists this into saying that the economic element is the only determining one, he transforms that proposition into a meaningless senseless phrase. The economic situation is the basis, but the various elements of the superstructure ... also exercise their influence upon the course of the historical struggles and in many cases preponderate in determining their form. There is an interaction of all these elements in which, amid all the endless host of accidents ... the economic movement finally asserts itself as necessary ... ' (Carver 1981).

In his later writings Engels gave even more support to the influence of ideas on history, while in his later years Marx accepted the possibility not only of a Soviet road to socialism but also of a peaceful, democratic one. This debate reflects an underlying conflict in the theory of historical materialism and Marxism generally in its attempt to be both a theory and a revolutionary guidebook. If historical materialism is correct, if socialism is inevitable, if political factors are subordinate to economic developments, why engage in revolutionary action?

Engels added to this impression of determinism by his increasing use of scientific terminology and concepts and by his claim that dialectical materialism was '*the Science of the general laws of motion and development of nature, human society and thought*' (Carver 1981). Marx, at least in his less deterministic mood, would reply that while economic developments create the framework for change, only men can actually make it happen. Therefore *not* to engage in the class struggle is to impede social progress.

The role of the state

THE state in advanced capitalist and especially socialist countries has not 'withered away' but grown in size and intervention. Within capitalism the state, the key political force, has become the major institution managing the economy and ensuring not only physical control of the masses but ideological control. This political dominance of the economy is even more profound in centrally planned economies and there, despite ideological claims to the contrary, the state is an oppressive totalitarian force suppressing rather than promoting human rights. Marx and Engels' views on the state and on its role as either the right hand of the ruling class or simply as a mediator protecting the interests of the system rather than those of any particular class, has been a major debate in post-war Marxism, notably in the writings of Gramsci, Poulantzas and Ralph Miliband.

The polarisation of classes

THE prediction of the polarisation of advanced capitalist societies into two major classes has obviously not come about. Rather the reverse, with the middle class growing, the working class shrinking and the whole class system becoming fragmented and truncated by such non-economic forms of stratification as age, race and gender.

Moreover, far from the working class growing in unity and revolutionary consciousness, it has remained highly conservative. The 'communist' revolutions of the twentieth century have occurred not in the prosperous industrial West but the poor agrarian societies of the East and the Third World, more often by political force than economic revolution.

Modes of production

THE concept of modes of production as an analysis of historical development has not proved as easy to apply to real societies as predicted. Few societies neatly fit this scheme. Few can neatly be labelled capitalist or feudal. Even Marx recognised this problem and allowed for mixed modes and even for the possibility of some societies skipping a stage in the great leap forward to Socialism. Communist societies of the twentieth century have proved neither classless nor liberating, but introduced some of the most ruthless and authoritarian regimes ever seen. The collapse of socialism in Eastern Europe in the late 1980s seemed to reflect the inherent hollowness of Marxian ideology and the superiority of Western capitalism.

Marx's actual writings, however, are more mature, more subtle, than his critics often give him credit for. His early work on alienation reflected his underlying focus on conscious human action and on the power of ideas. His dialectic methodology itself was non-deterministic by nature, and Marx constantly argued that 'man makes his own history', that history is not explained in terms of impersonal forces but man's purposeful activity. The future lies in the possibility of communism but only if the proletariat fights for it.

Much of the criticism of Marx is more of his followers and of the schools of Marxism that followed, those who derived from the structural and economic determinism of his later work (e.g. Althusser) and those that sought to explain post-war capitalism in terms of the ideological control of the superstructure and cultural realm (e.g. Frankfurt School). Marx and Engels distanced themselves from 'vulgar' materialism, arguing that the relationship between the base and the superstructure is more complex than the rigid, one way economic determinism some Marxist followers attempted to adopt. Marx did, however, adopt a more scientific and structural approach in his later writings, focusing in on the objective laws of development and arguing that *'life is not determined by consciousness but consciousness by life'* (quoted in Swinglewood 2000: 39).

Marx's analysis of capitalism is an abstract scientific one seeking to describe as an ideal type the main characteristics of the very spirit of capitalism rather than a specific historical example. At the heart of his analysis is his description of the social relationships that a particular mode of production generate – the relationship within capitalism of capital and labour, of bourgeoisie and proletariat and the underlying class conflict over ownership and private property.

Although Marx's initial analysis of class in a capitalist society is a relatively simple two-fold one, in his later writings he identified a much more complex structure which embraced small producers, petty bourgeoisie, managers and even the ideological or intellectual classes. He equally predicted the growth of the middle classes as important functionaries in managing bourgeois society: *'the constantly growing number of the middle classes which situated between the workers on the one side and the capitalists and the landlords on the other [living] mainly and directly on revenue . . . press like heavy burden on the labouring class, enlarging the social security and power of the upper ten thousand'* (Marx 1964–72: 573). In studying actual capitalist societies, notably nineteenth-century Britain, Marx fully recognised that capitalism in reality is far more complex than his ideal type and that even the bourgeoisie is never a unified, coherent and organised class but is itself driven by internal factions and fraction.

Though class struggle and revolutionary overthrow were the key themes in Marx's political analysis, towards the end of his life he did concede that in the developed democracies such as Holland, England and the USA, the working class may come to power by parliamentary means.

However, whatever its shortcomings in theory and practice, historical materialism has proved central to Marxist theory and a major stimulus to social scientists (and revolutionaries) throughout the world. It continues even today, 100 years later, to inspire debate, research and the hopes of millions of people for a freer, more rational and just society. Very few sociological ideas have had anything like as much influence, and as Terrell Carver (1981), one of Engels' biographers, concludes, *'The materialist interpretation of history is the main item in the intellectual legacy left us by Engels.'* Unfortunately, today there is no unitary *'interpretation of this famous view of history on which all Marxists agree. Rather the materialist interpretation of history represents a set of shared disagreements'* (Carver 1981).

Inequality – its causes, effects and potential solutions – was the driving force in Marx's and Engels' analysis and revolutionary polemic. This conflict and this revolutionary ideology led to two great political doctrines of the twentieth century, the societies and regimes created in Marx's name and the ideological Cold War that nearly destroyed mankind. Marx and Engels may have rejected Hegel's notion of the power of ideas to transform history, yet they and their ideas did more to change society as we know it than any philosophers, historians or economists before or since. *'Before the fall of Eastern European communism and the dissolution of the Soviet Union in 1989–91, more than one-third of the people on earth lived under regimes that claimed they intended to implement the theories of Marx'* (Manson 2000: 30).

Despite limited influence during his life, Marx's ideas came to dominate the twentieth century. With the Russian Revolution in 1917, the control of Eastern Europe under communism after World War II, the Chinese Revolution in 1949, and the Cuban Revolution in 1959, large parts of the world's population adopted various forms of Marxism. These developments associated Marx with totalitarian systems of society and an economy controlled by state bureaucracies – results at odds with Marx's goal of human freedom. The end of communism in the Soviet Union and Eastern Europe in the 1990s as well as the movement toward free markets and democratic governments almost everywhere else has reflected a near-unanimous rejection of Soviet-style Marxism (Pampel 2000).

 **See Also**

- **STRUCTURAL MARXISM** (p. 265), **RELATIVE AUTONOMY** (p. 250), **HEGEMONY** (p. 121) and **CRITICAL THEORY** (p. 84) as contrasting modern and post-modern versions of this thesis.
- **SOCIAL SOLIDARITY** (p. 72), **SOCIAL DARWINISM** (p. 67) and **STRUCTURAL FUNCTIONALISM** (p. 190) as very different evolutionary theories of social change and development.

Suggested Reading

ANY of the original works by Marx and Engels are worth trying (see Further Reading, below and on p. 21). The following are readable summaries of their key ideas:

CAREW HUNT, R.N. (1950) *The Theory and Practice of Communism,* Penguin, Harmondsworth.

PAMPEL, F.C. (2000) Karl Marx and the Centrality of Social Class, Ch. 1 in Pampel F.C., *Sociological Lives and Ideas: An Introduction to Classical Theorists*, Macmillan, Basingstoke.

RUIS (1986) *Marx for Beginners,* Unwin Paperbacks, London.

The following are short outlines of Marx and Engels' life and times:

MCCLELLAN, D. (1973) *Karl Marx: His Life and Thought,* Macmillan, London.

MCCLELLAN, D. (1977) *Engels,* Fontana, Glasgow.

Further Reading

CALLINICOS, A. (1983) *The Revolutionary Ideas of Karl Marx,* Pluto Press, London.

ENGELS, F. (1845) *The Condition of the Working Class in England*, Blackwell, Oxford.

ENGELS, F. (1942) *The Origins of the Family, Private Property and the State* [1884], International Publishers, New York.

JESSOP, B. (1998) Karl Marx, Ch. 1 Part I in Stones, R. (ed.), *Key Sociological Thinkers*, Macmillan, Basingstoke.

MARX, K. AND ENGELS, F. (1967) *Manifesto of the Communist Party,* Taylor, A.J.P. (ed.), Penguin, Harmondsworth.

SCHMITT, R. (1997) *Introduction to Marx and Engels: A Critical Reconstruction*, Westview, Boulder, CO.

STEGER, M.B. AND CARVER, T. (EDS.) (1999) *Engels after Marx*, Manchester University Press, Manchester.

The Iron Law
of Oligarchy

Robert Michels

The Idea

T HE THEORY OF THE IRON LAW OF OLIGARCHY WAS AN IDEA DEVELOPED BY THE
political theorist Robert Michels, writing in the early twentieth century during
and after the First World War, and the intense political, economic and social upheavals
that followed. Originally an active socialist and member of the German Social
Democratic Party, Michels became increasingly disillusioned with radical politics and
particularly revolutionary organisations. Instead he became a scathing critic of
socialism and Marxism and eventually an apologist for fascism, as his faith in revolutionary action and in the masses disappeared and drained away.

This disillusion with democracy and with radical action is clearly explained in his
theory of oligarchy and in his major work, *Political Parties*, published in 1911. Michels'
thesis is that oligarchy, the rule of the few, is inevitable at all times and in all places,
however democratic the organisation may seem to be. Worse than that, this rule of the
few is not only inevitable, is not only an Iron Law, it is always ultimately a rule in
the interests of the few.

Even in the most revolutionary of organisations, even in socialist parties in the 1920s,
however radical their aims and ambitions, however democratic they seem to be,
ultimately these organisations will be redirected to serving the needs and ambitions of
those at the top rather than those they represent. '*He who says democracy, says organisation; he who says organisation, says oligarchy*' (Michels 1911).

Like fellow political theorists Pareto and Mosca, Michels was writing at the turn of the
century, at a time when mass democracy seemed to be sweeping Europe, when
socialist and communist ideas were all the fashion, and when many were proclaiming
the advent of true democracy – government of the people, by the people, for the
people. But like Pareto and Mosca, Michels increasingly came to see such democracy
as impossible and oligarchy as inevitable. The basis of his thesis was that there is a
fundamental contradiction in mass democracies between the need for organisation

(*'democracy is inconceivable without organisation'*) and the inbuilt tendency of large-scale organisations to become oligarchical (*'Who says organisation, says oligarchy'*). In a mass democracy, the individual on his own is powerless. Only by joining others in organisations can he make his voice heard, and this is especially true for the working classes who lack the education, money and connections to pull political strings. However, within such mass organisations not everybody can be involved in making decisions so delegates have to be elected 'to represent the masses and carry out its will'. Moreover, to be efficient such organisations need full-time officials and an administrative hierarchy of rules and regulations. Among both officials and the organisations' leaders, however, oligarchical tendencies soon develop.

- Increasingly, officials begin to use their expertise and power over information to influence decision making.

- Increasingly, a career structure develops within bureaucracies and amid 'the mania for promotion', deference to one's superiors soon counts for more than simple ability. Individuality and criticism are thus soon excluded or crushed and the power of those at the top increased.

- Increasingly, those at the top of such organisations become more interested in maintaining their own powers and privileges than in promoting the causes of the organisation. The organisation becomes an end in itself rather than a means to an end; the policies of the organisation become increasingly conservative for fear that radical actions will lead to its destruction; the leadership dominates all decision making and appointments, dismantles any checks on its power and, where possible, votes itself into office for life.

- Increasingly, the ordinary members find themselves excluded from the organisation, from decision making. They find the rules, procedures and jargon of meetings and documents incomprehensible and react by not attending, not participating and so increasing the power of the leadership. Those at the top of organisational structures begin to adopt an elite lifestyle and so find it very difficult even to consider returning to the shop floor. They come to believe in their own omnipotence, come to accept mass adulation as natural, come to see themselves as invincible and to believe in their own propaganda that they alone know what is best for the organisation, for the 'people'.

Michels' thesis combined a structural and a psychological analysis of organisations. It therefore rested on three key elements:

1. the technical factors involved in establishing and maintaining an organisational machine, one which inevitably develops a 'life of its own';

2. the psychology of the organisational leadership and the way that having achieved power, leaders seek to cling on to it at all costs;

3. the psychology of the masses, the rank and file who need strong leaders, need to be told what to do.

There is a process of "goal displacement" by which the original often radical or idealistic goals of the organisation are replaced by the lesser goals needed to maintain the organisation and to keep the leadership in power. Democracy is smothered, the members excluded and the goals and needs of the organisation and its leadership increasingly supercede those of the people it purports to represent. Ultimately as a number of revolutionary leaders have come to believe, *'Le parti c'est moi'*, the Party is I.

To support his thesis Michels (1911) made a detailed analysis of the German Social Democratic Party and the trade union movement organisations, which in the 1900s seemed to epitomise radical policies and true democracy. They claimed mass democracy: they claimed to represent the working classes. They claimed to be organisations designed to overthrow capitalism and establish socialism. But, in practice, their actions and policies were reformist rather than revolutionary and conservative to the point where the leaders of the SDP became part of the German 'establishment'. Thus in Michels' view, just as democracy inside organisations is bound to fail, so democracy in society at large is doomed and this is true whatever type of society is involved, capitalist or communist. Democratic leadership is simply a new type of elitism, and socialism a new form of ideology to be used to control the masses. The rise of totalitarian governments in both fascist and communist countries in the 1930s only confirmed his theory. Initially Michels had hoped that such an analysis would inspire the rank and file to seize back control of socialist parties and trade unions and force the leadership into radical action. However, in later years he came to the conclusion that the masses were inept and apathetic, that they had a psychological need to be led and that decisive leadership was to be admired: *'leaders never give up their power to the mass but only to other, newer leaders'* (Michels 1911). Hence his esteem for the new fascist regimes of Hitler and Mussolini and his shift from analysing power in terms of organisational features to an analysis of its psychology, the charisma of leadership and the deference of the masses.

The Idea in Action

THE VAST MAJORITY OF STUDIES OF ORGANISATIONAL POWER HAVE SUPPORTED Michels' thesis:

- Philip Selznick's (1966) study, for example, of the Tennessee Valley Authority set up as part of the New Deal in America during the 1930s depression, found that though this organisation was established to represent and promote the interests of ordinary people in the area, it quickly came under the control of the wealthier white farmers. Only by accepting such a takeover, such 'goal displacement', argued Selznick, could the TVA survive, because to have opposed the farming establishment would have meant its death. Robert McKenzie's (1964) study of British political parties used Michels' thesis to argue that, despite their enormous ideological differences, once in power the British Labour and Conservative parties adopt very similar policies.

- Studies of socialist and communist societies from Soviet Russia to present-day China show the same tendency to oligarchy, and Eva Rosenfeld (1974) found this even in the highly democratic Israel kibbutzim.

Classic examples of Michels' thesis include the French Revolution, Soviet Russia under Stalin and the Khmer Rouge in Cambodia, when in the 'name of the people', revolutionary and democratic organisations were used to purge and exterminate millions of people under the banner of revolutionary socialism and in the interests of the leadership.

In Britain, Mrs Thatcher's attacks on the trade unions and the new laws on secret ballots in the 1980s struck a chord in the hearts of many trade unionists who felt ignored and poorly represented by their leaders.

The only major study to identify real democracy in a mass organisation was Lipset et al.'s (1956) study of the International Typographical Union (ITU), a craft printers' union in America which ensures active mass membership and prevents oligarchy by numerous elections, referenda and a two-party system. However, as Lipset et al. themselves concluded, the ITU is rather exceptional. It has a long tradition of very active membership politically and socially and it is highly unlikely that such a structure of internal democracy could be transplanted to other unions or organisations: their leaders at least would oppose such a threat to their powers.

The major criticism of Michels' theory is that the strength of the Iron Law of Oligarchy, the extent to which the leadership is able to hold on to power, is able to reorientate the organisation to its goals rather than pursuing the interests of its members, may vary from organisation to organisation. Within political parties, for example, in liberal democracies the leadership is subject to regular voting and tests of its competence and direction at general elections. In contrast, trade union leaders and top businessmen are less open to scrutiny, less likely to be controlled, even rejected by their members or shareholders. Michels' analysis therefore failed to distinguish clearly between different types of oligarchy. At least in Western democracies there is some possibility of accountability as the electorate has a choice of parties and regular elections; in dictatorships no such popular power exists save through revolution.

Despite such criticisms – or more accurately, refinements – Michels' thesis has stood the test of time remarkably well and stimulated a wide variety of studies into elite theory and the distribution of power. Whether it has yet achieved the status of being a 'sociological' let alone an 'iron' law is another question. What it has done is forced all concerned in running democratic societies or organisations to constantly question those in power and to check whether they are being run for the people, even if they are not being run by them.

 See Also

- **BUREAUCRACY** (p. 27) – Max Weber's view of power in industrial society.
- **POWER ELITE** (p. 171) – C.W. Mills' view of power in post-war America.
- **RELATIVE AUTONOMY** (p. 250) – Marxist views on power and the modern state.
- **DISCOURSE** (p. 208) – a post-modern view of power in the late twentieth century.

Suggested Reading

MCKENZIE, R. (1964) *British Political Parties*, Mercury Books, London.

Further Reading

MICHELS, R. (1911) *Political Parties*, Free Press, New York – Michels' own study of oligarchy.

Positivism

Auguste Comte

![The Idea]

POSITIVISM IS THE PHILOSOPHICAL VIEW THAT THE ONLY VALID OR TRUE FORM OF HUMAN knowledge is that discovered by empirical science. Just as empirical science and its scientific methodology has unveiled the laws of nature and revealed the causes and effects of natural forces in the fields of physics, chemistry and biology – so positivists have sought to apply the same methodology to the social sciences to try and explain how society has developed and to discover the underlying causes and effects of social change. Positivism is based on the fundamental belief that the social world is essentially the same, essentially as real as the natural world and so open to the rigorous, objective and impartial analysis empirical scientists use to investigate nature and the universe. Subjective perceptions, feelings and interpretations have no place in a positive perspective because they cannot be observed, measured and tested. Positivism therefore rejects abstract philosophising and speculation in favour of logical reasoning and testable hypotheses based on hard facts and objective analysis in the search for causal relationships in social behaviour – a search for the underlying laws of history and society comparable to the great theories of Charles Darwin and Albert Einstein in natural science. Positivism aspires to being the science of society and the means to discovering the nature of man and the nature (and future) of society.

The notion of positivism – and in fact the concept of sociology as a subject and as an academic discipline – dates back to the nineteenth-century philosopher Auguste Comte. Born in Montpelier, Southern France, the son of an aristocratic and conservative family, Comte pursued an independent academic career centred almost exclusively around developing and promoting his theory of

Auguste Comte

positivism, not simply as an academic thesis but as a blueprint for a new social order and a new 'religion' of humanity. Living as he did among the chaos and upheavals of the Agrarian, Industrial and French Revolutions, his was a search for 'order and progress' for social evolution rather than political revolution; his was a search to establish sociology as the science of society, the queen of all the sciences.

In his major works – *Cours de Philosophie Positive* (1830–42) and *Système de Politique Positive* (1848–54) – Comte set out his famous 'Law of Three Stages', an historical analysis of the evolution of society and of human thought.

- The *theological* stage (the period in world history up until 1300), during which all natural phenomena and social events were explained in terms of supernatural forces and deities, culminating in the Christian theory of one almighty God.

- The *metaphysical* stage (from 1300 to 1800 AD), during which abstract and even supernatural forces were still the main source of explanation but they were more consistent and systematic than the capricious gods of the past.

- The *positivist* stage (from 1800 onwards), during which thought and explanation are based on science not speculation, empirical experimentation not abstract philosophising. Only then will the world be demystified and reality truly exposed.

According to Comte, all branches of human knowledge have evolved through these three stages, but not simultaneously. The lower, more basic sciences adopted the positivist spirit of inquiry first; the higher, more complex disciplines later because they depended on the groundwork in the lower sciences for their development. Thus astronomy and mathematics preceded physics, which laid the foundations for chemistry and, in turn, biology, and finally sociology. Chemistry and the lower sciences constitute 'analytical' disciplines because they deal with fundamental laws and the most elementary components of natural phenomena. Comte referred to biology and sociology as 'synthetic' sciences because they deal with complete organisms and offer an overall picture.

Moreover, these very varied scientific disciplines form a natural hierarchy, rising from generality to complexity, from autonomy to interdependence and culminating in sociology as the ultimate explanation of human and social development.

According to Comte's thesis, human society has followed similar stages of evolution, and each stage has been associated with one particular mode of thought (a view he later modified as he sought to explain the emergence of each new stage as a struggle between traditional and progressive ideas). Using an organic analogy, he argued that through the division of labour, society has become more complex, differentiated and specialised. A social solidarity or sense of community has evolved based on an underlying consensus, and the increasing interdependence of its constituent parts – the family, education and all the other institutions which comprise the social system and all the aspects of culture and language which provide its fabric. The role of sociology is to provide an overview, to analyse both the *statics* (laws governing social order) and *dynamics* (laws governing social change) of society.

Comte's sociology increasingly developed into a search for the essential principles of both social order and social change, and came to reflect an underlying tension between traditional conservatism's opposition to science, reform and revolution, and radicalism's belief in a new golden age based on science and industry. Comte became increasingly sympathetic to the conservative view of social order as requiring an under-lying set of common moral values. Accepting the view that, through the decline of traditional religion and rise of revolutionary philosophies, Europe was undergoing a moral as well as a social crisis, Comte sought to offer positivism as a means for creating a new moral consensus as the basis of his new social order, even going on to propose that sociology become the new 'religion of humanity'.

This concern with values equally underlies Comte's view of social theory and research. He rejected pure empiricism, the simplistic collection and measurement of social facts for their own sake. Unlike many later positivists, he argued for the inter-relationship of facts and theory. He equally recognised that social research could never imitate the methods of natural science in all their purity, could not conduct pure experi-ments. He therefore proposed indirect or 'natural' social experiments and identified such scientific principles as observation, analysis and, in particular, comparison, as the foundations of his new science of society. He equally recognised the limitations of positivism, recognised that it could not claim absolute truth, only partial or provisional statements of fact. *'Finally, in the positive state, the human mind, recognising the impos-sibility of obtaining absolute truth, gives up the search after the origin and hidden causes of the universe and a knowledge of the final causes of phenomena. It endeavours now only to discover, by a well-combined use of reasoning and observation, the actual laws of phenomena – that is to say, their invariable relations of succession and likeness'* (quoted in Callinicos 1999).

Nevertheless, Comte ultimately believed that *'the social universe is amenable to the development of abstract laws that can be tested through the careful collection of data'* (Turner 1985). What he proposed to develop was a *'science of social development'*.

Though Comte's search for underlying laws of social development implies historical fatalism – that even if it is possible to understand how society is developing, it is not possible to change it – his ultimate aim was to provide policy makers with the knowl-edge and ideas to control and improve social conditions. Just as scientific method had provided natural scientists with the tools for mastering as well as understanding nature, so, believed Comte, positivist sociology would enable man to become master of his social and political destiny. Comte was not therefore opposed to change as such, rather he welcomed and predicted it as the outcome of the positivist stage. What he feared and opposed, however, was unnatural, man-made or revolutionary change that threatened the natural evolution of society and so generated the chaos and disorder he perceived in nineteenth-century Europe. He contrasted the 'positive' features of progress through order, with the negative and destructive chaos he saw all around him.

The Idea in Action

COMTE'S IDEA OF POSITIVISM HAS HAD A CONSIDERABLE IMPACT BOTH ON PHILOSOPHY and on sociology. It laid the foundations for the French tradition of positivism, influenced such leading English philosophers as J.S. Mill and Herbert Spencer, and pre-dated the Vienna School of Logical Positivism in the 1920s. It attracted considerable attention in Europe, Latin America and the USA. Comte's motto, 'Order and Progress' is emblazoned even today on the national flag of Brazil. It stimulated the notion of positive economics, a notion that still has some influence on modern economic theory.

Comte's influence within sociology has been even more profound. He founded the positivist tradition which has dominated British, European and American sociology right up to the present day. His use of the organic analogy, his use of such concepts as social consensus and social statics laid the basis for functionalism as propounded by Emile Durkheim and developed by American structural functionalists such as Talcott Parsons (see p. 190) in the 1930s and 40s. His emphasis on scientific method still influences both sociological and anthropological research. His faith in scientific knowledge as the basis for a more rational, just and stable society pre-dates many modern theories of post-industrial society.

However, his own attempts to outline an ideal society were somewhat less successful, even somewhat absurd. Comte envisaged a 'sociocracy', a society run by sociologists, and a 'sociolatry' – a series of festivals paying homage to a new religion of humanity. He was an eccentric and his personal eccentricity extended to his confident belief that the Pope would resign in his favour. Such extremes lost Comte many supporters, and led even Emile Durkheim to deny that he was a positivist.

Positivism's dominance over Western sociology, however, came under increasing attack in the late 1960s. Marxists criticised its conservative bias and failure to acknowledge the class conflict underlying capitalist societies. Phenomenologists went deeper and attacked its very foundations, its belief in a social reality above and beyond any group of individuals, its faith in scientific method and objective analysis for uncovering the truth about the fundamental laws governing social structure, social change and human behaviour. In contrast, phenomenologists argued that social reality is fundamentally different from nature; that it is no more than the interpretations and meanings given by people to their everyday lives. From such a perspective, objective analysis becomes impossible and scientific method a distortion. Rather the aim of sociological research should be to discover the very subjective factors so totally rejected by scientific sociology – meaning, feeling and interpretation. Such a relative view of knowledge, even of physical knowledge has received increasing support from philosophers, from historians of science such as T.S. Kuhn (see p. 151) and from recent developments in sociological theory such as post-modernity.

This fall from both philosophical and sociological grace was partly due to the way the term 'positivism' has been both used and abused by many of those following in this sociological tradition. It has been used to justify a narrow concentration on quantification and an obsessive faith in social facts. Human values and interpretations have been discounted in an obsessive belief that the facts will speak for themselves. Human action and the ability of the individual to influence and change social events is often ignored or discounted in positivist explanations and so social science often appears highly deterministic, inhuman, even as it portrays society as an entity in itself, above and beyond the people it controls. Man from this perspective often seems no more than a puppet on a string dancing to the tune of a social order and a social future he no longer controls.

Whatever its weaknesses and criticisms today, however, positivism established sociology as a respectable and respected academic discipline, as a 'science' of society capable of analysing and even predicting social change. As such it established sociology and contributed enormously to its development and its debates, its dynamism and its ongoing future. No mean achievement, and one deserving full recognition. Positivism often seems like the 'Big Brother' of sociology. Ironically Comte himself emphasised the inter-relationship of fact and value, the need for moral evaluation in conducting social research, but this aspect of his work is often forgotten and has been long lost. Nevertheless though now considered arcane by many sociologists and philosophers, positivism continues to draw strength from its scientific status, continues to influence, though no longer dominate, mainstream sociology.

 See Also

- **STRUCTURAL FUNCTIONALISM** (p. 190) as a version of positivist sociology.
- **PHENOMENOLOGY** (p. 165) and its offshoots, **SYMBOLIC INTERACTIONISM** (p. 195) and **ETHNOMETHODOLOGY** (p. 104), as critiques of positivism and its theory of scientific certainty.
- **PARADIGMS** (p. 151) and **FALSIFICATION AND CONJECTURE** (p. 109).
- **CRITICAL THEORY** (p. 84).
- **POST-MODERNISM** (p. 245).

Suggested Reading

BRYANT, C. (1986) 'What is Positivism?', *Social Studies Review*, January.

Further Reading

PICKERING, M. (1993) *Auguste Comte: An Intellectual Biography*, Cambridge University Press, Cambridge.

The Protestant Ethic

Max Weber

The Idea

THE IDEA OF THE PROTESTANT ETHIC WAS ONE OF THE KEY IDEAS OF MAX WEBER (1864–1920), one of the most famous of the classical sociologists and undoubtedly one of the founding fathers of sociology as we know it today. He was a leading German academic and a joint founder of the German Sociological Association in 1902. One of the key themes arising from his vast and extensive study of comparative societies was a search for 'the spirit of the modern age', a search for the key dynamic and the one key feature that distinguishes modern society from societies in the past. This, Weber believed, was *rationality*, the rational and logical way of thinking and of organising that characterises modern society in its relentless pursuit of efficiency and effectiveness and its desire to organise and control its people and its institutions. While previous societies relied on apparently irrational faiths or systems of thought such as religion, tradition or personal charisma, modern society rests on logic and the application of reason as the very foundation of its system of thought and organisation. Modern science and technology, modern law and business are classic examples of rationality and the way it has been applied in enabling modern society to advance in the way it has, and at the speed it has. This theme underlay Weber's studies of religion, bureaucracy and, in particular, capitalism; this thesis lay behind his major work, *The Protestant Ethic and the Spirit of Capitalism* (1930).

While other writers of the late nineteenth century, particularly Karl Marx, sought to explain the Industrial Revolutions that swept Western Europe mainly in economic terms, Weber tried to show the influence of ideas on such enormous historical change, in particular the influence of religious ideas and values. In a massive comparative analysis of past and present civilisations and religions, he concluded that while certain religious ideas promoted, or at least did not obstruct, social change, others did. The ancient civilisations of China and India possessed the necessary economic preconditions for industrial 'take off' (cheap labour, capital, inventions, mass markets) but failed to do so – why? Similarly the Industrial Revolution took place initially, not throughout the whole of Western Europe but primarily in such northern and Protestant countries as England, The Netherlands and Germany. Weber therefore concluded that the ethics of Protestantism, in particular those of the more puritanical sects such as Calvinism, provided the vital spark that ignited the Industrial Revolution.

For Weber, the key characteristic of modern capitalism is that it is rational, it is based on the competitive dynamic of market forces, the costs and benefits of such factors of production as wages and labour, on the likely returns of a given amount of investment and, in particular, on the pursuit of profit. This spirit of capitalism is not limited to a few adventurous entrepreneurs but is all-pervasive, underlying the way of life of whole societies. In his essays on early Protestantism Weber noted a strong 'affinity' between such economic values and those of the more puritanical sects that arose after the Protestant reformation – Calvinists, Lutherans and Wesleyans.

- While Catholicism taught that poverty was the pathway to salvation and that heaven was in the next world, Puritanism declared personal wealth to be a sign of God's favour, a visible symbol of the elect few who were predestined for salvation. By working hard and growing rich, Calvinists sought to convince themselves that they were the chosen few, and so profit-making became a psychological release from the fear of damnation. However, and this was crucial to the spirit of capitalism, such wealth must not be squandered but saved and invested as a means to further profits and for the greater glorification of God. In contrast to the riches and extravagance of the Catholic Church, Puritans were noted for their thrift and frugality, their strict rejection of all forms of pleasure. This desire to save rather than spend provided the spirit of investment so vital to the development of the Industrial Revolution.

- While highly structured and collectivist religions such as Catholicism and Islam subordinated the individual to the greater good of the whole, Protestantism was much more individualistic and democratic. In contrast to the authority of the papacy and the power of priests, Protestants were encouraged to seek their own salvation and to talk to God directly.

- While traditional religions rested on faith, ritual and even magic, Protestantism is much more rational, rejecting extravagant rituals and all forms of irrational explanation.

- While in medieval times work was seen as a necessary evil undertaken simply to maintain existing standards of living, and money-making was viewed with suspicion, for Puritans hard work and the accumulation of profits were the pathway to salvation, signs of God's favour for the Chosen Few.

From such comparisons Weber drew out the similarities between an ideal-type capitalist and ideal-type Protestant – their individualism and veneration of profit, their 'Puritanism', determination to succeed, and inner faith or self-confidence, involving where necessary risk-taking in pursuit of their 'calling'.

Weber's notion of the Protestant ethic therefore rested on the premise that, unlike religions based on magic or those that promoted asceticism, or other worldliness such as Catholicism, salvation for Protestants rested ultimately on individual behaviour and communication with God on this earth and in this world, not in the next. Such salvation was either predestined as in Calvinism, or earned as in other Protestant denominations by hard work and Christian conduct. For Protestants, too, achieving a state of grace is an intensely personal process and although the church or the ministry may help, ultimately it rests in the hands of the believer. Fear of eternal damnation, the need to work ceaselessly and frugally in the service of God, distinguished Protestant faiths in Weber's view from Catholicism and other mass religions where salvation could only be achieved through the church and its priests.

Weber therefore constructed and compared two ideal types – the Protestant ethic personified by John Calvin and the Calvinists, with the spirit of capitalism captured in the autobiography of American capitalist Benjamin Franklin, *Advice to a Young Tradesman* (1748). The Protestant ethic in Weber's view helped transform wealth accumulation, as it traditionally existed, into the *capital* accumulation needed to promote modern capitalism by saving and reinvesting profit, not spending it on extravagant personal and conspicuous lifestyles.

The Idea in Action

T HE VALUE OF WEBER'S THESIS WAS THAT IT RESTORED THE REALM OF *IDEAS* TO EXPLA-
nations of social change (and social order) and re-emphasised the importance of 'individual' action at a time when sociological theories based on economic determinism relegated cultural factors to the sidelines. The thesis of the Protestant ethic has yet to be totally disproved as a major explanation of industrialisation and there are many examples, even today, of societies where religion still seems to be the major obstacle to modernisation – Iran, India and even Ulster.

The idea that certain values, a *capitalist ethos*, is as vital to industrialisation as technical factors, has profoundly influenced many Western theories and policies for promoting modernisation in developing countries. The American psychologist David McClellan (1961), for example, argued that an orientation to achievement, the 'N-ACH factor', was the secret ingredient, the vital spark necessary for industrialising the Third World. He even set up training programmes to instil in local businessmen the necessary drive and determination so that they, in turn, could teach the local population the values of hard work, punctuality and motivation. Such programmes have been criticised by radical writers as ideological nonsense, blaming the lack of industrial progress in Third World countries on their own people's laziness when in fact the real cause of their backwardness is their exploitation by the First World, in particular by the giant multinationals that drain away such countries' natural resources and keep them in a state of poverty and dependence. From a socialist viewpoint it is capitalism and its market forces that are irrational and unjust and only through some form of planned economy will order be restored.

Many other criticisms of the Protestant ethic thesis, however, rest on a misunderstanding of Weber's ideas – not always that surprising, given the ambiguities surrounding much of his writings:

1. He has been criticised for saying that Protestantism *caused* the Industrial Revolution. In fact he merely said that he perceived an 'elective affinity' between the Protestant ethic and the spirit of capitalism, though, as one of his biographers,

Frank Parkin (1982), argues, Weber does oscillate between a weak and strong thesis, between seeing Protestantism as merely one of several influences on capitalism and seeing it as the decisive factor. Certainly his thesis fails to explain industrialisation in Catholic countries and why Scotland, one of the most puritanical of countries, failed to 'take off' in the way neighbouring England did.

2. He has been criticised for giving insufficient attention to economic and political factors in industrialisation but again this is not true. He was fully aware of the importance of technical factors, pointing out that Western societies of the nineteenth century not only had the culture of capitalism but the material base and rational framework, the legal, administrative and financial institutions necessary for the flow of capital and making of contracts. He merely sought to ensure that the importance of cultural factors was also recognised. Despite his reputation as a critic of Karl Marx, he greatly respected Marx. It was the crude economic determinism of many of Marx's followers he was opposed to. In particular, Weber's thesis sought to challenge the Marxian belief in historical change as the inevitable progress of underlying economic forces over which man has little control. Instead he proposed an alternative analysis, one which sought to capture the Spirit of the Age – in this case the Protestant ethic – and so clarify the role and meaning of human action and motivation in historical development. The notion of the Protestant ethic in particular sought to show the impact of cultural forces on economic change and to show how human motivation and a particular moral outlook – in this case Calvinism and the pursuit of profit – underpinned economic development.

   In contrast to Marx, Weber put human action and the individual at the heart of this analysis of capitalism, its character and its origins. In contrast to one-dimensional approaches, Weber argued for a pluralistic analysis of historical change. In his view, economic or material forces alone do not drive history; cultural and political forces equally have a part to play – and a life of their own. In contrast to Marx, Weber did not see the rise of modern capitalism as either inevitable or predestined. Rather it arose out of the congruence of a number of forces coming together in 'elective affinity' at a particular point in history. Weber contrasted the development of Western capitalism with economic development in the East, notably traditional China and India where despite the existence of comparable economic conditions, capitalism did not emerge. In contrast to Protestantism, Eastern religions do not encourage worldly pursuits nor material gain. Rather they promote other worldliness and individual spiritual harmony above and beyond material life.

   Weber's thesis is thus often portrayed as an idealist theory of historical change in contrast to Marx's more materialistic approach. Such a perspective is too simple. Just as Marx recognised the power of ideas in promoting change, so in his later writings particularly, Weber developed a very powerful analysis of economic history.

3. He has been criticised for failing to recognise the various forms of capitalism, some of which existed before the Industrial Revolution. In fact Weber did make such a distinction identifying the 'booty' capitalism of the buccaneers, the pariah capitalism of Jewish communities and the traditional capitalism of ancient civilisations. While many others had pursued wealth and riches – entrepreneurs, traders, bankers, pirates and the like – none had done so with the ascetic rigour and dynamism of Protestants such as Calvinists. In contrast to others, ascetic

Protestants rejected the consumption of wealth in favour of thrift and investment and pursued profit not for personal gain but to achieve religious salvation. They were totally dedicated to hard work and capital accumulation. They could not rest or ease off for fear of losing God's favour. They could not sin, gamble or lapse into self-indulgence for fear of his wrath. For Weber the spirit of capitalism is not a way of making money; it is a way of life, a cultural and moral set of ethics, duties and obligations; a single-minded and relentless pursuit of an economic and business vocation that required continual investment and reinvestment. Capital accumulation and the pursuit of profit is thus converted from greed and avarice to a moral crusade and a sign of God's favour. The rich have a right and a duty to become richer and the poor deserve to be poor. Weber therefore identified an 'elective affinity' between Protestantism and the spirit of capitalism. Puritanism, and in particular Calvinism, reflected the 'ideal type' Protestant and captured exactly the needs of capitalism because it legitimised individual profit making, promoted rigorous hard work and self-discipline and an austere lifestyle, and asserted the need for investment and saving for capital accumulation rather than luxury and conspicuous consumption – all in the name of and for the glory of God. Poverty was seen as a sign of moral failing and weakness. Pursuing profit became a moral duty, not a dirty deed. Wealth was a sign of God's favour. It is not greed but addiction to the pursuit of salvation that underpinned the dynamic drive of Protestant businessmen. Calvinism, to Weber, was a form of worldly calling, a vocation in the service of God that had to be renewed daily by hard work, thrift and moral rectitude. Although salvation for Calvinists was predestined it still had to be earned, earned by good works every day if the individual was to achieve a place among the Elect, and not be condemned to eternal damnation.

Weber's thesis, therefore, is that the Protestant ethic helped to produce modern capitalism and the business and organisational practices that support and promote profit-making and capital accumulation; specialisation, the division of labour, mass production and other forms of rationalisation. Once it was underway, however, modern capitalism no longer needed the drive and spirit of Protestantism and increasingly religion was marginalised in favour of secularisation. The Protestant ethic helped move society forward from feudalism to capitalism. Where traditional religions had obstructed and forestalled rationalisation and economic progress, Protestantism promoted it. However, once that cultural transition had been made and the values of Protestantism had been institutionalised, then religion as we know it is no longer needed – even though in the USA, that most capitalistic and materialistic of modern societies, Protestant-based religious groups and 'churches' have survived and thrived.

4. He has been criticised for the apparent internal inconsistencies in his thesis, in particular Weber's failure to explain in detail how Protestant attitudes actually influenced capitalists (and workers), why Protestants invested in profits rather than churches as a way of glorifying God, how Protestant attitudes arose in the first place. Historical studies, for example, have sought to show that the features of acquisitiveness and individualism associated with Puritanism actually predated the Protestant Reformation, and that such features could equally be found in other religions, including Catholicism.

Nevertheless this thesis and Weber's overall emphasis on rationality and individual action remains a key explanation of modern society and a key perspective in modern sociology.

 **See Also**

- HISTORICAL MATERIALISM (p. 43) as the Marxian thesis of industrial/economic change that Weber so vehemently disagreed with.
- GLOBALISATION (p. 214), MODERNISATION THEORY (p. 146) and DEPENDENCY THEORY (p. 92).
- INFORMATION(AL) SOCIETY (p. 220) and the way modern/post-modern global capitalism seems to be developing.

Suggested Reading

MACRAE, D. (1974) *Weber,* Fontana, London.

PARKIN, F. (1982) *Max Weber,* Tavistock, London – brief but useful summaries of Weber's life and work.

PAMPEL, F.C. (2000) Max Weber, Ch. 3 in Pampel, F.C., *Sociological Lives and Ideas: An Introduction to the Classical Theorists,* Macmillan, Basingstoke.

Further Reading

LEMANN, H. AND ROTH, G. (1993) *Weber's Protestant Ethic: Origins, Evidence, Context,* German Historical Institute, Berlin.

MANSON, P. (2000) Max Weber, Ch. 6 in Andersen, H. and Kaspersen, L.B. (eds.), *Classical and Modern Social Theory,* Blackwell, Oxford.

SCAFF, L.A. (1998) Max Weber, Ch. 2 in Stones, R. (ed.), *Key Sociological Thinkers,* Macmillan, Basingstoke.

TURNER, B.S. (1992) *Max Weber: From History to Modernity,* Routledge, London.

WEBER, M. (1930) *The Protestant Ethic and the Spirit of Capitalism* [1905], Allen & Unwin, London.

Social Darwinism

Herbert Spencer

THE IDEA OF SOCIAL DARWINISM DERIVES FROM THE THEORIES AND WRITINGS OF Herbert Spencer (1820–1903), a Victorian writer and philosopher who sought to apply Charles Darwin's ideas of evolution to the social sciences. Spencer argued that like nature, societies have evolved according to the laws of natural selection, survival and adaptation. Like biological organisms, societies have evolved from simple to complex structures by a process of natural selection, have adapted to their environment by a process of internal differentiation and integration, have progressed from the homogeneous to the heterogeneous. Human societies have evolved from the simple and homogeneous tribal units of primitive man to the advanced, integrated and heterogeneous social systems of modern civilisation.

Like Darwin, Spencer used the organism as the basis of his explanation. He likened society to an organism in a variety of ways:

- Both grow in size and evolve into more complex, differentiated structures.

- Both differentiate and become more specialist. Just as the brain evolved as the biological mechanism for control and decision-making, so has government emerged as the key social institution for this task.

- Both evolve – both societies and organisms learn to adjust and adapt to their environment in their search for survival.

Herbert Spencer

Spencer also incorporated certain elements of contemporary physics, including the idea that there is an inherent tendency for all things to move along the line of least resistance, and the principle of the rhythm of motion. In addition, like Auguste Comte

(p. 56), Spencer believed that the heart of social order is an underlying social consensus, an inherent agreement about fundamental values and morality.

These ideas were blended into a final theory of social evolution based on the key concepts of:

- natural selection, or, as Spencer called it, 'survival of the fittest';
- the inherent instability of all social systems.

As in nature, argued Spencer, social order and stability require a natural equilibrium, a sense of balance. Social change occurs because of a disturbance in that equilibrium, in the balance between the various parts of the social body or between society and its environment. Following a period of instability, a new social order emerges as a new equilibrium, a fresh moral consensus, and a new relationship between increasingly differentiated social parts is established.

Thus, like species in nature, argued Spencer, human societies have evolved from simple tribal units into the complex societies of today. Those that failed to adapt, those that were unfit, died out in the face of competition from more advanced and aggressive social units. Thus the caveman gave way to the tribesman and farmer, the great empires of Rome, India and China to the European powers of Britain, Spain and Germany. Through this law of the 'social jungle' only the fittest societies survived; through this law of social evolution human society 'marched forward'. *'Warfare among men, like warfare among animals, has had a large share in raising their organisations to a higher stage'* (Spencer 1873).

However, not all societies evolve at the same rate or in the same way. As in nature, evolution produces variety and diversity. Different societies may evolve differently according to their particular environment, neighbouring states and their own individual characteristics, be they racial or cultural. All, however, are following the same law of social evolution, will follow the same evolutionary stages, or will die out. Here Spencer distinguished between two types of society at different stages of evolution:

- The militant, controlled and integrated from the centre, as in those societies run by the military.
- The industrial, where social order is more organic and spontaneous, based on co-operation rather than force, or market forces rather than military might.

Thus, while early militant societies had to fight for survival against warring neighbours – as the Romans had to against the Goths and Vandals – more advanced industrial ones have learned to evolve peacefully through economic competition rather than war and conflict.

Finally, Spencer's theory had a psychological as well as sociological theme. Just as societies evolve, he argued, so do people. Modern man represents thousands of years of physical and psychological evolution as he has adapted to and survived his physical and social environment and so evolved into a superior being to his forefathers, the ape and the caveman.

Spencer's model of society was organismic. Societies are like living bodies which evolve out of a state of undifferentiated unity to highly complex, differentiated structures in which the individual parts, while increasingly autonomous and specialised, nevertheless come increasingly to depend on each other. While differentiation is limited in simple societies – men may be both warriors and hunters – modern societies are highly specialist. Human society evolves naturally to a state of complex hetero-geneity. He sought to develop a theory of universal evolution. In particular Spencer identified the pressures of population growth as a key dynamic on social evolution. In his major work, *The Principles of Sociology* (1893), Spencer defined society as a 'thing' which grows from simple to complex, differentiated structures in which the parts depend on the whole. The whole system needs to be in balance, in equilibrium and nothing, not even the government should disturb it. He distinguished between the simplicity, centralisation and rigidity of militant societies and the complexity, decen-tralisation and individualism of industrial societies. Spencer rejected any notion of state regulation in favour of the 'hidden hand' of the market and the freedom of the individual – just as many naturalists and environments today argue that man should not interfere with nature or its underlying laws of natural evolution.

Herbert Spencer's overall aim was to unify all theoretical sciences and create a compar-ative sociology based on the theory and methods of Charles Darwin. He sought to combine this organic model of social development with an emphasis on individual rights. Social Darwinism offered a highly structured and apparently scientific approach to social research, stressing the value of comparing societies at different historical and evolutionary stages. Politically, Spencer's thesis represented a rejection of state intervention. Social planning and state welfare threatened to distort the natural and progressive forces of social evolution, threatened the rights of the individual. Underpinning Spencer's evolutionary theory was the ultimate search for a new ethical and moral order. Through evolution, man would perfect his capabilities and his morals. This required the maximisation of individual freedom, including in his view the right to 'ignore' the state. Hence his opposition to social reform and to the Poor Laws and his view that suffering is useful and ethically right because it leads to perfect balance and adaptation. The appeal of social Darwinism was thus as much a political doctrine as a contribution to scientific sociology.

The Idea in Action

HERBERT SPENCER WAS AN IMPORTANT FIGURE IN THE DEVELOPMENT OF MODERN sociology. Social Darwinism gave early sociology a strong theoretical base and extensive academic status by allying it to developments in the natural sciences. Like Comte, Spencer believed that certain underlying laws of nature govern the social world just as much as the natural one. For Spencer, that underlying law was evolution.

As one of the earliest attempts to produce laws of social order and change, Spencer's theory had a major impact on nineteenth-century social philosophy. It pre-dated and strongly influenced functionalist theories and, through William James and W.G. Sumner, had a significant influence on American sociology in the early twentieth century. It is a classic example of Victorian ideas and attitudes, and many of its key concepts are still both popular and influential today: the Thatcherite beliefs in market forces, a rejection of state intervention and survival of the fittest being but a few examples.

However, by the late nineteenth century, Social Darwinism and its underlying views of man and society were under increasing criticism:

- Spencer's attempt to combine a holistic analysis of society with *laissez-faire* individualism produced theoretical contradictions between individual rights and freedoms and the needs of society at large to evolve and progress.

- His use of a biological analogy was at times absurdly over-stretched; his use of Darwinian concepts was often superficial, inaccurate and contradictory, arguing, for example, that while all societies are subject to evolutionary forces, some may skip certain stages or even regress from heterogeneity to homogeneity.

- Spencer's analysis was tautological, that is, the evidence he used and the classification he created for different types of society and institution derived from the very principles that the examples were supposed to prove.

- His ideas of natural selection have been used to support racist and anti-humanitarian views and policies. They reinforced the Victorian idea of white superiority, of the supremacy of the British Empire over its subject nations, especially black ones. Elements of this doctrine could be found in the racial policies of Nazi Germany and in the apartheid policy of white rule in South Africa. The thesis of 'survival of the fittest' has been equally used to justify policies of abandoning the weak, sick, poor and criminal, portraying them as biologically inferior and a threat to man's evolutionary development. *'Fostering the good-for-nothing at the expense of the good, is an extreme cruelty. It is a deliberate stirring-up of miseries for future generations. There is no greater curse to posterity than that of bequeathing to them an increasing population of imbeciles and idlers and criminals . . . The whole effort of nature is to get rid of such, to clear the world of them, and make room for better . . . If they are not sufficiently complete to live, they die, and it is best they should die'* (Spencer, cited in Abrams, 1968: 74). Spencer's advocacy of evolutionary struggle, of inferior and superior races, of the survival of the fittest in terms of both societies and races, underpinned the philosophies of numerous racist and extremist groups, notably in the form of the racist theories and practices of the German Nazis. Inevitably the collapse of such societies and their social philosophies undermined both the theoretical and the ethic value of social Darwinism.

- Social Darwinism is often seen as a conservative, even reactionary philosophy, justifying the existing order and existing inequalities as both natural and right.

- The decline of the British Empire, the eclipsing of England as a world power by Germany and America produced a decline, too, in support for social Darwinism. The rise of communist societies based on central planning contradicted Spencer's thesis of evolution by market forces. This thesis was further undermined by the adoption of state planning of the economy, welfare provisions and social democracy in advanced industrial societies at the turn of the century.

Criticism of Spencer has therefore focused on three key areas:

1. The inherent conflict between his individualist perception of man and that of society as an organism. Selfishness and self-interest alone cannot be the binding forces of a stable and progressive society.

2. The notion of ethical naturalism – the idea that those who survive are naturally morally superior – attracted extensive criticism and accusations of racism.

3. The conceptual and methodological approach of using biological concepts such as 'natural selection' and 'survival of the fittest' to analyse social and cultural development has proved increasingly impractical.

In particular the association of Social Darwinism with theories of eugenics and colonial warfare in the late nineteenth century, early twentieth century, undermined its theoretical attractiveness although Spencer himself sought to distance himself from such extremism. He subscribed to the equal rights of races and he was deeply depressed about the growing number of wars during his lifetime, 'a period of social cannibalism' as he described it, and a severe contradiction of the belief that industrialisation would bring with it greater peace and harmony.

Thus, even by 1900, social Darwinism had lost its popular appeal and much of its political support. It now looks anachronistic, a left-over from the Victorian era of the British Empire and white superiority. 'Herbert Spencer belongs to the category of thinkers who gained a large reputation and influence in their lifetime but who have since been almost forgotten' (Heine Andersen in Andersen and Kaspersen 2000: 35). A radical liberal in inspiration, Spencer's theories ironically were increasingly used to support conservative ideologies.

Nevertheless, it was a major contribution to establishing sociology as an academic discipline and its underlying themes have re-emerged in recent years in the form of such neo-evolutionary theories as structural functionalism, modernisation theses, cultural anthropology and more recently, socio-biology and game theory.

 See Also

- STRUCTURAL FUNCTIONALISM (p. 190) as a modern version of some of Spencer's key concepts.
- MODERNISATION THEORY (p. 146) as a theory of world development using Darwinist ideas of global evolution.
- DEPENDENCY THEORY (p. 92) as a scathing critique of evolutionary theory of world development.

Suggested Reading

PEEL, J.D.Y. (1971) *Herbert Spencer: The Evolution of a Sociologist*, Heinemann, London.

Further Reading

ANDERSEN, H. (2000) Herbert Spencer, Ch. 3 Part I in Andersen, H. and Kaspersen, L.B., *Classical and Modern Social Theory*, Blackwell, Oxford.

GRAY, T. (1996) *The Political Philosophy of Herbert Spencer: Individualism and Organicism*, Avebury, Brookfield, VT.

Social Solidarity

Emile Durkheim

The Idea

ONE OF THE CENTRAL ISSUES FOR SOCIOLOGY HAS BEEN THAT OF SOCIAL ORDER – OR as Emile Durkheim called it, 'social solidarity' – How does society maintain order?; how, amid the millions of people in society, how, out of all the multitudes of activities we engage in daily, does social order arise and how, given its immense complexity, does society hold together and change? For Durkheim, born and brought up in a period of intense change, this was a key question. Durkheim was born in Alsace-Lorraine, a part of eastern France that was partitioned by Prussia in 1870. He was brought up as a Jew but converted in his teens to Catholicism and later became an agnostic. A quiet, serious but very able student, he was educated at the elite École Normale Supérieure, and adopted an academic career becoming Professor of Education and Social Science at the Sorbonne, the first academic chair in the new science of sociology. His only son died in the First World War and he himself died shortly afterwards from grief and a heart attack at the age of 59.

Durkheim was intensely aware of the importance of social order and he devoted his entire academic career to analysing and explaining it. He made *social solidarity* the heart of his theory of functionalism, and the very basis of the new science he was proclaiming at the Sorbonne and across France. In particular, Durkheim sought to analyse how social order is established, maintained and in particular, after a period of severe and rapid social change, re-established; how do traditional societies evolve into modern ones, rural communities into mass industrial-urban ones? In particular, how, amid all this transitional change, are the individual rights and freedoms so characteristic of advanced industrial societies promoted and protected in the face of mass society's need

Emile Durkheim

for social order and social control? The answer, argued Durkheim, lay in 'a transformation of social solidarity due to the growing development of the division of labour'.

Durkheim devoted his first major publication, *The Division of Labour in Society* (1893)
to the topic of social solidarity, and he drew up two ideal types of social order –
mechanical and organic solidarity – as the basis for comparing and analysing the
simple social structures of traditional societies with the complex divisions of labour of
modern ones.

In traditional societies, communities or groups, relationships are essentially face to face
(or mechanical), the division of labour very simple, with most people involved in
essentially the same occupation, be it hunting or farming. There is a common lifestyle,
a common set of beliefs, customs and rituals, known and practised by all. There is an
underlying common consensus which Durkheim referred to as *'conscience collective'* –
a term which, whether translated as 'common consciousness' or 'collective conscience',
still evokes the same essential idea of a common morality or set of values upon which
social solidarity is based and which guide and control individual behaviour. In mechanical societies, the *conscience collective* is all-dominant because within such simple social
systems everyone is essentially the same. There is little individuality, social differences
are few and far between, private property is almost unknown and so conformity is both
'natural' and easily established through socialisation and such key social controls as the
family and religion. Deviations are severely and publicly punished.

However, as societies grow and modernise, adopt industrial economies and complex
divisions of labour, and people move from the country to the city, so they outgrow
mechanical solidarity. Similarity gives way to differentiation, homogeneity to heterogeneity, as the variety of occupations, lifestyles and sub-cultures proliferates and multi-
plies. Collectivism gives way to individualism, common ownership to private property,
communal responsibility to individual rights, commonality to class and status differences. Face-to-face relationships and informal social controls are no longer enough to
hold society together; power and authority have shifted from the family and the church
to the law and the state. Just as in nature, such differentiation and complexity requires
a new basis for social solidarity, an *organic* one that can successfully combine social
order and individual freedom.

For Durkheim, the heart of organic solidarity is the complex division of labour that
underpins the industrial economies of modern societies where everyone is interdependent. In today's advanced industrial-urban societies, no individual is totally self-
sufficient (in contrast to the self-sufficiency often displayed by people in simple
societies). While we are all very different, we all depend on a complex economic
system that requires us to specialise in a multiplicity of occupations and allows us
the freedom to live very different lifestyles. It is the economic interdependency, this
reciprocity and co-operation for mutual benefit, survival and prosperity, argued
Durkheim, that forms the foundation of modern organic societies. However, he totally
rejected the utilitarian arguments, particularly those of Herbert Spencer, that economic
self-interest alone is enough to cement and stabilise a civilised society. In his view, self-
interest alone would produce conflict and social chaos. Underlying the contracts and
economic exchange of advanced industrial societies there has to be some form of
morality, some ethical code of generally agreed principles, norms and values upon
which a system of trust and justice could be based. Man is as capable of altruism as of
greed and the role of society is to encourage as much as to restrain such human traits,

according to its own particular stage of evolutionary development. Durkheim thus proposed the notion of the duality of human nature, the idea that we all have two consciences – a personal one and a social one, one based on self-interest, one on the interests of society. Moreover, while in mechanical societies the individual and collective conscience are virtually synonymous, in organic societies the two consciences are both distinct, separate, and often in conflict. Formal social controls, therefore, become more necessary in organic than mechanical societies. Not everyone can have everything they want when they want it or else there would be chaos and society would fall apart.

But how, with the decline of traditional social controls – the family and the church – is social solidarity to be enforced and maintained in advanced societies? Durkheim put his faith in the state and the law at the societal level and in occupational and professional associations or guilds at the industrial level. While the government and courts promote the law as the fullest expression of the social consensus, Durkheim hoped that it would be the professional associations that would establish and enforce the essential codes of ethics and behaviour of organic societies. Therefore, in contrast to many of his contemporaries, he did not see social change as a destructive force, as the demise of social order, traditional morality and civilised society. He was optimistic that the new industrial order would be a step forward, both progressive and liberating. Durkheim's solution to the potential breakdown of social order, therefore, was moral regulation through the establishment of national and occupational or professional corporations akin to medieval guilds (as mediators between the individual and the state) and for the state to assert its collective and overall moral authority. The state is the highest form of collective consciousness; education and democracy are the means by which individual needs and aspirations would be reconciled with the collective good. The associations and corporations in Durkheim's view would act as intermediaries drawing together groups with common interests, developing professional codes of conduct and linking them to the state and the collective order via a moral code of civic duty and responsibility.

Having identified the two main types of social order and their underlying moralities, Durkheim then sought to monitor and measure scientifically the transition from mechanical to organic solidarity and the instrument he attempted to use was the law. While moral phenomena do not easily lend themselves to precise observation, legal codes do provide an external and measurable index because they are a formal expression of moral values. They tell us what society thinks is right and wrong. In particular, all laws involve sanctions and Durkheim identified two contrasting types of sanction:

- repressive sanctions, which involve punishment and suffering, be it loss of liberty, or of life!;
- restitutive sanctions as in civil or common law, which involve readjustment rather than punishment, restoring matters to their previous state prior to a transgression (e.g. returning goods or property).

Durkheim argued that legal codes based primarily on repressive sanctions reflected a strong underlying *conscience collective* of the type predominant in traditional societies, while restitutive law reflected the 'organic' morality of more modern societies and their need for contractual relationships. He was, therefore, able to draw up an index of social solidarity, a continuum for plotting society's evolutionary progress from religious to rational morality, from social regulation by the family to social direction by the state. In modern societies the state and its agencies, the police and the courts, embody an organic *conscience collective*, symbolise the people's will and moral values in the way that the church did in mediaeval Europe.

Durkheim saw modern morality, modern legal systems, as a superior basis for social order, justice and development than either mechanical solidarity or self-interest. However, he was deeply concerned that the transition from mechanical to organic solidarity was neither always successful nor painless. It often produced social strain, even social conflict, as the old order was replaced by the new. During this period of structural transition there is a severe danger of a period of normlessness – or as Durkheim called it, *anomie* (see p. 22) – as the old morality and traditional social controls declined but the new social consensus was still in its infancy. Durkheim believed that many of the early capitalist societies in Western Europe were undergoing just such a transition and were suffering the problems of anomie and of a forced or artificial division of labour: one imposed on the economic structure by the old ruling class as it struggled to stay in power rather than one that arose naturally to reflect the needs of industrialisation. This created unjust social inequalities and so led to an escalation of social conflict, and possibly, as in many nineteenth-century European countries, revolution.

Durkheim saw the role of social science as being that of identifying such problems and helping to overcome the problems of social transition by proposing effective solutions and social policies. However, by the end of *The Division of Labour in Society* he was showing doubts about the possibility of organic solidarity emerging automatically from an increasing division of labour. He accepted that it may require direct planning and direct control.

Mechanical and organic solidarity were, therefore, the two ideal types that Durkheim used to explain scientifically his theory of social order and change. He was increasingly aware, however, of the inherent problems and potential sources of conflict produced by this transition from an old to a new division of labour, from traditional to modern society.

The Idea in Action

THE CONCEPT OF SOCIAL SOLIDARITY, THIS CONCERN WITH SOCIAL ORDER AND EVOLU-tion has been at the heart of functionalist writings from Durkheim onwards. Durkheim's emphasis on morality and social consensus as the foundation of a successful social order has remained a central theme in modern sociology while his attempt to analyse scientifically and to monitor social change – its causes, effects and sources of strain – has inspired the whole positivist tradition within sociology and stimulated a mass of research into anomie, suicide and religion. The major exposition of his analysis of social solidarity and anomie was Durkheim's classic study of suicide and the extent to which, in his view, suicide rates vary inversely with social solidarity – the lower the degree of social solidarity, the higher the rate of suicide.

Much of Durkheim's analysis is within the sort of evolutionary framework proposed by August Comte and Herbert Spencer, notably the use of biological analogies and concepts. A healthy society is one where solidarity is high and a sick society is one where anomie runs riot and social order breaks down. The role of the statesman, he concluded, is akin to that of the doctor: *'he forestalls the outbreak of sickness by maintaining good hygiene, or when it breaks down, seeks to cure it'*. A primary goal of Durkheim's approach, therefore, was the practical application of sociological ideas to the body politic, particularly to the tensions, crises and dilemmas of France and Europe in the late nineteenth century. In particular he sought to promote moral reform in the face of the breakdown of religion and traditional order.

Durkheim's primary occupation was not on the structure and functioning of the social order but on its underlying moral regulation; on the system of rules of right and wrong that determine individual conduct. As he declared in his first major work, *The Division of Labour* (1893) his aim was *'to constitute the science of morality . . . To treat the facts of moral life according to the methods of the positive sciences'*. Hence his focus on anomie (see p. 22) and the absence of moral regulation as part of his overall analysis of social solidarity, *'men's passions are stayed only by the moral presence they respect'* (quotes from Callinicos 1999: 126). The object of sociology for Durkheim was *'to determine the conditions for the conservation of society'* although Durkheim himself was a liberal democrat rather than a political conservative. Society for Durkheim is essentially a moral reality that needs to be preserved and to evolve 'naturally'. Hence the description of his sociology as an attempt to establish a new civic ethic. This deep and lifelong interest in morality and in the moral crisis facing modern society was acutely reflected in Durkheim's public involvement in the infamous Dreyfus case in 1894. He was deeply offended by this case and by the underlying anti-Semitism – a symptom, as he saw it, of the moral sickness he perceived in French society at the time.

'When society undergoes suffering, it feels the need to find someone whom it can hold responsible for its sickness, on whom it can avenge its misfortunes: and those against whom public opinion already discriminates are naturally designated for this role. These are the pariahs who serve as expiatory victims. What confirms me in this interpretation is the way in which the result of Dreyfus's trial was greeted in 1894. There was a surge of joy in the boulevards. People celebrated as a triumph what should have been a cause for public mourning. At least they knew whom to blame for the economic troubles and moral distress in which they lived. The trouble came from the Jews. The charge had been officially proved. By this very fact alone, things already seemed to be getting better and people felt consoled' (Lukes 1972: 345).

Equally, although interested in socialism, Durkheim's kind of socialism was very different to that of Karl Marx. It was simply a system in which the moral principles discovered by scientific sociology were to be applied.

While Marx saw the division of labour as divisive, Durkheim believed it could increase interdependence and co-operation and so reinforce social solidarity. Mutual interest alone, however, is insufficient to guarantee stability. Social order requires moral order, an underlying and agreed set of moral codes which inform and promote co-operation and restrain the individual. The exchange of goods and services needs an ethical framework to work properly, or else it is pure self-interest and exploitation, 'a war of all against all'. Durkheim saw the development of contracts as the beginning of a new industrial economic and moral order governed by shared beliefs in right and wrong, and regulated by law.

However, the concept of social solidarity and its use in sociological theory and research has also been the subject of extensive criticism:

- Durkheim's use of an organic analogy and his belief that all societies would follow the same evolutionary path have been severely criticised as socially and historically inaccurate. In his defence, though, Durkheim was only using mechanical and organic solidarity as ideal types, useful for analytical purposes but not necessarily prescriptive. He fully recognised that not all societies neatly fitted these models and that societies may well evolve in different ways.

- While the concept of social solidarity offered a major framework for analysing social order, it lacked the depth for explaining social change and social conflict. 'Social solidarity' could explain gradual evolutionary development but not sudden or revolutionary change. It explained change in terms of social adaptation or the re-establishment of equilibrium but offered little explanation of class or political conflict save as a social problem (as in the concept of anomie). In contrast, Marxist and more radical writers have put the class struggle at the heart of their theories of social development. Durkheim tended to perceive class conflict as simply a symptom of the social strain created by an artificial division of labour and a perpetuation of existing social inequalities. In fact, he was very sympathetic to socialist ideas and, like St Simon, predicted the emergence of a classless society in the future based on organic solidarity and equality of opportunity. Recognising that such a mature society may not emerge naturally he came to support the idea of state planning to create a more rational division of labour, a fairer system of social justice.

While anthropological research has tended to support Durkheim's concept of mechanical solidarity, his faith in economic reciprocity and occupational ethics as the basis of organic solidarity now seems somewhat optimistic, if not utopian. Recognising this criticism, Durkheim gradually shifted his analysis of the moral and social consensus of organic solidarity from economic interdependence to a re-creation of religious values in modern societies and to the rise of moral universalism represented by such social mores as nationalism and the power of education and citizenship to create the sense of common humanity needed to bind the individual to society. Unfortunately, the *conscience collective* of modern societies often seems too varied, changeable and superficial to support the organic solidarity required to stabilise and order advanced mass societies.

Durkheim has also been accused of exaggerating the contrast between repressive and restitutive law as a basis for measuring mechanical as opposed to organic solidarity. Critics have argued that many of the traditional societies he cited had forms of restitutive law while others, like the Trobriander Islanders, did not use repressive sanctions at all. Equally, many modern states have used highly repressive legal codes to enforce their authority and suppress individual rights, notably South Africa under apartheid and many communist societies.

Despite all these criticisms, Durkheim's concept of social solidarity, his evolutionary theory of social change and his attempt to analyse and monitor social development have proved a major stimulus to sociological ideas and research ever since. Durkheim established sociology as a respected and respectable academic discipline. He was truly one of its founding fathers; truly part of the Holy Trinity that gave birth and life to sociology in the twentieth century.

 **See Also**

- **STRUCTURAL FUNCTIONALISM** (p. 190) as a modern version of many of Durkheim's key ideas.
- **HISTORICAL MATERIALISM** (p. 43) as a radically different theory of social order and social change.
- **ANOMIE** (p. 22) – Durkheim's companion thesis of the effect on society and the individual of a loss of social solidarity.

Suggested Reading

GIDDENS, A. (1978) *Durkheim,* Fontana, Glasgow.

PAMPEL, F.C. (2000) Emile Durkheim and Morality in Modern Societies, Ch. 2 in Pampel, F.C., *Sociological Lives and Ideas: An Introduction to the Classical Theorists,* Macmillan, Basingstoke.

PARKIN, F. (1992) *Durkheim,* Oxford University Press, Oxford.

THOMPSON, K. (1982) *Emile Durkheim,* Tavistock, London.

Further Reading

DURKHEIM, E. (1951) *Suicide: A Study in Sociology* [1897], Free Press, Glencoe.

DURKHEIM, E. (1960) *The Division of Labour in Society* [1893], Free Press, Glencoe.

GUNERUSSEN, W. (2000) Emile Durkheim, Ch. 5 Part I in Andersen, H. and Kaspersen, L.B. (eds.), *Classical and Modern Social Theory,* Blackwell, Oxford.

LUKES, S. (1972) *Emile Durkheim: His Life and Work,* Allen & Unwin, London.

POPE, W. (1998) Emile Durkheim, Ch. 3 in Stones, R. (ed.), *Key Sociological Thinkers,* Macmillan, Basingstoke.

– Modern –

Conflict Theory
Ralf Dahrendorf

The Idea

THE IDEA THAT IT IS CONFLICT RATHER THAN CONSENSUS THAT UNDERPINS SOCIAL order and social change has been the key feature of a wide range of sociological theories, most notably those of Karl Marx and Max Weber. Ralf Dahrendorf (1929–), a German academic and politician and, more recently, Director of the London School of Economics and a member of the House of Lords, has sought to take this theory of conflict further. Like Marx and Weber, he has identified class conflict as the key dynamic for social change in industrial societies. Unlike Marx, however, he has based his analysis not on the ownership and non-ownership of the means of production but on participation in and exclusion from power, and in particular from positions of authority.

In any organisation there are those who hold power, who make decisions, hire and fire, allocate resources. Such power is not personal but depends on the position one holds. Such office-holders have authority – what Weber called 'legitimated power'. While those in power seek to maintain their position, authority and control, those without power or authority strive to attain it – or at least to resist it, especially if they disagree with the way it is being used. Thus, even in a stable, democratic society, there is a constant underlying power struggle going on in which those in authority – be they head teachers or prime ministers – have to face constant resistance – be it from staff and pupils or opposition politicians and voters. This power struggle takes place at all levels of society from the Cabinet and Houses of Parliament through to the rivalries and conflicts in the local tennis club – and in the home!

For Dahrendorf, authority does not reside in individuals but in positions of legitimate power; positions of authority that confer power on the holder and expectations of obedience on his or her subordinates. Authority brings with it control and the avail-ability of sanctions to enforce it. However, positions of authority are not constant and while a person may be dominant in one situation or relationship, he may be subordinate in another. A political leader, for example, all-powerful in his own country, may be summoned before an international judge to answer accusations of genocide or crimes against humanity.

The notion of superordination and subordination created by the distribution of authority led Dahrendorf to develop the concepts of associations and of interests. In every association or organisation those in authority seek to maintain the status quo while those in subordinate positions seek change. A constant conflict of interest under-pins – and on occasions undermines – their relationship. This conflict of interest will be latent most of the time but may become manifest – or open warfare – when the legitimacy of authority, or at least of the postholder, is challenged. Dahrendorf distin-guished between three types of group – quasi groups, interest groups and conflict groups – or stages of grouping from loose associations, to common interests, to groups that actually challenge the social order. In contrast to Marx, Dahrendorf did not believe that the 'lumpenproletariat' would ultimately and inevitably form a conflict group or a revolutionary class. The conditions had to be right.

Thus in Dahrendorf's theory, while conflict underpins the status quo through an inter-minable balance of power, it also has the potential to generate social change and devel-opment. When and where conflict is intense, then change may be radical; when it is accompanied by violence, it is likely to be sudden.

This interminable contest between those in and out of power only erupts into class conflict when individuals find that the only way to protect or promote their own inter-ests is by collective action. Such group conflict develops in degrees and takes a variety of forms from trade unions going on strike to pressure groups demonstrating. Only in the most extreme situations does collective action explode into class conflict or revolu-tion. However, according to Dahrendorf, such class solidarity may equally disintegrate into competition between individuals when opportunities for individual advance-ment improve, as, say, during periods of economic prosperity. Thus, while Marx predicted that as industrialisation advanced in capitalist societies, so would class solidarity and class conflict, Dahrendorf (1959) predicted the opposite – that with technological development the working class would become increasingly heteroge-neous and fragmented, *'increasingly complex machines require increasingly qualified designers, builders, maintenance and repair men'*. With such increasing specialisation, the working class becomes highly differentiated, divided rather than united by differ-ences of pay, status and skill. Competition between the different levels of the working class – skilled, semi-skilled and unskilled – is likely to become even more intense than that between the middle and working classes. Dahrendorf (1959) even went on to claim that *'it has become doubtful whether speaking of the working class still makes much sense'*. Dahrendorf's picture of society is thus one of the interminable conflict at the personal, group, organisational and class level. It is chaotic and it is characterised by apparently random conflict between those in and out of power, between the dominant and the subordinate. Yet such conflict has a purpose.

- First, it holds society together. For Dahrendorf, the basis of social integration is not, as Talcott Parsons argues, consensus, but coercion, the power of those in authority to force the masses to obey them. Though, in his view, social conflict is endemic to all societies, for the majority of the time it is confined within boundaries based on some general agreement, or at least acceptance, of basic values and institutions. It rarely spreads across the whole of society, rarely explodes into violent revolution.

For example, trade unions go on strike over economic and industrial disputes but they rarely enter 'politics' itself; for them to enter directly the political arena would be seen as illegitimate and unacceptable in a democratic society.

- Secondly, this struggle for power, this balance of power, is a key mechanism in a democracy for preventing tyranny and the abuse of power, for promoting individual rights and the rule of law. It keeps a check on those in authority and encourages the ordinary citizen to question and on occasion resist those in power.

Therefore, for Dahrendorf, constant conflict is not only normal and inevitable, not only the source of gradual and occasionally radical social change, it is also the basis of social order and social integration – a form of eternal tension between chaos and order, stability and change. Dahrendorf therefore sought to bridge the gap between consensus and conflict theories and to update conflict theory as a struggle between those in and out of authority as much as a struggle over the ownership and distribution of wealth.

The Idea in Action

AMID THE INTENSE SOCIAL AND POLITICAL CONFLICTS OF THE 1960S AND 1970S – student riots, strikes, industrial unrest and mass unemployment – Dahrendorf's analysis seemed inadequate compared to more radical and Marxist predictions of class upheavals and impending revolution. He was even accused of being reactionary. However, with the aid of hindsight, looking back from the 1980s and 90s, it is clear that, in some ways, Dahrendorf's predictions have so far shown as much strength and accuracy as the more radical ones of neo-Marxists.

Far from the conflicts of the 1970s paving the way for proletarian revolution and uniting the working class in defence of jobs and pay against new technology and big business, the last 30 years have seen the British working class fragment and divide. Even those most classic of working class struggles – the miners' dispute in Britain in 1984, and that at Wapping in 1985 when over 6,000 printers were made redundant at a stroke – failed to unify the British working class or even get unswerving support from the trade unions. Rather, with the support of a powerful Conservative Government led by Mrs Thatcher, new machinery was installed, manning-levels cut and the workers left defeated and dispirited, as capitalism and Rupert Murdoch marched on anew.

As Dahrendorf predicted, the prosperity of the 1980s and 90s has created greater economic and social opportunities for individual and group advancement, epitomised by that most upwardly mobile of social creatures, the British 'Yuppie'. Traditional class formations are disintegrating and the working class in particular seems to be shrinking and fragmenting in the face of new technology, the growth of service industries, and the shift of population from the north to the south, the inner cities to the suburbs. New 'class' lines appear to have emerged based on employment/unemployment, private/public consumption of housing, education and health, private ownership and shareholding.

Dahrendorf's conflict theory has therefore much to offer even today in explaining 'modern' conflicts; conflicts which seem to be based more on civil rights, the environment, housing and welfare issues, nuclear power and genetics than on the traditional ones of ownership and non-ownership of the means of production. Bureaucracy as much as big business is now the target of protest.

Dahrendorf's neo-Weberian analysis, however, only offers an explanation of social conflict and social division. It fails to provide:

- Any detailed analysis of the basis of social conflict beyond competition for power and authority. Social order, therefore, seems to be more a matter of chance than organisation. As Ian Craib (1984) has pointed out, while Dahrendorf recognises that subordinate groups may or may not challenge those in authority, he provides little explanation of why they choose one course of action rather than another. Dahrendorf's response that it is a matter of individual choice seems an inadequate response in a structural theory. Neo-Marxists, like Westergaard and Resler in Britain, rejected Dahrendorf's claim that Marx's theory is no longer applicable to contemporary societies. In their view the class struggle is still the main form of social conflict, and class the main dynamic behind it.

- Any programme of action, any solutions to social conflict in the way functionalism and even Marxism attempted to. Conflict is simply accepted as natural and inevitable. Just as structural functionalism has been criticised for over-emphasising order and stability, conflict theory has been criticised for over-emphasising conflict and change. Ironically, many of the criticisms applied to functionalism have been equally heaped on conflict theory – Dahrendorf's emphasis on systems and structures, its conceptual tautologies and its failure to assign a role and an importance to the individual actor. Ironically, too many of Dahrendorf's ideas seemed to derive more from structural functionalism than from the father of conflict theory, Marx. And like functionalism, his theory failed to satisfy the sociological need for a theory that embraced and defined both change and order, conflict and consensus.

So, while Dahrendorf's analysis appeared to offer a real alternative to Marxist ideas of social conflict and fragmentation in the 1960s and 70s, its lack of analytical depth limited its sociological influence and use during that period though it stimulated significant interest thereafter. Ultimately, however, the picture painted by conflict theory is that of a society in constant chaos with no one apparently in control. Such a picture is as difficult to accept as the one portrayed by structural functionalists of perfect social order and harmony. Conflict theory lacked the coherence and breadth of other major theories and so has fallen out of fashion and out of use as a result.

See Also

- **STRUCTURAL FUNCTIONALISM** (p. 190) and **HISTORICAL MATERIALISM** (p. 43) as two key ideas of consensus and conflict that influenced Dahrendorf in very different ways.
- **STRUCTURATION** (p. 271) as Tony Giddens' attempt to combine action and structure in a theory of social development.

Suggested Reading

DAHRENDORF, R. (1959) *Class and Class Conflict in an Industrial Society*, Routledge & Kegan Paul, London – difficult but worth trying.

Further Reading

STRANDBAKKEN, P. (2000) Conflict Theory: An Alternative to Functionalism, Ch. 16 Part II in Andersen, H. and Kaspersen, L.B. (eds.), *Classical and Modern Social Theory*, Blackwell, Oxford.

Critical Theory

Frankfurt School

The Idea

THE TERM 'CRITICAL THEORY' DERIVES FROM THE WRITINGS AND PUBLICATIONS OF A group of Marxist academics working together as the Frankfurt School of Social Theory at Frankfurt University from 1923 through to the work of Jürgen Habermas and his colleagues in the 1980s and 90s. Though the Frankfurt School was never a single school of thought nor a constant and consistent team of members, it was bound together by an attempt to reappraise traditional Marxist thinking in the light of contemporary events and in particular by an abhorrence of totalitarianism and the threats to individual freedom and humanity presented by the authoritarian regimes of Nazi Germany and Soviet communism and the repressive ideology of post-war capitalism. Many of its key figures, notably Max Horkheimer, Erich Fromm, Herbert Marcuse and T.W. Adorno, were themselves political refugees. As Marxists and Jews they were forced to flee from Nazi Germany in the 1930s and the Institute itself was relocated at Columbia University in America from 1934 to 1949.

In the post-war period the Frankfurt School became the vanguard of the New Left, inspiring radicals and students alike with its neo-Marxist critical theory and its anti-capitalist, anti-America polemic. While the original school had all but died out by 1973 with the deaths of Adorno and Horkheimer, the writings of Jürgen Habermas have inspired a revived interest in its works and its ideas (see p. 225).

It is difficult to categorise *critical theory* as a single and unified set of sociological ideas in the traditional way. Rather, it represented a theoretical framework, an interdisciplinary approach combining Marxism with Freudian concepts, philosophy with psychoanalysis, economic research with historical and cultural analyses across a wide variety of sociological fields from the family to the media, the economy to the state. Critical theory included a powerful psychological analysis as to the type of psyche or personality needed by the authoritarian state or consumerist society. Hence the work by Erich Fromm and later Theodore Adorno on *The Authoritarian Personality* (1950) and by Herbert Marcuse on *One Dimensional Man* (1964).

The underlying theme of critical theory, however, was a 'critical' analysis of all forms of domination in modern society.

This overriding concern reflected the times the Frankfurt theorists lived in – the rise of totalitarian societies, the horrors of the Nazi concentration camps and Stalin's purges, the spread of authoritarianism and suppression of individual thought and freedom. Advanced capitalism and Soviet socialism emerged as the most powerful social systems ever developed by man, capable of fulfilling all the material needs of their mass populations, yet capable too of controlling and manipulating people on a scale that seemed to realise all the worst fears of George Orwell's *1984*.

While the new communist states used Marxism as the basis of their ideological control of the masses (as well as physical force and terror), Western capitalism used the more subtle ideologies of consumerism and individualism to lull the working classes of America, Britain and Western Europe into a sense of 'false consciousness' and material satisfaction. The critical theorists sought to analyse such dominant ideologies and to try and explain why all the attempts to date to break the power of the ruling classes or the dominance of the state, be it by revolution or democracy, had failed.

Critical theory was, thus, in the same tradition as Marx's concept of 'alienation', Durkheim's 'anomie' and Weber's 'iron cage', a cry for the freedom of the individual amid the all-pervasive and stifling forces of bureaucracy, technology, the media and the state. The modern world is portrayed as a spiritual desert within which the individual is a lost soul searching for meaning and understanding amid material abundance, struggling for freedom and control against the faceless forces of technical progress, bureaucracy and mass culture. The Frankfurt theorists sought to show that far from existing reality being real, it is an ideological distortion that conceals and legitimates the power of the ruling class; that far from existing society being rational, free and progressive, it is irrational and oppressive because it takes away or destroys the basic freedoms of human life – our ability to choose and make collective and rational decisions. Far from Western capitalist societies being the bastions of individual freedom as their propaganda proclaims, they are just as powerful an example of the 'totally administered society', as the communist societies they so revile and criticise. They too have created 'one dimensional' men subservient to the state and to the dominant ideology.

The aim of critical theory was to liberate the individual in modern society by critically analysing such forces of domination, highlighting their weaknesses and so raising class consciousness about such ideological conditioning. By also outlining what a truly liberated and rational society would look like they equally hoped to inspire the masses to revolutionary thought and action.

The Frankfurt theorists used a Marxist framework as the basis of their criticism but they were as critical of traditional Marxism as of any other ideology. They criticised classical Marxism for being too deterministic, for overplaying the power of economic forces in historical development and underplaying the role of the individual, for becoming a repressive ideology used by tyrants like Stalin to suppress the masses, and the truth! However, they did not intend to undermine Marxism, but to reinvigorate and revive it in the light of contemporary developments, to humanise and enliven it as the basis for predicting and promoting a more individualistic socialist society, '*a community of free human beings*' (Horkheimer 1937). Critical theory thus became a code word for neo-Marxism, a major attempt to liberalise official Marxism and create a more flexible, humanistic and radical interpretation of Western society that combined the ideas of early Marx with such non-Marxist ideas as those of Freud and Weber.

Tom Bottomore (1984) has identified four key themes in critical theory:

1. *Critique of positivism and empiricism.* A fundamental critique of positivism and empiricism as the basis of modern scientific analysis, as a theory of knowledge and as the basis of modern sociology. In such key works as *Traditional and Critical Theory* (1937) and *Reason and Revolution* (1954), Horkheimer and Marcuse, respectively, rejected the idea of sociology as a science, arguing that positivism is too deterministic a basis for analysing human behaviour. Positivism treats people as things within a highly deterministic scheme of causes and effects, fails to distinguish between fact and value and, by presenting what is in society as what should be, legitimises the existing social order and obstructs change. In particular, the power of science has been subverted to support and promote a new form of 'technocratic' domination, by which technological, economic and political decisions are now sanctified by the stamp of 'scientific' approval, all criticism suppressed by a welter of unchallengeable scientific jargon and technical detail, all 'progress' justified in the name of science. The ruling elites now use science to obscure and legitimise their control, to make modern society seem impersonal and all-powerful while, in fact, they control and direct it. Instead of positivism being a means to discovering the truth, be it about nature or society, it has become a source of 'instrumental reason' used by the capitalist class (and the communist state) to increase exploitation of man and nature, profits and controls, to promote an image of reality supportive of the ruling elites. Science no longer involves itself in philosophical debates about the rights and wrongs of decisions about nuclear weapons, chemical pollutants, or space research. It merely serves the decisions of the powerful, irrespective of the effect on mankind – yet it gives the appearance of pursuing truth and knowledge. In contrast to positivism, Horkheimer (1937) propounded 'dialectical theory', a critical approach to all knowledge as the basis for both promoting pure reason and for liberating human thought. By never accepting any argument, fact or theory as totally proven, dialectical theory hoped to provide a basis for both criticising and changing the world.

2. *Analysis of new forms of domination in advanced societies.* Like Weber, the Frankfurt theorists saw modern man as being overawed by a new form of control – the forces of techno-rationality, an inner logic of all modern social systems, be they capitalist or communist, democratic or totalitarian, that has seen the rise of scientific techniques and technology as the overriding powers in society, sweeping aside individual opposition, rights and freedoms in the name of logical progress. They cited as examples of this trend the growth of monopoly capitalism, the growth of state control and planning of the economy, the spread of bureaucracy, of automation and mechanisation – all rational and apparently sensible developments, but all of which create an increasingly impersonal and alienating world in which the individual seems increasingly powerless, isolated and frustrated. Social control and centralised planning become all pervasive but no one seems to be in control, so opposition becomes pointless. Like Weber, Horkheimer and Marcuse became increasingly pessimistic about man's ability to resist such domination. In *One Dimensional Man* (1964), for example, Marcuse argued that the two main classes in capitalist societies have disappeared as effective historical agents. Domination is no longer by class but by the impersonal forces of scientific–technological rationality. There is no opposition as the working class has been assimilated by mass consumption and rational production processes.

3. *Analysis of the culture industry*. The culture industry is seen as a key form of mass manipulation and deception whereby all forms of culture have been reduced to mass culture, fused into being merely a form of entertainment, devoid of any form of qualitative statement about the human condition, of any form of social criticism, and subverted by the advertising industry into a new form of consumer control. Adorno, in particular, sought to analyse all forms of culture, be they literature, art or music, to highlight the fact that in contrast to the great works of the past, modern culture no longer offers a critical analysis of the present or a vision of the future. It doesn't even reflect individual talent and creativity but is simply mass produced to sell on the mass market, to entertain the masses and keep them under control. Marcuse went on to highlight the way the culture industry produces and satisfies 'false needs' as a means to creating new markets for monopoly capital, to perpetuating consumerism and materialism and so averting criticism and dissatisfaction with capitalism. Modern man is encouraged to pursue pleasure and luxury, sex is no longer just a source of human reproduction and personal relationships but a major form of mass sales, for example of cars or magazines. At one point Marcuse himself put his faith into sexual freedom as the basis of a counter-culture and a more liberated society (1955) as he became something of a guru to the student revolutions of the 1960s.

4. *Fear of the decline of individuality in modern society*. Horkheimer and his associates were committed to the value of individuality but became increasingly pessimistic about its survival amid the forces of mass society and *'the trend to a rationalised, automated, totally managed world'* in an age *'which tends to eliminate every vestige of even a relative autonomy for the individual'* (Adorno et al. 1950). Using psychoanalytical concepts they even identified a trend to particular character types produced by society to promote conformity. Their classic study here was *The Authoritarian Personality* by Adorno et al. (1950), an analysis of the personality traits that helped give rise to fascism, aggressive nationalism and racial prejudice – a standardised individual whose thinking is rigid, stereotyped, superstitious and blindly submissive to authority. In contrast, individuals in the past were more autonomous and critical. This decline of individual and strong personalities is seen as a result of a change in the socialisation process. As capitalism develops, the role of the family and, in particular, the authority of the father, declines in the face of the growth of state power. With the father's power weakened, especially by the length of time he is away from home at work, the son turns to other role models and sources of identification such as heroes or stars promoted by the state or culture industry. Lacking a true father-figure the son is less able to stand up for himself, more self-conscious and anxious to prove his manhood, but by submitting to authority rather than by challenging it. Hence, argued Adorno, the mass support of Germany's youth in the 1930s for Hitler and the magnetic power of other fascist demagogues in this period and since!

Indeed the Frankfurt theorists themselves became increasingly despairing about this process. Horkheimer turned to religion while Marcuse put his faith for liberation in student and sexual revolution, and Adorno pinned his hopes on critical and authentic artists. They were equally fearful that despite all its rational and centralised planning, capitalism was driving Western society to catastrophe through its underlying cycle of overproduction, anarchy, depressions, unemployment and war.

As it developed, critical theory increasingly distanced itself from Marxism, and in the post-war years Horkheimer abandoned Marxism altogether, notably its notions of class struggle and the revolutionary role of the proletariat. Rather, their analyses focused on the development of capitalist societies controlled absolutely by the authoritarian state and the cultural controls of mass conformity and consciousness, cultural indoctrination as described by Marcuse in *One Dimensional Man* (1964). Modern society has become in their view *an iron cage* of total administration, mass consumerism and mass apathy – a truly totalitarian society made possible by science and rationality, and used by the ruling class to control man rather than liberate him.

Positivism as developed by traditional sociology was therefore a key target of critical theory, not so much as a method for conducting social research but for being a means for increasing technological rationalisation and social control by the state and the media. Modern culture was seen as dehumanising and decadent, the perversion of reason and human creativity in service to consumerism and the authority of the state. Under post-war capitalism the masses may be economically better off (and so less revolutionary) but intellectually and spiritually they have been impoverished and indoctrinated. Worse, argued writers like Adorno, modern man seemed to worship authority and to flock to support such authoritarian movements as Nazism and fascism as evidenced in the totalitarian regimes of the 1930s. A new dark age seemed to have fallen on Europe in the inter-war years in which repression and thought control were endemic. While post-war capitalist societies like Britain and America seemed more liberal and tolerant, this in their view was an illusion, a form of 'repressive tolerance' according to Marcuse (1964) that tolerated, even encouraged new ideas provided they were non-revolutionary and had commercial potential. Ideas were thus converted by post-war capitalism into commodities to be marketed and sold at a profit, and culture had been converted from artistic expression into a new mass industry – a leisure industry to amuse, entertain and divert the masses from the realities and alienation of modern life and work. Culture, like science, has been subverted by modern capitalism into an instrument of mass indoctrination and class control. Science liberated by the Age of Enlightenment as a means for freeing man from the toils and burdens of life had been converted into yet another capitalist industry for making profit and for improving social controls and bureaucracy. Hence the reaction of students and militants in the 1960s against developments in modern science which seemed to be either increasing the power of the state and the military or the markets, and profits of the chemical, food or oil industries. Even social scientists in seeking to develop social reforms were portrayed as servants of the state, increasing managerial control of the working classes through welfare programmes and state education.

The Frankfurt School thus sought to combine Hegel's focus on the power of ideas with the early Marxist notion of alienation and with Weber's pessimism about the power and use of rationality. Critical theory accepted Weber's disenchantment with the rationality of modern capitalism and his fears about the iron cage of serfdom, an iron cage based on thought control and state control of class consciousness rather than on force, as such. '*Reason had been captured by capitalism*' (Cuff et al. 1998: 197) through a process of creating a 'one-dimensional man' in a mass society that promotes mass culture and mass conformity. Choice is an illusion, personality a product and style a marketing strategy – a 'virtual reality' created on the basis of image, illusion and Hollywood dreams; a false reality in which individuality and individualism are illusions in a world of mass conformity and standardisation. Thus the working class had in their view been incorporated into post-war capitalism and lost its historic revolutionary role in favour of mass consumerism.

The Idea in Action

C RITICAL THEORY AND THE WRITINGS OF THE FRANKFURT SCHOOL BECAME A MAJOR force in radical thought in post-war Europe and America, inspiring both neo-Marxism, the New Left and student revolution. It reflected post-war fears about materialism, cultural decline, irrationality and imminent destruction through the nuclear arms race. It spawned a mass of critical studies into all forms of post-war culture and control, a rich and diverse array of analyses centred around the framework of critical theory and around the notion of culture (and science) as ideology and ideological control. Such studies, notably Adorno's work on art and on the psychology of conformity, still offer rich insights into modern life.

Its key themes of the growth of mass society, increase in social controls and ideological conditioning and decrease in individuality; its critique of monopoly capitalism, the state and the role of science and technology, reflected currents of thought elsewhere in the Western world, and its fears for the individual in the face of big business, big government and big brother inspired the young and other frustrated groups.

However, critical theory and its theorists themselves inspired criticisms that:

- Their theoretical work lacked coherence and structure, was based more on generalisations than detailed analyses. It failed to put events into their historical context, be it fascism in the 1930s or anti-Semitism in the 1940s.

- Despite their claim to its being an interdisciplinary approach, critical theory was in fact quite a narrow analysis limited to contemporary society and primarily philosophical in nature. It lacked historical depth, and breadth, and was weak on economic analyses of advanced capitalism despite the contributions of Friedrich Pollock and Franz Neuman. They often looked back to a golden era of early capitalism as a period of true individualism, but never analysed such a speculative claim.

- It tended to ignore economic factors and so over-emphasise the power of culture and psychology.

- While claiming to make a major reassessment of Marxism the Frankfurt theorists left out its core component – an analysis of class in capitalist societies and, in particular, the role of the working class as a revolutionary force. Critical theory has been described as 'Marxism without the proletariat'. The Frankfurt School lost faith in such revolution and tended to assume that class (and so class conflict) would disappear in the face of the totally administered society. While critical theory moved Western Marxism on in seeking to account for the loss of revolutionary zeal in Western society, it failed to offer any alternative force for change beyond the radical students inspired by Marcuse in America and his colleagues in Europe – students who quickly conformed once they graduated and became the new captains of industry, the new consumers of American culture.

Even in its chosen sphere of social control and conformity:

- It failed to analyse historically or empirically whether the condition of the individual in modern society was actually worse than in the past, or worse under capitalism than communism. Critical theorists tended to use a middle-class bourgeois model of modern man rather than the 'man in the street', and tended to ignore the very real growth in individual freedom in post-war Western society. The decline they talked of was more that of the intellectual and the educated middle class than that of the mass of the population.

- It over-emphasised the power of the culture industry and dominant ideology, ignoring its weaknesses and the way people have resisted and obstructed such conditioning.

- It ignored the wide variety of attempts by the working class and subject groups in post-war society to resist capitalism and domination: the growth and power of socialist and communist parties in Western Europe, the power of modern trade unions, the rise of women's liberation and other radical movements, such as students, ethnic groups or environmentalists, against the power of the state, big business, bureaucracy or technology. In trying to explain why a Marxist-type revolution had not occurred in the West, they tended to over-emphasise the power of the 'system' to crush or absorb opposition, to control people's thoughts and behaviour.

- Finally, while studies like *The Authoritarian Personality* (1950) and *One Dimensional Man* (1964) were significant contributions to analyses of the relationship between modern man and mass society, of social control and conformity, fascism and prejudice, they lacked the detail and depth of theoretical analysis to have a lasting influence.

Essentially, critical theory was a defence of individuality, a plea for consideration of the individual person in both mass society and modern social theory. It defended subjectivity and attacked the power of positivism in both sociology and Marxism. It proclaimed the individual amid the crushing forces of conformity and rationality inherent in the modern social system. However, it was only one among several post-war social analyses, one among a variety of Marxist reappraisals and though initially very influential, its growing pessimism and its theoretical weaknesses saw its decline in the face of more radical theories and successful social movements such as the revolutions in the Third World, the student revolution of May 1968 and other attempts to defeat or overthrow the 'system'. Its preoccupation with culture and philosophy has now been bypassed by more recent developments in Marxist thought more in tune with such central concerns as economic, historical and class analysis. Thus Tom Bottomore declared in 1984 that 'the Frankfurt School in its original form and as a school of Marxism and sociology is dead'. While it may have died as a distinct school of Marxism, however, many of its ideas have informed modern Marxism and even mainstream sociology. The work of Jürgen Habermas in particular embodies and maintains the spirit of critical theory even if Habermas has now taken it in new directions.

At heart the Frankfurt philosophers believed that man is essentially a rational being who could only live and breathe, be truly human, in a rational and free society. They lost faith, however, in the possibility of such a society ever emerging.

 See Also

- HISTORICAL MATERIALISM (p. 43) as the parent theory of this revision of classical Marxism.
- STRUCTURAL MARXISM (p. 265) as a radical alternative interpretation of the master.
- ALIENATION (p. 14) as a reflection of Marx's early views that provides the basis for the humanist themes of critical theory.
- LEGITIMATION CRISIS (p. 225) shows how Jürgen Habermas has extended and revised the ideas of the Frankfurt School of the 1930s.

Suggested Reading

BOTTOMORE, T.B. (1984) *The Frankfurt School,* Tavistock, London – a concise and readable overview.

McINTYRE, D. (1970) *Marcuse*, Fontana, Glasgow.

Further Reading

ADORNO, T.W. ET AL. (1950) *The Authoritarian Personality*, Harper, New York.

BERNSTEIN, J. (1994) *The Frankfurt School: Critical Assessments,* Routledge, London.

BOWIE, A. (2001) Theodor Adorno, Ch. 5 in Elliott, A. and Turner, B.S. (eds.), *Profiles in Contemporary Social Theory*, Sage, London.

BRONNER, S.E. (1996) *Of Critical Theory and its Theorists*, Blackwell, Oxford.

KELLNER, D. (2001) Herbert Marcuse, Ch. 4 in Elliott, A. and Turner, B.S. (eds.), *Profiles in Contemporary Social Theory*, Sage, London.

MARCUSE, H. (1964) *One Dimensional Man,* Routledge & Kegan Paul, London – a popular version of 'critical' ideas.

RAMSAY, A. (2000) The Frankfurt School, Ch. 10 Part II in Andersen, H. and Kaspersen, L.B. (eds.), *Classical and Modern Social Theory*, Blackwell, Oxford.

WIGGERSHAUS, R. (1994) *The Frankfurt School: Its History, Theories and Political Significance,* Polity Press, Cambridge.

Dependency Theory

Andre Gunder Frank

DEPENDENCY THEORY IS A KEY IDEA IN THE SOCIOLOGY OF DEVELOPMENT AND underdevelopment of the Third World. While a variety of theories have been developed about the dependence of the Third World on the rich countries of the West, Andre Gunder Frank, Professor of Development Studies at the University of East Anglia is generally considered the leading exponent of dependency theory. It is his version that is outlined and discussed in this chapter.

Traditionally, economic development was seen as a series of stages through which every country must progress if it is to 'take off' as an industrial nation and move from the poverty of the Third World to the wealth of the First. From this perspective the failure of the Third World is not only due to a lack of skills and technology but also to ignorance and superstition, to a lack of enterprise and ambition. What the poor countries of the world need, argued modernisation theorists (see p. 146) is support, aid and trade with the Western nations so that they can become part of a global, capitalist economy and so be transformed from backward agrarian societies to progressive industrial ones.

In a stream of publications dating back to his pioneering work *Capitalism and Underdevelopment in Latin America* (1969b), A.G. Frank rejected modernisation theory and all that it stood for. He argued instead that the key reason the Third World has not developed is not because of its own inadequacies but because the Western nations *deliberately* underdeveloped it. Such a relationship of exploitation and dependency can be traced back to the sixteenth century when the great European powers like Britain, France and Spain conquered and colonised the continents of Africa, Asia and Latin America and made them an integral part of their worldwide empires. Such colonies supplied the mother country with cheap food and raw materials and in turn acted as new markets for the industrialised country's manufactured goods. There thus developed a world capitalist system based on an international division of labour by which the colonial powers made 'their' colonies specialise in one or two primary products on terms highly advantageous to the mother country and through such a system of unequal exchange the Western economies developed and the Third World ones under-developed. An unequal exchange existed whereby the prices of Third World products were kept artificially low, yet they had to pay inflated First World prices for manufac-tured goods and technology. Thus the advanced nations made huge profits or surpluses by exploiting and so creating the poverty of the developing nations of the world. The First World grew rich as the Third World grew poor. Where necessary the colonial powers even destroyed local industries that might compete against theirs, the classic example of this being the destruction of the thriving Indian textile industry by the British to ensure the success of the Lancashire cotton mills.

There thus developed, argues Frank, a world system of dependency and underdevel-opment by which such core nations as Spain exploited such peripheral ones as Chile in a chain-like system of expropriation by which these satellite countries became totally dependent on the metropolis. The key link in this chain was (and still is) the city. The colonial powers used existing cities (or built their own) as the main means not only for governing such areas but for draining them of their surplus. The rich ruling elites of such colonies lived in the cities and generally collaborated with the colonial powers, using their control of local markets (and after independence their control of the government) to exploit the peasantry in the countryside, buy up their produce cheaply and export it to the West. Thus the cities were used to exploit the countryside and the ruling families of the Third World became more closely linked to the Western way of life than to their own people. So, to preserve their own privileged life-styles and maintain their elite rule, they often use the military to protect Western interests and factories against their own people. In return the West supplies such dictatorships with aid and even weapons. There has thus developed a chain of dependency that through the world capital cities stretches across the globe and deep down into the villages of the Third World. Through such countries economic surplus is sucked upwards and outwards to the wealthy West: *'a whole chain of metropolises and satellites, which runs from the world metropolis down to the hacienda or rural merchant who are satellites of the local commercial metropolitan centre but who in their turn have peasants as their satellites* (Frank 1969a).

Today with the decline of colonialism, it is the multinationals who govern this system. In their relentless pursuit of profit they search the world for cheap labour, raw materials and new markets – Volkswagen in Brazil, for example; Coca-Cola in India – but the profits always go to the West. Dependency is also maintained by the Third World's reliance on the West for aid. Despite appearances, aid to the Third World does not come cheaply as interest charges or Western factories have to be paid for. Soon these debts outstrip the poorer countries' ability to repay and so they default as Brazil and Mexico have done, and Argentina is now doing, creating a world financial crisis. They cannot repay their debts because their exports do not earn much. It is the First World that controls the world prices of food and raw materials and deliberately keeps them low to maintain their own high standards of living. The only way for the Third World to break this monopoly is to form their own power bloc, as the Organisation of Petroleum Exporting Countries (OPEC) did in controlling oil in 1972/73. This, however, is very difficult as only the industrial nations of the West are rich enough to buy the goods of the Third World.

Thus, according to Frank's model, 'satellite' countries can never develop so long as they remain part of the world capitalist system. One solution is 'isolation' – refusing to be part of the world trade system – as in the examples of Paraguay or China. Another is to 'break away' at a time when the metropolis country is weak, as in times of war or recession – as happened in the two World Wars and 1930s depression. This may require a socialist revolution to overcome the *comprador*, the ruling classes of the Third World, but to achieve this requires extensive organisation of the new urban proletariat or landless peasantry. Here Frank is rather pessimistic, believing that sooner or later the metropolis will reassert its control. For him the most 'ultra-developed' areas, the poorest countries of the Third World are precisely those that had the closest ties with the mother country in the past but have now been economically 'scrapped' as no longer useful (e.g. north-east Brazil).

Thus for A.G. Frank, development and underdevelopment are two sides of a world process by which the First World has developed at the expense of the Third World and having got the upper hand uses its economic power to keep the Third World poor, in debt and dependent. Such poor countries are so locked into this system that it is almost impossible for them to escape.

The Idea in Action

THIS RADICALLY ALTERNATIVE EXPLANATION OF DEVELOPMENT TO THE MODERNISATION theory of such Western writers as W.W. Rostow (see p. 146) inspired a whole generation of radical writers and Third World leaders. It offered a highly detailed analysis of the way they were being exploited and oppressed and, in depicting each link in the chain, offered the hope of breaking it. A host of subsequent studies found strong evidence in support of Frank's thesis. Barnet and Müller's (1975) study of the multinationals, for example, identified the way that companies like ITT and General Motors, far from spreading jobs and technology in the Third World, in fact 'drained off' local investment capital. Teresa Hayter's study of aid (1971) revealed the very high cost to Third World countries of such loans and the way Western technology (and arms) are used more to bolster oppressive dictatorships than to lay the basis of development. New hospitals, airports and hotels are not only of no use to the ordinary peasants of the Third World but actually distort their economies and turn them into debtor nations. According to the World Bank, the Third World in the 1990s paid $21 billion more in paying interest on loans from Western banks than it received in aid.

Hayter further cites evidence of the way the economies of the Third World are distorted, of how the dependence of poor countries on a few cash crops serves the West's need for cheap food but leaves their own people starving. The key here is that the West keeps world food prices low, but the price of technology high. Eight hundred million people live in absolute poverty and near to starvation today while the West suffers from overeating. As Cardinal Arns pointed out at the 1985 International Development Conference in Rome, every time the US raises its interest rates, '*thousands die in the Third World because money that could be used for health care and food is sent outside*' to pay off debts to the First World. When Third World governments attempt to break away from Western control, financial controls are tightened and ultimately the CIA or the American army is sent in to restore 'order' – in for example the Bay of Pigs, Chile, El Salvador, Nicaragua, to name but a few examples of American intervention. Many Latin American scholars have tried to formulate economic policies by which their governments can get better trade relations with the West or even, like OPEC, gain control of their own export prices.

However, Frank's thesis has also been extensively criticised by both right- and left-wing writers. Frank's theoretical concepts like dependency, metropolis and satellite are very vague and even circular because the present international system leaves the First World countries as dependent on the Third World as it is on them. The First World needs the raw materials of the Third World as much as these countries need new technology and financial aid.

Modernisation theorists argue that both the multinationals and Western aid do bring considerable benefits, citing the examples of 'economic miracles' in both Brazil and Mexico in the 1970s (though both went bankrupt in the 1980s) and the growth of newly developing countries like Taiwan and South Korea, the 'Asian Tigers'.

Similarly, liberal writers like John Goldthorpe et al. (1980) and the Brandt Commission (1980) believe Frank's ideas are too radical, too Marxist. Colonialisation did benefit many poor countries and the First World needs the Third World to grow and industrialise as a source of new investment and new markets. What is required, argues the Brandt Report, is a 'rebalancing' of the world economic and financial system in favour of the south, not its abolition.

Marxist writers have criticised both Frank's theory and his failure to provide a revolutionary programme for breaking the chains of the world capitalist system. Writers like Samir Amin (1976) have criticised Frank's historical analysis as too generalised. It fails to show the 'unevenness' of Third World development which ranges from the total backwardness of Ethiopia to the growing industries of South Korea and Taiwan. Similarly by concentrating only on North–South relations it ignores exploitation and dependency within the Third World (e.g. Asian multinationals dominating Eastern markets).

Ernesto Laclau (1977) has argued that dependency theory is not a true Marxist analysis. It only describes how the surpluses of satellite countries are extracted and distributed. It fails to provide the heart of a Marxist analysis, an explanation of the relations of production and of the modes of production, the economic stages from feudalism to capitalism that Third World countries have gone, or are going, through. Frank's theory only analyses the external feature of the world capitalist system, not the internal dynamics of the class struggle so vital to Marxist revolutionary practice. Taylor (1979) in turn has argued that the key concept of economic surplus as developed by dependency theorists is weak and lacking in detail or rigour.

Bill Warren (1980) goes even further, arguing that far from underdeveloping the Third World, capitalism and imperialism are 'progressive' forces, helping backward nations along the inevitable historical path from feudalism to capitalism and eventually socialism. Just as in the Western nations, early capitalism produces extreme poverty and exploitation, but these are short-term transitory problems. Through Western expansion the Third World has not only acquired the skills, capital and technology for industrial progress but become conscious of and increasingly organised against Western capitalism. The Third World is developing an industrial and urban proletariat, developing a 'typical' class struggle, seizing control of its own resources and as the newly industrialising countries have shown, stimulating the present crisis within Western capitalism. The mass unemployment and deep economic recession of the First World is ironically partly a reflection of Eastern competition from Taiwan, South Korea and Singapore.

In more recent works such as *Crisis in the World Economy* (1980), Frank has acknowledged such criticisms and the possibility of industrial development in the Third World, if the multinationals can be brought under control. But, whatever its shortcomings, dependency theory as developed by A.G. Frank has proved a major contribution to both the theory and practice of development and offered a radical alternative to modernisation theory.

Dependency theory as such developed as part of a wider framework of radical analysis, one that took the world system as its primary focus of attention in seeking to analyse the way the modern world economy evolved and is currently constituted. Alongside Frank's theory of dependency, the work of Immanual Wallerstein, notably in *The Modern World System* (1974), is particularly prominent and his notion of core, semi-periphery and periphery reflects a similar analysis to Frank's of how the West controls and exploits the Third World in the interests of profit and power over the world economy. Wallerstein's detailed historical research into the origins and underpinning structure of relations of both the modern capitalist economy and its predecessor, the world empire system, has inspired a generation of younger scholars, and he himself has moved on to analyse the power and predominance of post-war American capitalism. He predicts a fundamental restructuring of the world system over the next 50 years as the nations of the southern hemisphere seek greater equity with the north and greater control over their own economies and lives from the major multinationals.

While world system theories such as Frank's and Wallerstein's have been subject to criticism from both liberal and radical writers, this framework of analysis and the underlying relationships of dependency and exploitation between the First and the Third Worlds have proved – and continue to prove – to be a very powerful and fruitful basis for analysing world relations – and changing them!

 See Also

- **MODERNISATION THEORY** (p. 146) – W.W. Rostow's thesis of global development that A.G. Frank so scathingly denounced.
- **INFORMATION(AL) SOCIETY** (p. 220) and **GLOBALISATION** (p. 214) – late-modern theories of global development today.

Suggested Reading

BENNETT, J. AND GEORGE, S. (1987) *The Hunger Machine,* Polity Press, Cambridge.

FOSTER-CARTER, A. (1985) 'The Sociology of Development' in Haralambos, M. (ed.) *Sociology New Directions,* Causeway Press, Ormskirk.

HARRISON, P. (1981) *Inside the Third World*, Penguin, Harmondsworth.

HAYTER, T. (1985) *Aid: Rhetoric and Reality*, Pluto, London.

HERTZ, N. (2002) *The Silent Takeover: Global Capitalism and the Death of Democracy*, Arrow Books, London.

Further Reading

FRANK, A.G. (1969a) *Latin America: Underdevelopment or Revolution?*, Penguin, Harmondsworth.

FRANK, A.G. (1969b) *Capitalism and Underdevelopment in Latin America*, Monthly Review Press, New York.

FRANK, A.G. (1981) *Crisis in the Third World*, Heinemann, London.

HAYTER, T. (1981) *The Creation of World Poverty*, Pluto, London.

Deskilling

Harry Braverman

A S MODERN INDUSTRY HAS ADVANCED AND NEW METHODS OF PRODUCTION HAVE BEEN introduced, many writers have speculated whether the new industrial technologies would liberate the modern worker from the drudgery of manual labour or whether it would deskill him, rob him of his traditional skills and crafts and turn him into a human robot, just another cog in the industrial assembly line.

One of the leading critics of modern industrial technology was Harry Braverman, an American Marxist who began his working life as a coppersmith in a New York naval yard and then progressed onto becoming a sheet metal worker, pipe-fitter and freight car repair man before moving into left-wing journalism with the *The American Socialist* magazine. His experiences of both manual and non-manual craft work inspired and informed his major publication *Labor and Monopoly Capital* in 1974, a book he subtitled 'The Degradation of Work in the Twentieth Century'. He was not against technological change – he recognised it as both inevitable and necessary. What he objected to was *'the manner in which (such) changes are used as weapons of domination in the creation, perpetuation and deepening of a gulf between classes in Society'*. He took this process of deskilling of the labour force not just as an injustice but as a 'personal affront'.

Braverman adopted a Marxist view of the capitalist mode of production and saw its prime aim as the increase in efficiency that would bring an increase in profits. Within the capitalist work system the worker is not a human being with needs, feelings and potential. He is simply a unit of production, a source of surplus value or profit. The purpose of new technology, however, argues Braverman, is not only to increase productivity, but to increase management's control of the work force. It is a system of class control as well as of class exploitation. *Labor and Monopoly Capital* (1974) is a detailed outline of how the capitalist labour process actually works.

The traditional craftsman of the early Industrial Revolution was, in a sense, self-employed and independent. He owned his own tools and place of work, bought his own raw materials and sold the finished product direct to the consumer. He alone possessed the necessary skill and knowledge required for the whole production process, from conception through to execution. He had a certain status and power in relation to his employer. However, such a system of production was not only expensive and inefficient, but difficult to control. Although centralising the workforce within the modern factory improved managerial control, the traditional workgangs still had considerable autonomy and independence.

All this changed with the introduction of the scientific management techniques of F.W. Taylor in the early twentieth century (see p. 175). These techniques had one prime aim, to increase efficiency by deskilling the workers and centralising all knowledge and information in the hands of the factory management. This revolutionary labour process was based on three key principles:

1. The 'dissociation' of the labour process from the skills of the worker. Henceforth it was to be the management who held all the technical knowledge required and this was then imposed on the workforce in the form of 'rules, laws and formulae'.

2. The separation of conception from execution, of mental from manual work. Henceforth, the initiation and planning of the work process is controlled by management. Work tasks are divided and sub-divided, simplified and fragmented, the worker divorced from overall planning and understanding and reduced to a cog in a massive assembly-line process.

3. The use by management of this knowledge to control each step of the labour process and its mode of execution. Henceforth, every work-task is planned in minute detail by management and the role of the worker is reduced to simply executing written instructions.

Scientific management, argued Braverman, deskilled the industrial worker and left him helpless, powerless and skill-less, controlled from above by factory managers and reduced on the shop floor to simply a unit of production. The epitome of scientific management was Henry Ford's giant assembly lines and the mass production of the early Ford motorcar.

The new technologies of today – the computer and the industrial robot – have merely extended this process of automation and control.

Braverman extended his thesis to other areas of industrial work arguing that deskilling is affecting all walks of industrial life and is reducing even the modern office worker to being a cog in a giant industrial wheel. From being a person in the past of some importance, knowledge and power, the clerk today is merely part of a huge assembly line of paper controlled by Head Office through its computers and fax machines.

With the introduction of time and motion studies, open-plan offices and new technology, even non-manual workers have lost their skills, status and control of the work process. They too have been degraded, routinised and replaced. They are left unskilled, powerless and alienated, subject to external controls while undertaking meaningless and mindless tasks, devoid of any intrinsic job satisfaction. Consider the effect, and purpose, of automated cash points and direct line banking on the traditional role, status and numbers of the bank cashier. Consider how easily both the modern factory and office worker are now replaced by new machinery or by unskilled and semi-skilled labour.

Braverman went on to develop his theory of deskilling into a contribution to the broader Marxist theses of *proletarianisation*. This is the theory that within advanced capitalist societies the modern worker is not becoming more middle class, more affluent and independent, but is in fact being proletarianised, being reduced to being an employee of capital, whether it be as a servant of some private enterprise or a servant of the state. Using this definition, Braverman calculated that some 70 per cent of the American labour force can now be categorised as proletarian and that even the 15–20 per cent who constitute the intermediate classes as lower level managers, technicians and state employees, while receiving '*its petty share in the prerogatives and rewards of capital . . . also bear the mark of the proletarian condition*'. Eventually they, too, will be deskilled and fully proletarianised as monopoly capital continues its relentless pursuit of profit. Such intensified pressure of deskilling, decontrolling and degrading the mass of the population through control of the labour process, through new machinery and technology, will ultimately create the conditions for a proletarian uprising – though Braverman was careful not to predict when. As he summed up: '*The mass of humanity is subjected to the labor process for the purposes of those who control it rather than for any general purposes of "humanity" as such. In thus acquiring concrete form, the control of humans over the labor process turns into its opposite and becomes the control of the labor process over the mass of humans. Machinery comes into the world not as the servant of "humanity", but as the instrument of those to whom the accumulation of capital gives them ownership of the machines. The capacity of humans to control the labor process through machinery is seized upon by management from the beginning of capitalism as the prime means whereby production may be controlled not by the direct producer but by the owners and representative of capital. Thus, in addition to its technical function of increasing the productivity of labor – which would be a mark of machinery under any social system – machinery also has in the capitalist system the function of divesting the mass of workers of their control over their own labor*' (Braverman 1974).

While recognising that similar processes were occurring in socialist countries, Braverman argued that these were transitional, created by the imitation and use of Western technology. The essential difference is that the ultimate aim is not relentless profit nor the degradation of the worker. Where the means of production are in common ownership then new work techniques will be used to enrich the work experience and extend worker control. Braverman was not against technical advance; only against its misuses as a form of exploitation and profit making.

The Idea in Action

*L*ABOR AND *M*ONOPOLY *C*APITAL HAS BEEN HAILED AS A CLASSIC, AS A MAJOR ADVANCE in Marxist analysis of class and the labour process: '*one of the two most important works of Marxist political economy to have appeared in English in the last decade*' (Rowthorn 1976). It offered a radical, forceful and passionate critique of the prevailing liberal claims that modern work techniques were enriching and reskilling the work experience, yet fragmenting and defusing the working class. It contrasted sharply with the optimism of post-industrial writers and their predictions of a life of leisure for workers liberated from the chains of work. It inspired a wealth of studies into the work process on all levels and in all occupations. It provided the focus for a major debate on the labour process and even led to what Graeme Salaman (1986) has called 'Bravermania'. Research into many of the new, non-manual occupations showed little improvement in the level of skill, control and job satisfaction: *'The chemical operator is singled out time and time again as the outstanding beneficiary of automation . . . yet few have stopped to think whether it is harder to learn to read a dial than tell time'* (Braverman 1974). Braverman's thesis offered a major theoretical explanation for various workers' attempts to resist deskilling, such as the printers' dispute in Britain in the mid 1980s. It revived the Marxist analysis of class formation and class relations and restored it to the centre of radical analysis.

However, once the initial flush of academic and left-wing enthusiasm subsided so the criticisms of the deskilling thesis began.

Definitions

FIRST, the very term 'skill' is ambiguous. It can refer to real attributes of knowledge and/or manual dexterity, or to labels used by management or workers to up- or down-grade a particular job. Skills may be technical or personal and often a job is labelled 'skilled' even though the work involved is largely unskilled. Jobs may be deskilled but workers not – they may be reskilled or redeployed. Such ambiguous definitions make an analysis of 'deskilling' highly problematic.

Secondly, Braverman's definition of the proletarian class has been heavily criticised as too simple, too broad. He tries to include all 'classes' of worker in it and so ignores the diversity and tensions of class perceptions.

Work strategies

BRAVERMAN has been accused of both overestimating the resources, knowledge and will of capitalists to so relentlessly pursue a strategy of deskilling and controlling the work force and underestimating the ability of many work groups to resist such a process. While some managers have sought to improve the work situation by, say, job rotation or human relations approaches, others have used alternative strategies to deskilling and Taylorism for controlling the work force. Equally, historical research shows how many unions, especially craft unions, have successfully resisted, or at least, manipulated deskilling attempts. By solely concentrating on scientific management, Braverman ignored different management strategies, different industrial relations as, for example, in Sweden. As Graham Winch (1983) and David Knights et al. (1985) have argued, employers are not simply motivated by a desire to control their work-forces. They face stiff competition from rival firms and have to adopt new technology to survive.

More recently, writers like Michael J. Piore (1986) and John Atkinson (1985) have sought to identify the move in the post-Fordian era of the 1980s and 90s towards flexible specialisation, towards the 'Flexible Firm' operating with teams of highly trained specialists within a management structure that gives them high degrees of autonomy, control and responsibility. High levels of industrial competition and the intense growth of new technologies are forcing firms to be more flexible and worker-oriented if they are to survive. Multi-skilling, subcontracting and relocation are the watchwords of modern management. Worker control and management is far more varied and diverse today than Braverman envisaged in the 1970s. The advent of the Internet and of e-commerce is adding a further revolutionary dimension to the whole debate about skill specialisation and management control.

Analysis of clerical work and clerical workers

WHILE studies like Crompton and Jones (1984) and Goldthorpe et al. (1980) support Braverman's view that most clerical work is routine and involves little skill, control or satisfaction, many groups of office workers welcome new technology as relieving them of the most boring tasks and freeing them to develop and expand their skills and authority (National Economic Development Office Study, 1983). Moreover, office workers do not constitute 'a large proletariat in a new form', but rather are stratified by age, qualification, gender and level of post. Like most non-manual workers, they are highly mobile and can (and do) move up into more intermediate or supervisory positions. They have greater self-control, are more organised to resist deskilling and a loss of job status. They are less class conscious than the working class. White-collar workers may have become more unionised in the 1970s, but this was to protect their class/status differences with manual workers, not eliminate them. They still identify with the capitalist class, not the proletariat; with those in authority rather than with their subordinates.

Marxist criticisms

MARXIST writers have criticised Braverman's analysis of class, first for failing to analyse the modern working class in terms of class consciousness as well as class position, and secondly for failing to place such an analysis within the framework of a broader analysis of other forms of political domination and of the class struggle. By only analysing the modern working class as a class 'in itself', not 'for itself', Braverman ignores all the subjective elements of class consciousness, portrays the working class as essentially passive, unable to resist control from above. Such a deterministic picture fails to put the class struggle and class conflict at the heart of what is supposed to be a Marxist analysis and fails to offer any glimpse of the underlying dialectical process and struggle for control.

Feminist criticisms

FEMINISTS have applauded Braverman for including female labour in his analysis, for highlighting their role in monopoly capital as a reserve army of labour used to replace men and so reduce the status, skill and cost of many jobs. At last sexual stratification has been used in a class analysis. However, they too criticise him for failing to take a broader perspective, for failing to include the domestic division of labour, women's unpaid work in the family, the degradation of housework, in his analysis of the labour process. Equally, his analysis of class fails to give sufficient weight to differentiations and cleavages within the working class other than those of gender.

Historians' criticisms

HISTORIANS have criticised Braverman's account on two main grounds:

- for being historically inaccurate, particularly about the timing, extent and pace of deskilling;
- for glamourising the traditional craft worker and postulating a sort of 'golden age of work' in pre-industrial societies. Work in the past was often far more onerous, exploitative and oppressive than even the twentieth-century factory Braverman describes.

Though Braverman's deskilling thesis is now considered somewhat dated in the light of recent research and new developments in the work place, it has rightly been acclaimed as a major contribution to this sociological and radical debate and still informs, even 25 years later, much of modern analysis of the nature of work and the labour process. Braverman was not, however, a critic of technological progress, nor did he yearn for a past era of skilled crafts. Like Marx, he sought to embrace new technology and science. What he objected to was the way the new methods of production were being used by capitalism '*as weapons of domination in the creation, perpetuation and deepening of a gulf in the classes in society*', rather than as a means to enriching work and freeing the worker from bondage to the machine. Only in a socialist society, he believed, would such liberation occur. Post-Fordian writers (see p. 234) have often agreed with Braverman's fears but some have identified even in post-industrial capitalism, signs of greater control and freedom for the modern worker as modern work methods have had to adapt to the challenges and pressures of technological and industrial change in the age of the Internet, global production and world-wide communication.

Dated as Braverman's work may now seem, its insights, concerns and questions continue to inform the ongoing debate about work, control and the labour process.

 See Also

- SCIENTIFIC MANAGEMENT (p. 175) as the target of Braverman's critique.
- POST-FORDISM (p. 234) as a post-modern view of industrial development.

Suggested Reading

BRAVERMAN, H. (1974) *Labor and Monopoly Capital,* Monthly Review Press, New York. Try Braverman's own study as it is well worth the effort.

WOOD, S. (ED.) (1982) *The Degradation of Work? Skill, Deskilling and the Labour Process*, Hutchinson, London.

Further Reading

RITZER, G. (1993) *The McDonaldization of Society*, Pine Forge Press, Thousand Oaks, CA.

RITZER, G. (1996) *Sociological Theory*, Ch. 8, McGraw Hill, New York.

SALAMAN, G. (1986) *Work*, Tavistock, London.

Ethnomethodology

Harold Garfinkel

The Idea

T HE TERM 'ETHNOMETHODOLOGY' REFERS TO 'THE METHODS PEOPLE USE TO MAKE sense of the world about them'. It is the study of *everyday* life, the routines and rules people use to go about their everyday business, the norms and values they employ to deal with and relate with other people as friends or family, colleagues or customers, strangers or acquaintances.

This approach to sociological research and theory stands in stark contrast to the grand theories of Marx, Weber and Durkheim and seems to capture little of the excitement and revolutionary fervour of the more radical theories some left-wing sociologists have proposed. A sociology of everyday life, a study of social routines and habits and the everyday way people interact seems at first glance quite boring and tedious and yet this field of study has proved one of the most innovative, challenging and profound fields of sociological research since the Second World War.

The founding father of ethnomethodology was Harold Garfinkel, an American sociologist who studies under Talcott Parsons but who was heavily influenced by the phenomenological ideas of Alfred Schutz (see p. 165). Fascinated by the minutiae of everyday life, Garfinkel launched ethnomethodology as a distinct and deliberate approach to sociology in 1967 with his book *Studies in Ethnomethodology*.

Most sociologists and most people take the order of everyday life for granted and rarely question or examine it in any detail. Instead they usually focus their attention on the unusual events, activities or happenings – crime, terrorism, catastrophes and crashes – and rarely question what it is that keeps us all together and how day after day millions of people across the world routinely go about their daily lives. While most sociologists focus their attention on the great underlying forces of social change and disruption – the economic system or political revolution – ethnomethodologists have made everyday reality the heart of their investigations. In their view, without the common agreements, the mutual expectations and the shared meanings behind the routines and common sense of daily life, there would not be any social order to study. We would live in chaos, in constant conflict and disorder, a brutish life, a jungle of threat and fear through which no change, no progress could be made, no peace established.

Harold Garfinkel was inspired to investigate this much neglected, even 'extraordinary' area of social life by his study of a group of jurors and the 'common-sense' methods they used to make sense of the evidence before them. A key feature of his research was his use of 'natural experiments' to bring to light the highly precarious nature of social order. So, for example, to highlight the importance of routines in daily life he would get his students to deliberately disrupt them – by singing on a crowded bus or asking old ladies and pregnant women to give up their seats for them. You can just imagine the response they got and the chaos they caused. To illustrate the extent to which we all use a vast store of background knowledge and essentially depend on the context of a conversation or action in order to interpret it, Garfinkel set up an experiment in which ten students were sent to see a counsellor, ostensibly about their personal problems. The counsellor sat behind a screen, gave only *yes* and *no* answers and even these were at random. Yet the students made sense of this 'nonsense' by using their own background knowledge of the problem and what they thought a counsellor would say. Had they known the counsellor was a fake, their 'interpretations' of his answers might have been very different.

From such experiments Garfinkel developed three key concepts to explain how ordinary 'members' of society not only have the capacity to interpret reality but to create (and recreate) it daily: *documentary method, reflexivity* and *indexicality*. By documentary method Garfinkel referred to the way we identify certain underlying patterns out of the enormous variety of phenomena we see and experience every day. We then use such general patterns to make sense of the individual phenomena we experience in the future. Social life is therefore reflexive – each individual item is seen as a reflection or evidence of a more general theme and vice-versa. Thus, not only is 'each used to elaborate the other' but a self-fulfilling prophecy develops. Our general idea of reality directs us to select and interpret individual items of evidence in a predetermined way that tends to confirm our original picture of life. Finally, argued Garfinkel, no words or actions make sense outside the context of the conversation or situation involved. Such indexicality occasionally has to be 'repaired' as, for example, when a gesture or phrase has been misunderstood or misinterpreted. Consider, for example, how differently people might interpret the expression 'you're dead', depending on the context, manner and tone in which it is said.

Thus, for Garfinkel and most ethnomethodologists, language and the 'activity' of talk is a central means by which we not only make sense of the world but actually 'create' it. Words are not just symbols of what is going on but are the very means by which things get done, by which society functions. So central is this notion to ethnomethodologists that writers like Harvey Sacks have tried to establish 'conversational analysis' as a distinct sub-discipline.

Garfinkel was especially at pains to refute the traditional sociological assumptions that social order has a reality of its own above and beyond the views and accounts of it by ordinary people and that sociologists' interpretations of life are any more accurate and scientific than those of ordinary members of society. Far from ordinary people being 'cultural dopes' simply acting out the dictates of society, they, by their interpretations, actions and accounts, are actually 'creating' it. Thus, in Garfinkel's view, the sociologists' methods of making sense of society are essentially no different (and certainly not superior) to ordinary people's. The man-in-the-street is therefore in a sense his own sociologist. The role of the sociologists is therefore simply to describe and explain how people daily create and recreate the 'worlds' they live in.

Ethnomethodologists' critique of mainstream sociology was therefore fundamental. Instead of treating social order as a given, as something existing above and beyond social behaviour, as social facts, ethnomethodologists sought to make social reality itself the primary objective of sociological study. In the view of ethnomethodologists, traditional sociologists impose their views and interpretations of social life on the social world rather than seeing it from members' point of view or how they actually behave. Their perceptions, therefore, tend to be distorted and biased. *'Statistics simply do not do justice to the elegance and sophistication of the real world'* (Ritzer 1996: 393). Actors do not just respond to society's rules and regulations, they create them and even break them in everyday life or work. Social order in Garfinkel's view is not the result of the workings of imperatives within the social system or common culture as depicted by writers such as Talcott Parsons and structural functionalism (see p. 190). People are not passive dopes controlled and conditioned by society – rather they are active participants in its daily creation and re-creation. The object of study for ethnomethodology is the common-sense activities of ordinary people. The aim of ethnomethodology according to Zimmerman and Wieder (1974) is to explain *'how members of society go about the task of seeing, describing and explaining order in the world in which they live'*. The research methods employed by ethnomethodologists have therefore reflected this focus on everyday life, methods such as:

- the documentary method used by Garfinkel (1967) and Atkinson (1971) to draw out the underlying patterns of understanding used to make sense of the world.
- the 'rule-breaking' technique used by Zimmerman (1971).

The Idea in Action

ETHNOMETHODOLOGY IS GENERALLY SEEN AS PART OF THE INTERPRETATIVE TRADITION in sociology. It starts from the phenomenological assumption that society only exists in so far as its members perceive its existence and that therefore the best way to understand how it works is to study it from within, subjectively, from its participants' point of view. Garfinkel's prime aim, therefore, was to put the ideas of Alfred Schutz and phenomenology (see p. 165) into practice and to develop a sociology of everyday life. The central object of sociological study, argued Garfinkel, is the methodical character of everyday life, the way people make sense of everyday life by classifying and typifying the processes around them and by drawing on assumed common understanding or knowledge.

Everyday life is based on a web of common assumptions and understandings that are taken for granted. The only way to expose such assumptions, argued Garfinkel, was to use provocation as a sociological method, breaching experiments to break everyday norms methodically and deliberately. Act in an abnormal manner and all of a sudden all the underlying 'taken for granted' assumptions of everyday life come to the surface because they are being challenged and exposed – the person who laughs and tries to 'party' at a funeral, the cheat in a game of cards, the student who asks pregnant women to give up their seats on a bus.

Initially, ethnomethodology stimulated enormous interest as it severely challenged the very foundations of traditional sociology. It argued that nothing in social life should be taken for granted; that even the 'hardest' of data on social reality should be scrutinised in terms of the social processes by which it was collected. Aaron Cicourel (1976) showed, for example, that far from the official statistics on crime being an accurate reflection of the amount of criminal behaviour, they were more a reflection of the activities and interpretations of the officials collecting and interpreting such facts and figures, in particular the police. Thus, in a sense, the police (and behind them the politicians and courts who make and administer the laws) create our image of the reality of crime. Maxwell Atkinson (1978) reinterpreted suicide statistics in a similar manner.

Inevitably, such a challenge to the basis and superiority of traditional sociology incurred the wrath, criticism, even derision of 'established' approaches. Ethnomethodology was criticised as:

- Tedious, boring and leading nowhere. It offers only descriptions, no grand theories.
- Portraying people as creative but failing to give them any sense of purpose or motive as to why they acted or interpreted in a particular way.
- Failing to give any real consideration to the influences of power and social differences on people's behaviour or the structure of society.
- Portraying life as no more than a multitude of individual everyday existences, untouched by such external forces as war or unemployment.
- Ethnomethodology's own approach can be turned back on itself. If ethnomethodologists' descriptions of 'life' are no better than ordinary people's and only further add to reality, rather than explaining it, what is the point of doing such study, why bother employing ethnomethodologists?

Nevertheless Garfinkel and his students have highlighted a vital but neglected area of study – everyday life – and shed new light on accepted assumptions. Thus, while some see it as a 'flash in the sociological pan' with little more to offer, its supporters like Benson and Hughes (1983) see it as a *fundamental break with a whole tradition of social scientific thought* and one that is here to stay. It still illuminates modern thinking and, argues Tim May (1996), informs such contemporary thinkers as Anthony Giddens. According to John Heritage, the ideas of Garfinkel have *permeated almost the whole of sociological theory today'* (in Stones 1998: 187). And in terms of research methodology, ethnomethodology has proved more successful than traditional sociology in penetrating the inner worlds of science, law, music and art. It has been particularly successful in analysing conversation and communication and even in informing such recent developments as artificial intelligence and studies of human–computer interface and cyberface. It has stimulated a whole tradition of sociological research, research that has included:

- Behavioural studies such as those by Jefferson (1984) on laughter, Heritage and Greatbatch (1986) on applause and G. Clayman (1993) on booing.

- Conversational analysis and the unwritten rules underpinning understanding and communication notably in the work of Harvey Sacks (1963), Atkinson and Heritage (1984), Boden and Zimmerman (1993).
- Studies of professional and institutional practice, notably in the fields of deviancy and suicide reflected in the works of Aron Circourel (1964), Jack Douglas (1967) and Peter McHugh (1974).
- Feminist studies such as those of Dorothy Smith (1993) and Garfinkel (1967) himself on gender, notably his ethnography of Agnes the transsexual.

Within ethnomethodology, however, a number of stresses and strains have emerged. There are those like Paul Atkinson (1988) who believe that it has lost sight of its phenomenological roots, has lost sight of the importance of people as motivated actors, has lost sight of its radical and critical edge and settled down '*into the suburbs of sociology*' (Pollner 1991: 370). While conversational analysis is ploughing ahead within mainstream sociology, ethnomethodology is in danger of becoming peripheral to its main concerns. There has been a trend within ethnomethodology in the 1990s towards theoretical synthesis, such as that of Boden (1990), to integrate symbolic interactionism and conversational analysis, and of Hilbert (1990) to link its micro-sociology with macro-sociology. Nevertheless the impact of ethnomethodology on sociology has been profound and ongoing.

 See Also

- **PHENOMENOLOGY** (p. 165) and **SYMBOLIC INTERACTIONISM** (p. 195) as the parent theories that gave birth to this strand of interpretative sociology.
- **STRUCTURATION** (p. 271) as a 'late modern' attempt to integrate structure and action.

Suggested Reading

ATKINSON, M. (1971) Societal Reactions to Suicide: The Role of Coroners, in Cohen, S. (ed.), *Images of Deviance,* Penguin, Harmondsworth – sums up Atkinson's ideas.

ATKINSON, M. (1978) *Discovering Suicide,* Macmillan, London – an excellent example of an ethnomethodologist at work.

SHARROCK, W.W. AND ANDERSON, R. (1986) *The Ethnomethodologists,* Tavistock, London.

Further Reading

BENSON, D. AND HUGHES, J. (1983) *The Perspective of Ethnomethodology,* Longman, London.

GARFINKEL, H. (1967) *Studies in Ethnomethodology,* Prentice Hall, Englewood Cliffs, NJ.

HERITAGE, J. (1984) *Garfinkel and Ethnomethodology,* Polity Press, Cambridge.

HERITAGE, J. (1998) Harold Garfinkel, Ch. 13 Part II in Stones, R.(ed.), *Key Sociological Thinkers,* Macmillan, Basingstoke.

Falsification and Conjecture

Karl Popper

THE TRADITIONAL VIEW OF SCIENTIFIC DISCOVERY AND KNOWLEDGE IS THAT OF A process of *verification*. The scientist observes the results of carefully controlled experiments from which an idea, hypothesis or theory emerges about the behaviour of a particular type of matter. The scientist searches by further experiments for evidence to verify his hypothesis which, if successful, grows in stature into a scientific theory or law upon which he and other researchers can not only accumulate further knowledge about the wonders of nature but can actually 'predict' its behaviour. This process of accumulating fresh facts, this constant searching for new ideas by observation and experiment is known as induction, and this method is seen as the dividing line between scientific and non-scientific knowledge.

In *The Logic of Scientific Discovery* (1959), Sir Karl Popper pointed out two key flaws in this traditional picture of scientific method and knowledge:

1. That, in reality, many of the major scientific discoveries had resulted not from systematic observation and analysis but from wild speculation, inspiration and chance.

2. That no matter how scientifically arrived at, no theory can be totally verified, absolutely correct. Rather as the eighteenth-century philosopher, David Hume, argued, there is always the possibility that sometime in the future it will be 'falsified', proved

Sir Karl Popper

wrong. All it takes is one or two contrary examples. It only takes the observation of one black swan (as has occurred in Australia) to refute the thesis that all swans are white. Equally, while we can predict that the sun will rise tomorrow, we cannot prove it will happen until it does. Thus, in Popper's view, all scientific hypotheses are only temporal and as yet unrefuted: all scientific knowledge is provisional, workable and the best available so far.

Popper therefore proposed that the real essence of scientific method was not and could not be verification but was and should be *falsification*, that good science would involve a process of trial and error or *conjecture* and *refutation* by which scientists were actively encouraged to develop bold new ideas and hypotheses and then set up tests and experiments, not to prove them correct but to refute or falsify them. In this way weak and inadequate theories could be swiftly eliminated and only the strongest ideas would survive for future testing and form the basis for some temporary advances in scientific knowledge and understanding.

A good scientific theory for Popper, therefore, is one that is falsifiable, one that makes definite claims and predictions about the natural or social world that can then be put to the test. Newton's theory of gravity fulfilled such a criterion by making a wide variety of highly testable claims which survived examination for over a century, and so became the basis for major advances in scientific knowledge. Falsification, however, gradually eroded its authority and opened the way for Einstein's grandiose and spectacular theory of relativity which, so far, has survived the tests of the twentieth century. A bad scientific theory is one that is not empirically or rationally testable, one that is so general and wide-ranging that there is nothing definite to test, or one whose supporters ignore such criticism and simply keep amending it whenever its predictions prove false. Popper was especially scathing here about Marxism and psychoanalysis, both of which he regarded as pseudo sciences because they were untestable and made grandiose predictions about a utopian future but offered no basis for evaluating them.

Thus for Karl Popper, what distinguished science from non-science was the falsifiability of its ideas and knowledge and, though this meant that we could never absolutely prove any scientific theory, such continual testing did bring us gradually nearer to the truth, slowly peeling away the many layers of reality. More important, for immediate, practical purposes it gave us 'relatively' solid ground upon which to base our technology and social policies; ground solid enough for piecemeal social reform but not solid enough for the sort of large-scale social engineering proposed by more radical writers. Popper therefore believed that the social sciences are capable of becoming 'scientific' provided they adopted the scientific approach he proposed of conjecture and refutation. He was scathing, however, in his criticism of sociological theories, particularly Marxism that went beyond this and sought to claim that their predictions of future society were both scientific and inevitable. In *The Open Society and its Enemies* (1945) Popper launched a major critique on such historicist theories and argued that the closed mentality of such dogmas excluded alternative or critical perceptions or evidence – the very essence in Popper's view of falsification, the only practical way to prove and establish scientific theories. Falsification, by definition, could only operate in an open society encouraging open minds so that all theories are continually subjected to an ongoing process of conjecture and refutation. Those that survive such a rigorous process deserve critical acclaim. The longer a theory survives the test of time, the closer it is likely to be to the truth. Closed societies in his view had closed minds. They deliberately exclude criticism and alternative views in favour of a faith and belief in the governing orthodoxy. Such societies, such creeds could not, in his view, progress or find the real truth. Hence his virulent and passionate opposition to Marxism as a philosophy and as a basis of future society.

As an Austrian by birth and having seen the devastation caused by fascism in his home country and by communism in Eastern Europe, the passion that Popper brought to his criticisms of Marxism and other 'totalitarian' theories is perhaps understandable.

The Idea in Action

KARL POPPER HAS BEEN ACCLAIMED BY SIR PETER MEDAWAR AS '*INCOMPARABLY THE greatest philosopher of science that has been*' (Magee 1973). His idea of science as a process of falsification rather than verification has been widely accepted as an accurate description of what scientists actually do and should do. Such a thesis supports the popular view of scientific method as highly rational and objective, and of scientific knowledge as being tried, tested and true compared to the untestable claims of such 'disciplines' as religion and mysticism. The distinguished mathematician and astronomer Sir Hermann Bondi declared: '*There is no more to science than its method and there is no more to its method than Popper has said*' (Magee 1973).

Others, however, have severely criticised Popper's model of scientific discovery. First, it is in practice very difficult to falsify a theory. Although a particular experiment may disprove a hypothesis, its author could rightfully claim that the experiment was at fault, not the idea; that under different conditions the hypothesis would have stood up. More important, while a theory may seem false now, with the development of more accurate scientific techniques it may well be proved correct sometime in the future. As A.F. Chalmers (1982) points out, if falsification had been strictly adhered to, some of the now most respected of scientific theories would never have been developed, including Newton's gravitational theory and Bohr's theory of the atom.

Secondly, writers like Kuhn (1962) and Feyerabend (1975) have argued that far from scientific discovery being a process of rational, critical and open-minded enquiry, scientists are in fact a very closed and conservative community very opposed to outside criticism. Feyerabend criticises the sloppiness, secretiveness and lack of imagination of modern scientific method and calls for a far more speculative and 'abandoned' approach. T. S. Kuhn has argued that during any one period of 'normal science' scientists are locked into a particular theory or paradigm (see p. 151) which is taken for granted and from which alternative ideas are excluded or rejected. Only when this dominant paradigm reaches a 'crisis' point, when the evidence against it is so overwhelming that it cannot be ignored does a 'scientific revolution' take place and a new paradigm (and with it a new generation of scientists) take control and re-analyse all existing scientific knowledge. Thus, while Popper accepts that existing knowledge is relative and provisional, he does believe that ultimately we will discover an objective reality and truth. However, for writers like Kuhn all knowledge, even scientific knowledge, is relative, depending for its existence and meaning on the theoretical framework through which it is interpreted.

Despite such criticisms Popper's thesis of falsification has been a major advance in the philosophy of science and still has a lot of popular appeal, not least because it recognises the limitations and fallibility of human understanding and because it proposes a gradual and critical improvement in human knowledge and society rather than the all-embracing claims of some less rigorous theories.

 See Also

- **POSITIVISM** (p. 56), **PARADIGMS** (p. 151) and **PHENOMENOLOGY** (p. 165) as three ideas that form part of the debate about sociology as a science.

Suggested Reading

MAGEE, B. (1973) *Karl Popper,* Fontana, London.

Further Reading

POPPER, K. (1945) *The Open Society and its Enemies*, Routledge & Kegan Paul, London.

POPPER, K. (1963) *Conjectures and Refutations: The Growth of Scientific Knowledge*, Routledge & Kegan Paul, London.

POPPER, K. (1972) *Objective Knowledge: An Evolutionary Approach*, Clarendon Press, Oxford.

Gender

Feminism

The Idea

T HE TERM 'GENDER' IS USUALLY USED SIMPLY TO REFER TO THE PHYSICAL AND SOCIAL distinctions between men and women. Sociologists, however, and feminists in particular, are keen to define it more exactly and to try and determine the extent to which gender behaviour is natural and innate or social and 'man'-made.

Sociologists, therefore, use the terms:

- 'sex' to refer to the physical and biological differences between men and women (e.g. physical features, sexual organs);
- 'gender' to refer to 'social' and cultural differences in behaviour and roles, in the personal attributes we call masculinity and femininity.

The central issue in the gender debate is whether the behaviour of men and women in society is determined by biology or by culture. Are men and women *naturally* different or are they *nurtured* differently by the society they live in? Are men naturally the 'doers' – the workers, warriors, writers and decision-makers – and women the natural 'carers'? Are men naturally aggressive, rational and logical, and women naturally passive, intuitive and emotional? Is a man's place out in the world – working, fighting and organising – while a woman's place is in the home, bearing and looking after children? And most especially, are men naturally the dominant sex, and so entitled to rule society – and to rule women?

This naturist–nurturist debate, as it has been called, has raged throughout the social sciences for decades.

The naturist argument

THE naturist argument rests on the assumption that the social differences in society between the two sexes are a direct reflection of biological differences. Men are physically stronger than women, so they organise society; women produce children so they have a natural maternal instinct to be passive, caring and dependent. Thus the present gender division of labour of men at work and women at home is both naturally and socially efficient as each specialises in the tasks they are best at. As Sigmund Freud proclaimed, '*Anatomy is destiny*', and a vast array of biological, genetic, psychological and sociological evidence has been produced to support this thesis, from Tiger and Fox's (1972) concept of the human biogrammer – a genetic predisposition for men to be 'masculine' and women 'feminine' – to E.O. Wilson and the development of sociobiology – the study of the way our biological characteristics determine our social behaviour. In intelligence tests and exams, boys used to out-perform girls, especially in the hard and logical disciplines of maths and science, so 'apparently' proving their natural right to positions of authority and decision-making in society at large.

The nurturist argument

THE nurturist argument in contrast rests on the belief that gender roles are not biolog-ically determined, but are culturally determined and socially constructed. Nurturists see human behaviour as largely a reflection of the social and cultural environment within which a child was brought up. As Ann Oakley argued early in the 1970s (1972), the sexual division of labour is neither universal nor biologically pre-ordained. Evidence for the nurturist view includes the following:

1. Studies that show that the biological and psychological differences between the sexes are not that great. Though, for example, men, on average, may be physically stronger than women, women survive better in tests of endurance and stamina. Wars like those in Vietnam and Israel have shown women to be just as aggressive, just as capable of killing as men, when put in such situations. And as for intelli-gence, it is, in fact, girls who are the brighter sex – up until puberty when they tend to give way to boys for fear of appearing competitive and unfeminine. The two sexes do, however, tend to think differently: boys are generally better on visual-spatial tests and girls have superior verbal skills, while personality tests often reveal that boys are just as emotional and sociable as girls, they just don't like to be seen as being so. As reviews such as Maccoby and Jacklin (1974) or Lloyd and Archer (1982) clearly show, though, there are natural differences between the sexes, they are not that great, and certainly not great enough to explain existing social differences or justify gender inequality.

2. Anthropological evidence which shows that in other societies and cultures, even other times in a society's history, men and women behave differently and even swap roles. Thus, for example, in Margaret Mead's (1950) classic study of three tribes in New Guinea, she found extensive differences in sex-roles and gender behaviour. While the Arapesh (both men and women) were compassionate and caring, the Mundugumors were harsh, violent and aggressive. And among the Tchambuli tribe there was a virtual exchange of roles as the men did 'women's work' and painted and decorated themselves while the women went out hunting and fighting. In many primitive societies it is the women who do the heavy, physical work, even during pregnancy, and among the Triobander Islanders it was the women who were sexually aggressive, who took the sexual initiative.

3. Studies of the socialisation process which reveals the extent to which male–female differences are socially constructed (or at least socially exaggerated) and identify

the ways in which boys and girls are brought up to be distinctly different and socially divided. In the family, for example, from the moment of conception, the two sexes are treated differently: dressed in different clothing, even different colours, given different toys, punished differently and even touched and spoken to in a different manner. At school, work, in the media and even in the very words we use, boys and girls are treated differently and react accordingly. We don't (usually) have a 'Page 3' for women or a problem page for men; the terms 'tomboy' and 'cissy' are fearful sexual sanctions, and few Western men today would wear skirts, though some of the greatest fighters in history quite happily did so – the Romans, the Greeks and even the Vandals.

It is evidence and arguments like these that have reinforced and bolstered the feminist case that sexual differences do not explain gender differences. There is, in their view, no natural division of sexual labour and therefore no natural justification for the sexual inequalities that exist in Western society today.

4. At work, although over 40 per cent of the British workforce is female, they are heavily concentrated in 'women's work' – the caring professions such as nursing and teaching, or in subordinate roles such as secretaries. Relatively few women get to the top of the major professions; few get in to such male preserves as engineering and science, even fewer get on to boards of directors. Women still suffer low pay, poor promotion, worse conditions, and even trade unions often discriminate against them despite equal opportunity legislation. A similar picture is evident elsewhere in Europe and other Western societies.

5. At school, sex stereotyping has been, until recently, fairly rampant, with girls usually 'opting' for such 'female' subjects as cookery and typing, often doing badly in mathematics and the 'hard' sciences and being advised by careers personnel to look for a job rather than a career, on the assumption that their primary post would be as a mother and housewife. Although much has now changed and although girls have outstripped boys in many subject areas, sex stereotyping is still evident in many career choices.

6. In government: despite comprising over half the population, women are only represented by 100 or so MPs out of 658 in the British Parliament. America has yet to elect her first female president. Politics is still primarily a male preserve in Western society.

It is evidence like this that has led feminists to reject the idea that it is nature that is behind such extensive gender inequalities and to argue instead that it is power, male power to control society, to fashion it in a 'masculine' image, that is really at work. And for this analysis they have developed the concept of 'patriarchy' (see p. 156).

The Idea in Action

THE CONCEPT OF GENDER HAS PROVED CRUCIAL IN HIGHLIGHTING ONE OF THE KEY elements in human society and social stratification: the distinction between men and women, a distinction that predates and cross-divides all other forms of social difference, be it class, status or race.

It has revived the nature–nurture debate and helped highlight inadequacies in the naturist argument. It has also stimulated the feminist argument that we live in a 'man-made' society in which male dominance is not only institutionalised but taken for granted as 'normal', even by women!

If gender differences are socially constructed and not biologically determined, there is at least the hope of a 'sexual revolution' and the liberation of women from sex roles, sex stereotyping and patriarchy.

However, two main sets of criticisms of the use of this concept have emerged in recent years:

1. Writers like David Morgan (1986) and Linda Birke (1986) have expressed concern that the distinction between sex and gender, between biological and social influences on human behaviour, has been made too rigidly. Rather than either sex or gender being the only influence, they should be viewed as 'interacting' factors. No one can seriously argue that physical, genetic and especially hormonal factors have no influence on gender behaviour. The opposite view would equally be an exaggeration. Rather it is the balance between these two views, and more especially, how humans culturally interpret that balance, that is crucial. As Linda Birke argues, no woman can escape her own biology; what feminists should therefore be analysing is the way female biology is interpreted, the way gender identity is constructed and reconstructed in a constant and dynamic process of social interpretation. To see women simply as 'passive victims' of sex stereotyping and socialisation is as deterministic and as simplistic a view as arguing that 'anatomy is destiny'. Rather, women must recognise their biological experiences and gain control of the way their resultant gender identity is interpreted.

    This shift in emphasis from the *content* of sex stereotyping to the *processes* by which feminine images are constructed is reflected in a whole range of recent feminist work on the arts and mass media (e.g. Betterton 1987; Beechey 1986). Modern advertisements and television programmes, for example, are no longer so stereotyped. They now attempt to portray 'real' women in situations outside the home and kitchen, 'doing' things, working alongside and even organising men. Images of women are, therefore, changing, but the question remains as to who controls our pictures of women and femininity, and in whose interests? Modern gender analysis needs to adopt a more complex and dynamic approach to keep pace with such changes in role modelling and self-perception.

2. The concept of gender has been used very narrowly. Until recently it has been used almost exclusively to analyse women. Men, by and large, have escaped its searchlight and only a limited amount of work has been done, in sociology at least, on homosexuality, transsexuals and all the other possible forms of gender. Recent studies have attempted to break out of this male–female stranglehold.

First, a true sexual revolution will not merely involve liberating women, but men too. It is men's notions of gender and sexuality that imprison women in images of femininity. According to the patriarchy argument, so long as men continue to think of women as mothers, home-makers and sex objects, and so long as they control the 'means of cultural reproduction' (i.e. mass media), what hope do women have of a more positive and equal image?

Secondly, as writers like Andrew Tolson (1977) have argued, men are as much a victim of sex stereotyping as women, possibly more so. They are brought up to live up to a 'macho' image of strength and power. They must not admit weakness or show their feminine side, their emotions or their feelings. They thus lose a key element in their humanity. As Sheila Rowbotham (1979) has pointed out, *'Men are ashamed of their own sensitivity to suffering and love because they have been taught to regard these as feminine. They are afraid of becoming feminine because this means that other men will despise them and they will despise themselves.'*

Men are as imprisoned in their work roles as women are in the home. They lose out a lot on family life and fatherhood and it is argued that it is the *absence* of the modern father as a person and role model which forces young males to turn to images of masculinity outside the home, especially on television; for example to follow shallow and stereotyped representations of how to be a 'man'.

Attempts have been made to set up 'men against sexism' groups such as 'Achilles Heel', but so far they have had very little success. While women can feel the anger and passion of oppression, men can only feel guilt. As the French writer Emmanuel Reynaud (1981) argued: *'When a man finds himself stifled by the meaninglessness of his life and makes an effort to put a final end to his patriarchal power, he will not have far to go to find the enemy. The struggle has to start, above all, in himself. To get rid of the "man" embedded in himself is the first step for any man getting out on the path towards getting rid of power altogether.'*

Within sociology men, too, have been almost invisible as a distinct social category. There have been relatively few attempts to study masculinity, especially by men. One notable exception is an article by Carrigan et al. (1985) that extensively criticises the male liberation approach, arguing instead for a more dynamic analysis of what they call 'hegemonic masculinity'. Hegemonic masculinity is a concept that not only involves analysing the dominant image of men over women but the way men who fail to live up to the male stereotype – the young, unemployed, and especially the homosexual – are marginalised and suppressed. There is now a wider recognition even in the media that 'masculinity is in crisis', that men are under threat, from women, modern life and especially unemployment, and that gender images are changing. *'Over the last two decades . . . social attitudes and images of masculinity have loosened up in Britain. Men are expected to show more interest in fashion, in childbirth, in their children, are encouraged to express their emotions and to pay more attention to women's needs. The soft and gentle man is not such a rare creature'* (Segel 1981).

More recent studies such as those by David Gilmore (1990) and Victor Seidler (1994) have shown the potential for masculine studies. However, as yet this is an underdeveloped area of gender study, one reflecting perhaps male sociologists' own feelings about self-examination. While studies of masculinity have been few and far between in contrast to feminism, Bob Connell's (1995) analysis does attempt to take gender studies a step further forward. He rejects both biological and cultural determinism, arguing instead that in reality gender behaviour is a fusion of both and may vary at different stages and ages in life. He goes on to argue that masculinity – like femininity – is no longer a fixed entity but takes various forms and style. While hegemonic masculinity – the type of masculinity that seeks to be dominant in any given social situation and to be based on relationships of dominance and subordination through physique, violence or economic and political power – has traditionally dominated gender relations, it has increasingly been challenged in the Western world by feminism and the gay movement. Connell's (1995) study of a range of Australian men highlighted the growing tensions, fears and insecurities prevalent among modern men about their gender and self-image, leading some to assert their masculinity in more extreme and violent forms and others to seek to recognise and to reconcile themselves to the arguments of the feminist movement concerning sexual equality, the celebration of sexual differences and even of the virtues of recognising feminine traits in men. As Connell concludes, while patriarchy as a structure of power is still very evident in modern society, its legitimacy has 'crumbled'; even men have doubts about it.

Thirdly, as 'gay liberation' so clearly highlighted in the 1960s and 1970s, a gender revolution does not only involve men and women, but all other 'genders'. Again, this topic is a key element in the nature–nurture debate, in the argument whether homosexuals, transsexuals and the like are born or made. As Anthony Smith (1976) concluded, 'No-one knows whether [homosexuality] has a genetic cause or not . . . but most biologists would put heavy bets on the environment as the main contributor.' Hence the extensive delving by psychiatrists and others into the background of homosexuals in search of the event or incident that turned them from the 'normal' path of hetero-sexuality. Ken Plummer (1975) and others using a symbolic interactionist approach, however, point to the way that society has created 'homosexuality' by the way in which, only very recently, it has labelled certain forms of sexual behaviour deviant. Homosexuality was accepted as 'normal' in Roman and Greek times. It is only in modern times (the late nineteenth century onwards) that homosexuals have had to 'hide in the closet' or come out fighting for gay liberation against the ideological and physical oppression of heterosexual society.

The study of transsexuals (people trapped in the body of the opposite sex) highlights these points even more. Jan (James) Morris's (1974) description of his own transition from a male to a female body is a fascinating account of sexual liberation, while anthropological studies of the Xaniths of Oman and the Mohave Indians of North America have postulated the possibility of a *third* gender, people who are biologically male but act and look like women. Ironically, such societies seem far more capable of coping with and tolerating such gender variations than our own.

Fourthly, the notion of gender as defined purely in terms of male and female, mascu-line and feminine, is a conceptualisation characteristic more of Western societies than of cultures and societies at large. Primitive and even modern societies increasingly recognised that the gender traits associated with men and women are not necessarily restricted to one sex or the other and that these forms of behaviour may vary according to time, place and role. No male is all masculine and it is quite permissible, even encouraged in society today for men to reveal, even use, their 'feminine side' in finding and being their true self and in fulfilling their role as a father, husband and even employer. Equally, women are now encouraged to assert themselves more and to use their gender traits to good advantage in a society and an economy where inter-personal and technological skills have replaced brute force and physical power as the dominant modes of production. Violent aggression is no longer tolerated, and emotional intelligence is increasingly valued as the means to ordering highly techno-logical and knowledge-based societies.

Moreover, while men may now be free to show tenderness in their relations to children and their partners, women increasingly assert themselves at home, at work and in public life showing the capacity to at least influence, if not control, gender definitions and the prevailing notions of what is acceptable. The concept of gender today is far more diverse and complex and it is no longer capable of stereotyping the behaviour of one sex or the other. Some post-modern feminists call for the abolition of a term that no longer captures the richness and diversity of female – or even male – behaviour in societies and in a global world where class, ethnicity and even age are producing as many differences in the experiences of women as similarities. Other writers, feminist – and increasingly those seeking to develop gay rights and masculine perspectives – adopt an 'essentialist' position; they still see in the notion of gender the potential to capture and analyse the essential nature of being male, female or androgynous.

Gender studies have ultimately inspired a greater respect for and appreciation of sexual differences and their potential to contribute positively to the development of 'man'-kind in the broadest and richest sense of the word. As feminists have long argued, where and when women are able to contribute fully to public life then *the world will be a safer more humane place for all of us*' (Riker 1996).

Studies today of gender relations and increasingly of homosexuality reflect what Anthony Giddens (1993) has referred to as 'reflectivity' on the ability of each individual to reflect on and manage his or her social image. In contrast to traditional analyses which portrayed homosexuality as deviant, writers like Jeffrey Weeks (1986) see gays as being today in a positive and confident position with the capacity to deter-mine their own public image rather than living under the label bestowed on them by society at large and the media in particular. There has thus been the development of 'Queer Theory' though, as yet a marginal field of sociological study. As Seidman (1998) has concluded, '*In practice sociologists have tended to relegate the study of sexual minorities to the analytical sidelines rather than treating such study as a window onto a larger world of power, meaning and social organisation*'.

David Bouchier (1983) distinguished three key, and often different, objectives for the feminism movement:

- an integrated or egalitarian society where sex differences no longer count (Marxist and socialist feminists);
- an androgynous society where sex differences no longer exist (radical feminists);
- a separatist society where men and women no longer share the same world (radical feminists).

Since then, however, the whole movement, its objectives and the nature of debate has changed significantly. There has been a backlash against the more extreme forms of feminism, a fragmentation of feminist groupings with the rise of black, lesbian and eco-feminists, a softening of demands in the light of the apparent improvements in women's opportunities and influence, and a revolution in theoretical and political approach as a result of the development of post-modern feminism. The development of men's studies and the changing attitude of men to masculinity and to women has only added to the range and diversity of the current debate on gender and patriarchy. The richness of this debate and the rise of post-modern thinking reflect both the strengths of such traditional concepts as gender and patriarchy in stimulating debate and action. How far they will continue to inform debate in the twenty-first century has yet to be seen.

The concept of gender in its broadest sense, therefore, moved from the margins of sociology into the mainstream, from being a minor topic to ranking alongside 'class' as a key concept in analysing social stratification, ideology and knowledge. It has highlighted the fact that a truly liberated society will not only be free of class divisions, but of gender roles and gender stereotypes. It would need to be an androgynous as well as a classless society. However, while feminists and gays may have grasped the analytical value of this concept with both hands, many male sociologists still seem fearful of this nettle – fearful, possibly, of the impact it will have on sociology as a discipline and possibly on their own academic reputation and self-perception. Moreover the future of this concept is under debate. Does the notion of gender still have relevance in societies that are changing so rapidly that all notions of stable social roles are increasingly meaningless?

 **See Also**

● **PATRIARCHY** (p. 156) as a key idea in the debate on gender and power.

Suggested Reading

CLARKE, E. AND LAWSON, T. (1985) *Gender: An Introduction,* University Tutorial Press, Slough.

GARRETT, S. (1987) *Gender,* Tavistock, London – a useful overview of the whole topic from a female perspective.

GRAY, J. (1992) *Men are from Mars, Women are from Venus*, Thorsons.

LLOYD, B. AND ARCHER, J. (1982) *Sex and Gender,* Penguin, Harmondsworth – summarises and assesses much of the biological and sociological evidence.

MACCOBY, E.E. AND JACKLIN, C.N. (1974) *The Psychology of Sex Differences,* Stanford University Press, Stanford.

Further Reading

BOUCHIER, D. (1983) *The Feminist Challenge*, Macmillan.

CONNELL, R. (1995) *Masculinities*, Polity Press, Cambridge.

GIDDENS, A. (1992) *The Transformation of Intimacy, Sexuality, Love and Eroticism in Modern Society*, Polity Press, Cambridge.

MORRIS, J. (1974) *Conundrum,* Faber, London.

RIKER (1996)

SEIDMAN, S. (1996) *Queer Theory/Sociology*, Blackwell, Oxford.

TOLSON, A. (1977) *The Limits of Masculinity,* Tavistock, London – the topic of gender seen from a male perspective.

WEEKS, J. (1986) *Sexuality,* Tavistock, London – covers the whole topic of sexuality.

Hegemony

Antonio Gramsci

THE TERM 'HEGEMONY' ORIGINATED IN GREEK TIMES. IT REFERS TO THE DOMINANCE OF one state or ruler over another. Antonio Gramsci, a radical socialist living in Italy during the reign of Mussolini in the 1920s and 30s adopted the term to refer to the ideological rule of one social class over another. He made the notion of hegemony the centrepiece of his major work, his *Selections from the Prison Notebooks* (1971), 33 notebooks written in appalling conditions when imprisoned by Mussolini in 1926 for forming and leading the Italian Communist party. He was finally released in 1937 but died shortly afterwards from a cerebral haemorrhage and the awful conditions he suffered under in prison.

Antonio Gramsci is considered one of the greatest Marxist theorists of the twentieth century. His aim was to develop an alternative approach to scientific Marxism, a humanist approach that gave radical socialists and the masses – both the peasantry and the working class – a real and an active role in promoting revolutionary change. A socialist revolution, he argued, would not happen automatically. It is not the inevitable outcome of the laws of historical and economic determinism. It needs popular participation and in particular it needs moral and ideological leadership to enlighten and inspire the masses and to create a national popular and collective will.

Gramsci therefore defined hegemony as ideological rule as well as military rule, as the control of dominant ideas as well as control of the means of production. From his point of view the power of capitalism in the twentieth century is not only its power as the dominant economic system in the Western world, but its control over people's way of thinking and behaving as workers, consumers and as citizens.

Capitalism today is a way of life as well as an economic system. Its concepts of commercialism, consumerism and profit-making permeate all aspects of everyday life, from culture and sport to working life and leisure. Making money, shopping and aspiring to the lifestyles of the rich and famous are the very values and motivating forces of life in Western society, while the giant corporations of Ford, Sony and McDonald's seek to entice all of us to buy more and consume more as they seek new markets and new profits. Ideological control, argued Gramsci, not military might nor economic dominance, is the highest form of hegemony, a form of consent rather than coercion – and Western societies today have taken capitalism to their hearts as well as their heads and it will take a great deal of persuading to convince them that socialism is a better way of life.

Writing in the 1920s, however, in the period when Western societies were in economic turmoil, when the working classes in Italy, Germany and elsewhere in Europe were in revolutionary mood as mass unemployment, hyperinflation and the aftermath of World War I left them poor, exploited and homeless, Gramsci's ideas made powerful sense. Gramsci argued that no ruling class could dominate by economic control, or even by political force alone. Such naked oppression would only inspire revolution. What is also needed is ideological control, the consent of the governed, and this is achieved through such important socialising agencies as the family, church, law, media, schools, and even trade unions. They all promote and legitimise the ideas of the ruling class to the point where such values are accepted uncritically and unconsciously as normal. They form the basis of everyday life, its core values and norms, and even underlie our notions of 'common sense'. Thus, while the ruling class can ultimately enforce its rule through the state (the law, police, army, etc.), its real control lies through its intellectual dominance over civil society.

Complete ideological dominance, however, is rare and never complete. It always faces new challenges from alternative groups, new ideas, new crises. It rests on gaining the support of the mass of the population through establishing an 'historic bloc' of shifting alliances between the dominant class and other sectors of society; alliances which are always open to dispute and collapse. This opens the way for subordinate classes like the working class to seize the moral, intellectual and political high ground, establish leadership, win widespread support and overthrow the ruling class intellectually and morally as well as physically. In capitalist societies the working class is in a particularly strong position to resist and expose bourgeois indoctrination. Their everyday experiences of working life under capitalism have revealed its essentially exploitative and oppressive nature. However, to turn such knowledge into revolutionary action will require sustained education of the masses by radical intellectuals to raise such proletarian understanding into revolutionary class consciousness and, ultimately, action. A true working-class revolution will, therefore, first require an intellectual struggle to expose bourgeois ideology; a cultural revolution in which the working class seizes philosophical and moral leadership before gaining political and economic control of the state and society. The role of the Communist party is, therefore, in Gramsci's view, to help promote working-class consciousness and help win the support of other groups in forming a revolutionary alliance.

Thus, Gramsci recognised that hegemony can never be complete, that struggles for ideological control will always exist – among the ruling class as well as among the proletariat. All ruling classes have to make concessions if they are to maintain popular support and remain in power. Total indoctrination is never possible, even in a totalitarian state. Although capitalist ideas permeate all aspects of modern society, people's own experiences clearly reveal the weaknesses, the evils and the exploitation of capitalist economics; its effects on the environment, its rampant consumerism and its isolating and alienating effects on many individuals and groups. People can see through capitalist propaganda, can see the need for reform if not radical change; can see life as it is and as it might be.

According to Gramsci, therefore, true hegemony is never possible until reality and ideology are as one. Capitalism cannot achieve full hegemony because of its underlying contradictions and exploitation. It has to make concessions, it has to gain consent and legitimacy to maintain power. Once it loses that hegemonic influence, once it loses its legitimacy then revolution became possible. However, while the Bolsheviks succeeded in seizing power in Tsarist Russia due to the complete collapse of public support for Tsar Nicholas and his family, the ruling classes in modern capitalist societies have a much stronger hold on the public mind. It is this ideological stranglehold that Gramsci saw as the key to a proletarian revolution and this needed an alliance of the intellectual and the working masses uniting within and behind the Communist party to challenge and overthrow capitalist hegemony and replace it with a new revolutionary vision of world order and social justice.

The Idea in Action

GRAMSCI'S CONCEPT OF HEGEMONY HAS HAD A MAJOR INFLUENCE ON POST-WAR Western Marxism, offering a major alternative to the rigid orthodoxy of Soviet communism. It offered new insights into the complexities of advanced capitalism, and in particular into the lack of revolutionary consciousness among the working class of Western Europe even under the fascist regimes of the 1930s. It equally offered an alternative, non-violent socialist strategy, more in keeping with the liberal freedoms and individual rights of Western society than the Bolshevik model of a political revolution based on the use of violent force to seize and sustain power.

Gramsci argued that before winning power the working class would have to undermine the hegemony of the ruling class by developing its own alternative hegemony or worldview, a new socialist 'commonsense', which could be used to challenge and undermine the culture of capitalism, expose its flaws, its exploitation and its oppressive nature and so provide a basis for a new liberated social order – a counter-hegemony to lead the revolution and to stabilise and legitimise workers' power thereafter. The bourgeois view of the world needed to be replaced by a socialist one if true class consciousness was to be achieved.

Ideological victory thus becomes a precursor to class conquest in the battle for 'hearts and minds' as well as bodies and heads. It may therefore obviate the need for physical revolution and allow for a bloodless, non-violent victory for the workers and the Communist party. It offered an alternative strategy for achieving socialism, one that combined theory and practice.

Thus in Gramsci's view, the struggle of ideas is as important as the struggle for economic and political control. Without it, class consciousness cannot be achieved nor the working class consent to the rule of the Communist party.

Gramsci's use of the term 'hegemony' therefore differed from that of more orthodox Marxists such as Lenin and Mao Zedong, who used it to refer to political leadership or state domination. His interpretation and strategy differed in the following respects:

- Its emphasis on ideological, moral and cultural factors as opposed to simply political and economic ones, on the importance of an intellectual revolution, of promoting mass class consciousness within civil society as well as seizing control of the state.

- Its emphasis on the masses, on groups other than the working class being involved in the revolution, so allowing for the inclusion of non-proletarian and radical groups such as students, women, blacks, etc. Such a broad analysis, one that extended beyond the working class alone, greatly helped Western Marxists explain the student revolutions and the Women's Liberation movement of the 1960s and 1970s.

- Its emphasis on creating a National-Popular movement dependent on the conditions in each country helped stimulate the growth of independent Communist parties and socialist groups with national strategies which did not need to wait for a world revolution nor require directives from Moscow.

- Its emphasis on the unity of theory and practice encouraged radical intellectuals to get involved with the working class and promoted the idea, as Marx said, that men make their own history rather than wait for underlying, impersonal historical forces to do it for them.

Gramsci's analysis tried to show not only how ruling classes seized power, but how they sustained it, not only by force and economic control, but by ideological leadership which, if successfully broken, usually preceded its political downfall. In the *Prison Notebooks*, for example, Gramsci contrasted the success of the Jacobins in the French Revolution who, by including in their own propaganda the aspirations of the masses, were able to gain the support of the peasantry, with the failure of the Italian Risorgimento which failed to broaden its support, and so collapsed. He pointed out how the bourgeoisie, the ruling class under capitalism, has been able to retain power, despite the instability of the capitalist economy, primarily by maintaining its intellectual ascendancy even against socialist challenges; how conservative governments have achieved passive revolutions without the use of force, but by convincing the masses, even large sectors of the proletariat, that its ideas are their ideas. Mrs Thatcher's Conservative government of Britain in the 1980s not only used the state and the law to roll back the welfare state and crush militant trade unions and local authorities, but established an ideological climate in which the values of liberal capitalism were dominant, in which market forces, privatisation and inequality were not only accepted, but promoted. Socialism was in danger of being driven out of modern Britain as even the working classes deserted the Labour party. Thus, to gain power, the working class must transcend its own immediate interests, combine with other sectors of society and win over the majority of the population to the moral correctness of its cause. A modern socialist revolution, in Gramsci's view, is as much one of ideas, of 'hearts and minds' as of political force, as much one requiring mass support as minority leadership. For him, the ideal society is one in which the laws of the state coincide with the dictates of individual conscience.

Gramsci has been called the 'superstructure, theoretician' of modern Marxism. He saw the intellectual as having a key role in developing an alternative socialist hegemony capable of challenging bourgeois ideology and helping educate the class consciousness of the working class. He distinguished between *organic* and *traditional* intellectuals, between those who become experts in legitimation and in raising class consciousness and those who have traditionally been independent of society and who have sought to maintain its culture and its traditions. A revolutionary party needs the support of both types of intellectual to achieve hegemony and to win over the masses.

Gramsci was highly critical of orthodox Marxism, its positivism, its economic determinism and rigid attachment to historical materialism. He rejected the idea of automatic or inevitable historical development. Man had to make his history, not just wait for it to happen. The masses had to act if revolutionary change was to be achieved and to do that they had to become class conscious; conscious of their place in history and willing to struggle for it actively, not passively. Led by intellectuals, they needed to develop a revolutionary ideology, a hegemony that links philosophy and practice, a philosophy of praxis that provides cultural leadership in the style and manner advocated by Lenin and the Bolsheviks. His version of Marxism was much more flexible, optimistic and liberating than the orthodox Marxism of his time, much more relevant to contemporary society. Hence its attraction.

Inevitably Gramsci's more humane, open and gradualistic analysis of socialist strategy has been subjected to severe criticism by more orthodox Marxists for being too liberal, for denying the historical importance of the laws of historical materialism, and by the Communist party for compromising the revolutionary purity of the proletariat. Structuralists like Louis Althusser (see p. 265) and Nicos Poulantzas (see p. 250) have been especially scathing. Nevertheless, this concept has provided Western Marxists with a major means of analysing the complexities of advanced capitalism, of explaining the lack of revolutionary fervour among the European working class and the success in gaining and holding power of such New Right governments as Margaret Thatcher's in Britain and Ronald Reagan's and George Bush's in America. Gramsci's ideas have inspired the New Left in Western Europe and the growth of Eurocommunism, providing a strategy for promoting peaceful revolution by exposing the exploitation, oppression and inequality of Western capitalism, and so winning over radical groups to the socialist cause. Ironically some of the best examples of 'bloodless revolutions', of revolutions where the ruling elite lost hegemony, lost their right to rule, lost the battle for the moral highground, have been in East European societies rather than in the West. The collapse of the Berlin Wall, the collapse of the communist governments of Eastern Europe and, more recently, the resignation of Slobodan Milosevic in Serbia, all represented the collapse of the ideological power of the ruling class and the refusal of the masses to continue to accept their hegemony, their moral and intellectual leadership. As their right to rule collapsed, so did their military might, and many of the post-war dictators have chosen to resign rather than resort to attempting to maintain regimes that had become morally and politically bankrupt.

The notion of hegemony has inspired academic research as much as radical action. Examples of the influence of the notion of hegemony on academic study include the work of the Centre for Contemporary Cultural Studies at Birmingham University in the UK in analysing youth culture and the power of the media.

Probably Gramsci's greatest legacy has been the emergence, ten years after his death, of the Italian Communist party as a major force in post-war Italian politics; a true reflection of his desire to combine theory and practice.

- **ALIENATION** (p. 14) and **IDEOLOGY** (p. 131) as background ideas to Gramsci's theories.
- **STRUCTURAL MARXISM** (p. 265), **CRITICAL THEORY** (p. 84), **RELATIVE AUTONOMY** (p. 250) and **LEGITIMATION CRISIS** (p. 225) as four very different versions of this key Marxist idea.
- **DISCOURSE** (p. 208) and **SIMULATIONS** (p. 260) as post-structuralist/post-modern perspectives on the power of ideas.

Suggested Reading

BOCOCK, R. (1986) *Hegemony,* Tavistock, London – a broad analysis of the whole idea of hegemony.

JOLL, J. (1977) *Antonio Gramsci,* Fontana, London – a short, readable study of his life and work.

Further Reading

GRAMSCI, A. (1971) *Selections from the Prison Notebooks*, New Left Books, New York.

Human Relations Theory

Elton Mayo

The Idea

T HE IDEA OF A 'HUMAN RELATIONS' APPROACH TO THE ORGANISATION OF WORK ORIGI-
nated from research by Elton Mayo and his colleagues into industrial relations and
productivity at the Hawthorne plant of the Western Electric Company in Chicago
during the period 1927 to 1932.

The dominant theory of industrial relations at this time was that of scientific management, the key idea of F.W. Taylor (see p. 175). Taylor's theory of industrial productivity
was based on two important premises:

- that workers' primary motivation for working is economic need and financial
  reward;
- that men work primarily as individuals rather than as part of a team or social
  group.

Scientific management theory therefore argued that the main way to raising productivity is by offering workers financial incentives and encouraging every individual to
work harder. Elton Mayo's researches contradicted such assumptions and led to a
whole new school of thought, a human relations approach to industrial relations.

Mayo and his team initially began their research on the basis of scientific management's assumptions that the main determinants of productivity were the physical
conditions of the work environment, the aptitude of the worker and the financial
incentives available. A variety of experiments were set up to establish causal relationships between variables such as the levels of lighting and heating, bonus payments,
rest periods and productivity. However, the results proved inconclusive and, at times,
contradictory. For example, in one experiment not only did changes in lighting not
appear to have a direct effect on productivity, but at one point a gradual dimming of
the lights led to workers working harder and producing more, rather than less, as any
normal 'scientific' hypothesis might have predicted. It appeared that the workers

involved were responding more to social factors than to physical conditions, were working harder because they were being watched, rather than because the lights were getting low. The presence of the researchers made the workers feel that, at last, the management was taking an interest in them as people, not just as factors of production.

Another study, of the Bank Wiring Room, revealed that, far from men working as individuals, they operate as part of a social group, and that such informal work groups are a greater influence on productivity than either the ability or motivation of any individual. The Bank Wiring study involved observing a team of wiremen connecting wires to banks of terminals. Tests relating output to the men's intelligence or dexterity produced no positive relationship, nor did the group incentive scheme appear to have a dominant influence. Rather, everyone seemed to work towards a uniform weekly rate of production, rather than maximising their own individual output, and so, pay. The worker's output, it appeared, was determined not by bonus schemes, but by an informal norm established by the work group as a whole. In this way the group ensured that all its members achieved a reasonable bonus and, most especially, prevented the management raising productivity targets on the basis of the ablest workers' output – a tactic which would have saved the company money, lost most workers bonus payments, and possibly led to the sacking of weaker workers. These groups' norms and sense of solidarity against management were reinforced by such informal social controls as sending 'deviant' workers to 'Coventry', disrupting their work, or even using threats of verbal/physical intimidation to bring them into line.

Such results led Mayo and his chief researchers, P.J. Roethlisberger and W.J. Dickson, to conclude that social factors are far more important than economic ones, that man is essentially a 'social being' rather than an 'economic animal'. Thus, argued Mayo, the poor output and resistance to supervision evident in the Hawthorne plant and factories elsewhere in America were due to the impersonal treatment created by the management techniques of scientific management. Workers felt as though they were merely cogs in a giant industrial machine, felt alienated in factories where teamwork and social collaboration were frowned on. Drawing on Durkheim's ideas of anomie and social harmony, Mayo and his researchers proposed a radically different approach to scientific management, that of the Human Relations School of Management. Roethlisberger and Dickson argued that, to achieve industrial harmony and maximise output, managers must pay far greater attention to:

- Social and personal factors: fulfilling workers' social needs for friendship, status, recognition and group support; releasing workers' talents and creativity rather than suppressing them; making the factory or workplace a social unit as well as an economic one.
- Industrial relations: establishing consent and co-operation between management and workers, and so overcoming the present divisions and conflict between 'us' and 'them'. Greater harmony at work, argued Mayo, may ultimately help to reduce disharmony and anomie in society at large.

The Idea in Action

MAYO'S IDEAS BLOSSOMED INTO THE HUMAN RELATIONS SCHOOL OF INDUSTRIAL Relations, and even into a social movement which has had a profound effect on Western capitalism. It even influenced personnel management in socialist societies, and led to the development of personnel work as a specialist area of modern management; it encouraged major firms to radically alter the basis of their industrial relations. Such harmony and staff care has become the by-word of such leading British firms as the John Lewis Partnership, Marks & Spencer and Sainsbury's. Many industrial organisations and mass production factories, especially in Scandinavia, began to radically rethink their organisational structure – to abandon their 'assembly lines' and austere environments in favour of teamwork, job rotation and enrichment schemes, worker participation, social clubs and friendlier, more pleasant surroundings. The social needs of the worker – job satisfaction, good staff relations and a 'happy family' atmosphere began to take precedence over immediate profits.

Academically, the idea of human relations inspired a whole series of experiments and researches into group dynamics, social psychology, leadership styles and social factors, not least at Chicago University's own School of Human Relations. However, it was also extensively criticised:

- Research into the application of human relations techniques produced inconsistent results. Coch and French's study of the introduction of new production methods and piece rates in a pyjama factory showed that where the workers were actually involved in the change-overs, rather than merely being informed of them, then productivity rose accordingly, with minimum staff upset. Similar studies, however, produced different or inconclusive results.

- Goldthorpe et al. (1968) criticised the human relations approach for failing to look beyond the factory gate out into society at large, for factors influencing workers' attitudes and motivations. Their study of 'affluent workers' in Luton showed that workers' needs vary and depend as much on the culture of society and the individual's place in the social structure as on anything that goes on in the workplace. Different workers have different needs. Their affluent workers were motivated primarily by financial reward. They neither sought nor expected any intrinsic satisfaction at work, be it group solidarity or job satisfaction. They had come down to Luton simply for the money. Their social needs were satisfied at home.

More radical critics went further, castigating human relations ideas:

- For being pro-management and anti-union, for being a new, subtle form of worker manipulation and control. Rose and Marshall (1988) has described Elton Mayo as a *'popularizing publicity officer'*.

- For assuming that, at heart, there is no conflict of interest between management and workers; that by simply reorganising social relationships within organisations, treating workers as human beings, industrial discord can be eliminated and harmony established. Marxist writers, in particular, reject such an assumption. For them, there is a fundamental conflict between employers and employees in a capitalist society that can only be eliminated when the class structure and owner-ship of the means of production are radically altered. Personnel work and worker participation are merely more subtle forms of social control and indoctrination. The end result is still the same – profit and exploitation.

While the human relations movement enjoyed its heyday in the 1940s and 1950s, by the late 1960s it had been severely undermined academically. It still, however, enjoys some prominence in both industrial theory and practice as major corporations continue to espouse and use new techniques of worker–manager groupings and collab-oration, continue to try and involve or win over the workforce, aided in the 1970s and 1980s by the threat of mass unemployment and in the 1990s by the development of new technology.

Recent research such as that by Rose and Marshall (1988) has drawn attention to the way work tasks today and new technology is influencing, if not determining, working relationships. This broader more inclusive approach, one that seeks to inter-relate technology and group behaviour, offers a bridge between the precision of scientific management and the sensitivity of human relations approaches.

 **See Also**

- **SCIENTIFIC MANAGEMENT** (p. 175) as the theory that ironically gave birth to human relations theory.
- **DESKILLING** (p. 98) as a Marxist perspective on both scientific management and human relations approaches to industrial relations.
- **POST-FORDISM** (p. 234) as a post-modern view of industrial relations today.

Further Reading

MAYO, E. (1932) *Human Problems of an Industrial Civilization*, Macmillan, London.

MAYO, E. (1949) *Social Problems of an Industrial Civilization*, Routledge & Kegan Paul, London.

Ideology

Karl Mannheim

The Idea

THE TERM 'IDEOLOGY' IS USUALLY USED TO REFER TO A SET OF IDEAS ABOUT THE nature of man, the nature of society and how life is or *ought* to be. Ideologies may represent a very structured or systematic set of ideas, such as communism or fascism, or they may reflect underlying feelings, even prejudices about power, politics and social order. Ideologies usually try to make sense of existing society and often represent theories, creeds or political manifestos about how society and life in general *ought* to be lived or might improve. Ideologies usually reflect a particular view about the nature of mankind and often reflect strong and heartfelt views about morality and social justice. Ideological perspectives are usually seen as biased viewpoints, as a particular, often partial or closed view of the world through which facts and figures are interpreted selectively to support one particular ideology and to reject another. Consider, for example, the very different interpretations and arguments that a socialist would have compared to a conservative about the distribution of wealth in modern Britain, or the causes of crime and the breakdown of family life. Compare, too, a scientific approach to facts and figures with an ideological one. In the scientific approach academics and scientists adopt a purely objective and impartial methodology designed to let the facts speak for themselves. Ideologists on the other hand are openly biased and often appear to use facts and figures selectively and partially to support their predetermined arguments and to undermine those of their political opponents.

Karl Mannheim – a Hungarian refugee in the 1930s who fled to England in 1933 to escape the Nazis and who became Professor of Sociology at the London Institute of Education – used the concept of ideology to argue that all knowledge is ideological; all knowledge, with the notable exception of mathematics and physics, is simply a reflection of the values, aspirations and interests of the wide variety of social groups that make up modern society. No facts or figures 'speak for themselves'. They cannot speak for themselves. They have to be interpreted. They have to have some form of intellectual framework to make sense of them. There is therefore in Mannheim's view no such thing as objective knowledge or absolute truth, only at best an approximate truth, a synthesis of the enormous variety of beliefs about what life is really like and what ought to be done. Mannheim therefore saw intellectuals as no more than the most articulate spokesmen of class or group interest; though he later accepted that they may be sufficiently independent as to be able to synthesise rival views and establish some sort of intellectual harmony. The role of the sociology of knowledge, therefore, was to try and identify which ideas derived from which social groups and from such evidence piece together their overall ideology and show how such a world view helped promote the group's own interests. All truths, therefore, are ideologically biased, all truths ultimately reflect the interests and biases of particular social groups. The question is, whose interests, and how powerful some groups are compared to others in promoting their interpretations of the world.

Karl Mannheim therefore sought to develop a sociology of knowledge, a sociological analysis of how knowledge is created and promoted – and in whose interest. His ideas were outlined in his key work *Ideology and Utopia* (1929). Here Mannheim used the term 'ideology' to refer to the beliefs and values of the ruling class and the term 'utopia' to mean the beliefs and values of the rest of society, particularly the underclasses; the oppressed and those seeking a radical alternative or utopian society. Both perspectives in his view are biased. Both rely on strong underlying ideologies about how society ought to be organised – and in whose interests. Both obscure and distort truth and reality to promote and support their own arguments and positions. Such ideologies are inherently in conflict, are diametrically opposed and represent a form of ideological warfare. Their relationship, argued Mannheim, is a dialectical one. The weaknesses and injustices of any dominant social order give birth to criticism and demands for change. Such demands, if unmet, give rise to radical, even revolutionary ideologies aiming for a new social order, a Utopia in which the people will be free and fulfilled. With revolution comes a new social order, a new ruling class, a new ruling ideology and eventually a new radical alternative, a new utopian vision and ideology. Just as the French Monarchy gave way to the Jacobins, and the Russian Tzars to the Bolsheviks, so in the twentieth century capitalism has faced the Cold War ideology of communism. Thus in Mannheim's thesis, life is a process of continual struggle for power between rival social groups backed by competing ideologies and interests. He sought to trace the social origins of such competing ideologies as the basis of his sociology of knowledge from Chiliasm through to the modern ideologies of liberalism, conservatism and communism.

The Idea in Action

MANNHEIM'S VIEW OF KNOWLEDGE HAS PROVED IMMENSELY INFLUENTIAL, AND HE and Karl Marx are generally seen as the founding fathers of the sociology of knowledge. Together they broke the traditional assumption that knowledge and ideas have an independent life of their own. Rather, they highlighted the social roots of knowledge and ideas, and the power of ideas to influence and control people's behaviour. Though heavily influenced by Marx, Mannheim rejected the idea that class alone was the basis of ideology, nor did he see the possibility of a 'scientific' analysis that would unveil the distortion of class ideology and reveal the truth.

He did not, however, go to the other extreme. He did not support the relativist view of knowledge nor the notion that no true and objective knowledge is possible. Rather he sought to rescue his thesis from relativism and strengthen its potential for unveiling the truth in the following ways:

- He exempted the exact sciences – sciences involving precise measurement such as mathematics and physics – from his theory of the sociology of knowledge.
- He introduced the notion of 'free floating intelligentsia', enlightened intellectuals capable of liberating themselves from class interests and so seeing the truth.
- He introduced the concept of relationism in preference to relativism, the notion of a relation between social position and social views – the insight into this relation will ultimately lead to more universally valid knowledge.

He was not as systematic a thinker as Marx and he lacked a theory to explain why certain groups adopted one ideology rather than another or why human societies are perpetually involved in a struggle for power. Yet his insights and analyses of individual ideologies were often quite brilliant. His essay on 'Conservative Thought', for example, is considered a classic.

Partly because of his refugee existence, partly because European thought, especially in Germany, was shattered by Nazism and the Second World War, he never created a new generation or school of sociologists in the way that Max Weber did. He had no immediate successors to continue and extend his analysis, though his influence on the sociology of knowledge today is considerable and is reflected in such phenomenological studies as those by Berger and Luckman. As George Ritzer (1996) concludes, '*He is almost single-handedly responsible for the creation of the contemporary field known as the Sociology of Knowledge*'.

 **See Also**

- HEGEMONY (p. 121)
- STRUCTURAL MARXISM (p. 265)
- CRITICAL THEORY (p. 84)
- LEGITIMATION CRISIS (p. 225)
- RELATIVE AUTONOMY (p. 250)
- DISCOURSE (p. 208)

as modern and post-modern views of the power of ideology today.

Suggested Reading

KETTLER, D. (1986) *Karl Mannheim,* Tavistock, London – a short overview of Mannheim's life and work in the Tavistock series of key sociologists.

Further Reading

LOADER, C. (1985) *The Intellectual Development of Karl Mannheim,* Cambridge University Press, Cambridge.

Labelling Theory

Howard Becker

The Idea

IS DEVIANCY – ANTI-SOCIAL BEHAVIOUR THAT *THREATENS* THE NORMS AND VALUES OF society – or criminality – anti-social behaviour that *breaks* the laws of society – the result of innate characteristics, or is it behaviour that is created by the social environment into which a person is born or brought up? Are people born deviants? Are they born criminals, or does society make them anti-social by the way it treats and responds to them?

This is the central question that has confronted the sociology of deviance and crime and underpinned all its theories and propositions about crime and the causes of crime. Traditionally, positivist sociologists have tended to see deviance and criminality as innate – people are born criminal or deviant – it is in their genes. Phenomenologists, particularly those operating within a symbolic interactionist framework, however, have tended to view anti-social behaviour as environmental, as a reflection of the social environment into which a person is born, and the way they are treated by significant others, notably parents, friends, teachers and those in authority. From this perspective people are not innately and irredeemably bad or evil. Rather they become anti-social as a result of the way they are treated – or at least the way they perceive such treatment. From this viewpoint, deviants and criminals can, with the right treatment and response from others, be rehabilitated and even 'cured'.

As symbolic interactionism grew in popularity in the 1950s and 60s, a range of sociologists, particularly those operating at the University of Chicago, began to develop the theory that it is 'labelling', that it is the social 'labels' that we apply to certain people and the way we treat them thereafter that causes and amplifies deviancy, rather than any genetic characteristics they may have been born with. One of the leading figures within the labelling theory movement was Howard Becker, educated at the University of Chicago, and later Professor of Sociology and Urban Affairs at North-West University, Illinois.

In his ground-breaking book *Outsiders* (1963), Becker set out to develop a systematic theory of labelling and deviancy. He argued that there is no such thing as deviancy per se. Rather, deviancy is a form of behaviour created by the way other people define and label it. *'Deviance is not a quality of the act a person commits but rather a consequence of the application by others of rules and sanctions to an offender. The deviant is one to whom the label has successfully been applied; deviant behaviour is behaviour that people so label.'*

From this perspective there is no such thing as a deviant act; deviancy is simply behaviour others disapprove of and label as anti-social, abnormal or criminal. It all depends on who does it, when and how and in front of whom. So, for example, it is perfectly normal to be naked in the bath or shower, but if you sat down to dinner with your family with no clothes on, your parents, brothers or sisters might be slightly surprised. Similarly raucous or outrageous behaviour might be expected or even encouraged at a party or a rave, but be frowned on and reprimanded at a funeral. Even killing another human being is not innately wrong nor inevitably punished. It all depends on the circumstances, the motives of those involved and the way others, particularly those in authority, view it. Killing someone, therefore, may be labelled as murder or at least manslaughter and punished accordingly. It may equally be accepted, even celebrated as heroism, if it occurs in wartime or as an act of self-defence. What is critical is the reaction of those in authority, those who have the power to define and label behaviour as acceptable or deviant – the judge and the policeman, the doctor and the teacher, the government and the media – and their relationship with those subject to them as citizens or patients, children or readers. As Becker argued, *'Deviance is not a quality that lies in behaviour itself, but in the interaction between the person who commits an act and those who respond to it.'*

Becker went on to outline the stages by which a person is transformed from being seen as normal to being perceived and labelled as deviant.

First, there is the initial 'public' labelling, a process that is often quite informal at first but one that gains momentum and usually leads to a public ceremony and official definition of a person as not only acting in an odd or deviant manner but being a deviant person: the delinquent who ends up in court and is sent to prison as a criminal; the drunk who is diagnosed by a doctor or psychiatrist as an alcoholic; the 'potty' aunt who is diagnosed as schizophrenic and sent for treatment to an asylum.

Secondly, once such official labels are applied, they become the master label and override all the other symbols and statuses a person previously held as father, friend or employer. People react very differently. They see the person involved in a totally new light, translate all previous behaviour in a very different way and react accordingly, usually by rejecting, isolating and castigating him or her as a deviant and someone with whom they no longer have a relationship. The alcoholic who is rejected by his family and ends up homeless; the ex-convict who is unable to get a job or buy a house.

Thirdly, such rejection inevitably affects the individuals' own perception of themselves, their own self-image. Many respond by living up to their deviant label, by becoming deviant and adopting a deviant lifestyle or even a deviant 'career' – the juvenile delinquent who becomes a professional criminal, the drug-user who becomes a junkie and a drug addict. Such individuals often withdraw from 'normal' society and go to live in alternative lifestyles or go underground, seeking support and status among fellow-deviants living in deviant sub-cultures.

Thus a cycle of labelling can lead to a self-fulfilling prophecy. Label someone as a deviant and ultimately they may become one; they may even adopt it as their 'controlling' label and live up to their deviant image as a master-criminal or a madman. Labelling is not an inevitable process – some criminals do go straight, some addicts do kick the habit – but, argues Becker, it takes a very strong personality to resist and overcome the labelling process – the public pressure and the social rejection – once it is underway, particularly when you are in prison or in an asylum living among criminals or the insane.

Howard Becker drew together many of the key themes within labelling theory and gave it a structured and systematic framework for future debate. Other writers adopted and developed this theory and sought to apply it to sociological research and practice. Edwin Lemert, for example, has made the key distinction between primary and secondary deviance, between deviant acts *before* they are publicly labelled (and if they are) and the effect of societal reaction on an individual's personal self-concept and status *after* being labelled. In Lemert's view most people at some time or another commit deviant acts but only a few are caught and publicly labelled, so much primary deviance has little effect on their self-image or daily life. Therefore, delving deeply into the backgrounds of criminals for the 'causes' of crime, as traditional criminology does, is irrelevant. Rather, the cause of deviance is public labelling and its effect on the individual (secondary deviance).

In his study of the way police and juvenile officers handle potential delinquents in California, Aaron Cicourel (1976) outlined the key stages by which criminal labelling takes place – the way both policemen and juvenile officers, guided by a stereotypical view of the typical delinquent as male, black and working class, create a self-fulfilling prophecy because most of those they arrest are of this type. Moreover, the police seem to be influenced by the individual's ability to negotiate and resist arrest and prosecution. 'Justice is thus negotiable' and the white, middle class youngsters, particularly girls, seem better able to talk the police out of arresting them than their working class counterparts. They don't fit the stereotype so they are less likely to be arrested, particularly as their parents have more influence and 'clout'. Far from reflecting the reality of crime, official statistics are therefore more a reflection of police stereotypes in interaction with relatively powerless social groups. Hence the inclusion of young, working-class and black males in the majority of crime statistics and the exclusion of white middle-class youngsters and girls from most of them.

Erving Goffman (1968) revealed how *total* institutions such as prisons, mental hospitals and reform schools seek to dehumanise inmates, to destroy their individuality and self-identity and reduce them to an institutional number, cell and status through a process of *mortification* – stripping new entrants of their clothes, hair and personal possessions, putting them into uniforms and making the daily routine of the institution so controlled that the inmates have no freedom, involvement or initiative. Far from reforming them, such institutional organisation only confirms and cements their deviant identity, making re-entry to normal society even more difficult and so significantly increasing their chances of reverting back to crime and, eventually, to the sanctuary of prison. Hence the very high rates of recidivism of the criminal and insane returning to prison or asylum on a regular basis – to perhaps, ironically, a place they feel safe and secure!

Thomas J. Scheff (1984) and Thomas Szasz (1987) applied labelling theory to psychiatry and to studies of mental illness. According to Scheff, while minor violations of normal behaviour may be labelled as 'odd', more serious persistent abnormality may well lead to diagnosis as mental illness, insanity and ultimately incarceration. Rosenthal and Jacobson (1968) sought to illustrate this process by applying for admission to a variety of psychiatric hospitals in America, complaining of hearing voices. They were all hospitalised, diagnosed as mentally ill, possibly schizophrenic and their every action was interpreted as pathological. Even boredom was interpreted by the hospital staff as 'anxiety'. The researchers' deception was never discovered, although some of the 'real' mental patients became increasingly suspicious. Szasz used labelling theory to criticise traditional psychiatry and its underlying assumption that mental illness is an individual sickness rather than, as he saw it, a problem of modern living created by the stresses and strains of life today.

The Idea in Action

SUCH A DRAMATIC RE-ANALYSIS OF CRIME AND DEVIANCE, SHIFTING THE FOCUS OF attention from the individual to societal reaction and the agencies of social control, had a major impact on the sociology of deviance. It stimulated a wealth of studies modifying and extending the idea of labelling, not only in the field of criminology, but in the study of medicine, race, education and feminism. Like its parent perspective – symbolic interactionism – labelling became one of the new sociologies of the 1960s and, for a period, dominated the sociology of deviance. It even influenced social policy and the practices of such institutions as prisons and asylums. It had a particularly strong influence on the study of mental illness and education. Modern psychiatric treatment cautions professionals in the field about the dangers and consequences of labelling patients at too early a stage while educational research into the impact of labelling or streaming pupils at school at too early an age underpinned the development of comprehensive school systems throughout Europe and America.

However, labelling theory equally inspired a growing flood of criticism over the vagueness of its theory and its lack of empirical evidence:

- Labelling theory fails to explain the 'origins' of deviance; what motivates certain individuals to break society's norms and laws when the majority of society conform and obey the law without question.
- It seems to be very deterministic, to put all the blame for crime and deviance on the labellers and to portray deviants as innocent victims. As Ronald Ackers (1975) has so succinctly put it: *'One sometimes gets the impression from reading the literature that people go about minding their own business and then – "wham" – bad society comes along and stops them with a stigmatized label.'* Those who take drugs or steal are fully aware that they are breaking the law and are often quite proud of their defiance, yet labelling theory tends to portray deviants as passive, as unaware of the deviant nature of their acts until arrested. Rather, argue critics, the individual chooses to commit a murder, the vandal chooses to deface a bus or shop window, a pupil chooses to truant from school, and then and only then does society and its agents of social control react and respond.

- It does not fully explain 'societal reaction' – why the police, teachers, etc. react in the way that they do, where they get their attitudes and stereotypes from, why they label some individuals and not others. More important, it does not explain who makes the rules that define deviance. For Marxists and other radical writers it is this failure to analyse the *power* of rule-making and in particular to show the 'class' basis of such power that is the key weakness of labelling theory. Becker and Lemert fully recognised that certain groups have the power to impose rules and labels on other, weaker sections of society (the old on the young, men on women, the middle class on the working class) but they failed to extend such an insight into a detailed analysis of the social system at large. Instead labelling studies tend to concentrate on the 'underdog', on the hippies, delinquents and homosexuals who are labelled, rather than on those who enforce the laws on labels and in particular those who make them – politicians, top businessmen, media magnates, etc. It has been left to Marxist writers to develop a full-blown critique of crime and deviance in capitalist societies and this approach increasingly replaced labelling theory as the dominant influence on the sociology of deviance in the 1970s and 80s.

- Labelling theory has equally come under strong criticism from more traditional perspectives for the weakness of its concepts and its lack of detailed evidence. There tends to be a wide array of labelling definitions, some of which overlap and even conflict. Some theorists like Becker and Lemert even reject the idea that labelling is a theory, arguing instead that it is merely a sensitising concept designed to stimulate more detailed analysis. Moreover, as Walter Cove (1976) and his colleagues argued, actual studies tend to refute many of the claims of labelling theory, showing that at most it is a marginal influence compared to personal or background factors and in particular that *'the available evidence indicates that deviant labels are primarily a consequence of deviant behaviour and that deviant labels are not the prime cause of deviant careers'*.

Labelling theorists have sought to respond to such criticism arguing that it is a much more sophisticated and flexible theory than its critics give it credit for. In his article 'Labelling Theory Reconsidered' (1974), Becker himself sought to outline the choices as well as the processes through which the 'labelled' went in the course of their rite of passage to a new identity, career and lifestyle. At any stage a criminal, patient or drop-out could decide to abandon passage towards a deviant career and seek to re-establish his or her original identity. Becker concluded, however, stating that he regretted the way that his style of research had been 'labelled' and stigmatised, preferring instead that it be seen as a critique of positivist approaches and as a contribution to the overall development of the interactionist school of sociology.

Labelling theory has therefore contributed enormously to the development of the sociology of deviance in a wide variety of fields, redirecting attention from rule-breakers to rule-makers, from an acceptance that the norms and laws of society are natural and given, to a recognition of their relative nature. It has led to a recognition that far from deviance being a minority activity it is in fact quite widespread. What is abnormal, as official statistics show, is getting caught and being publicly labelled. Labelling theory contributed significantly to the debate over positivist and determin-istic theories of deviance as inherently anti-social and a characteristic alone of sick or deviant individuals. It showed the potential for society to influence, even change the processes by which individuals adopted or were forced into anti-social behaviour. It helped to influence social policy in a variety of fields from criminology to education and mental illness, forcing professionals in such areas to think again about their own procedures and behaviour and how far they were contributing to the deviant behaviour exhibited by their patients, pupils or criminals. What labelling theorists like Howard Becker failed to do, however, was to develop this brilliant insight into a full-blown theory of crime and deviance. Hence their replacement in this field by the more powerful theories such as those of the more radical and Marxist writers of the 1970s and 80s and the post-modernists of the 1990s.

- **SYMBOLIC INTERACTIONISM** (p. 195) as the philosophical source for this idea.
- **STIGMA** (p. 185) as an example of this theory in practice.
- **SIMULATIONS** (p. 260) as a post-modern view of the power of images and labels.

Suggested Reading

BECKER, H.S. (1963) *Outsiders,* Free Press, New York.

COHEN, S. (ED.) (1971) *Images of Deviance,* Penguin, Harmondsworth.

Becker's own study is readable and stimulating while among the Further Reading, the following are some examples of sociologists applying this theory to a particular field of study.

Further Reading

GOFFMAN, E. (1968) *Asylums*, Penguin, Harmondsworth.

SCHEFF, T.J. (1984) *Being Mentally Ill: A Sociological Theory*, Aldine.

SZASZ, T. (1987) *Insanity: The Idea and its Consequences*, Wiley.

Linguistic Codes

Basil Bernstein

The Idea

THE IDEA OF LINGUISTIC CODES DERIVES FROM THE THEORIES AND WRITINGS OF BASIL Bernstein, Professor of Sociology and Education and Director of the London Institute of Education and Sociological Research.

Drawing on his own experiences as a working class child living in East London in the 1930s and his teaching experience in Shoreditch, Bernstein developed a theory of sociolinguistic codes in four major volumes between 1971 and 1990.

The essence of his idea is contained in the title of his works *Class Codes and Control* (1971–90), namely that the way you speak, the linguistic code that you use, reflects your position in Britain's class structure and controls your access to power, privilege and wealth. How you speak determines who you are and what you will become, and Bernstein focused his analysis on education as the prime source of knowledge, power and opportunity in post-war society.

Bernstein argued that social class is not only determined by wealth and occupation, it is also cultural and linguistic. Speech patterns reflect class and Bernstein made a key distinction between middle-class speech patterns and working class ones in terms of formal or public – or as he later called them – elaborate or restricted codes of speech.

- *Restricted* codes tend to be limited or restricted speech patterns 'short, grammatically simple, often unfinished sentences' with limited and repetitive vocabulary and an extensive use of gesture and voice intonation. Meaning is often taken for granted, implicit or particular to a given situation or relationship. It is therefore difficult for an outsider to understand what is going on.

- *Elaborate* codes are far more elaborate, far more grammatically accurate, logical and descriptive. Meaning is made explicit by a wider vocabulary, greater use of detail and an individualistic explanation selected to fit the needs and knowledge of a particular listener. Elaborate codes are therefore universalistic, they can be understood by anybody; they do not depend on existing knowledge of a particular context or social group.

Bernstein explains the origins of these social class speech codes in terms of family relationships, socialisation practices and the nature of manual and non-manual occupations. In working-class families, relationships and authority are clear cut and distinct; what Bernstein calls 'positional'. The father asserts his authority merely by a command ('shut up') rather than by discussion. In middle-class families relationships are more personal and less rigid. Communication is more elaborate and fluid, decisions are discussed and rules negotiated. Such class–family differences in turn reflect the different work situations of the middle and working classes – the manual skills of the blue-collar worker, where conversation is limited to a few direct instructions, compared to the verbal skills of the white-collar worker where decision making, negotiation and the development of ideas are the very essence of his job. Thus their respective children are socialised into both a particular form of communication and a very different structure of authority.

Such an analysis reflects Durkheim's idea of mechanical and organic forms of solidarity whereby in working-class communities relationships are more face-to-face (mechanical) and so a lot of meaning can be left out. The middle-class 'world', in contrast, is much more mobile, impersonal and individualistic so communication has to be more formal and explicit (organic). Thus Bernstein (1961) suggested that if we look into the work relationships of this particular group, its community relationships, its family role systems, 'it is reasonable to argue that the "genes" of social class may well be carried less through a genetic code but far more through a communication code that social class itself promotes'.

Bernstein used these codes initially to explain social class differences in educational attainment. Schools are very middle-class institutions based on 'universalistic orders of meaning'. Teachers are essentially middle class and communicate primarily in an elaborate code. So, while the middle-class child feels 'at home' at school, the working-class child feels in an alien environment faced by a 'foreign' language. Moreover, their restricted style of speech not only hinders the learning of school-type knowledge – abstract ideas and concepts from textbooks and teachers – but it gets them into trouble (and the lower streams). Their 'slang' language is downgraded and discouraged by teachers. They are constantly being corrected and their limited vocabulary interpreted as both ignorance and rudeness. They are therefore more likely to be labelled, more likely to be punished. They cannot relate to teachers in the way the middle-class child can but come to see them purely as authority figures. As Bernstein puts it 'this may well lead to a situation where pupil and teacher disvalue each other's world and communication becomes a means of asserting differences'. The working-class child is therefore more likely to end up in a lower stream, excluded from the fullness of academic knowledge (and the resultant qualifications), made to feel inferior and so socialised into future subordination at work.

Linguistic codes therefore function as a form of class reproduction providing a means of creating and maintaining the identity and unity of the middle class while excluding the working class from power, privilege and opportunity.

Bernstein and his colleagues at the London Institute have conducted numerous experiments to try and identify exactly how linguistic codes operate in a variety of contexts – in the description of pictures, the playing of games, in a theft situation and even in the different modes of control used by middle- and working-class mothers. But Bernstein himself has moved on from this to an analysis of educational knowledge as a key form of class control and reproduction. Whoever controls the school curriculum not only has better access to it but can actually control what is defined as knowledge. Schools and teachers promote academic knowledge which requires an elaborate code to gain access to it. You have to speak 'proper' and use language, especially written language, to do well in our examination system and so get into university and into top jobs. The middle class therefore have an inbuilt advantage and so can be sure that their children maintain their existing class dominance. Equally, working-class children fail in our school system not, as was implied in Bernstein's earlier work, through their own inadequacies, their restricted speech and language, but because the system makes sure they fail by selecting out the middle-class student on the basis of middle-class knowledge and elaborated speech codes. In *Class Codes and Control* (Vols. 1–4, 1971–90), Bernstein and his colleagues went on to analyse the way in which the school curriculum is classified and taught, and how that too reflects and reinforces social relations in a class-based society. In Bernstein's view the curriculum can be conceived of as tight 'collections' of knowledge with strict boundaries separating them from other subjects or as 'integrated' or interdisciplinary codes that seek to combine and cross over subject boundaries. Compare, for example, the tight boundaries surrounding physics or chemistry with the breadth and diversity of combined science, social studies or expressive arts. *Collection* codes are often taught as received knowledge, as facts and figures to be learnt rather than challenged or debated while *integrated* codes tend to be more student-centred, encouraging discussion and debate. In the more formal and controlled situation, the teacher is in charge, the font of all knowledge; in the latter the student has more power, more say and is encouraged to develop his/her own views and style of learning. The curriculum, the way it is organised and taught, therefore reflects the relations of power in the classroom between teacher and pupil, relations that in Bernstein's view reflect the power structure in society at large. When it comes to subject options, for example, the working class pupil is more likely to choose integrated subjects rather than the more theoretical disciplines of single science or mathematics. He or she is therefore less likely to get the subject grades needed for A-level study and progression onto university.

Thus, far from schools being 'classless' institutions processing pupils purely on the basis of merit, they are, in Bernstein's view, an integral part of a system of class reproduction and inequality operating under the guise of equal opportunity.

Bernstein's overall aim now is to explain '*how power relationships penetrate the organisation, distribution and evaluation of knowledge through the social context*'. While Durkheim and Mead influenced his early work on linguistic codes, Marxism is predominant in his more recent analyses. By this intermingling of interpretative and structural ideas, what he is attempting is nothing less than a complete theory of the cycle of class reproduction.

The Idea in Action

B ASIL BERNSTEIN'S IDEA OF LINGUISTIC CODES HAD A MAJOR IMPACT ON BRITISH sociology of education. It inspired a host of empirical studies and added a new dimension to the perennial debate about educational achievement.

It derives and draws from both of the two main traditions in the post-war British sociology of education.

- The attempt in the 1950s and 1960s to explain the great differences in educational achievement between middle- and working-class children in terms of their home background and level of parental support.
- The attempt by the 'new' sociology of education in the 1970s to reveal how knowledge is an integral part of class inequalities, reproduction and social control in a capitalist society.

However, it also inspired a number of quite fervent criticisms, some of which are due to exaggerated or distorted versions of his thesis.

Although Bernstein never said working-class speech patterns were either inferior or inadequate, never said that because 'the working class don't speak proper, they can't think clever thoughts', he did imply it and other writers like Carl Bereiter have used this theory to argue that low income groups and blacks fail in the American educational system because their speech pattern is incapable of dealing with the higher level concepts and modes of communication needed in an advanced industrial society. Their speech patterns in Bereiter's view retard their intellectual development and make it difficult for them to understand abstract ideas. Harold Rosen (1974) and William Labov (in Keddie 1973) launched furious attacks on such claims. Rosen argued that Bernstein's definitions of social class were so vague as to be useless – at times Bernstein lumps together all non-manual workers as middle class and all manual as working class, at other times he refers only to the lower working class – and his evidence of such codes is so sparse and weak at times that it can in no way meet the claim of middle-class superiority. Labov's analysis of black American speech patterns show that far from being incoherent, ungrammatical or illogical, they are as rich and rational as the elaborate code, just as rule-bound and capable of handling complex ideas. It is simply that the middle class has the social power to claim that their form of English is superior.

Bernstein himself described working-class language as warm and vital, simple and direct: *'My own view has always been that code restriction where it does exist, does not constitute linguistic or cultural deprivation, for there is a delicacy and variety in cultural and imaginative form.'* Moreover in an article entitled 'Education Cannot Compensate for Society' (1970) he attacked the concept of compensatory education, of attempts like Education Priority Areas to overcome the educational deficiencies of the poor working class, because it blamed parents rather than asking why schools failed such children. He argued that there was nothing in the 'working class dialect as such' to prevent a child from learning the elaborate code, though not having it does put such children at a considerable disadvantage in our education system. He similarly distinguished linguistic codes from regional dialects, though, again, speaking in a Scouse or Cockney accent rather than standard middle-class English can often be a handicap and be labelled a sign of unintelligence and inferiority.

Other writers have criticised certain ambiguities in Bernstein's definition of linguistic codes, in his presentation of them as polar opposites when in fact speech seems more a continuum from slang to fluent and articulate expression, and, most important, that his experiments do not provide enough evidence to prove conclusively that such codes are the key to social class differences and relations. His colleagues are using this concept less in their experiments and even Bernstein now puts more emphasis on 'modes of control' than sociolinguistic codes. Moreover, studies like David Hargreaves et al. (1975), show that schools do not necessarily use only the elaborate code but also rely heavily on 'implicit' understanding and short sharp commands, which should, according to Bernstein's theory, make working-class pupils feel more at home in school!

Despite his recent use of a Marxist framework, radical writers like Rachel Sharpe see Bernstein's work as essentially functionalist or Weberian. In her view he fails to provide a proper Marxist definition of class, make proper use of a dialectical analysis or clearly relate such codes to the underlying relations of production in a capitalist society. Research (by Pap also and Pleh (1974)) shows that elaborate and restricted codes exist even in such apparently classless societies as Hungary. As Karabel and Halsey (1977) argue, while Bernstein's thesis makes a lot of sense in an obviously class-based society like Britain, it would be difficult to apply, for example, to America or Communist China.

Since the original exposition of this idea in the 1960s and 70s, Bernstein and his colleagues have moved on from analysing educational achievement and the school curriculum to using the notion of linguistic codes to explain the broader structures and processes of power and control in a class-based society at home and in the workplace. In particular they have sought to identify the processes by which power and control in society at large operates at the institutional and personal level; how through linguistic codes the social relations of a capitalist society are transmitted and reproduced within the family and at work to the point of influencing, if not determining, individual behaviour and relationships. Bernstein aims to define more precisely the concept of linguistic codes and to identify the principles behind them: how they are created and how they help legitimise and promote inequality. He argues that, while relatively simple divisions of labour give rise to 'restricted' linguistic codes and relationships, the more complex the social division of labour and the more impersonal the relations of production between employer and worker, the more elaborate becomes the linguistic code of communication and control. Consider, for example, the short sharp commands and communication used on the shop floor of a factory between the boss and the workers compared with the elaborate discussions found in modern boardroom meetings between managers and chairman.

However, while linguistic codes are an essential mechanism of class control and repro-duction, they can also generate 'oppositional' codes both in school (for example, pupil subcultures) and at work (trade unions) as groups of pupils or groups of workers use language to defend themselves and to organise opposition to those in power. This notion of oppositional codes highlights the potential for resistance by oppressed classes and even the potential internal contradictions and conflict within ruling classes. Code controls are not established in a passive manner; they involve a continuous interaction – even struggle – between 'transmitters' and 'acquirers'. Ultimately Bernstein's theory includes the possibility of resistance to and even revolt against class controls, be they symbolic, economic or political, through the use of language.

Bernstein's theory of linguistic codes has therefore moved on to a much broader and deeper analysis. While it still has its roots in education, it is now more explicitly focused on analysing power, control and communication in capitalist societies at large. It has travelled a long way, it is still having a major impact and it still informs much sociology teaching, even if some GCSE candidates have described working-class children as not only linguistically deprived but linguistically 'depraved'.

- **POST-MODERNISM** (p. 245), **DISCOURSE** (p. 208) and **SIMULATIONS** (p. 260) as post-modern theories of the power of language and symbols.

Further Reading

BERNSTEIN, B.B. (1970) 'A Sociolinguistic Approach to Social Learning', in Worsley, P. (ed.), *Modern Sociology Introductory Readings,* Penguin, Harmondsworth – Bernstein outlines his own ideas.

BERNSTEIN, B.B. (1971–90) *Class, Codes and Control,* Vols 1–4, Routledge & Kegan Paul, London.

SHARPE, R. (1980) *Knowledge, Ideology and the Politics of Schooling,* Routledge & Kegan Paul, London.

Modernisation Theory

W.W. Rostow

The Idea

WALT WHITMAN ROSTOW WAS A LEADING AMERICAN ACADEMIC IN THE 1950S AND special adviser to Presidents Kennedy and Johnson in the 1960s. In his most famous publication *Stages of Economic Growth: A Non-Communist Manifesto* (1960) he set out his proposals for modernising Third World countries as both a blueprint for economic growth and as a 'capitalist' alternative to the state planned model on offer from the Soviet Union and Communist China. His theory of modernisation was therefore as much part of the ideological battle between East and West to win over the countries of the Third World as it was an exercise in economic theory and policy.

Modernisation theory is not a new theory of social and economic development. Its basic ideas of how societies grow and develop date back to the functionalist ideas of Emile Durkheim and Talcott Parsons and the view that like natural organisms, like human beings, societies grow in stages, maturing gradually from birth and infancy through to childhood and adulthood, through some sort of internal dynamism. True maturity only occurs when such physical (or in society's case economic) development is accompanied by appropriate psychological (or cultural) development. Just as we often talk of a child being immature, even retarded, when its mental development doesn't match its physical growth, so too we talk of underdeveloped even backward societies, of Third World countries held back by illiteracy, ignorance and superstition. They have failed to develop what Max Weber called the Protestant or work ethic (see p. 61) and what David McClelland (1961) called the achievement factor – the 'culture of enterprise', the drive and ambition that seems to us so vital in getting economic progress, industrialisation, off the ground.

Walt Rostow's contribution to modernisation theory, both as an economist and a presidential adviser, was to outline in detail the five main stages of economic growth', through which all societies must pass:

- *Stage 1: Traditional society.* Here he lumped together all pre-industrial societies because, whatever their differences, they are all basically agricultural societies with low output, ancient technology and poor communications. The social structure is highly traditional and hierarchical and there is little social mobility. It is based on strong family and kinship networks and value systems geared to traditional religions and 'long-run fatalism'. Political power is highly centralised but the local landlord rules his own roost.

- *Stage 2: Preconditions for take off.* Gradually change occurs, triggered by some internal mechanism or outside stimulus, such as a foreign invasion which 'shocks' traditional society, sows the seed of an idea of economic progress and sets in motion the growth of trade and the establishment of infant industries. *'A new breed of businessmen emerges, men of enterprise ready to take risks in the pursuit of profit and modernisation'* (Rostow 1960) and a new political elite arises determined to overthrow the traditional landed classes (or colonial government) and lead the people into the 'modern' world.

- *Stage 3: The take off.* A period of about 20 years during which, as the economy gathers pace, as traditional obstacles and practices are overthrown, as industry begins to replace agriculture as the core of the economy, so a country *'takes off economically and industrialisation becomes a self-generating force'.* 'Market forces', supported by the state, sweep away traditional economic, political and social structures. Investment grows to at least 10 per cent of national income and economic activity spreads into the development of new technologies and the exploitation of previously untapped natural resources. Agriculture is commercialised, the economy shifts from an agrarian to an industrial base, and the people move from a rural to an urban environment and lifestyle. Britain was the first country to 'take off' (1783–1803) followed by countries like America (1843–60), Japan (1878–1900) and Russia (1890–1914).

- *Stage 4: The drive to maturity.* This stage covers a period of about 40 years during which a country both consolidates and builds on such progress. Investment grows to between 10 and 20 per cent of national income, technology and science spread to all branches of the economy and the economy becomes part of the international economic system.

- *Stage 5: The age of high mass consumption.* As the economy matures and prospers the population can start to enjoy the benefits of mass consumption, a high standard of material living and, if it chooses, a welfare state. There is a shift in the economic structure from primary and secondary industries to services and, in the stage 'beyond consumption' society will have to choose between 'babies, boredom, three-day weekends, the moon and the creation of new inner human frontiers'.

Rostow's dynamic theory of economic development is essentially an evolutionary one based on the assumption that all societies must progress through a set of 'fixed' stages – there are no 'leaps' or short cuts in his model – driven by an underlying 'internal' dynamic. However, he does allow for some choice in economic strategies and for a distinction between the self-generating Industrial Revolutions of the First World and the Third World's need for outside help. In fact, as the subtitle of his book indicates, *Stages of Economic Growth* is not merely a theoretical treatise but a manifesto of the way Western aid (especially American) should be organised to fight off the threat of communism, the 'disease of transition' as he called it. Such aid should not only be economic, in the form of technology, investment and expertise, but political, supporting non-communist elites, democracy and pluralism against one-party dictatorships. Thus he helped influence American foreign policy in the 1950s and 1960s in its fight against communism in Asia and Latin America.

The Idea in Action

WALT ROSTOW WAS IN THE HIGHLY UNUSUAL POSITION OF BEING ABLE TO PUT HIS theory of development into practice. As an adviser to two American Presidents during the 1960s, he was able to inform American policy on economic development in Latin America and South-east Asia as America 'fought' to win over the Third World to capitalism and the Western way of life. Unfortunately American foreign policy and aid programmes in the 1960s and 1970s fell increasingly into disrepute following the disastrous war in Vietnam and charges of 'imperialism' and dictatorship in South America. As American policy fell into disarray and disrepute, so criticisms of Rostow's thesis grew on two main grounds:

1. *Economic analysis*. His idea that industrialisation can only occur through one predetermined pathway has been heavily criticised. As Alexander Gerschenkron argued, late developing countries can quite easily learn from the mistakes of the West, borrow Western skills, technology and expertise and so leap a stage or two. Secondly, though Britain and America may have 'taken-off' through their own 'steam', most of the rest of Europe did so under state control and planning. Thirdly, if the Third World also begins to industrialise, the strain on the world's resources may well prove intolerable. Finally, although the First World nations may well have faced an 'open market' when they industrialised, the Third World countries today face an international economic system firmly under Western control. If they restructure their economies they face the danger of not only being unable to compete on the world market (and so going bust) but of losing their capacity to feed their own people as land is given over from food production to industry or 'cash crops'. If, however, they are successful then the West may suffer not only a loss of supplies of cheap food and raw materials but of jobs, as the cheap labour industries of the East make Western ones redundant.

2. *Western – especially American – bias*. Rostow tended to assume that the only true model of industrialisation is the Western one, so ignoring the success in the East of a variety of communist and centrally planned systems. Secondly, while promising freedom and democracy, Western aid all too often has involved 'propping up' corrupt dictatorships and allowing Western multinationals to dominate and exploit Third World economies. His theory has been criticised as simply an ideological justification for American imperialism and as totally ignoring conflict, not consensus, over the distribution of wealth both *within* nations and between the First and Third Worlds.

Such criticisms reached their peak in the 1970s in the critique of modernisation theory by world system theorists such as Immanuel Wallerstein and dependency theorists such as Andre Gunder Frank. A.G. Frank (see p. 92) is especially severe in his criticism arguing that Rostow's various stages are largely 'fictional' and highly deterministic. His first stage, 'traditional society', totally ignores the enormous variety and diversity of pre-industrial societies. To assume that they were all initially as undeveloped as the Third World today is historical nonsense. More important, Frank totally rejects this idea of *internal* economic development. Rather, the West, in his view, developed by colonising and exploiting poorer countries and it now uses the world capitalist system not to help the Third World develop but to keep it *underdeveloped*. A chain of dependency and exploitation has been set up from the cities of the West (the Metropolis) to the capitals of the East down to the villages of the Third World (the satellites) by which the First World expropriates the surplus of the poorer countries, locks their economies into supplying the West with cheap food and raw materials and, far from aid helping them, it increases Western control and burdens poor countries with intolerable debt. Therefore, in Frank's view the dynamic of development is not an internal one depicted by Rostow but an external one, a world capitalist system which once helped the West 'take off' but which now keeps the Third World shackled and dependent, poor and exploited.

Immanuel Wallerstein (1974) took this critique of modernisation theory even further, arguing that although stages of development could be identified historically, they were neither uniform nor necessarily sequential. Although societies prior to the development of modern capitalism in 1500 may have been relatively self-contained 'minisystems', the development of modern capitalism transformed the world into a global economy based on world transportation systems and the military power and empires of the Western nations. The world economy that has emerged since is based on a core, a semiperiphery and a periphery whereby the powerful manufacturing nations subjugated and exploited the poorer, less developed 'periphery' of Third World countries where raw materials and labour are cheap and so profits high. The poorer nations, according to Wallerstein, are now locked into a world economic system from which they can neither escape nor control their own economic development. Studies like Sidney Mintz's (1985) of the global system of the sugar industry have shown how from the colonial period onwards the Western nations reorganised their colonies and forced them to concentrate on products like sugar for which there was high demand and high profits using cheap or even slave labour in areas such as the West Indies and southern states of America. Similar analyses have been made of the cotton and tea industries showing how Britain, a major example of a core country, exploited its colonial periphery India. We in Britain enjoy cheap tea and cheap clothing because the workers in India suffer poor pay and long hours. This framework of core-periphery analysis can equally be applied to the economic and political relationships *within* a particular country or nation; the slave economy of the southern states of America in the production of cotton and tobacco being a classic example.

In its time Rostow's thesis was immensely influential and very powerful. Today it has fallen into disrepute as typical American propaganda used to justify Western imperialism and exploitation. It still finds some favour with Western development policy makers, and within academic circles modernisation theorists have added a sixth stage – a post-industrial stage to try and update Rostow's model. The debate therefore continues but within a newer framework, a paradigm within which evolutionary theories of dependency compete directly with those proclaiming more radical and revolutionary ideas.

 **See Also**

- **THE PROTESTANT ETHIC** (p. 61) as Max Weber's original idea of the 'spirit' needed for capitalism to take off.
- **DEPENDENCY THEORY** (p. 92), A.G. Frank's critique of the modernisation thesis.
- **GLOBALISATION** (p. 214), **RISK SOCIETY** (p. 255) and **INFORMATION(AL) SOCIETY** (p. 220) as more recent views of global development.

Suggested Reading

FOSTER-CARTER, A. (1985) 'The Sociology of Development' in Haralambos, M. (ed.), *Sociology New Directions,* Causeway Press, Ormskirk.

HARRISON, P. (1981) *Inside the Third World,* Penguin, Harmondsworth.

Further Reading

FRANK, A.G. (1981) *Crisis in the Third World*, Heinemann, London.

ROSTOW, W.W. (1960) *The Stages of Economic Growth: A Non-Communist Manifesto,* Cambridge University Press, Cambridge.

Paradigms

Thomas Kuhn

THE TERM 'PARADIGM' REFERS TO A SET OF IDEAS, A THEORETICAL FRAMEWORK, A theoretical model of how society or nature works. Almost all academic or scientific disciplines operate within a particular paradigm or involve a debate between competing paradigms as to the nature of society or the underlying forces of the physical or natural world. Examples of major paradigms would be Albert Einstein's theory of relativity in physics and Charles Darwin's theory of evolution in biology. Examples of competing paradigms would be Marxism and structural functionalism in sociology and behaviourism and Gestalt theory in psychology.

In his key work, *The Structure of Scientific Revolutions* (1962), Thomas Kuhn, an American philosopher of science, used the concept of paradigms not to simply explain how scientific and academic research develops but to challenge the accepted view that science and the accumulation of scientific knowledge is a gradual, evolutionary process based on objective and impartial analysis in which scientists and academics collaborate on an agreed agenda in the pursuit of truth and the discovery of facts. Instead, using the notion of paradigms, Kuhn proposed the radical and quite revolutionary thesis that in fact the history of modern science is not a gradual and cumulative one, rather it is one of *revolutions* in thinking, as new theories overturn old ones and new schools of academics rise up and overthrow accepted thinking and the professors that go with it. Far from the academic world being one all embracing community, Kuhn describes it as an inner world of competing theories and competing communities racing to make the next great discovery, plotting to take over and dominate academic theory in their particular discipline or science. As traditional theories and practices are discarded in favour of a new paradigm or supertheory, so a new very different view of the world of nature emerges and with it a new approach to scientific research and a new team of key theorists.

Thomas Kuhn defined paradigms as '*universally recognised scientific achievements that for a time provide model problems and solutions to a community of practitioners*'. A paradigm is a unified and coherent framework, a way of thinking that a particular field of science has about the universe and the way it works. It guides scientists towards certain problems and provides many solutions; it governs their research programmes and is increasingly reinforced by the theories that develop from it. It is like a puzzle. It sets out the rules of the game, poses the challenges for each new generation of scientists and the aim is to solve the problems it poses and to discover the missing pieces required to complete its picture of nature. It sets the standards against which new discoveries will be acclaimed or rejected. It is the accepted view of what constitutes science in a particular discipline and the members of each scientific community are so committed to it, so take it for granted, that it is rarely questioned or criticised. Modern examples of paradigms would be the dominance of Einstein's theory of relativity in physics or Darwin's theory of evolution in biology. New generations of young scientists are socialised into the paradigm's underlying theory and research methods by their teachers and their textbooks. They are taught only the paradigm's principles and theories and rarely exposed to alternative ones. They gain entry to the 'scientific community' by producing the expected solutions in their experiments, passing examinations set by professors steeped in the paradigm's principles and setting up research projects directed at the paradigm's problems. The picture Kuhn therefore presents of modern science is of a series of tight-knit academic communities each based on a rather closed, even dogmatic, view of reality from which alternative visions are rigorously excluded and in which the standard of judgement is not objective reality but the subjective evaluation of one's peers.

Kuhn divided the development of science into three main stages:

1. Pre-paradigm – a state in which there is no general consensus or agreed theoretical framework within a particular discipline but a wide variety of competing theories as to the nature of their subject matter, appropriate research methodology and the types of problems that require solutions.

2. Normal science – the mature stage at which a particular scientific community agrees to unite behind a particular paradigm, its achievements and its guidelines as to research. The general aim is to fill in the puzzle and 'mop up', rather than to innovate. Though anomalies in the paradigm do arise they are either forced into the existing framework or the scientist involved is blamed as incompetent.

3. Paradigm revolution – however, in time, as the anomalies grow, as more and more questions arise that the dominant paradigm cannot answer and new phenomena are discovered that it cannot explain, so a crisis develops in the discipline to the point where even its 'leading lights' feel uneasy. There follows a period of hectic debate about fundamentals and a sudden willingness to try anything which is solved either by a new development in the existing paradigm or the emergence of a new paradigm with a new view of nature and a new puzzle to solve. During this revolutionary stage the discipline tends to divide into traditionalists and radicals and a battle for power and allegiance develops. This takes place at two levels: the theoretical and the political. Gradually, more and more of the scientific community are won over to the new paradigm, not by reason – because initially it lacks substantial proof and cannot by definition be tested by the old methods – but by 'conversion', a leap of faith, what Kuhn (1962) calls a *'Gestalt* shift', a sudden vision of the new wonders offered by the new paradigm – *'Lavoisier . . . saw oxygen where Priestly had seen dephlogistated air and where others had seen nothing at all'* – and, once converted, not only is it impossible to revert back to the old view of

nature, but it is impossible to hold, simultaneously, two paradigm visions because people holding different theories 'see different things and they see them in different relations to one another'. After a paradigm revolution scientists simply see and so respond to a different world. Such incompatibility of paradigms Kuhn called 'incommensurability'.

As conversions to the new truth spread, as evidence and research experiments in its favour grow, so too, in time, the older traditional professors of the discipline will have to give way to the new young converts eager for power and ambitious for authority. Once in power they will now preach the new orthodoxy, select the research projects and teams, rewrite the textbooks and set the exams. As the dust settles and the new paradigm gains general acceptance so a further phase of normal science is set in motion as a new generation of scientists explores the fresh challenges and novel problems posed by the new framework, until that too reaches its limits. As Max Planck remarked: *'a new scientific truth does not triumph by convincing its opponents and making them see the light, but rather because its opponents eventually die, and a new generation grows up that is familiar with it'* (quoted in Kuhn 1970).

As examples of scientific revolutions, Kuhn cites the developments associated with the names of Copernicus, Newton, Lavoisier and Einstein, each of which involved the overthrow and rejection by the scientific community of one time-honoured theory for another, each of which produced a shift in the problems available for scrutiny and the standards by which their solutions were to be judged, each of which transformed the scientific imagination in such a way as to transform the world within which scientific work was done.

THOMAS KUHN'S IDEA OF PARADIGMS REVOLUTIONISED OUR UNDERSTANDING OF SCIENCE and scientific knowledge. It inspired a wealth of detailed studies of major scientific advances and has been a major contribution to both the sociology of science and the sociology of knowledge: Hollinger (1980) in history; Serle (1972) and Falk and Zhao (1990) in linguistics; Stanfield (1974) in economics; and Friedrichs (1970) in sociology. It also generated a storm of controversy and a major debate between Kuhn and Sir Karl Popper (see p. 109), because it appeared to challenge the very foundation of modern science. In the second edition of his book (1970) Kuhn sought to reply to his critics but, in doing so, he so modified much of his original thesis that many writers now distinguish between the early and the later Kuhn.

The main criticisms of Kuhn's idea (and his later amendments) can be listed as follows:

- That his key concepts were too vague to be workable. One writer counted 22 versions of the term 'paradigm' in Kuhn's original work and though Kuhn (1970) tried to define this term more precisely, he later argued that it be dropped in favour of the term 'disciplinary matrix'. The concept of scientific community proved equally elusive with Kuhn referring both to the whole scientific community and to particular sub-disciplines, some with as few as 25 members. Similarly it proved difficult to distinguish a full-blown scientific revolution from a simple theoretical advance. Kuhn's answer was that this could only be done by more detailed studies of key advances and that ultimately it was for the scientific community involved to assess how 'revolutionary' an impact a new theory had on their discipline. He even conceded the possibility of micro-revolutions.

- That Kuhn's concept of 'incommensurability', that no one paradigm can be used to judge or evaluate another, made independent evaluations of alternative theories impossible and so left as the only standard of judgement the subjective evaluations of the scientific community. For critics such as Sir Karl Popper such a standard reduced scientific evaluation to 'mob psychology' and replaced the power of logic with the rule of power, so fundamentally challenging the authority of modern science. Though Kuhn later accepted the idea of 'partial communication' between paradigms and that standards do exist in science, he continued to argue that ultimately a scientific community is won over to a new paradigm not by proof but by persuasion, by experiencing and using its theoretical framework and vision of reality.

- That Kuhn's concept of paradigms is *relativist*, that it denied the possibility of objective knowledge because, according to his thesis, all knowledge, all understanding of nature depends on the paradigm through which it is viewed. No fact speaks for itself. It depends for its discovery and existence on the meaning given to it by the paradigm involved. All knowledge, therefore, must be partial knowledge and absolute, total knowledge is impossible. Far from compromising on this relativist view of knowledge the later Kuhn developed it by arguing that knowledge depends not only on the paradigm used but the language involved – and we have no culture-free language in which to communicate. Kuhn's theory therefore seemed to deny the possibility of sociology as a science, of sociology being objective and value free. Rather, it supports the phenomenological perspective that all knowledge is relative and culture bound. It equally seems to portray sociology as an infant science, pre-paradigmatic and so pre-scientific. Sociology seems to be in a constant state of flux, or permanent revolution with no one agreed or dominant theoretical framework but several competing ones.

Despite such criticisms Kuhn's idea of scientific paradigms has proved a major contribution to our understanding of science and the sociology of knowledge. Moreover, far from trying to undermine the achievements of modern science he was simply trying to describe how they actually occur, rather than how scientists claimed they appeared. As he argued, it is this very unity of approach, this paradigm consensus, that has enabled science to advance so rapidly while other disciplines have stagnated. Moreover, behind this scientific commitment to one paradigm also lies the scientists' desire to be original, to discover that earth-shattering new theory, and it is this tension between preservation and innovation that lies at the heart of science's monumental progress today.

Kuhn's thesis inspired intense debate on the nature of science and the nature of knowledge in the 1960s and 70s, and although he later modified many of his ideas, writers such as George Ritzer (1996), and Robert Friedrichs (1970) have sought to revive this concept and use it to analyse and describe sociology as a multiple paradigm discipline without an overarching theory of society and history but with a variety of competing theses, all of which contribute to a healthy and progressive debate on the nature of man and the nature of society.

- **FALSIFICATION AND CONJECTURE** (p. 109) as the basis of an ongoing debate between these two philosophers of science and knowledge, Popper and Kuhn.

Suggested Reading

BARNES, B. (1982) *T.S. Kuhn and the Social Sciences,* Macmillan, London – an overview of Kuhn's work and contribution to social science.

Further Reading

KUHN, T.S. (1962) *The Structure of Scientific Revolutions,* Chicago University Press, Chicago; 2nd edn, 1970.

RITZER, G. (1996) *Sociological Theory*, McGraw-Hill, New York.

Patriarchy

Feminism

The Idea

THE TERM 'PATRIARCHY', LITERALLY, MEANS 'RULE OF THE FATHER' (OR PATRIARCH) BUT has been adopted by feminists to refer to male domination over women in all its forms – physical, political, psychological and ideological. In particular, it refers to the social and political structures, cultural institutions and social forces which keep women oppressed and powerless in male-dominated societies.

Patriarchy can be traced back to the Bible, to the assumption that God is male and to the Book of Genesis where, after Eve ate the forbidden fruit in the Garden of Eden, God condemned her and all womankind to subordination to men, *'in sorrow thou shalt bring forth children, and thy desire shall be to thy husband and he shall rule over thee'*. Every known society is ruled by men and, although examples of female equality can be cited (e.g. the Tchambuli tribe of New Guinea), there is no known example of female rule, or matriarchy.

Feminist writers, however, totally reject the idea that patriarchy is either inevitable or natural. They have instead developed a variety of theories to show that patriarchy is man-made, a physical and ideological force used by men to keep women in their place in the background of society and historically invisible. The notion of patriarchy has provided feminism with a core concept for identifying, explaining and ultimately changing sexual inequality and oppression and for inspiring women to be female in the fullest and freest sense of the word. Within the feminist movement, however, a wide and diverse range of theories have emerged, each identifying different causes and so different solutions to patriarchy.

Traditional and liberal feminism

TRADITIONAL feminism pointed to the family as the key source of male domination and female oppression. In the past the right of the father to rule the family, and in particular his wife, was sacrosanct, enshrined in custom, tradition and often law. He could rightfully demand complete obedience and exercise his authority, and punishments, in any way he saw fit. In many primitive and traditional societies, women were a form of exchange, their marriages arranged and their rights to free speech and divorce non-existent. Even today in advanced democratic societies women as wives and daughters are governed by men in the home as their husbands and fathers make the key decisions and generally control finances. Feminists have equally highlighted the extent of domestic violence and even rape endured by women in the home and the way that, by bringing girls up to be passive and feminine, the traditional socialisation process idealises and reinforces male dominance. Hannah Gavron, for example, highlighted the prison-like nature of the home for many women by calling her 1966 study *The Captive Wife*. The patriarchal nature of society, therefore, merely reflects and reinforces male domination in the home. As Kate Millett (1971) concluded, '*Patriarchy's chief institution is the family*'.

Traditional feminists have further highlighted numerous examples of male domination and female segregation outside of the home. For example:

- Most working women do only 'women's work' (e.g. nursing, secretarial work, etc.) and are almost always in subordinate positions to men.

- In almost every field of work – even such apparently female areas as nursing and catering – men hold the top jobs. Fewer than 5 per cent of architects, engineers, scientists and solicitors in Britain, for example, are women and, in every field, the higher up the hierarchy you go the fewer women you find.

- Just as at home, men dominate most key posts and key decisions, be it in the board-room or Parliament. Although Britain has now had her first female prime minister, America still awaits her first female president. Although New Labour in Britain campaigned hard for women MPs, even today only 100 or so women hold seats in Parliament compared to the remaining 550 men.

And so the list goes on. But patriarchy's real power is not physical force but institutional control. It is the power of an all-pervasive ideology which proclaims that male dominance and female subordination are both natural and normal; that for women to be dominant or aggressive is deviant and unfeminine. Such sex stereotyping is promoted not only in the media (e.g. 'Page 3') but through the socialisation process. It is even reflected in our everyday language. Girls are brought up to be passive and feminine. Key terms such as *history* and *mankind* are symptomatic of the inbuilt assumption that men are the dominant gender. Such terms simply assumed that they include women but as the passive, almost invisible segment of the human race. Those who deviate from such gender roles are often socially chastised, be it by gossip, by being ostracised or stigmatised as a tomboy, single parent or prostitute. So all-pervasive is this ideology of patriarchy, this ideological hegemony, that it is rarely criticised, and most women defer to it without question!

The driving force for liberal feminism has been equality of opportunity, the fight for women's rights and the right to be given the same opportunities as men. And it is here that they have enjoyed their greatest success. Equality of opportunity is now enshrined in the legal systems of the main Western societies and acknowledged as an essential concept for improving and liberating society from all forms of inequality, discrimination and oppression. Sexual discrimination has now been legally outlawed but, as modern research shows, it still exists beneath the surface. Research into sexualized violence has sought to redefine traditional concepts and views of gender relations as disparate and wide ranging as prostitution, pornography and sexual harassment. Studies into women battering, incest and sexual abuse, for example, have highlighted male violence, made the use of sexual violence more visible, socially repugnant and increasingly subject to legal control – even for those practising sexual harassment at work.

Such research has also focused on men as much as on women; on the men who abuse, batter or harass – and on men who themselves are victims of sexual power. However, while the ideological battle may have been won, the campaign to give women equal opportunity with men in all places, at all times has still some way to go, particularly at the highest levels of politics, society and the economy. Men still hold the ultimate positions of power and control the agenda for social control and political direction.

Marxist feminism

MARXIST feminists, however, take a broader, more theoretical view. They see patriarchy as simply a further division and form of exploitation and oppression generated by the capitalist mode of production. Like social class, patriarchy is rooted in the ownership of private property and, according to Friedrich Engels (1942), Karl Marx's lifelong collaborator, monogamous marriage developed not to unite men and women in marital bliss, but to protect private property.

Monogamy arose out of the concentration of considerable wealth in the hands of one person – that of a man – and out of the desire to bequeath that wealth to this man's children and to no-one else's.

Men, therefore, needed to use marriage to control women and to ensure 'undisputed paternity'. For Engels, male dominance was, therefore, based on economic dominance; remove that and patriarchy would collapse. While arguing that true sexual equality could only come about in a socialist society where property was communally owned, Marx and Engels did see some elements of capitalism as progressive. The demand for female labour, they argued, would bring women out of the home, give them some economic independence and bring them together with male workers as socialists, conscious of and united against exploitation and inequality. Marxists and socialist feminists have used, added to and re-analysed traditional Marxist concepts from a female perspective view, highlighting the way women, especially as wives, help capitalism function more efficiently by acting:

- As a *reserve army of labour* in the sense that they can be employed in times of boom and dismissed in times of slump more easily than men. Moreover, they accept low wages, part-time and unskilled work, rarely join unions and are relatively compliant. They can be used, too, to break male unions and strikes. Their whole socialisation process has not only taught them to be obedient and passive, but to regard work as secondary to their primary role as housewife and mother.

- As a source of *social control*: as (unpaid) housewives, women ensure that the male labour force is kept both healthy and compliant. No husband takes strike action or any other form of rebellious act lightly, knowing the effect on their wives and children. Instead of taking out their frustration with capitalism on their bosses, men often take it out on their wives.

- As a source of *ideological control and hegemony*: sexist ideology helps rather than threatens capitalism because it helps divide the working class into men versus women, and so makes them easier to control. A dominant gender-based ideology exists that assumes and asserts male dominance and leaves women, like the proletariat, subordinate to a false consciousness, a self-perception of inferiority and passivity. From a Marxist feminist perspective, women are in a double bind. Depending on their position within the class structure they are not only underprivileged and exploited as women but they are doubly so treated if they are working class – or worse, black! Capitalism and patriarchy combine to imprison and oppress working class women.

However, evidence from socialist societies where the 'means of production' are communally owned and even where the traditional forms of family and marriage have been abolished, does not show the automatic collapse of patriarchy. Though in communist countries, and particularly in Israeli kibbutzim, women are much freer, more equal and more likely to hold high office, the key positions, the key decisions, are still made by men. No women sit in the Politbureau, the main policy-making body in Soviet Russia, and even in kibbutzim it is still women who are most likely to be doing the cooking and child-minding. As David Lane (1970) has argued, collective ownership of the means of production is '*a necessary but not sufficient condition for female liberation*'.

Radical and revolutionary feminism

RADICAL and revolutionary feminism developed out of dissatisfaction with this Marxist feminist analysis, in particular its claim that patriarchy is like class, rooted in economic power and so, like class, can be abolished by socialism. In their view, patriarchy is a distinct form of oppression that pre-dates capitalism and all other forms of social stratification. Its roots are many and varied – economic, political, sexual, cultural, ideological, and even biological – but they all add up to the same thing. Men as a class have power over women as a class. Men control society, hold all the key positions, make all the key decisions. Men control women at home and at work as subordinates; women still primarily do 'women's work' (e.g. nurse, secretary), still see the housewife role as their prime duty and are both kept subordinate and brought up to be passive by an all-pervasive patriarchal ideology that assumes male dominance, assumes that a woman's place is in the home, reinforces gender distinctions of masculinity and femininity, assumes heterosexuality is normal and severely punishes any woman who deviates from such 'natural' norms (e.g. single mothers, lesbians, career women). Some radical feminists go further and see the roots of patriarchy as biological. As Schulasmith Firestone (1972) argues, '*unlike economic class, sex class sprang directly from a biological reality*'. Because women bear children they are dependent on men physically and economically. Men enjoy 'power over women' and so have reinforced their domination throughout the social structure. From a radical perspective, male dominance ultimately depends on force and on physical violence – or at least the threat of it. This sex class system, in her view, can only be eliminated ultimately by freeing women from their most basic biological role, having children, and while birth control techniques are a step in this direction, true liberation will only come with artificial reproduction, when babies can be born *outside* the womb.

Radical feminists, therefore, see patriarchy as a much deeper form of social stratification than Marxist feminists and so are far less optimistic about uprooting it. In their view, whatever the society, social group or even social situation, for example even simple conversations, men dominate women, and only by raising women's conscious-ness (and men's) can women even begin to liberate themselves.

Analyses like these have increasingly uncovered the deep roots and multi-faceted layers of patriarchy, revealing not only the extent to which all social institutions are male dominated (even such areas as nursing and midwifery), but the extent to which male assumptions lie behind our very language and consciousness, rendering women invisible and powerless. Only by uniting behind a programme of radical, even revolu-tionary change will the sisterhood eventually challenge and overcome the brotherhood of man and show the superiority of women. Some extreme feminists have gone as far as to argue that true liberation can only come about in a matriarchal society where women are dominant. Others go further, advocating a women-only society; arguing that lesbianism is the only real path to sexual freedom.

Black feminism

BLACK feminism has grown out of dissatisfaction with earlier forms of feminism which seem to assume that the experiences of white middle-class intellectuals applied to all women in all parts of the world at all times. In actuality, the experiences of black women, particularly black, working-class women in America and the Third World with a historical and social background steeped in slavery, the caste system and racism, are a world away from those of their white sisters in middle-class universities. Oppression and inequality for black women is often multi-layered and multi-faceted, reflecting race and class as well as gender. Moreover such dimensions may divide and fragment feminism as much as unite it as black feminists seek liberation from the racial power structure of which their fellow white feminists are a part. Black feminists have identi-fied a 'racist bias in feminist theory' and for them liberation from white rule is as critical as freedom from patriarchy or capitalism.

Post-modern feminism

MORE recently a number of feminist writers have turned from structural analyses based on Marxism or patriarchy and embraced post-modernism, a process Barret and Phillips (1992) describe as 'destabilising theory', a rejection of all embracing theories like Marxism developed originally by men for men and applied in passing to feminist concerns. Moreover many modern feminists have rejected the prevailing assumption that the objective of feminism is to create a more sexually equal society. Rather, they take a more positive, even assertive position and seek not only to illustrate the differ-ences between men and women but the superior qualities of femininity. Post-modern frameworks and approaches to study offer the opportunity to develop a more explic-itly female, a more sensitive approach to the study of women in their everyday lives.

Post-modern feminism rejects the belief in a single all embracing theory of society as the means to explaining the position of women. It even rejects the idea of a single essential woman. Rather, women are all very different, living very different lives and therefore beyond the analytical embrace of one single stereotype or theoretical frame-work. They reject male approaches and concepts – be they the use of reason or notions like justice; they even reject traditional feminist thought as being infused with, if not contaminated by, masculine styles of thinking. Their focus in true post-modern style is on language and on deconstructing male language and the masculine view of the world. Whereas in the past male language and perceptions were taken for granted and regarded as normal, post-modern feminists seek to turn such a world view, such uncon-scious bias or hegemony on its head and to put feminist perspectives on top. The term 'ugly', as traditionally applied to women, is very much based on a male view of beauty – tall, glamorous, slim etc. Women have traditionally subscribed to such stereotypes and sought to emulate them, often to the detriment of their own health and well-being. Post-modern feminists reject male-based perceptions and argue instead for women to be themselves, to identify and support their own views of beauty even if they conflict with men's – to fight for the rights and attractiveness of a size 16 in prefer-ence to the media and male ideal of a size 10!

Such writers go further and challenge the whole notion of truth by claiming that all our social and legal concepts have been devised by men and that language is not neutral but used by men to control our view of the world. Women are the invisible 'other' in the history of the world. By making the voices of women – different women – heard, post-modernists believe that women can escape this 'ideological strait jacket and develop a feminist language that truly expresses women's ideas in their own words not those of men', a truly feminist view of the world. Such ideas derive from the works of French philosophers and post-structuralists Jacques Lacan and Jacques Derida, and their theories of the power of language to define and create reality.

Feminist writers like Hélène Cixous (1981) have argued that women must learn to express sexuality not in male terms of penetration and orgasm but in the multitude of ways women experience and enjoy sexual pleasure or *jouissance*. Female sexuality has traditionally been repressed in the service of men, its full array and beauty untapped in the belief that it was deviant and inappropriate for women to be sexually assertive and for them to deliberately explore their own bodies sexually. Such assertiveness, she argues, does not necessarily threaten men; rather men may gain considerably from exploring their feminine side. Writers like Helen Haste (1993) have gone further, arguing that rationality and the search for truth through reason is very much a male approach. Female approaches based on intuition or emotional intelligence tend to be rejected and portrayed as irrational when in fact the world would gain – men as well as women – from a recognition that female perspectives have as much to contribute as male. What is needed is not a single perspective but an encouragement of all points of view in improving our understanding of history and society. Thus, while structuralist writers have sought to liberate women by identifying the source of their oppression – be it class or patriarchy – and removing it to make men and women more equal, post-modern feminists have focused on language as the source of ideological hegemony and sought to liberate women not by making them equal to men but by celebrating their differences and their diversity, encouraging women to be themselves, to be individuals free of male-based stereotypes of ideal or typical womanhood. Post-modern feminists have therefore adopted a very different approach to sexual inequity and sexuality, one based on language rather than social structures, one that rejects the idea that there is a single pathway to female liberation. Women are too diverse for that; they may have to find their own way, as individuals as well as a 'class', to health, happi-ness and freedom.

Within feminism the political agenda has shifted from trying to make women equal to men, to debates about diversity and differences within as well as between the sexes. While patriarchy, therefore, may no longer be a dominant theme or battlecry, it has helped women to unite in trying to understand their social position – and in trying to change it.

The Idea in Action

THE CONCEPT OF PATRIARCHY HAS BEEN CENTRAL TO FEMINIST UNDERSTANDING AND analyses. It clearly highlights male domination and power in the home as well as in society at large. It combines the force of male authority with the subtleties of paternal care, so highlighting the way women's subordination rests on ideological and emotional power, on personal relationships as well as on physical force.

However, as the review above clearly shows, it is also a concept which has inspired a multitude of very different definitions and theories – so much so that some feminists have called for its elimination from the 'feminist dictionary', proposing such alternatives as 'sex-gender system', 'phallocracy' and simply 'sexism'. Its usage led to a fierce debate within feminism in the late 1970s because it seemed to hide as much as it revealed. It implies that male domination is universal and mono-causal (i.e. that it is caused solely by biology or capitalism), so obscuring the multitude of forms in which female oppression has occurred in contemporary and past societies. Moreover, it takes the concept of gender for granted, failing to recognise that this, too, is a social construct. Finally, it fails to portray gender relations as varying and as being a continuous struggle in which women do resist, occasionally successfully. *'Patriarchy . . . suggests a fatalistic submission which allows no space for the complexities of women's defiance'* (Rowbotham 1979).

The wide variety of solutions advocated for abolishing patriarchy have equally undermined the power and force of this concept, not least with extreme feminists advocating the abolition of biology, as well as segregation from men.

As this debate has abated, however, as feminist studies in the 1980s and 1990s have turned from theoretical overviews into detailed empirical studies, a Third Wave of feminist debate has arisen which has sought to identify and analyse the intense and immense diversity of women's experiences depending on their social location – their class, race, age, culture and sexual orientation. Women do not suffer equally from patriarchy and there are as many differences between women as there are between men and women. Moreover, these differences, this diversity, should be celebrated and encouraged at both the macro level of women's experiences as a social 'class' and at the micro level of the individual experience of simply being a woman. So the concept of patriarchy has become less controversial and, once clearly defined, more useful. It is now, according to Sarah Fildes (1985) more generally accepted because, at the very least, *'it highlights and names the areas around which we need to construct theoretical accounts'*.

Patriarchy remains a key idea in feminist analyses, although such analyses are increasingly sophisticated and complex. Sylvia Walby (1990), for example, has sought to interrelate the major feminist perspectives into a more dynamic and up-to-date concept of patriarchy, combining six underlying dimensions or structures: paid work; patriarchial relations within the household; patriarchial culture; sexuality, male violence towards women; the state. While women have made gains in all six spheres, the state in her view is still patriarchial as well as capitalist and racist. Patriarchy may have changed – it may be less obvious and less oppressive and all pervasive, particularly in the home – but it still exists as a powerful and interrelated system within the public sphere where men continue to predominate and to control power at the highest level. In Walby's view (1990) women have gained the freedom to move from the private sphere of the home into the public sphere of society at large in ever increasing numbers. However this has not in her view reduced sexual inequality and exploitation but spread it – *'women are no longer restricted to the domestic hearth but have the whole society in which to roam and be exploited'*.

In her more recent work (1997) Sylvia Walby goes on to highlight the generational differences. Older women are more likely to be restricted by the constraints of private patriarchy, to be more domesticated and less likely to be independent and out in the workplace. Younger women are more highly qualified, more likely to be in higher education, full-time employment and to be financially independent. They are less dependent on men, better protected by the law and more socially visible and sexually confident. However, such freedom and independence, she argues, has also led to higher rates of divorce and single mothers and it has still not led to equality in pay or in top jobs. Patriarchy still exists but it has changed shape and form; it affects different women differently depending on their age, class or race.

Walby's theory is a recent attempt to update the notion of patriarchy by using a range of feminist perspectives from radical to liberal approaches to show that while women have made advances in both the private and the public sphere, patriarchy remains as powerful as ever – even if it is less visible and less overt.

In contrast to Walby, Anna Pollert argues in *The Poverty of Patriarchy* (1996) that the whole notion of patriarchy is bereft of analytical value because it ignores the fact that it is the overarching and overriding structure of capitalist society that promotes and underpins inequality, exploitation and oppression. Patriarchy in her view is simply another example, another feature or secondary inequality of an inegalitarian society. It has no 'agency', no dynamic or driving force of its own. Rather it is an agent of capitalism in the same way that race, age or other social divisions are generated and used by capitalism to divert attention from its exploitative nature and to create divisions within and between the mass of the population. Rather in her view class is the dominant structural division in a capitalist society and *'class relations are infused with (rather than separate from) gender, race and other modes of social differentiation'*. Dual systems theories, theories that distinguish between patriarchy and capitalism and describe patriarchy as a separate system of inequality are, in her view, missing the point, missing the real source of social and gender division, capitalism and its inherently divisive class system.

In contrast to Walby's analysis of public power, other writers continue to see women's liberation as essentially a personal and private matter involving freedom from traditional gender roles and stereotypical images of what it is to be a woman, celebrating and rejoicing in the diversity of family types and female forms rather than focusing solely on equal pay or equal opportunity. Writers such as Susan Faludi (1992) have gone further and warned of a potential backlash against feminism and against the extremes of the women's liberation movement. Women appear to be freer at home and at work but no happier. The stresses and strains of modern life ranging from divorce to anorexia seem greater than ever and many women as well as men blame the excesses of feminism for the growth of gender-related diseases and depression, and blame Women's Lib for undermining the traditional roles and responsibilities of men and women in family life.

Within sociology, the concept of patriarchy has generated a whole new paradigm, a whole new set of sociological questions and a new agenda for analysis. Like Marxism, patriarchy is a concept that has revolutionised sociological theory and social practice because it highlighted the structure of power and gave the 'underclass' a basis for challenging and changing that structure in practice as well as in theory. Women today are freer because of feminist ideas and campaigning. Equal opportunity is a driving force in Western societies that even politicians and employers now subscribe to. Women in the West are more self-consciously and self-confidently female and feminine and less prepared to accept male dominance physically, socially or ideologically. The impact of feminism on the Third World, however, is still in its early stages, still part of the national and global struggle for social, sexual and racial liberation and equality.

 See Also

- **GENDER** (p. 113) as a background to feminist theories of power and gender relations.

Suggested Reading

ABBOT, P. AND WALLACE, C. (1997) *An Introduction to Sociology: Feminist Perspectives,* Routledge.

GREER, G. (1971) *The Female Eunuch*, Paladin, London.

GREER, G. (2000) *The Whole Woman*, Anchor Books.

Further Reading

GIDDENS, A. ET AL. (EDS.) (1994) *The Polity Reader in Gender Studies,* Polity Press, Cambridge.

GOLDBERG, S. (1977) *The Inevitability of Patriarchy*, Temple Smith, London – a very different and, from a feminist point of view, controversial account.

POLLERT, A. (1996) The Poverty of Patriarchy, *Sociology*, 30 (4).

WALBY, S. (1997) *Gender Transformations*, Routledge.

Phenomenology

Husserl and Schutz

The Idea

P HENOMENOLOGY IS A PHILOSOPHICAL THEORY DEVELOPED BY THE GERMAN PHILOSO-
pher, Edmund Husserl (1859–1938) and his 'disciple' Alfred Schutz (1889–1959),
an Austro-American businessman and social philosopher who, in combining Husserl's
ideas with those of G.H. Mead (see p. 195), developed phenomenology as a leading
school of 'interpretative' sociology in the late 1960s and 1970s. During this period,
phenomenology became the major challenge to positivism (see p. 56) and the idea of
sociology as a science.

The word 'phenomenon' has two meanings. It is an object
of perception, something we see, feel or perceive through
our senses. Secondly, however, a phenomenon is
something 'extra'-ordinary, something out of the normal
which we cannot yet explain or understand – a spiritual
force, an ESP, a UFO.

The first definition is the scientific everyday one based on
the assumption that the world around us actually exists
and has a reality of its own that we perceive objectively,
through our senses. The second definition is the 'interpretative' view; that far from the physical world having a
reality of its own, we, through our senses, make sense of

Edmund Husserl

it and so in a sense recreate it according to our own interpretation. There is, for
example, according to phenomenology, no such thing as a chair or a table, or even a
mountain or a tree. They are all names or labels we have given to man-made or nature-
made objects to make sense of them. Phenomenology therefore takes the philosophical
view that the physical world is not a 'real' world that never changes and is the same
to all people. Rather it is a 'relative' world dependent for its existence on human
interpretation and the meaning we give to it. Consider, for example, all the rich and

varied meanings we give to a building or a house – as a towerblock or a royal palace, as a bungalow or a family home – when in reality they are all no more than a box of bricks.

Phenomenologists see the 'social' world in even more relative terms than the physical world. While objects in the physical world do physically exist, 'objects' in the social world do not. Concepts like crime, love and family are entirely human creations, entirely dependent on human perception, interpretation and meaning for their existence. There is, for example, no such thing as a crime; it all depends on human interpretation of a particular act in a particular situation (e.g. killing someone may be self-defence, an accident or heroism as well as murder). All human knowledge is, therefore, relative. Equally, society is not a thing out there with an existence of its own as portrayed in positivist analyses but is something we create and recreate in our everyday lives through our routines, interaction and the common assumptions we share with others. The key to such interpretation and communication is language and we learn our particular societies' common assumptions about life through social-isation. The social world is a world known in common with others through lived experience.

Phenomenology, therefore, is the study of human consciousness and the way people make sense of the world around them. Edmund Husserl's aim was to go 'back to basics' and to discover the very essence of man's 'Life World'. Alfred Schutz sought to apply such ideas to the study of society and in particular to analyse how, if our social world is so relative, so fluid, it all holds together on a daily basis. How does society keep going if it is all down to interpretation, if it is all in the mind? Here Schutz identified three key elements in everyday social order:

- common sense – a common stock of knowledge about how to interpret and act in our own particular society or social group;
- typifications – common ways of classifying objects (house, man) and experiences (hate, nightmare) which build up into 'stocks of knowledge';
- reciprocity – common assumptions that others see the world in the same way that we do.

All three elements of this intersubjectivity create the apparent order of everyday life. It is a shared world, a common sense world. We learn such common sense through social-isation and language, and we adapt, alter our perception of it, as and when necessary. Social order for phenomenologists is thus a 'negotiated' order, a practical framework forming the basis of most people's 'life world' as they seek to go about their daily lives and work. We all have our own individual backgrounds, interests and motiva-tions, our own view of ourselves and the world, but we can only execute them, only live as human beings, by working together, using common meanings and assumptions. When such common assumptions break down, when this underlying consensus collapses, then social confusion and disorder arise, either on a very limited scale as, for example, when you misinterpret what someone said or did, or on a massive scale when, say, the value of money is no longer commonly agreed (e.g. hyperinflation in Germany in the 1930s).

Schutz's view of the social world was, therefore, a highly interpretative one in which social order was a negotiated reality based on common assumptions and inter-pretations.

The role of the social scientist is that of understanding it in its essence. To do this he must suspend or 'bracket off' his own attitudes, taking nothing for granted but trying to see the world, or a particular social situation, as those involved in it do, because it is they (and their assumptions/interpretations) who are creating it. The researcher must, on the one hand, withdraw from the social world in order to study it objectively and without preconceptions, and yet use his own human consciousness, understanding, and even intuition to make sense of the world as other humans see it. He must, in a sense, act like a stranger, someone coming from outside, anxious to understand how people in society act, feel and see, so that he too can participate fully within their world. Consider, for example, what it is like to go and live in a foreign country where you not only do not understand the language, but have to 'make sense' of some apparently strange customs and ways of living. In such a situation you have to almost 'suspend' your normal ways of thinking and acting in order to properly learn a new way of life. The phenomenological researcher is as concerned with people's motives, feelings and imagination, with all forms of sense perception, as he is with actual behaviour and action, if he is to understand not only how people behave, but why. The subjective elements of human behaviour and social life are as important, if not more important, than the 'objective facts'. Open-mindedness, seeing before thinking, are crucial to phenomenological research if all phenomena, all assumptions in and about the social world are to be revealed and understood in their essence.

Schutz sought to uncover and to understand the underlying assumptions that underpin everyday life, the 'typifications' by which people organise their lifestyles, routines and construct common-sense knowledge as the basis of communicating with and living with others. People operate in and make sense of the world about them on the basis of a general presumption of a common world. They assume that others see and interpret the everyday world in the same way as they do and so there is a 'reciprocity of perspective', a 'natural attitude' that underpins and holds together social order and intersubjectivity. The role of the researcher, argued Schutz, is not to study life objectively and externally by devising abstract concepts and scientific theories remote from life itself, but to go out into the world and see it as its members do. The social world is not a thing with a life of its own 'out there' but a living ever-changing social experience created and re-created daily by its members living active and informed lives on the basis of common understandings and relationships. It is 'a Lifeworld', an everyday world of experience and culture. The meaning of life is the meaning its members give it as they consciously and actively live it, day in, day out.

The focal point for phenomenology, therefore, is everyday life, the normality that traditional sociologies tended to take for granted in studying the more unusual or abnormal and exciting aspects of life. Whirling and swirling though the social world may be, it is stable and it does have an underlying structure built around a stock of common-sense knowledge, a practical understanding of how the world works and how people relate that is communicated through language, culture and constantly reinterpreted shared meanings.

'We' are our own world. Our everyday world is not something out there, isolated and separated from us, even though at times it may feel like that. The social world is our world, our relationships, our actions and our understandings that make the social world the world it is. It is not, however, a single and common reality but what Schutz called a community of 'multiple realities' based on a common culture that binds them together and forms the basis of social order. There is in Husserl's theory a common social consciousness. So even though children, women, farmers and the old perceive the world differently and may live in very different realities, lifestyles or subcultures, there are common perceptions and common cultural features in social life that bind them together as a community, nation or species. We each live in our own world but we share that world – and many others – with other people daily and through our consciousness and empathy we are equally able to conceive of the world as they see it (intersubjectivity). Such understandings are not always correct nor harmonious; people misunderstand, misconstrue and make mistakes in their relationships with others. Nevertheless they are able to recognise and repair such misunderstandings and misconceptions and to so restore order and harmony. *'The life world is neither my private world nor your private world, nor is it my world and your world added together, but the world of our common experience'* (Schutz and Luckman 1979).

Schutz used the example of strangers meeting for the first time and subsequently to illustrate the way in which people seek to establish a common understanding upon which they can build a relationship for future communication. Given his own background, having to flee from the Nazis in Austria and living in involuntary exile in the USA, Schutz was acutely aware of the difficulties of intercultural communication and how difficult it often is to establish common understandings, even when speaking a common language; and how easy it is to misunderstand and so create conflict rather than consensus. Our everyday knowledge is therefore never fixed. It is constantly in flux, requiring re-interpretation and recreation and repair as we actively and consciously live life to the full. Life has to be worked at; it never stands still. Relationships are fragile and ever changing; they need constant nurturing and repair.

As Alfred Schutz points out there are different forms of rationality in the lifeworld; the most basic is its commonality, the common commitment to society and to a social life without which we would all live like hermits and there would be no society.

The Idea in Action

PHENOMENOLOGICAL SOCIOLOGY HAS HAD A MAJOR INFLUENCE ON MAINSTREAM sociology since the 1960s, offering a major challenge to scientific sociology and to positivism. However, rather than developing a sociological school of its own, it has spawned a variety of 'interpretative' approaches such as ethnomethodology and symbolic interactionism, and stimulated interpretative and subjective elements within such existing 'sociologies' as Marxism (e.g. Habermas's interpretation of critical theory). The works of Berger and Luckman in particular reflect a deliberate attempt to maintain and develop the concepts and insights of Husserl and Schutz.

Phenomenology challenged 'scientific' sociology on two key fronts:

- its view of man and society;
- its method of research.

Positivist or scientific sociology tends to portray society as similar to the natural world, as something above and beyond the individual, something with a reality of its own, a world in which the individual is something of a puppet, his behaviour determined largely by external forces. Positivism, therefore, argues that the scientific methods of the natural sciences are as appropriate to understanding the social world as the physical one, since both are essentially of the same nature and governed by similar forces of cause and effect, from which can be discovered laws of nature capable of sustaining predictions about future behaviour. Phenomenologists utterly reject such an analysis. In their view, man is a conscious being, free, independent and rational, capable of constructing and controlling his social world. Man's actions are not externally determined or programmed, but purposeful and motivated. Man is not a puppet.

'Human beings are not merely acted upon by social fact or social forces ... they are constantly shaping and creating their own social worlds in interaction with others [so] special methods are required for the study and understanding of these uniquely human processes' (Morris 1977).

Thus phenomenologists equally reject scientific method, whatever its claims to objectivity, as totally inappropriate to understanding society or a social situation from within, in terms of the meanings and interpretations of the social factors involved. The sociologist should ideally *involve*, not detach, himself in order to perceive the social world, its underlying assumptions, culture and typifications as others do. Hence phenomenologists' preference for techniques like participant observation and qualitative research. They equally reject the positivist claim to objectivity as a philosophical impossibility. In their view no human being can totally suspend his or her own cultural assumptions and frameworks of thought without producing a distorted and humanless version of reality. By such an approach the social scientist merely imposes his interpretation on a situation, ignoring the views and motives of those involved. Similarly, social facts such as crime or marriage cannot exist, or be studied, as independent things with a reality of their own, but only as social constructs created by human beings to make sense of the world. Phenomenology has put the subjective elements to the forefront of social analysis in the same way that positivism sought to insist on objectivity as the key to discovering the truth about the social world.

Inevitably, phenomenology itself has been attacked and criticised, not least by scientific sociology.

- Its concepts and language such as 'essences' and 'being in itself', are somewhat exotic for Anglo-Saxon tastes, hence the slow acceptance of its ideas in Britain and America.

- It can be both exciting and tedious – exciting to move from abstract theories to real life, from grand concepts to common sense, but then such analysis can become quite technical, even boring. Conversations, as we all know, can be extremely stimulating, until someone starts analysing your every word and what you 'really' meant.

- Its research projects have tended to be small-scale, concerned primarily with small group activity and interaction, and so lack the sweeping power of grand theory and its attempt to analyse the whole of society.

- It has been criticised as highly unscientific, as being little more than the subjective interpretation of individual sociologists studying a particular social situation. The results of such studies have no basis for generalising beyond that particular study, offer no basis for constructing laws about society and human behaviour.

- There is an inherent contradiction in the phenomenological mode of study, that not only must the observer highlight and explain the feelings and assumptions of his subjects, but his own, as the study progresses, so that the reader can fully understand the layers of interpretation involved in a particular situation. Not only may this process become an *ad infinitum* one, which can become quite futile, but it means that ultimately no-one can offer an objective and superior analysis, free of assumptions. If all analysis is no more than interpretation and no interpretation is superior to any other, then why do sociology?

Phenomenologists have replied to such criticisms by claiming that what their research projects might lack in objectivity, they make up for in terms of validity and quality by being highly accurate and detailed accounts of what really happens in given social situations. It is this emphasis on qualitative research, on insight and subjective factors, which has distinguished phenomenological theory and method from more 'scientific' approaches. Phenomenology has had a major impact on modern sociology. It has offered a real alternative to scientific and structural perspectives. Even today its theory and its method continues to inform and stimulate sociological debate.

 See Also

- ETHNOMETHODOLOGY (p. 104) and SYMBOLIC INTERACTIONISM (p. 195) as offshoots of phenomenology.
- POSITIVISM (p. 56) and STRUCTURAL FUNCTIONALISM (p. 190) as alternative approaches to sociological analysis and practice.
- STRUCTURATION (p. 271) as a 'late modern' attempt to integrate structure and action.
- POST-MODERNISM (p. 245) as a post-modern perspective on society and the individual.

Suggested Reading

PIVCEVIC, E. (1970) *Husserl and Phenomenology*, Hutchinson, London.

Further Reading

SCHUTZ, A. (1972) *The Phenomenology of the Social World*, Heinemann, London.

Power Elite

C.W. Mills

The Idea

THE STUDY OF POWER ELITES HAS BEEN A KEY TOPIC OF ANALYSIS THROUGHOUT THE
history of political sociology. It dates back to Plato and Aristotle, the great Greek
philosophers, and it has been the focal point of political theorists ever since from
Mosca to Pareto through to Robert Michels and Karl Marx. What was unusual about
C. Wright Mills' version of this key idea was that he analysed elite power in terms of
institutions rather than individuals and he identified and analysed the existence of a
power elite in *America*, the very home of democracy in the twentieth century and the
champion of life, liberty and the pursuit of happiness against the evil forces of communism in the Cold War of the 1950s and 60s. To claim that the home of the Statue of
Liberty was being run by an unaccountable political elite was not only radical but in
the post-war period of McCarthyism, positively dangerous.

A radical by nature and in spirit, C. Wright Mills not only criticised the American
Establishment but challenged the very democracy it was supposed to be leading. In his
book *The Power Elite* (1956), C. Wright Mills sought to show that America was not
ruled by the people but a power elite comprising three key institutions – the major
corporations, the military and the federal government. Moreover he argued that
though these three elites appeared to be separate, they do in fact constitute a single
and unified elite, a single and unified elite that governs America in its own interests
and without any real accountability to the electorate. The basis of these elites' unity is,
in his analysis, their 'institutional proximity' and their interdependence. The politicians
need the military to defend the country; the military need the politicians to fund their
military budgets and the major corporations need to make huge profits by supplying
military technology and new weapons. Such is the size of the American military budget
that the arms industry is one of the key components of the modern American economy;
a big business in itself that in the 1950s and 60s was escalating at an alarming rate as
America embarked on a 'Cold War' with Soviet Russia. These three elites, argued Mills,
not only needed each other to 'stay in business' but they came from similar social and

educational backgrounds, married into each other's families and moved around within each other's social circles and top jobs. It is not unusual for a top businessman to enter a presidential cabinet or for a top general such as Dwight Eisenhower to become president. George W. Bush, the current American president, has a business and legal background; his father was a president before him and his Secretary of State, Colin Powell, was a leading general in the Gulf War.

The fact that America was led – or is being led – by a power elite is not necessarily undemocratic provided it is accountable to the electorate in some way and it uses its power in the interests of the American people, rather than to preserve its own powers and privilege. In Mills' view, however, this military-industrial-political complex is not only unaccountable, it is autocratic and self-serving. Modern America in his view is 'government of the Power Elite, by the Power Elite, for the Power Elite'. It serves the interests of American capitalism and its major corporations while the masses are generally excluded from power and offered a sham of a democracy. The two major parties in America, the Republicans and the Democrats, offer no real political alternative and the mass of the population are seduced by consumerism and alienated from politics. Hence the low turnout even in presidential elections. Such a concentration of power had resulted, Mills argued, from the oligarchic tendencies of American capitalism destroying small businesses and creating giant corporations; from the growth of federal government and bureaucracy in post-war America and in particular from the Arms Race that followed World War II. For Mills the dropping of the atom bomb on Hiroshima showed both the enormity of elite power in America and its total unaccountability. The mass of Americans could, in his view, only look on in awe. They could do nothing about this decision except carry on with their daily business.

The concept of America being ruled by a power elite just as powerful, unaccountable and dictatorial as any she was fighting abroad was depressing enough, but then Mills went on to propose, in *The Causes of World War III* (1958), that the power elites in America and the Soviet Union not only had some sense of common interest, even some sense of common community, but that they might actually constitute some form of international power elite with a common ambition to rule the world whatever their ideological differences.

However ambitious and radical his analysis, C. Wright Mills' ultimate aim was to expose decision making and decision makers in America, make the citizens of America more aware of their 'ruler's' powers and incite public opinion to at least check such institutional power and to put the national interest at the forefront of political decision making rather than the self-interests of the power elite.

The Idea in Action

WHILE SUCH A DESCRIPTION OF MASS CONTROL FITTED THE AMERICAN PEOPLE'S image of Stalin's Russia, it was a devastating view of their own society and inevitably inspired a massive counter-attack. At an intellectual level critics argued that Mills' idea was purely circumstantial. There was no proof that such an elite existed, nor that it ruled America in its own interest. At a personal level Mills was portrayed as an academic maverick and an apologist for Marxism and communism. He had simply revealed the existence of elites at the top of American society, shown that they had the potential for mass manipulation but he had produced no proof that they had conspired together against the American people, no evidence that they had ruled in the strongest sense of the word. Only an examination of key decision-making could substantiate such a claim. So began what has come to be known as the 'pluralist–elitist debate', a debate over the distribution of power in advanced industrial democracies.

While pluralists like Robert Dahl (1961) and Arnold Rose (1967) in America and Chris Hewitt (1974) in Britain claimed that their analyses of decision-making at the local and national level revealed not a centralised structure of power but a highly fragmented, diverse and competitive one, elitists moved on from analysing the common backgrounds and values of top decision-makers to highlighting 'non-decision making', the idea put forward by Barach and Baratz (1962) that key decisions are not made (and certainly not debated) in public or in the political arena of Congress or Parliament but are made behind closed doors or simply never raised. Issues such as inequality, racism and nuclear weapons are so much a part of modern capitalism that the establishment takes them for granted and, through its control of the media, excludes debate or criticism.

One attempt to actually identify the American power elite, to name names, was that by Thomas R. Dye in 1979. He actually identified 5,416 individuals involved in controlling America's key institutions and resources, highlighted the power of such key families as the Rockefellers and Kennedys, their common background and outlook, the exclusion from elite power of women and blacks, and the way that political controversy is primarily over means not ends, over how to preserve American capitalism, not over how to change it. The political agenda is set even before debate begins. However, Dye also found evidence of social mobility into such elite circles, conflict between the various elites as well as consensus, and some limited influence on key decisions by the mass of the American people. Thus Dye concluded that the power elite is neither as coherent as Mills portrayed it nor as competitive as pluralists believe but rather an oligarchy requiring further examination. Elite research elsewhere has come to similar conclusions. Research in Britain, for example, by Butler and Kavanagh (1997) and by John Scott (1991) has shown that even today those from elite social and educational backgrounds have a power and pre-eminence in British government and politics well beyond their numbers or representativeness. However, as Jean Blondel concluded, such studies have yet to prove that elites rule in the 'strongest sense of the word'; that they rule purely in their own interests and not those of the country at large.

Therefore, as yet, Mills' idea has been neither proved nor disproved but, as he hoped, it has inspired a major debate throughout the Western world about the nature and distribution of power in modern society, a debate between pluralists and elitists, between liberals and Marxists about democracy today and in the future. It equally awakened the American people to the dangers in their midst of elitism and dominance. The land of the free, warned Mills, is not as free as it thinks it is. Act now and keep elitism in check. C. Wright Mills' legacy, therefore, was a public one as well as an academic one, a sociological contribution to the public 'imagination' and to the American system of checks and balances as well as a significant contribution to the academic study of elite theory.

 **See Also**

- **THE IRON LAW OF OLIGARCHY** (p. 52), **LEGITIMATION CRISIS** (p. 225) and **RELATIVE AUTONOMY** (p. 250) as alternative and complementary theories of the structure of power in the modern state.
- **DISCOURSE** (p. 208) as a post-structuralist perspective on power today.

Suggested Reading

ELDRIDGE, J.C. (1983) *C. Wright Mills,* Tavistock, London – a short readable overview of Mills' life and times.

MILLS, C.W. (1956) *The Power Elite,* Oxford University Press, Oxford – though dated, still worth reading.

Further Reading

BOTTOMORE, T. AND BRYM, R. (EDS.) (1989) *The Capitalist Class,* Wheatsheaf Press – an update on the pluralist–elitist debate.

DYE, T.R. (1979) *Who's Running America?,* Prentice Hall, Englewood Cliffs, NJ.

Scientific Management

F. W. Taylor

THE IDEA OF SCIENTIFIC MANAGEMENT ORIGINATES FROM THE WRITINGS AND industrial experiments of Frederick Winslow Taylor whose ideas on industrial and organisational efficiency informed and inspired a generation of factory owners and management theorists at the beginning of the twentieth century. Having worked himself as an apprentice, gang boss and chief engineer at the Midvale Steel Company, Taylor developed a whole range of ideas for a more scientific approach to organisational efficiency, which he put into practice in 'Johnstown', the first scientifically managed factory in America and which he developed in his subsequent lectures and publications, most notably his major work, *Principles of Scientific Management* (1911). A highly controversial figure, Frederick Taylor died in 1915, regarded by many alongside Henry Ford and Herbert Hoover as one of the trinity of early twentieth-century technician-philosophers.

Scientific management grew out of a particular period in America's industrial development. By the turn of the century, industrialisation was spreading in America with major advances in mass production techniques and the emergence of big business corporations and even multinationals. However, the organisation of production tasks *within* the workplace and factory was still very traditional and haphazard, with workers having considerable freedom to decide on their routines and speed of work. Such key decisions as hiring and firing were still left to individual foremen. The result was gross inefficiency and considerable unrest.

Taylor's objective, therefore, was to introduce a 'managerial revolution', a revolution of management and planning to match the technical advances of modern production, a revolution to break the power of the foreman. The basis of this revolution was to be:

- the fragmentation of work into simple, routine operations;
- the standardisation of each operation to eliminate 'idle time';

- the separation of conception from execution, of planning from operation, of management from worker.

His final system, as laid out in *The Principles of Scientific Management* (1911) can be summarised as follows.

Organisational

AT the shop floor level changes based on the 'scientific' analysis of every single task to maximise efficiency and production were introduced; what we today might call 'time and motion studies'. Experiments and stop-watch studies were conducted in the minutest detail to find the most efficient tools, ways of doing a task, rest periods and groupings of workers. One Dutch worker called Schmidt, for example, was used to analyse such basic tasks as digging a hole or shovelling pig-iron, to find the most efficient way of holding and swinging a spade, the best size of spade head and so on. Work tasks were simplified, workers 'scientifically' selected for the job they were best suited to and trained to perform the task exactly as specified in written instructions from the management. The quantity and quality of work produced was continually checked by a system of 'systematic supervision' and discipline maintained by 'functional foremanship'.

At managerial level, too, the division of labour became more specialised and decision-making more centralised. Control of both the work process and the workforce fell to management. They now had to plan production, hire and fire and co-ordinate the now-fragmented production line. Innovations here included standardising tool rooms and methods, a new accounting system and, in particular, the establishment of a separate planning department.

Motivational

TAYLOR assumed that men's prime motive for work was money and so, to maximise productivity and quality and to overcome worker resistance to his methods, he experimented with various incentive schemes, especially differential piecework (payment according to the amount of work done).

Ideological

HE believed that his methods would so increase industrial productivity and therefore profits and wages that workers and management would learn to collaborate for their mutual benefit, recognise the justice of his system of determining a fair wage and so an 'ideological' revolution would occur whereby the two sides of industry would learn co-operation instead of conflict. He therefore saw little need for collective bargaining or personnel work.

The Idea in Action

F.W. TAYLOR'S RATIONALISATION OF INDUSTRIAL ORGANISATION BECAME THE PHILO-sophical basis of the scientific management movement that swept through factories in America and Europe in the 1900s. It influenced the assembly-line production methods pioneered by Henry Ford and was acclaimed even by Lenin as the means of creating the abundance of goods necessary for a socialist society. Though only a few industrialists introduced his system wholesale, ideas like time and motion studies permeated the whole of industrial organisation and gave management the 'scientific' justification they needed for reasserting their control over the production process. In David Nelson's view (1980) he helped *'transform industrial management and to a lesser degree, industrial society between the 1870s and World War I'*.

However, Taylor's system was also the subject of extensive and often bitter criticism on two main levels:

1. His assumptions that money is men's prime motive for work and that workers act primarily as individuals were severely undermined by the famous Hawthorne experiments of Elton Mayo in the 1920s (see p. 127). The studies were, ironically, designed initially to improve productivity by introducing scientific management methods into a Chicago factory. They ended up showing that workers responded best when given some managerial 'attention' and that the key influence on a worker's output was not money but his workgroup and his fear of being ostracised by them. These findings laid the basis for the Human Relations School of Management which stressed workers' social as well as economic needs, the impor- tance of the workgroup, of good industrial relations and communication. It intro- duced such ideas as personnel management, job enrichment schemes and worker participation – industrial management with a 'human' touch.

2. His belief that such methods would increase industrial harmony has been severely challenged by the American Marxist Harry Braverman (1974, see p. 98) who argues that, far from enriching the work experience, the techniques of scientific management have deskilled, degraded and dehumanised the modern worker, shorn him of his skills, knowledge and autonomy and reduced him to the level of 'cogs and levers', a mere extension of the machine. In Braverman's view the key feature of such a system (and the chief attraction for employers) is not the increased productivity but the increase in managerial control brought about by the separation of mental from manual work, management from workers and, especially, conception from execution. Management is now a specialised skill with total control of the work process because it has extracted from the workers all knowledge about the work process. Therefore the ordinary factory worker now needs few skills, can be continually checked on and easily replaced. He is left skill- less and powerless. As the techniques of scientific management have spread into all forms of work, into offices, shops and the like, so, argues Braverman, the working class generally has become more open to intense supervision, exploita- tion and replacement by machinery. Scientific management has thus become a means of class control, a crucial weapon in the management of a capitalist society, 'masquerading in the trappings of science'. Scientific management has therefore been described as an ideological tool, a means for legitimising management control and for controlling workers through deskilling and the ultimate threat of replacing men with machines.

Thus scientific management has become a key idea in the sociology of work as well as the management of business. It is still the subject of passionate debate on such diverse issues as alienation and class control. However, in practice the principles of scientific management were rarely fully implemented. The theory was more a reflection of work practices in America than in British and European factories. Modern industrial practices have modified, if not abandoned, many of Taylor's essential principles as illustrated in the chapter on Post-Fordism (see p. 234).

 **See Also**

- **HUMAN RELATIONS THEORY** (p. 127), **DESKILLING** (p. 98) and **POST-FORDISM** (p. 234) as contemporary and modern contributions to the ongoing debates on industrial relations today.

Suggested Reading

NELSON, D. (1980) *F.W. Taylor and the Rise of Scientific Management*, University of Wisconsin Press, Madison, WI.

Further Reading

BRAVERMAN, H. (1974) *Labor and Monopoly Capital,* Monthly Review Press, New York.

Secularisation

Bryan Wilson

THE IDEA OF SECULARISATION IS NOT A NEW ONE. IT HAS ITS FOUNDATIONS IN CLASSICAL sociological thinking, most notably in the works of Auguste Comte and Emile Durkheim and the theories of social development proposed by Karl Marx and Max Weber. Writing in the 1960s, however, Bryan Wilson – a British academic – reignited this debate with the publication of his book *Religion in a Secular Society* (1966) and his claims that as Britain and other Western societies were entering the 'age of affluence' and the 'swinging sixties', so religion was losing its significance and in danger of becoming extinct in modern society.

Wilson defined secularisation as '*the process whereby religious thinking, practice and institutions lose social significance*'. The secularisation thesis is based on the theory that as societies industrialise, become more rational, scientific and specialist, so traditional values, beliefs and practices decline. Industrial societies no longer need religion to explain the meaning of life; they have science and logic, rationality and bureaucracy. God and the Church are no longer the centrepiece of society's values and lifestyle. Traditional ways of thinking are an obstacle, not an aid to solving modern social problems. Religion no longer has a purpose in a modern industrial and affluent society.

The secularisation thesis rests on five main arguments:

- That there has been a decline in religious practice and participation in advanced industrial societies. This form of decline is mainly measured in terms of statistics of church attendance and membership. For example, in Britain today only about one-sixth of the adult population belong to a Christian church and only about 10–15 per cent regularly attend church on Sundays. The 1998/99 UK Christian Handbook Survey of church attendance showed an ongoing decline in all aspects of church membership, attendance and ceremonial use, particularly among Christian denominations. Church attendance, for example, has apparently fallen from 10.2 per cent in 1980 to 8.1 per cent in 1995 and the survey estimates further falls by the year 2000 to 7.7 per cent.

- That there has been a decline in religious belief. As Wilson argues, *'religious thinking is perhaps the area which evidences most conspicuous change. Men act less and less in response to religious motivation: they assess the world in empirical and rational terms'*. Such rationalism has developed from the Protestant ethic, the growth of large-scale rational organisations, the growth of scientific knowledge based on reason, and the rise of rational ideologies, all of which offer practical solutions and appeal to logic rather than to faith and rewards in the afterlife.

- That there has been a decline in the church's status and functions as a major social and political institution. Compared to its dominant role in mediaeval Europe, the church in Western society has undergone a process of 'disengagement'. Many of the church's traditional functions have been replaced by secular organisations. Science now explains the inexplicable and has even given man control not only over nature but over the creation of life itself with the advent of test-tube babies and genetic engineering. The welfare state now cares for those in need and educates our children while the mass media preaches the new gospel of materialism and progress. Although Cardinal Wolsey governed the England of Henry VIII, the present Archbishop of Canterbury has little say in affairs of state.

- That there has been a process of 'secularisation' within the church. To survive in modern society and retain their congregations in the face of alternative competition churches today have both simplified and modernised their services. The Catholic Church, for example, now has the Mass in English rather than Latin and even involves women in its sacred rituals. Similarly some denominations are merging. As Wilson comments, *'organisations amalgamate when they are weak rather than when they are strong'*.

- That the growth in number of religious sects is further evidence of the fragmentation of religion, of the decline in power and influence of a single all-powerful church. So, instead of religion reinforcing social consensus and common values, it reflects the plurality of beliefs and truths in modern society. In Wilson's view sects are *'a feature of societies experiencing secularisation and they may be seen as a response to a situation in which religious values have lost social pre-eminence'*. For him the new religious movements of the 1960s and 1970s are irrelevant, catering merely for a few dropouts and contributing nothing to the moral regeneration and unity of modern society.

Thus by drawing heavily on Max Weber's thesis that as societies industrialise so they inevitably adopt a more rational and logical way of thinking and organising and traditional sources of authority such as religion are simply swept aside, Wilson hoped to explain the apparent process of decline of religion in modern society.

The Idea in Action

THE SECULARISATION THESIS HAS GAINED WIDESPREAD SUPPORT AND STIMULATED A lot of development from a variety of writers including Berger and Luckman (1969) and Will Herberg (1960). It has had a profound influence on both sociological theory and the sociology of religion and seemed to offer a major explanation for the fundamental shift in attitudes and values in Western societies compared to the still highly religious societies of the Third World. Such ideas even influenced the attempts by organised religions to recapture people's hearts and souls by more modern methods, be it 'singalong Masses' or TV religion.

However, the thesis itself and its five key arguments have also been fundamentally challenged.

First, the statistics on church attendance used by Wilson and others have been shown to be both unreliable and possibly invalid. Statistics on religious participation are notoriously unreliable and difficult to handle. They use different definitions and methods of collection and analysis. They can therefore provide equally strong evidence for and against secularisation. Not only are such facts and figures only sporadically collected (and usually by the churches themselves) but they do not necessarily indicate a lack of faith. It is quite possible to believe in God and be personally quite religious without joining an organised religion. While some religions insist on regular attendance, others do not. Similarly, attendance at church does not necessarily indicate strong religious views. Many people attend out of fear, habit or, in the case of births, marriages and funerals, for social reasons. Surveys have shown that 90 per cent of people believe in God and 60 per cent claim membership of the Church of England. Surveys on religious belief are equally vulnerable to criticism and reassessment. The 1995 British Social Attitudes Survey shows an ongoing decline in people's belief in God and Steve Bruce's (1995) analysis of earlier surveys shows a similar decline in beliefs in sin, the devil and eternal damnation. Peter Brierley (1991) in contrast has noted that while religious participation has declined, there is evidence that people still cling, however irrationally, to some form or some elements of religious or spiritual belief. Wilson himself has agreed that there is *'no adequate way of testing the strength of religious commitment'*.

Secondly, though the church today performs fewer social functions and is a more specifically religious body, this trend is only in keeping with a general movement to specialisation within all organisations in advanced industrial societies. Christian ethics still underlie the social values of most Western societies; and even in Britain, one of the most apparently secular of countries, the Queen is still Head of the Church of England, Bishops still sit in the House of Lords, 80 per cent of the people of Northern Ireland are devout Protestants or Catholics and people still come to church for the key *rites de passage* of births, deaths and marriages. In other Western societies – France, Italy and especially Eire – organised religion is still more powerful, having considerable influence over the national government. Similarly it has become a focal point of national unity and identity when countries are faced by an internal crisis or an external threat, as in Northern Ireland, Poland and Iran. The notion of disengagement, of the Church or churches losing their influence over society and the state, is thus controversial. While David Martin (1969) identified high levels of disengagement in Western societies today compared to the Middle Ages, Steve Bruce (1995) has equally pointed out that such distancing has enabled churches, notably the Church of England, to be more critical of modern lifestyles and even of the British Government in such diverse and controversial areas as nuclear power and urban poverty.

The influence of the Church may therefore not have declined but simply become more specialised, more focused on values and ethics and less on economic and political matters now considered the responsibility of the state. Writers such as José Casanova (1994) have gone further, arguing that while in the 1960s and 70s religion may have retreated into the private sphere of personal beliefs and convictions, in the 1980s the churches re-entered the public arena with a vengeance and contributed significantly to major debates in Western – and Eastern – societies on abortion, Northern Ireland, the Middle East and the collapse of communism. Rather than declining, argue Bruce and Casanova, religion has become differentiated, separated and free from the secular arena now occupied by the state. The revival of the New Right in America, of funda-mentalist Protestant 'churches' and their ability to influence American politics is yet another example.

Thirdly, the growth of religious sects may be a fragmentary process but it nevertheless also reflects a revived search for truth and meaning in a highly materialistic society. It may simply reflect a turning away from traditional religions rather than a rejection of God. Thus, for example, while membership of the major religions in Britain has continued to decline, breakaway movements like the House Church Movement have grown spectacularly and there are now well over one million members of such non-Christian groups as Muslims, Hindus and Jews in the UK. Evangelical movements and sects like the Mormons have swept modern America into a religious ferment and now have considerable political influence as part of the New Right majority. Critics, however, see much of this revival as simply an expression of love of America rather than faith in God, packaged and sold to the American public like any other commer-cial product with little real religious meaning. The original secularisation thesis implied the decline of one central church, one commonly acknowledged faith, be it Protestantism in Great Britain or Catholicism in Italy and Spain. While this form of decline may well have occurred, modern writers have noted the growth of religious pluralism, the growth of a wide variety of faiths, cults and churches for people to choose from in modern societies. Roof and McKinnay (1987) found this to be particu-larly true in the USA where religious choices seem to be part of the consumer mentality with 'churches' and sects even having their own television channels.

In turn, writers like George Chryssides (1994) have noted that while ethnic minorities in modern societies such as Britain have adapted their religious practices to accom-modate the host culture, they have not lost their faith or involvement, but have often used it as a source of strength and support when settling in.

Fourthly, the whole underlying argument of secularisation rests on the idea of a decline from some golden age of religion in the past. However, historians have shown that even in the Victorian period religion was not as strong as it appeared. While the middle classes may have seemed very puritanical and devout, the 1851 census showed only 40 per cent of the adult population regularly attended church. Possibly there has been no real decline; we simply never were a very religious society and so neither industri-alisation nor rationalisation caused its decline. While the general trend to secularisa-tion may be evident, as David Martin (1978) has argued, it is highly variable and not necessarily inevitable. His comparison of the USA, Britain and Sweden shows signifi-cant variations in the impact and extent of secularisation and this variation is evident elsewhere in the modern and modernising world. Even in countries as advanced as France, Italy and Spain, the Catholic Church remains a powerful force while in more pluralistic societies such as the Netherlands and Germany, Protestant and Catholic churches are still influential. In Third World countries, religions have experienced a widely contrasting fate as these societies sought to develop and modernise; in some, such as Tunisia and Egypt, religious faith has declined; in others, the religious leaders, such as those in Iran, have dominated political change and used moral and religious fervour to control and channel economic development to ensure that Western values do not contaminate Islamic beliefs. Secularisation in Martin's (1991) view is neither automatic nor universal.

The key problem with the secularisation thesis is that of adequately defining the term religion and finding a precise enough way of measuring religiosity – the strength of people's belief. Though writers like Glock and Stark (1965) have attempted to do this, it is almost an impossible task because belief is such a subjective concept. Moreover, even if a common definition could be agreed, be it on the basis of organised religion or religious beliefs, the inverse relationship with modernity would need to be measured and calculated and the term modern society itself defined. How modern, for example, is America compared to Africa and is religiosity in the USA proportionately smaller in significance and power than in South Africa or Uganda?

Thus, the very term 'secularisation' is so vague and ill-defined that it is open to a wide variety of interpretations, some of which simply reflect a particular writer's own biases and opinions. David Martin (1969) has therefore argued for the removal of this term from the sociological dictionary. In many ways those involved in the secularisation debate often seem to be talking about different things and while it may well be argued that *organised* religion has declined, *individual* belief and need for spiritual meaning seem as strong as ever. Advocates of post-modernism, for example, argue that as science and rationality lose their appeal and fail to deliver, people will begin to look again to the irrational and the spiritual. Religion – organised and cult-like – will enjoy a revival and a rejuvenation. Gilles Kepel (1994), for example, identifies the resurgence of major religious faiths in modern societies – Islam, Christianity and Judaism – as a reaction against the anonymous and impersonal nature of modern society. And even in America, that most modern and capitalist of societies, religious participation seems to hold steady at around 40 per cent.

Whatever conclusions this debate eventually reaches, Bryan Wilson's idea has helped stimulate one of the key debates in the sociology of religion of the past 30 years. The secularisation thesis has been neither proved nor disproved. Even today, 30 or more years after Wilson outlined his version of this theory, it still enjoys and stimulates debate and research. It has become more focused and analytical, looking at different experiences in different societies, particularly those experiencing religious revivals, nationalist movements or those where religious values have been used to counter the loss of community or ethical values often associated with modernisation and the consumerism of Western technology and business methods. The influence and significance of religion, however defined, remains a powerful force even in the most modern of societies.

- **THE PROTESTANT ETHIC** (p. 61) – Max Weber's thesis of the power of religious ideas on industrial development.
- **POST-MODERNISM** (p. 245) and Jean François Lyotard's fears about the future.

Suggested Reading

THOMPSON, I. (1986) *The Sociology of Religion,* Longman, London – overview of the whole topic of the sociology of religion.

Further Reading

BRUCE, S. (1995) *Religion in Modern Britain,* Oxford University Press, Oxford.

CASANOVA, J. (1994) *Public Religions in the Modern World,* University of Chicago Press, Chicago.

Stigma

Erving Goffman

The Idea

E VER BEEN STIGMATISED? EVER BEEN LABELLED AS ODD, DISFIGURED, DIFFERENT OR deviant? Ever been made to feel excluded, rejected or an outcast because of your physical features or the way you act? Then you know only too well not only the intense emotions that such labelling provokes but the sense of despair and humiliation that quite easily turns into anger and frustration, or worse, self-loathing and self-hatred. You come to accept that you are odd and abnormal, and you start to live up to the label, to dress strangely and to act in the manner expected, seeking out others of a similar nature and finding comfort and support in their company as a way of defending yourself, as a way of reaffirming yourself against the 'outside' world, where everyone seems to hate and despise you.

The study of stigma formed part of the study of the presentation of self that formed the unique focus and contribution of the American sociologist, Erving Goffman, to the study of sociology in the 1960s and 70s. Goffman's style of sociology was highly individualistic and difficult to categorise but influenced by the ideas of George H. Mead and symbolic interactionism. He sought to analyse human interaction and the way people 'present' themselves in everyday life, particularly in public situations. Self-image, its creation and its maintenance and defence formed the heart of his approach and in his pioneering work *Stigma* (1968; originally published in 1961) Goffman turned his eye from the way 'normal' people present themselves to the strategies employed by the 'abnormal', those with 'spoiled' identities or 'stigmas'; those cast out by society or locked away from normal life – the physically disfigured, the mentally ill, the drunk, the criminal, the disabled and the discriminated against.

Goffman (1968) defined a stigma as any physical or social attribute or sign that so devalues an actor's social identity as to disqualify him or her from 'full social acceptance'.

He identified three main types of stigma:

- physical defects such as being a cripple, a dwarf or deaf;
- personal weaknesses or blemishes on a person's character or background such as a prison record or being unemployed;
- social stigmas due to the company a person keeps or the racial or religious group he belongs to, for example ethnic minorities.

Stigmas may therefore be *ascribed* or *achieved*, something you are born with or something you 'earn'. It may be highly visible like having no nose or being known as a prostitute, or it may be an invisible but 'dark' secret like alcoholism. It may be a source of public sympathy like polio, or one of public shame, like being an ex-convict. Different implications inevitably follow for the stigmatised person depending on whether the stigma is visible or invisible. A physical defect, for example, is generally less easy to manage and control than a 'social' one; blindness is far more immediately visible than say insanity.

The essays in Goffman's study of *Stigma* are a rich and penetrating discussion of the wide variety of strategies people use in response to being stigmatised or to prevent such a label being applied in the first place. Much obviously depends on the defect involved and how visible it is. Some try to 'repair' it, for example, through plastic surgery or by going 'straight'. Some try to hide it by wearing special clothing, dark glasses or using an alias. Some learn how to pass it off in public or how to prevent the sneers and looks of others by joining in 'normal' society. Others withdraw – the handi-capped into homes, junkies into a drug culture – into the security of 'worlds' where their defects are considered normal. Some even fight back by forming pressure groups like Gay Lib or Black Power to force society to change its view of them and grant them equal rights with other humans. The stigmatised have to go through a special *moral career*, a particularly painful socialisation process, as they learn to live in a society where they are not considered complete, are looked down on and often segregated. Their self-image is often shattered, especially if stigmatisation occurs late in life, as the result say of a crippling car accident or an addiction to drink. Such individuals feel strangers in their own society and face enormous strain between their public images and their private lives. Their egos are rarely intact.

However, as Goffman emphasises, the stigmatised are only one of the two 'faces' of stigma. The other is society at large and its definitions of normality. We are the audience whose reactions force the abnormal and the deviant to act in an unusual manner. It is we 'normals' who discriminate, segregate and construct an ideology about the 'handicapped' as inferior or a threat, in order to justify our rejection, fear and prejudice about them. Yet we are all well aware of our own imperfections as we 'face up' to everyday situations. So, argues Goffman, the normal and the stigmatised are not two separate classes of people but the two faces of stigma, two ends of a continuum which varies according to the people, time, place and situation involved. What may be abnormal in one situation may not be in another. Thus we are all 'normal deviants', we all play 'two-headed roles' as we joke about or sympathise with the stigmatised.

Stigmas are not, therefore, a reflection of inherent weaknesses in a person's body or character. They are a social label created by the 'reaction' of others in society. The individual involved fails to live up to people's expectations and stereotypes about normal looks or behaviour and so is 'disqualified from full social acceptance'. The study of stigma, therefore, is not only an analysis of a special form of 'image management' but of a particular form of social control. The abnormal are labelled deviant and sub-human as a way of controlling or excluding them. Ironically, in Goffman's view labelling people in this way creates the very behaviour it was designed to suppress. Faced by the 'abnormal' reactions of ordinary people, the stigmatised inevitably act strangely!

While Goffman sought to identify and explain the various ways in which stigmas are applied and the highly creative strategies that the stigmatised use to resist or reject such social labelling, he was ultimately optimistic that the majority of those stigma-tised could recover and embark on relatively normal lives – even if on occasion this meant giving in to the stigma, admitting one's guilt or illness and asking for forgive-ness or treatment so that the professionals in control relaxed their pressure, adopted a more positive attitude and approach to rehabilitation because they had 'won' or been proved correct. The mental patient or prison convict, the alcoholic or drug addict, all enjoy a much more relaxed relationship with their doctors or prison officers once they admit their deviance and accept treatment or punishment. Goffman, however, was less optimistic about the attitudes of society at large. The general public – employers in particular – are less forgiving and the label ex-convict, ex-mental patient is a powerful stigma that may well last a lifetime.

The Idea in Action

ERVING GOFFMAN'S ESSAYS ON STIGMA (1964) AND SELF (1956) HAVE TO BE READ themselves to be appreciated. They are full of intricate and intimate detail and brilliantly convey the emotions and minute planning and interaction that goes into the way those in prisons or asylums respond, react and re-analyse themselves once they become stigmatised by normal society and try to restore some semblance of self-esteem, individuality and freedom against the crushing power of being labelled odd, deviant, insane or criminal. The book and the film of *One Flew over the Cuckoo's Nest* is a brilliant portrayal of the sorts of ideas Erving Goffman was seeking to describe, focusing as it does on the lives and characters of a mental institution and their attempts to take over the asylum and re-establish some control over their lives.

Goffman's work equally inspired enormous interest within the academic world and had a profound effect on many professions and their treatment of their patients. Whereas symbolic interactionism had tried to examine how people create or negotiate their self-images, Goffman focused on '*how society . . . forces people to present a certain image of themselves . . . because it forces us to switch back and forth between many complicated roles, it is also making us somewhat untruthful, inconsistent and dishonourable*'. He sought to explore and explain social action in terms of '*its meaning for others rather than in its causal origins*' (Burns 1992). He focused in on the relationship between social order, social interaction and the self, the interrelationship between society at large and everyday social intercourse, between macro and micro sociology. He wanted to provide what he regarded as a distinctly sociological account of the individual to analyse the distinction between the self as a character or personality and the self as a social performer, managing and defending his or her social image in a multitude of face-to-face situations. The self, therefore, is multi-faceted or multi-faced, capable of putting on the image or social mask the situation demands and moving in and out of different social situations as needed. Goffman's focus not only on the way people react to being labelled but the way labelling often creates 'abnormal' behaviour, forced many doctors, psychiatrists and social workers to re-examine the very basis of their relationships with their patients or clients. By labelling – or worse, stigmatising them as sick, insane or deviant – were they changing their self-image, making them feel odd and abnormal, isolating and humiliating them so that they lost the will to recover or reform and instead adopted a new lifestyle, self-image and friendship pattern that both insulated and isolated them from normal society – the homeless in a refuge, the hooligan in a detention centre, the terminally sick in a hospice. The labelling process has the inbuilt potential to be a self-fulfilling process, a process by which the label, the stigma, becomes the reality, those labelled insane 'become' insane, those labelled as sick or deviant become social outcasts forever. Stop labelling and stigmatising people in this way and possibly they will remain in mainstream society and re-establish normal lives and identities. Profound though Goffman's work was – and is – it too was subject to criticism and counterclaim.

Like its parent philosophy, symbolic interactionism, Goffman's theory of stigma was criticised for failing to explain where such social labels, such social stigmas come from, who has the power to stigmatise and why some groups suffer such discrimination and not others. It was more a study of social psychology than of social structure. For all that, works like *Stigma* (1964) and *Asylums* (1961a) continue to stimulate and entrance, are full of depth and colour and add enormously to our understanding of the various social 'worlds' that make up society. Few writers have given sociology such style, individuality and such insight; few have inspired the sociological imagination as much as Erving Goffman.

He died in 1982 at the peak of his fame. He had attained almost a cult status and was seen as something of a sociological maverick, a leading social theorist in the 1980s and elected President of the American Sociological Association in the year he died. Although often perceived as an exponent of symbolic interactionism, he himself would not have accepted any such label. Rather, his studies were highly original, highly individualistic, informed as much by anthropology and social psychology as sociology.

 **See Also**

- **LABELLING THEORY** (p. 134) and **SYMBOLIC INTERACTIONISM** (p. 195) as the parent theories of this idea.
- **SIMULATIONS** (p. 260) as a post-modern theory of the power of symbols and images.

Suggested Reading

BURNS, T. (1986) *Erving Goffman,* Routledge, London – a short and readable overview of Goffman's life and work.

GOFFMAN, E. (1956) *The Presentation of Self in Everyday Life*, Penguin, Harmondsworth.

GOFFMAN, E. (1961) *Asylums,* Penguin, Harmondsworth.

GOFFMAN, E. (1968) *Stigma* [1961], Penguin, Harmondsworth.

Further Reading

BRANAMAN, A. (2001) Erving Goffman, Ch. 8 in Elliott, A. and Turner, B.S. (eds.), *Profiles in Contemporary Social Theory*, Sage, London.

MANNING, P. (1992) *Erving Goffman and Modern Sociology*, Polity Press, Cambridge.

WILLIAMS, R. (1998) Erving Goffman, Ch. 11, Part II in Stones, R. (ed.), *Key Sociological Thinkers*, Macmillan, Basingstoke.

Structural Functionalism

Talcott Parsons

![The Idea]

THE CONCEPT OF STRUCTURAL FUNCTIONALISM DERIVES FROM THE WRITINGS OF Talcott Parsons, lecturer and professor of sociology at Harvard University from 1928 until his death in 1979. Structural functionalism inspired a whole generation of sociologists and between 1930 and 1970 it dominated sociological thinking in America and Western Europe to such an extent that it became 'the sociology', virtually unchallenged by any alternative theory or approach. The sociological perspective or school of thought known as functionalism did not originate with Talcott Parsons – that claim dates back to Comte, Spencer and especially Darwin. What Parsons did was to put the *structure* into functionalism, to make this rather general theme that society is a living entity with a life and structure of its own, above and beyond those of its members, theoretical and scientific. The usual analogy used by functionalist writers to explain how society works is that of a living organism which, to survive in an ever-changing environment, has to adapt and evolve, maintain its 'equilibrium' and ensure that every part of its body is 'functioning' properly (see Durkheim, p. 22).

Parsons, however, used a systems approach. He viewed all societies as distinct and self-sufficient systems made up of a wide variety of sub-systems, all interconnected and interdependent. Thus, for example, the economic system depends on the education system for its supply of skilled workers, schools depend on the family for their supply of future pupils and so on. Each of these sub-systems contributes towards four key functional imperatives or basic needs that a society must fulfil in order to survive: 'AGIL', as discussed below.

- *Adaption*. Every society has to feed, clothe and shelter its members and so it needs an economic system to produce and distribute its resources and adapt to the external environment.
- *Goal attainment*. Every society has to set goals for itself, make decisions and create organisations and so needs a political system.

- *Integration.* Every society has to create a sense of belonging, of community and common identity. It has to prevent the development of social divisions and conflict or it will disintegrate. It therefore needs systems for establishing codes of behaviour (religion), communication (media), and social control (the law, the courts, police and prisons).

- *Latency.* Like all species, every society seeks to perpetuate itself even though individual members are constantly dying and being born. It seeks to pass on its rules, customs and culture from one generation to the next and such pattern maintenance, in Parsons' theory, depends primarily on the kinship system, on the family socialising its offspring. This process is reinforced by such other social institutions as schools, the media, the church and the law. Not only must society at large fulfil these four imperatives but the sub-system (and sub-sub-system) must too, if it is to function properly.

Strongly influenced by Durkheim, Parsons saw the 'heart and life-blood' of a stable and efficient social system as its central value system: its code of values and set of norms which, if properly established, would not only ensure perfect synchronisation of all the various sub-systems but ensure the integration of the individual so that everything and everyone is in perfect harmony, ticking over perfectly. But how do societies integrate, harmonise and motivate, often millions of people, each with their own personality, ambitions and desires, into working hard towards a set of common goals along certain social guidelines? According to Parsons this is achieved by socialisation, social control and role performance. Every individual has to perform a wide variety of social roles – as a parent, a worker, a citizen – and although other people's expectations pressure the individual into effective role performance and the system of social control can force him/her to carry out these duties, real efficiency comes from people being committed to the social system. Such 'internal' motivation comes from effective socialisation, from parents bringing up their children properly, teaching them the prevailing norms and moral values of society to the point where they are internalised and become a part of the child's own consciousness, even conscience. Like Durkheim, therefore, Parsons emphasised the importance of morality in the central value system. While his study of Freud and behaviourism led him to see children as empty vessels into which the culture of society could be poured, he saw human behaviour and personality as open to moulding, particularly by parents, through punishment and reward, love and affection, teaching children how to fit into society. Deviant behaviour was thus portrayed as primarily due to inadequate socialisation, necessitating the use of the institutions of social control (the police and courts) to restrain or isolate such unhealthy and anti-social behaviour.

Parsons went on to divide social norms and values into two main categories:

- those like particularism, affectivity and collective orientation that are essentially expressive or emotional ones;
- those like achievement, self-discipline and individualism that are instrumental or task-orientated.

Such pattern variables, Parsons argued, represent different levels of integration and equilibrium and reflect different types of society. More advanced societies, for example, rely on instrumental values for efficient functioning, while small-scale societies are more personal and expressive. Similarly, different social institutions rest on differing values. The family, for example, is essentially expressive, an 'emotional haven', while factories are usually impersonal and mainly concerned with results and the production of goods.

Such a distinction is very similar to Durkheim's idea of mechanical and organic solidarity (see p. 73). Parsons further claimed that, by analysing a society's norms and values, sociologists could pinpoint sources of conflict and tension, areas where there was a lack of 'fit' between the values and norms of one sub-system and another, and suggest ways to improve integration, to help the transition of the individual from one social institution to another. Schools, for example, could prepare young people better for the changing world of work. The essence therefore of Parsons' social system is equilibrium, integration and consensus. All forms of conflict are generally seen as a threat to the stability and functioning of society and must be eliminated. He sought to show how society at large functions as a complete unit and how the individual fits into it. For Parsons, the social system is a pattern of institutionalised culture that has been internalised by the individual personality and acted out through the roles, norms, expectations and rules society has developed for him or her.

The Idea in Action

T ALCOTT PARSONS SET HIMSELF THE TASK OF PRODUCING A SINGLE COHERENT analytical sociological theory of voluntaristic social action. He repudiated behaviourist theories of human action as automatic, coercive or purely self-interested. Rather, building on the work of Durkheim and Weber he sought to develop a social systems approach that combined systematic analysis of the social system itself with a theory of social action in an attempt to explain how, out of all the chaos of individual and group activity, social order is established and maintained and how the individual is integrated into society.

From this framework, Parsons produced some excellent empirical studies of, for example, the nuclear family and the sick role. He inspired a generation of functionalist studies like Davis and Moore's (1967) analysis of social stratification and, even today, functionalist ideas are a major source of sociological debate.

However, by the late 1960s, as the consensus in American society was breaking down, with riots over black power, Vietnam and civil rights, criticisms of structural functionalism grew and grew:

- Parsons' view of human nature was criticised as overdeterministic, as making man seem like a 'puppet on a string' without any personality or free will of his own. Certainly this was the picture Parsons painted in his later works. Initially he had been heavily influenced by Weber's emphasis on social action, choice and meaning, on Freud's idea of tension between individual free will and society's need for control. However, by the time of *The Social System* (1951) such 'subjective' understanding (*verstehen*) had given way to descriptions of people as cogs in the social machine. While Parsons' work originated from a social action perspective, as his analysis developed, the social system became pre-eminent and the individual inactive, a passive component of the socialisation process.

- His theory over-emphasises social consensus and order. It ignores the influence of power and is unable to explain rapid, especially revolutionary social change. In response to such criticisms, Parsons did introduce 'evolutionary' ideas into his theory, arguing that societies, like nature, grow and mature through certain stages of evolution, and he did make some analysis of power but as an aid to collective action rather than a source of conflict.

- It is a very 'conservative' approach. It assumes that there is complete agreement on the goals and values of society; it assumes consent and not only explains how the existing social order works but justifies it, arguing that whatever social institutions exist, must do so because they have a function to perform. It thus ignores the 'power' of some to impose their goals and values on society at large and offers no real framework for reforming or criticising the existing social systems.

- It is a very 'American' approach, assuming that their system, their free enterprise economy and liberal democracy is naturally the best.

- His writings are often tortuous to read, full of 'scientific' jargon and abstract theory and much of his argument is teleological, explaining an effect as a cause, explaining all social institutions by their function. 'Opaque verbiage', as C. Wright Mills (1959) scathingly called it.

Attempts by students of Parsons, such as Robert Merton (with his notions of manifest and latent functions, and dysfunctions) and Lewis Coser (conflict as an integrating force) only temporarily stemmed the decline of structural functionalism and, by the 1970s and 80s, the more radical and conflict-orientated approaches of Marx and Weber were more in sociological fashion in Britain and Europe (though less so in America). In contrast to his critics, Parsons was well aware that the functioning and integration of society are problematic. Modern society is far too complex, especially in America, to be portrayed as a totally harmonious institution. Rather, his whole notion of system functioning, adaptation and equilibrium sought to show how out of all the tensions and conflicts of normal life, order is not only established but maintained. Parsons made culture the primary feature of the social system and sought to explain social change in terms of evolution and system adaptation. He rejected, however, Marxian ideas of class conflict and revolutionary change and wrote extensively on the social conflicts of his time – Nazism, racism and deviance – though his solutions were relatively liberal if not conservative in tone, involving adaptations to the social system and in particular the need to improve socialisation and education rather than its overthrow. He recognised the notion of conflict but reduced it to a notion of tension within the social system rather than one of its key features. He took a personal stand in support of liberal democracy and passionately opposed totalitarianism and racism.

While functionalism attracted extensive academic criticism, its legacy is considerable. As Heine Andersen (Andersen and Kaspersen 2000: 232) has put it *'several basic concepts, like role, norm and institution are still standard furniture in sociology, heavily carved by functionalist thinking'*. Many of Parsons' ideas have been revived and renewed in the 1980s by neofunctionalism, particularly through the work of Jeffrey Alexander and even the systems approach of writers like Habermas and Luhmann draw on his approach and concepts.

Though in today's conflict-ridden and divided world structural functionalism seems a highly conservative, even archaic and less relevant sociological explanation, it was a major step in establishing sociology as a separate and scientific discipline. It dominated post-war sociology in the Western world and even today it still has tremendous value as an explanation of social order and integration. Whether it will inform the twenty-first century in the way it influenced the twentieth remains to be seen. As Robert Merton (1980: 71) concluded: *'The death of Talcott Parsons marks the end of an era in sociology. When [a new era] does begin . . . it will surely be fortified by the great tradition of sociological thought which he has left to us'* (quoted in Ritzer 1996: 239).

 **See Also**

- **POSITIVISM** (p. 56).
- **SOCIAL DARWINISM** (p. 67) and Durkheim's ideas on social solidarity as background material to this modern version of functionalism.
- **PHENOMENOLOGY** (p. 165) and its offshoots.
- **ETHNOMETHODOLOGY** (p. 104) and **SYMBOLIC INTERACTIONISM** (p. 195) for very different interpretations of social structure and change.
- **HISTORICAL MATERIALISM** (p. 43) and its offshoots.
- **STRUCTURAL MARXISM** (p. 265) and **CRITICAL THEORY** (p. 84) represent a radically different view of social order and social change, an alternative one based on conflict rather than on consensus.
- **STRUCTURATION** (p. 271) as a 'late modern' attempt to integrate social structure and individual action.

Suggested Reading

HAMILTON, P. (1983) *Talcott Parsons,* Tavistock, London – an introduction and overview.

Further Reading

ANDERSEN, H. (2000) Functionalism, Ch. 14, Part II in Andersen, H. and Kaspersen, L.B. (eds.), *Classical and Modern Social Theory*, Blackwell, Oxford.

FAURKE, H. (2000) Neo-Functionalism, Ch. 15, Part II in Andersen, H. and Kaspersen, L.B. (eds.), *Classical and Modern Social Theory*, Blackwell, Oxford.

HOLTON, R. (1998) Talcott Parsons, Ch. 7, Part I in Stones, R. (ed.), *Key Sociological Thinkers*, Macmillan, Basingstoke.

ROBERTSON, R. AND TURNER, B.S. (EDS.) (1991) *Talcott Parsons: Theorist of Modernity,* Sage, London.

SICA, A. (1998) Robert Merton, Ch. 8, Part II in Stones, R. (ed.), *Key Sociological Thinkers*, Macmillan, Basingstoke.

Symbolic Interactionism

G.H. Mead

The Idea

TRADITIONAL SOCIOLOGY HAS ATTEMPTED TO EXPLAIN AND ANALYSE SOCIETY IN TERMS of its structure and the way that such structures influence, if not determine, social behaviour. The functionalist theories of Emile Durkheim and Talcott Parsons were based on the notion that society is an organic or structured being with a life of its own while scientific Marxism put the class struggle at the heart of its analysis of social change.

In contrast, symbolic interactionism focuses on the microscopic side of society, our everyday lives, our everyday worlds and how through 'symbolic interaction' people communicate, interact and create order and meaning in their daily lives. This socio-logical perspective rejects the scientific approach favoured by the classical sociologists in favour of analysing society from *within* and trying to see what motivates people in any given situation or lifestyle.

The theory of symbolic interactionism dates back to the teachings of the American philosopher and social psychologist George Herbert Mead and the publication of his lectures by one of his students, Herbert Blumer. In contrast to European sociology and its focus on social structure and social class, American sociology has been more concerned about the individual and his (or her) ability to express his freedom and capacity to create and control new frontiers, new challenges. While Europe has seemed to be a society run by its ruling classes, America has always seen itself as a classless society in which the individual roams free. Hence the development of very different, highly contrasting sociological perspectives from within the two continents.

G.H. Mead laid the foundations for symbolic interactionism with his interpretations of the workings of the human mind. According to Mead, what distinguishes man from the rest of the animal kingdom is this unique mental mechanism which enables man:

- to plan consciously and adapt his behaviour according to the situation in hand or the goals he has set himself;

- to communicate with others through a wide variety of symbols, the most important of which is language, and interpret the meaning behind what they say, do or indicate in reply;
- to be self-conscious; to be aware not only of his own feelings, motives and views but those of others; to be able to take the 'role of the other' and imagine how other people might interpret a particular act or situation and even to imagine how he looks to other people. We all therefore have a self and a 'self-image'.

It is this capacity that allows man to have some control over his behaviour and over his environment. Therefore, in Mead's view, human behaviour is not predetermined either by instincts or by external social forces. Rather, we are thinking, conscious beings, capable of pursuing a wide variety of aims and objectives and capable of communicating with each other in order to create some sort of social order and structure. We are capable not only of conveying meaning but of interpreting the words and actions of others and such meanings are neither fixed nor absolute. They vary from situation to situation, context to context. Consider, for example, the wide variety of possible meanings behind the word *strike* or the situation where two people are alone in a room. A strike could refer to an industrial dispute, a baseball game or the lighting of a match; two people alone in a room could be involved in an interview, a tutorial, or something more secretive or sexual. Humans are therefore in a continual process of negotiating over the definition of a particular situation or relationship and out of this process of daily interaction arises our 'social world'.

However, social order does not only arise out of direct communication, out of people talking to one another, but out of common expectations. We are usually already aware of what is expected of us in a particular situation. We have learnt through socialisation and role play how we ought to behave. As children grow up they learn through instruction, imitation and, in particular play, the roles of mummy and daddy, doctors and nurses. As they grow older and their minds mature, such social guidelines are 'internalised' and used as a means of both responding to and even manipulating others. Such control is especially evident when children play games and have to use the rules to interpret and predict the behaviour of others in order to win. As adults we act out a wide variety of fairly well-defined social roles, from being a husband and father through to being a foreman, friend and local sportsman. But in Mead's analysis none of these roles is fixed. They are simply general outlines within which individuals improvise according to their own images, motives and abilities.

Mead further distinguished between the 'I' and the 'me', between a person's real 'inner' self and his public front, the social image people put on in front of others. Every individual has his own private desires and wants but, because we are able to imagine what others think of us, we dare not act in an entirely selfish way. There is therefore a constant battle between the 'inner' I and the 'outer' me and this, argues Mead, is the basis of what we call self-control, the means by which we try to get our minds to govern our bodies and keep our emotions under control, though sometimes such self-restraint breaks down. However, it would be impossible to predict accurately the expectations of every other person we ever met, especially as most of them are not known to us personally. So we generalise, we create a *generalised other*, an image of what we think other people would think of us if, for example, we started singing on a bus or laughing at a funeral. But we do not religiously conform to others' expectations. As Mead emphasised, we have minds of our own and often defer only to the pressure of *significant others*, people who are especially important to us.

Thus for Mead man is essentially a social being and society is the world he has created about him, one that is in a constant state of flux, a continual process of creation and recreation, interpretation, negotiation and definition. We are both individuals and social beings. We both shape our society and are shaped by it. We all live in a wide variety of miniature 'worlds' – from the home to the office, the golf-club to the local bar, and yet are part of a broader and shared human culture. Each of these 'worlds' has an essential structure but may at any time change or collapse as, for example, when a factory closes or a family experiences divorce.

Thus at the centre of Mead's analysis is not the class struggle or the division of labour but the individual and his mind and its ability to communicate and interpret. Symbolic interactionism has no real vision of society at large but is more an analysis of group interaction and psychology, more an interpretation of the 'internal' dynamics of man's social behaviour than of broader social trends.

In Mead's view human thought, experience and action are all essentially social (i.e. they involve other people) and the basis of all social interaction is *symbolic interaction*, the sharing of meanings through symbols, notably language. No object, be it a chair or a house, lover or lust, has a meaning of its own outside that given to it by man in communication. Without shared meaning, without symbols there would be no human interaction, no human society. Social life and communication itself is only possible if the meanings of symbols are largely shared by members of society through what Mead called 'role-taking' and interpretation of a particular symbol, be it a gesture, a word or an observation. Through role taking, individuals develop the concept of self and an understanding of the perceptions of others, the ability to be both I and Me, the ability to be self-conscious and to have a self-concept. The notion of self is learned – it is not inborn – through play and games during childhood and through continual 'inner conversations' throughout life.

Self-conscious thought enables people to see the viewpoint of others and to so co-operate with others on the basis of what they think others think of them. Thus the community exercises control over the behaviour of its members as they absorb and reflect on the expectations – and perceived expectations – of others. However though culture, roles and social controls exist, in Mead's view people have choices as to how they respond. They are not mindless robots or puppets in the control of Big Brother. Such choices operate within certain freedoms and opportunities, be they about the clothes to wear or the jobs to take. Society therefore is a world of symbols that give significance and meaning to life and provide the basis for human interaction. Through education the 'common habits of the community', its rules and its expectations are internalised by the individual.

Students of Mead extended and refined this analysis. Herbert Blumer, for example, sought to develop the methodology to put such ideas into practice, arguing that sociologists should study society from the inside, from the participant's own viewpoint, within 'natural' situations so as to understand why people act as they do, rather than from the 'outside' using artificial laboratory experiments or simplistic 'cause and effect' analyses. Everett Hughes developed the concept of a *career* not only to explain the common features of a range of jobs but also to outline the stages people pass through to become a criminal, a mental patient and a variety of other lifestyles, and Charles H. Cooley developed the idea of the 'Looking Glass Self'.

The Idea in Action

GEORGE HERBERT MEAD'S CONCEPT OF SYMBOLIC INTERACTIONISM INFLUENCED A whole range of disciplines within the social sciences from psychology to philosophy. Within sociology, symbolic interactionism, the study of the individual as a social being, became the basis of numerous studies by the Chicago School in America in the 1920s and re-emerged in the 1960s and 70s as a major critique of the determinism of structural functionalism – its picture of society as a thing above and beyond ordinary people; its portrayal of the individual as a puppet; its abstract theory and jargon. Symbolic interactionism spawned a whole tradition of empirical analyses rich in detail and involvement and with a particular concern for the 'underworlds' of such deviant groups as delinquents and the insane. It produced such offshoots as labelling theory, ethnomethodology, phenomenology and dramaturgy. It contributed to debates on socialisation, role play and the nature of social knowledge. For Mead (1934), both mind and self were the social creations of everyday life. *'Human society as we know it could not exist without minds and selves.'* Mind and self generate self-consciousness; mind and self exist only in relation to others. The self is both the subject and the object of consciousness, the I and the Me as man *reflects* on himself and interacts with others and the 'generalised other' or the 'significant other'. Children learn through play to conceive of the other, to imagine how others see the world through role play. Through the 'generalised other', the individual in a sense carries society around in his or her head. Mead's writings emphasised the active and creative potential of the individual and underplayed conformity, passivity, coercion and conflict.

However, symbolic interactionism has also been criticised for failing to go beyond analysing the individual and small group behaviour, for failing to develop a picture or theory of society at large, for failing to explain large-scale social change or the distribution of wealth and power. It seems at times to portray society as merely something in people's heads. It is a very 'American' view of the freedom of the individual and the limited role of society. Symbolic interactionism focuses on the individual actor, tends to downplay the influence of social structures on human behaviour and so portray society as structureless consisting solely of the activities and interactions of numerous isolated and rootless individuals. The influence and power of class, government, law and the like over the individual are marginalised as a result. Of all the presumed difficulties of the symbolic interactionist paradigm, then, two stand forth as the most crucial: (1) limited consideration of human emotions, and (2) limited concern about social structure. In effect, the first of these shortcomings implies that symbolic interaction is not psychological enough, while the second implies that symbolic interaction is not sociological enough (Meltzer et al. 1975: 120).

Criticisms of symbolic interactionism therefore include:

• Its failure to put human interaction into context and into a social or historical setting so that at times it seems to be no more than a study of episodes, encounters and situations.

- Its failure to highlight the constraints on human behaviour, over-emphasising choices and freedoms.
- Its failure to show the origins of meaning, rather portraying the meaning of a given situation as emerging spontaneously out of interaction rather than out of the underlying social context in which it is situated. While European sociology emphasises the constraints of power, wealth and class, American sociologies like symbolic interactionism emphasise liberty, freedom and individuality.

Some of this criticism is unfair or based on extreme versions of Mead's ideas. Mead recognised the importance of social structure, of social institutions, but simply rejected the idea that they determined human behaviour.

Secondly, by definition, symbolic interactionism sees no social reality beyond that created by human interpretation and so rejects the possibility of explaining society at large.

Thirdly, the concept of power is integral to such analyses, if not always explicitly stated. It is an essential part of human interaction, of the ability of some to control how a situation is 'defined'. In fact such writers often argue that their studies concentrate on the 'underdogs' of society precisely because the powerful in society are already well able to make their voices heard.

During the 1970s, symbolic interactionism seemed to have lost steam and fragmented into a variety of directions as more powerful and critical perspectives like Marxism gained prominence – and, for a period, dominance. However, it has recently enjoyed a revival. Symbolic interactionism has now entered what Fine (1992) has called a 'post-Blumerian' age. On the one hand, this has involved refocusing Blumer's work onto the macro level; on the other hand it has involved an attempt to synthesise interactionism with other theories such as ethnomethodology, exchange theory and phenomenology at the micro level and with Parsons, Weber, Marx and Durkheim as well as post-modernism and feminism at the macro level. This new symbolic interactionism is a much more diverse and synthetic perspective than in the days of Mead and Blumer.

Writers like John Baldwin (1986) have gone further, seeking to develop Mead's ideas into a full-blown and integrated sociological theory, while Maines and Morrione (1990) have sought to show that Blumer's work, notably his unpublished study 'Industrialisation as an Agent of Social Change', had an objective and macro perspective as well as a subjective one. Writers like Stryker (1980) have sought to embed concepts like power, status and class within modern interactionism while Norman Denzin (1992) has sought to extend its perspective into the post-modern study of culture and media. Symbolic interactionism is as alive and vibrant today as it was in the 1920s and 30s. It may, as Gary Fine (1993) has argued, have fragmented and expanded, it may have been incorporated into or even adopted by other theoretical perspectives, but it is still distinct, still capable of informing and challenging sociological thought and method.

 See Also

- **PHENOMENOLOGY** (p. 165) as the parent theory to this form of interpretative sociology.
- **LABELLING THEORY** (p. 134) and **STIGMA** (p. 185) as examples of the development of symbolic interactionism.
- **STRUCTURATION** (p. 271) as a 'late modern' attempt to integrate social structure and individual action.

Suggested Reading

HAMILTON, P. (1992) *George Herbert Mead: Critical Assessments*, Routledge.

PAMPEL, F.C. (2000) George Herbert Mead, Uniting Self and Society, Ch. 5 in Pampel, F.C., *Sociological Lives and Ideas: An Introduction to the Classical Theorists*, Macmillan, Basingstoke.

Further Reading

COOK, G. (1993) *George Herbert Mead: The Making of a Social Pragmatist*, University of Illinois Press.

MILLER, D.L. (1973) *George Herbert Mead*, University of Texas Press, Austin – an overview of Mead's life and work.

ROCK, P. (1979) *The Making of Symbolic Interactionism*, Macmillan, London – assesses the contribution of symbolic interactionism to modern sociology. Interactionism has contributed enormously to such fields as deviance and education.

PLUMMER, K. (1998) Herbert Blumer, Ch. 6 Part I in Stones, R. (ed.), *Key Sociological Thinkers*, Macmillan, Basingstoke.

Urbanism

Louis Wirth

T HE IDEA OF URBANISM, THE IDEA OF A DISTINCTIVELY *URBAN* WAY OF LIFE – ONE THAT is distinctly different from that in the country – was first developed by Louis Wirth, an American sociologist working in Chicago in the 1920s. Cities are both exciting and frightening places. The sheer pace of life, the traffic, the hustle and bustle, the bright lights, are both fascinating and exhilarating. But cities are also lonely places. Amid the swirling crowds you can feel very lonely and lost, angry and irritated. No one has time for anyone else, everyone seems cut off from each other as they struggle to survive in the urban 'rat race', warding off such predators as the loan shark, the city slicker and the urban cowboy. Such an alienating and artificial lifestyle seems to be a million miles away from the friendliness, sense of community, peace and quiet of country life; yet Americans in the 1920s seemed to be attracted like moths to the bright lights and the teeming crowds searching for fame, fortune and excitement.

While fellow students like Park and Burgess sought to explain urban life in terms of human ecology, a Darwinian-type theory of human struggle, adaptation and survival, Wirth developed a more cultural theory arguing that the three key influences on urban life are:

- *Size.* By definition cities are large places containing thousands of people. This fact alone helps explain their impersonality, the highly transitory and segmental nature of urban relationships. People in the city are always on the move, rarely settle long enough to establish permanent friendships. They are in the city for a specific purpose, be it to make a purchase or for a business arrangement. They are 'on the make' so they don't have time for pleasantries. The city is a giant marketplace, a 'rat race' in which everyone is out to better themselves in the climb to the top and so they will either use or trample on others. It is easy, therefore, to feel a failure, rejected and powerless. The only way to cope and survive is to treat others in the same unsentimental way. To cope with the sheer size of cities people split up into smaller communities based on a particular area or neighbourhood with others of similar background – the ethnic groups in the Chinatowns and Italian quarters of the inner city, the middle and working classes in the outer and inner suburbs. Such social segregation provides a sense of community, identity and security in the 'naked city' but can also lead to social conflict when one group feels that its territory (and its status) is about to be invaded.

- *Density*. Not only are cities full of people but they are physically packed tightly together. There is barely space to breathe and so life tends to be very tense and irritable. All manner of people now live in close proximity to each other and, inevitably, this increases the potential for social conflict, be it between rich and poor, ethnic groups or neighbouring territories.

- *Heterogeneity*. The city attracts all types of people, from every ethnic group and from all types of background. It is the furnace at the heart of America's melting pot and such enormous variety of social groups is exacerbated by the intense division of labour and high degree of mobility of modern industrial society. Their differences outweigh their similarities as they all struggle for survival.

So, in his classic essay, 'Urbanism as a Way of Life' (1938), Wirth proposed a minimum sociological definition of the city as 'a relatively large, dense and permanent settlement of sociologically heterogeneous individuals'. He went on to lay one of the foundations of the theory of an urban–rural continuum, the idea that where you live profoundly influences how you live, '*the city and the country may be regarded as two poles in reference to which, one or other of all human settlements tend to arrange themselves*'. In other words, life in the city and the country are distinctly different because of their different environments and especially their differences in size, density and heterogeneity. However, Wirth also believed that eventually urbanism would become *the* way of life of modern society and would spread even to rural areas. Though he obviously feared that such a way of life was socially disruptive, a threat to society's moral values, sense of community and underlying consensus, he hoped that in time the cities of the 1920s would settle down and establish some sense of permanence of their own.

The Idea in Action

U RBANISM AND THE URBAN–RURAL FRAMEWORK INSPIRED A MASS OF COMMUNITY studies throughout the world over the next 30 years, detailing both urban and rural lifestyles, as generations of sociologists joined this quest for community, this search for the 'good life' free of the pressures, violence and squalor of the city. However, it was these very studies that increasingly undermined Wirth's theory.

Wirth used Chicago as his social laboratory but, as Herbert Gans (1968) has argued, Chicago in the 1920s was hardly a typical city. It attracted a particularly large influx of immigrants (and criminals) and so appeared especially disorderly.

Wirth's argument that population size and density inevitably create psychological stress is contradicted by examples such as Hong Kong and Singapore where overcrowding is intense but disease and social disorganisation are low. Studies like

Young and Wilmott's (1962) in East London and Herbert Gans' (1962) in Boston revealed the existence of 'urban villages': tight-knit communities in the heart of the urban sprawl. Equally, studies like Ray Pahl's (1965) of commuter villages in Hertford-shire and Oscar Lewis's (1951) in Mexico revealed that aspects of urbanism – social conflict, class divisions, alienation – could equally be found in the countryside.

As Gans and Pahl argued, neither urbanism nor a particular environment are the key influences on urban behaviour. People's social class and position in the family life cycle (whether they are young or old, single or married) have much more influence. For Marxist writers the source of all our urban problems is not the city itself but modern capitalism which generates class conflict, exploitation, alienation, urban decay and rioting. The city simply happens to be where most people live, where these divisions and problems are most intense and where the present class struggle is being fought out – on the streets. Amid the urban riots of the 1960s such radical theories soon became the basis of a new urban sociology that swept away the cultural and ecological theories of Wirth and the Chicago School.

Though no longer a dominant thesis in urban sociology, Louis Wirth's essay on urbanism still remains a classic, still has the strength of insight to possibly provide food for thought about the cities of today. Certainly he and the Chicago School have had a major influence on modern sociology and on modern urban planning.

 See Also

- GEMEINSCHAFT–GESELLSCHAFT (p. 39) as the original theory on urban-rural relationships.

Suggested Reading

WIRTH, L. (1938) 'Urbanism as a Way of Life', *American Journal of Sociology*, 44, 1–24.

Further Reading

WIRTH, L. (1928) *The Ghetto,* University of Chicago Press, Chicago.

YOUNG, M. AND WILLMOTT, P. (1962) *Family and Kinship in East London,* Penguin, Harmondsworth.

Cultural Studies

Stuart Hall

The Idea

DURING THE 1970S AND 80S, *CLASS* – THE CENTRAL CONCEPT OF CLASSICAL SOCIOLOGY – was under challenge from newer, more post-modern sociologies that focused instead on lifestyles and on social identities centred around non-class issues such as youth, gender and ethnicity. A new sociology, one based on the study of culture and modern lifestyles began to emerge, and at the head of this new school of thought were Stuart Hall and his colleagues at the Centre for Contemporary Cultural Studies (CCCS) at Birmingham University, a centre that soon gained an international reputation for the sheer volume and quality of the academic work it produced in the period 1964 to 1979. Cultural studies emerged as an academic discipline in its own right with a vast breadth of work that ranged from social and political theory through to studies of youth culture, mass media, class conflict and popular culture, all infused with a left wing, neo-Marxist perspective that enjoyed extensive and highly critical debates with the emerging New Right government of Mrs Thatcher – and with feminist and black writers of the late 1970s. Cultural studies and the CCCS were at the forefront of the New Left movement of this period.

Cultural studies developed from a diverse range of European traditions and it came to life amid the social, political and cultural 'revolutions' of the late 60s and 70s. The young and the radical were about to revolutionise post-war society, through the student riots in Paris in 1968, the anti-war demonstrations in America, the anti-nuclear marches in Britain and the Cultural Revolution heralded by Elvis Presley in the 1950s, and by the Beatles, the Rolling Stones, Bob Dylan and all who followed them in the decades thereafter. The idealism and romantic energy of the new movements led some to try and change post-war society, others to try and 'drop out' of it either through drugs or by adopting alternative, communal lifestyles. A whole new 'counter culture' emerged among the young in direct challenge to mainstream society; a youth culture expressed through music, literature, protest and lifestyle. Cultural studies was at the forefront of academic attempts to capture and embrace this new sociology.

The Centre for Contemporary Cultural Studies was originally founded by Richard Hoggart in the 1950s in an attempt to transform the traditional view of culture and to lift it out of its narrow and middle class obsession with classical music, traditional art and classical literature by focusing instead on contemporary and ordinary everyday life and in particular on the lives of those previously ignored and dismissed by academic study – the working classes. When Stuart Hall took over he sought to modernise cultural studies by using a neo-Marxist framework to highlight the critical importance of class, ethnicity and gender in analysing contemporary society, particularly the emerging youth culture. The concept of 'cultural resistance' became a focal point of this analysis in analysing the behaviour of 'working class lads' and their 'dumb' defiance of those in authority. In *Resistance through Rituals* (1976) Hall and his colleagues published a diverse and very focused collection of studies of the subcultures being developed by the young – the Mods, the Rockers, the Punks and their like. Beneath such diversity in attitude and lifestyle, argued Hall, remains the common theme of class resistance to modern capitalism. The generations of the 1960s and 70s may have used different ways of resisting capitalism from their parents – the new working class may have turned to their trade unions and the Labour Party as a way of resisting capitalism; the new middle-class youth of the 1960s in contrast turned to radicalising their university lifestyles, to radical protest or simply withdrew into drugs and communes. Both classes of youth, however, were seeking to express their opposition to capitalist control, were seeking to express their alienation, and in particular their rejection of the ideological assumption that capitalism is good for you and the only worthwhile and normal way of life. The ideas of Antonio Gramsci, particularly his notion of hegemony (see p. 121) and his concept of ideological control, therefore formed a key role in the critical analysis of the CCCS.

Hall himself, as an Afro-Caribbean, led the way in focusing in on black youth in Britain. *Policing the Crisis* (1978), for example, brought the issues of black power and race riots to the forefront of sociological and political debate. Hall portrayed black youth as a 'fraction' or element of the working class at large while equally recognising that race and colour divided the British working class rather than uniting it. For Hall, black crime like black riots was part of black resistance to both class rule and white supremacy.

While the CCCS approach to cultural studies, and in particular their neo-Marxist framework, may have come under increasing challenge in the late 1970s from other black writers, particularly feminists, what the Centre did do was to bring the concept of *culture* to the forefront of sociological analysis and debate and to infuse it not only with a radical Marxist critique but also with the post-modern ideas being developed elsewhere in Western Europe; ideas that focus in on style, demeanour and identity as much as on class and group conflict.

The Idea in Action

CULTURAL STUDIES, ITS CONCEPTS AND THEORETICAL PERSPECTIVES, IS NOW AN accepted part of modern sociology and in many universities it represents an academic discipline in its own right. Such acceptance and integration is largely due to the pioneering work of Stuart Hall and his colleagues at the Centre for Contemporary Cultural Studies. Cultural studies both in concept and in practice has not, however, been without criticism.

Redhead (1990) and Bennett (1999), for example, have strongly criticised the notion of 'subculture' as being too rigid and concrete a concept. In Bennett's view youngsters do not '*live simply in mainstream society or in one of its subcultures*'. Rather, most youth 'flit' between life at home or at work and 'social lives' that may well focus around subcultural lifestyles, clothing or music – the weekend rocker, the mini-skirted librarian or the punk vicar. Only a very small percentage of the young, even in the heady days of the 1960s and 70s actually became revolutionaries or professional hippies.

Secondly, the CCCS model seems to portray subcultures as essentially forms of resistance to modern capitalism and its cultural domination. However, as Hall and Jefferson themselves recognised, subcultures cannot solve the problems faced by the working class such as low pay, unemployment and educational failure. They are at best, ways of resisting authority and providing some form of escapism. They are not the basis for revolution. As Mike O'Donnell (2001) argues, this seems to render the notion of subcultural resistance redundant, except when applied to black youth and their willingness to use physical violence and rioting. Elsewhere, white subcultural resistance is at best anti-authoritarian and at worst racist and anti-foreign. As the economy and employment improved in the 1990s, white subcultures have all but disappeared as the working class young have enjoyed full employment and relative affluence. The working-class 'Lads' of the 1950s and 70s – the rockers and the punks – are now part of British social history. Rather than being the vanguard of a class revolution, the youth of the post-war period were simply seeking to establish teenage identities in contrast to the older generation, and even the more militant and radical middle-class youth quickly conformed once they left university and joined the capitalist 'rat race' – some of these having moved on to positions as captains of capitalism; Richard Branson being a classic example.

Finally, the CCCS model is equally overly rigid in its depiction of youthful behaviour. While the introduction of European ideas and structural Marxism gave cultural studies a very radical and post-modern framework to draw on, such modes of analysis tended to be highly abstract and deterministic. The behaviour of the youth at that time was often interpreted as a forerunner to radical, even revolutionary action; whereas in practice, many of the young were simply enjoying new freedoms, new affluence and new opportunities, experimenting with new lifestyles and identities rather than trying to change society at large. Few saw themselves as life-long revolutionaries embarking on a class war, even if many were prepared to march and protest for greater freedom and civil rights at the time.

More recent work within the cultural studies tradition, notably by Paul Willis (1990) and Angela McRobbie (1994) seeks to strike a more even balance between class and such factors as age, ethnicity and gender. More importantly such writers seek to provide the opportunity for the young to 'speak for themselves' rather than have their behaviour interpreted through a predetermined theoretical framework that claims superior understanding of why they act as they do. McRobbie's article 'Different Youthful Subjectivities' (1996) in particular seeks to use a multi-causal analysis, recognising that factors such as age, ethnicity, gender and class interact and are subject to flux and change throughout the various stages in a person's life. Work such as hers seems to reflect a shift towards the 'social actor', towards recognising that not only are the young a product of their times but also that individually and collectively, the young and their varying subcultures act on and influence, if not affect, modern and popular culture, taking it in new, unpredictable directions.

Cultural studies has thus come more of age. It is now more widely accepted as a discipline in its own right with its own curriculum and sense of direction. This is the legacy of Stuart Hall and his colleagues at the Centre for Contemporary Cultural Studies. This is also the irony that a sociological perspective that was so critical of British society and so determined to radically change it, should ultimately be embraced by it; an irony that was most clearly reflected in Stuart Hall's appointment as professor of sociology at the Open University. Hall, a black Jamaican, a radical and outspoken Marxist writer, a leading critic of Mrs Thatcher and the Tory Governments of the 1980s, was now able to use the BBC, the very heart of the British establishment, as a means for promoting and for popularising his radical ideas about a better Britain. He used this position to great effect and became a well-known TV personality and critic. Stuart Hall retired in 1997 after 30 years of developing and inspiring ideas about the culture and lifestyles of modern Britain and the people living in it.

Suggested Reading

WRITINGS in the field of cultural studies are not easy reading. Nevertheless they are well worth the effort and the following reflect the style and approach developed by Stuart Hall and his colleagues in the 1970s and 1980s.

HALL, S. AND JEFFERSON, T. (EDS.) (1976) *Resistance through Rituals: Youth Cultures in Modern Britain*, Hutchinson, London.

HALL, S., CRITCHER, C., JEFFERSON, T., CLARKE, J. AND ROBERTS, B. (1978) *Policing the Crisis: Mugging, the State, and Law and Order,* Macmillan, London.

HALL, S. ET AL. (1982) *The Empire Strikes Back*, Hutchinson, London.

Further Reading

THE following reflect more recent developments in cultural studies and in Stuart Hall's own thinking over the past 30 years.

HALL, S. AND DU GAY, P. (EDS.) (1996) *Questions of Cultural Identity*, Sage, London.

HALL, S. (ED.) (1997) *Representation: Cultural Representations and Signifying Practices*, Sage, London.

MCROBBIE, A. (1994) *Post-Modernism and Popular Culture*, Routledge, London.

WILLIS, P. (1990) *Common Culture: Symbolic Work at Play in the Everyday Cultures of the Young*, Oxford University Press, Oxford.

Discourse

Michel Foucault

The Idea

THE *OXFORD POPULAR DICTIONARY* DEFINES DISCOURSE AS '*CONVERSATION, LECTURE OR treatise – a way of communicating ideas*'. Michel Foucault, the French philosopher, used this term, however, as the basis of his theory of power and social structure. For Foucault, power and knowledge are not only intimately linked, they are indivisible. Not only is knowledge power, but those holding power control knowledge – '*Those who have power in any area of human activity have the capacity to define and control knowledge in their area of control and so subject others to their rule, be they a professor, a doctor or a military general*'; '*there is no power relation without the correlative constitution of a field of knowledge nor any knowledge that does not presuppose and constitute at the same time power-relations*' (Foucault 1980). This relationship in Foucault's view is particularly evident in the nature of the modern state. As the power of the state grows, so the state seeks to develop new types of knowledge, new forms of *discourse* to define, control and plan for the growing numbers of social groups within its boundaries.

In a series of disparate and wide-ranging studies, Foucault sought to develop this theme and the theory behind it. In *Madness and Civilization* (1965), for example, he attempted to show how society has sought to define, explain and control the poor and the unemployed, the sick and the mad. Before the nineteenth century, the state had no responsibility for such groups; as its responsibilities grew, however, modern systems of definition and control began to emerge – the poor and unemployed were labelled 'lazy' and sent to the workhouse to learn self-discipline and the work ethic; the sick were hospitalised and confined to bed; the mad were defined as deviant, sinful or sick and confined to the madhouse, isolated from society at large. Armies of new experts began to emerge claiming to have the knowledge and authority to diagnose and treat such 'social sicknesses' – the psychiatrist and the doctor, the social worker and the economist. A new *discourse* develops, a new professional language and body of knowledge emerges that enhances the power and authority of the professional to the point that not only are these 'patients' forced to subject themselves to state control under the threat of force or punishment, but increasingly they do so willingly and voluntarily. They too defer to the power and knowledge of the doctor, the psychiatrist and the social worker and go to them for treatment and cure.

In *Discipline and Punish* (1977a) Foucault sought to develop these ideas further by tracing the changing nature of punishment. The torture and public executions of the eighteenth century and before have given way to questioning and interrogation and to the abolition in many countries of the death penalty. Punishment has moved from physical pain to psychological suffering and the loss of liberty; revenge and deterrence have given way to reform and rehabilitation; judgement is now made not only on what crime was committed but the motive behind it. And in the wake of such changes in the field of punishment, a whole army of experts from psychologists and criminologists, to lawyers, judges and prison officers has emerged, each with their own specialist field of knowledge, power and discourse, each the servant of the state but expert enough to claim professional autonomy and authority.

With the growth of professional power also comes the growth of professional controls and disciplines. Foucault identifies three forms of disciplinary power:

- hierarchical observation – the power and ability of the experts to observe all aspects of their 'patients' or subject lives; the doctor in the clinic, the psychiatrist on the couch, the prison warden from the watchtower;
- normative judgement – the movement from arbitrary judgement to a system of rational, objective and agreed regulations and rules on how prisoners should be sentenced or patients treated;
- examination of patients or subjects using professional 'instruments', methods and diagnosis so that a judgement or treatment could be recommended.

These 'disciplines', this move to professional practice, is a common trend and the defining characteristic of all contemporary human and social sciences, be it modern medicine or current penal policy. Moreover such 'disciplines' in turn breed new technologies, new forms of control that not only increase the power of the professional but lead ultimately to self-control by the subject or patient in order to return to normal life or to regain normality. The sick, the insane and the imprisoned submit themselves to self-treatment or voluntarily submit to treatment at a hospital, asylum or probation service as a way of re-establishing normality and their re-entry back into normal society. To illustrate these processes Foucault produced an intensely detailed study of the *Panopticon* or prison watchtower. Through this instrument of control prison wardens can observe all their prisoners, all of the time. Fearing that they might be seen and punished, prisoners respond in model fashion and even become self-disciplined and self-motivated. Thus for Foucault the Panopticon symbolised all that characterised modern society and modern systems of discipline and punishment. 'Big Brother' rules OK as much by promoting self-discipline as by threatening control and punishment.

Power for Foucault is not, therefore, always negative or threatening. It can equally be positive, even liberating, 'encouraging' people to take control and responsibility for their own lives and actions, even if it is under the threat of confinement or punishment. Equally, power is not a one-way relationship. Even in the direst of circumstances a patient or a prisoner can resist, can refuse treatment, can challenge the authority of those in power – the patient by asking for a second opinion or seeking alternative treatment, the prisoner by calling his lawyer or appealing to a higher court. Power for

Foucault therefore does not ultimately lie in social structures or social systems; it lies in personal relationships and it pervades all aspects of social life.

Modern society for Foucault is therefore a highly *disciplined* society, a society in which social controls have grown and continue to grow, not arbitrarily but through the spread and knowledge of technology and the rationale and relationships that underpin and promote them. Modern society is a *self-disciplined* society in which fear of being caught and punished induces self-control and conformity to an all-seeing, all-knowing state with its surveillance cameras, speed traps and data banks. However, such complete control is a delicate balance. People are equally capable of resisting or evading 'Big Brother' if the occasion arises and even of openly rebelling if their privacy or rights are threatened. Beneath the apparent calm and control of modern society, beneath the authority of the government, the police or the teacher, lies the potential for social resistance and social chaos, be it by the demonstrations of protestors, the riots of the deprived or the dumb insolence of the resentful. Power and control are in a delicate balance between compliance and rebellion, and the power of the authorities is always open to challenge or refutation from a new or alternative source of knowledge or opinion.

Power-knowledge, therefore, underpins modern society and discourse is the means by which power is created, debated, controlled and distributed. The holders of power-knowledge control the agendas of debate and discourse and so enjoy ideological power as well as any physical or legal power they may hold. These ideological frameworks evolve over time as knowledge and so authority changes; the psychiatrist has replaced the faith healer; the chemist the wizard. And while such discursive and ideological 'frameworks' encourage debate and discussion, they often equally exclude and condemn alternatives that may threaten the power and authority of those within. The religious frameworks of the medieval world have given way to the scientific/rational frameworks of today; the modern university and professional body has replaced the power and authority of the church and the monastery. Such intellectual revolutions have reflected power struggles not only between power-holders but between those in power and those subjected to their laws and their rulings as the powerless – the victims of control, suppression and exploitation – have learnt over time how to resist and even overthrow controls, be it slavery or social exclusion.

In portraying power-knowledge as the essence of modern society and discourse as its mode of communication and distribution, Foucault also proposed a methodological approach based on *archaeology* (1972) by which the researcher might burrow down deep into the history, culture and psyche of each society to discover the very essence of its identity and character, the power-knowledge relations upon which it is based. This methodology required the historian to immerse him or herself in the assumptions and lifestyle of a particular culture and then to trace them back to their origins, using a genealogy or family tree of the dominant discourses throughout its history and its development. Only in this way would the researcher, in Foucault's view, truly understand the origins of the human sciences and avoid distorting them with his own cultural preconceptions. Foucault's *History of Sexuality* (1978) was an example of such an approach and through it he sought to show how the medical and scientific framework of discourse gained pre-eminence in the Victorian debate on sex, with Western Christianity and its moral framework of sin and guilt pervading all debate about what was or was not normal or socially acceptable in sexual behaviour. However, while the medical and religious discourse of today ebbs and flows at the social and legal level, the rise of pornography, of gay rights and other sexual liberation movements illustrates Foucault's point that beneath the discipline and controls of modern society lies resistance and challenge, lies an underworld and an alternative lifestyle and sexual behaviour that is not easily nor totally controllable – be it in Soho in London or in the red light district of Amsterdam.

Through studies such as those above, Michel Foucault sought to develop and refine his key themes and theories about power, knowledge and discourse and, while in his earlier works he adopted a structuralist, deterministic and quite pessimistic view of modern society as a 'police state', his later studies revealed a more optimistic view of man's (and woman's) capacity to resist and challenge those in power.

The Idea in Action

THE WORK OF MICHEL FOUCAULT HAS BEEN ACCLAIMED AS A FOUNDING STUDY FOR the post-structuralist tradition of thought. By analysing power as a form of social knowledge and as a form of social relationship, he sought to redirect attention from classical and modern studies and their focus on social structures and social positions. While pluralists tend to focus on decision makers and Marxists on ruling classes or power elites, Foucault sought to highlight the social nature of power and its importance in everyday social discourse as much as in the corridors of power; he focused on the micro-politics of society as much as the macro structures of political analysis.

Foucault's work equally exemplified and informed the post-structuralist tradition by drawing together a multitude of theories and concepts and synthesising them very powerfully into a radical new framework in which no one theory or perspective would dominate. His ideas drew as much on Nietzsche and Freud as on Marx and Weber but he rejected them all as much as he assimilated them; *'I have never been a Freudian; I have never been a Marxist and I have never been a structuralist'* (quoted in Swinglewood 2000: 194). For him, modern society is not part of the liberal tradition of evolution, of man's progress to enlightenment, truth and liberation. Rather, it is yet another form of domination and discipline, another example of power-relations and power-knowledge. For him, history is not a continuous process of change but a disorderly tale of struggles for power, of chaos and conflict beneath order and control. His early radicalism and belief in a communist utopia gave way to a critique of Marxism just as searing as that of capitalism and a view that the advance of reason is as great a threat to freedom as it is a source of liberation.

For Foucault, history is the story of domination and subjection and only in his later writings did he give the individual the power and the will to resist and to rebel. The study of 'subjectification', of the processes by which self-identity is defined and controlled is at the heart of all his work, and at the core of his analysis of 'the age of discipline' in *'organising a consciousness of self'* (Foucault 1989).

However, just as Foucault's work and mode of analysis inspired a cult following and generated libraries of post-structural writings and debates, so too it inspired vigorous controversy and criticism:

- His historical accounts have been criticised as poorly researched or even inaccurate and Foucault himself once described his studies as historical 'fictions' designed nevertheless to illustrate his thesis on the development of the disciplined society.
- Feminists have castigated Foucault for his lack of attention to gender inequality, sexual violence and the power-relations between men and women.

But most of the criticism focuses on his concept of discourse and the way it changes and fluctuates throughout his work. In his early structuralist phase he portrayed the state, its civil servants and its ideological control as all-powerful and all-pervasive. Little credence was given to the power of the individual to resist or to act consciously, rationally or responsively. People were depicted as *'virtual "dummies" and the structures as virtual ventriloquists'* (O'Donnell 2001: 123) controlling their every thought, word and movement. Later in life, inspired by the new social movements and the New Left, Foucault became more optimistic about radical change and the power of resistance. This inevitably contradicted some of the pessimism and determinism of his earlier work and left him open to questions about where these oppositional or reverse discourses come from, if those in power have excluded all alternative modes of thought or discourse. Moreover, his later theses – that ultimately power-relations lie not in structures but in relationships and in everyday life – gave the subject classes a power and a control over those in authority over them that contradicted the omnipresent approach that informed his earlier structuralist analysis and its 'de-centring of the subject'.

Despite the more liberal and optimistic strains in his later writings, however, the overriding legacy of Foucault's work is his gloomy pessimism, his lack of faith in the individual and in rational thought, and a personal despair bordering on anti-humanism. Modern man is not marching towards an enlightened utopia. Rather he faces a future of ever-increasing controls and surveillance in a disciplined society that has perfected indoctrination and used technology to such effect that the mass of the population are reduced to robotic compliance, to controls from above and controls conditioned from within, to ideological and cultural controls far more effective, far less obvious than the physical controls of the past, training us for *'automatic docility'* (Foucault 1977a: 169). This was the profound and provocative conclusion to the discourse that Foucault inspired across the breadth of the social sciences, a conclusion that equally informed his own very exotic lifestyle and search for the ultimate experience.

The concept of discourse was only one of the key ideas that he developed during his academic career. In fact Michel Foucault cannot be typecast within any one philosophical or sociological tradition; he spent his academic life avoiding such confinement. Rather he swept across the whole range of the human and social sciences – and beyond into the realms and depths of pleasure and punishment, madness and sexuality, power and death, areas of life he not only wrote about but personally experienced. He pushed himself mentally and psychologically to the limit in an obsessive search for inner meaning, most notably of himself and his life experiences. He openly flaunted his homosexuality and sadomasochism and deliberately sought out 'limit experiences', be they through drugs such as LSD or sadomasochistic activities in France or San Francisco. He died in Paris in 1984 at the age of 57, the victim of AIDS and his own radical and exotic lifestyle.

The range and volume of his writing was prolific and immensely influential not only on philosophy and social science, but on such professional fields as urban planning, medicine, criminology, mental health, architecture, education and public policy. This 'Foucault effect', as some writers have called it, has been so profound and so wide-ranging that few areas of academic and professional study have not been touched at some time by his ideas and his insights. This was the essence of Foucault's influence. He contributed to an enormous range of areas of study but was confined to none; he led a variety of 'lives' but restricted himself to none; he produced a treasure trove of ideas but left behind no single, comprehensive nor coherent theoretical framework which unified and underpinned all his thoughts and insights. Instead he preferred *discourse*, preferred to provoke debate and challenge existing ways of thinking and so stimulate new knowledge, new understanding. As Stephen Katz (quoted in Elliott and Turner 2001) has concluded, Michel Foucault was *'one of the most important and popular thinkers of the twentieth century'*.

- **BUREAUCRACY** (p. 27), **THE IRON LAW OF OLIGARCHY** (p. 52), **CONFLICT THEORY** (p. 79), **HEGEMONY** (p. 121) and **POWER ELITE** (p. 171) as classical and modern theories of power.

Suggested Reading

FILLINGHAM, L.A. (1993) *Foucault for Beginners*, Writers & Readers.

Further Reading

FOUCAULT, M. (1965) *Madness and Civilization: A History of Insanity in the Age of Reason* [1961], Pantheon Books, New York.

FOUCAULT, M. (1971) *The Order of Things: An Archaeology of the Human Sciences* [1966], Pantheon Books, New York.

FOUCAULT, M. (1972) *The Archaeology of Knowledge* [1969], Pantheon Books, New York.

FOUCAULT, M. (1973) *The Birth of the Clinic: An Archaeology of Medical Perception* [1963], Pantheon Books, New York.

FOUCAULT, M. (1977a) *Discipline and Punish: The Birth of the Prison* [1975], Pantheon Books, New York.

FOUCAULT, M. (1977b) *Language, Counter-Memory, Practice: Selected Essays and Interviews by Michel Foucault* (Ed. D.F. Bouchard), Cornell University Press.

FOUCAULT, M. (1978) *The History of Sexuality*. Vol. I: *An Introduction* [1976], Pantheon Books, New York.

Globalisation

Anthony Giddens

THE IDEA THAT WE ALL NOW LIVE IN A GLOBAL ECONOMY BASED ON A GLOBAL MARKET providing goods and services across the world is now commonplace. Moreover, Marshall McCluhan's concept of the world as a 'global village' in which we not only know what is happening on the other side of the world but can watch it live, as it happens, is a reality. Through modern global communications, through the Internet, people across the world can talk face to face – or at least monitor to monitor. The global world is now, and all aspects of life, society and culture have been affected if not redefined by 'globalisation'. Even the political world is now a truly global one. After two world wars, the Cold War, the Gulf War, the Balkan Wars and now the War on Terrorism following the 'bombing' of the World Trade Centre in New York in 2001, every war has implications for the whole world.

While America and the Soviet Union competed for military, economic and political dominance in the post-war period, the collapse of communism saw America and global capitalism dominate the 1990s. Such power, however, has not gone unchallenged and today America faces not only challenges from environmentalists and the Third World but from religious and cultural movements fearing that their very identities and beliefs will be submerged beneath a blanket of Western consumerism and global capitalism. The nature of globalisation, its causes, effects and future trends has fascinated sociologists throughout the late twentieth century and inevitably spawned a wide variety of theories and perspectives as to its causes and its effects.

Mike O'Donnell (2001) has divided theorists of globalisation into two broad camps:

- those who from a broadly liberal pluralist perspective see world society improving and evolving into a more egalitarian and global community – *the optimists*;
- those who from a Marxist or post-modern perspective see capitalism and its search for profit as a threat and a drive towards global control and world domination by the West and its capitalist allies – *the pessimists*.

Anthony Giddens, a leading British sociologist and social theorist, writes from a broadly liberal perspective and defines globalisation as follows:

'The world has become in important respects a single social system as a result of growing ties of interdependence which now affect virtually everyone. The global system is not just an environment in which particular societies – like Britain – develop and change.

The social, political and economic connections which cross-cut borders between countries decisively condition the fate of those living within each of them. The general term for the increasing interdependence of the world is globalisation' (Giddens 1997: 63–64).

Anthony Giddens

For Giddens, the modern world is not a 'post-modern' world fundamentally different from anything that has gone before. Rather it is a modern world at an advanced stage of modernity. It reflects the trends and forces of the past but it is a very different way from the world of Marx, Weber and Durkheim. Not only is it different in nature but in the speed and pace of change and in man's capacity to control it. Giddens describes modernity as a juggernaut: *'a runaway engine of enormous power which, collectively as human beings, we can drive to some extent but which also threatens to rush out of our control and which could rend itself asunder. The juggernaut crushes those who resist it, and while it sometimes seems to have a steady path, there are times when it veers away erratically in directions we cannot foresee. The ride is by no means wholly unpleasant or unrewarding; it can often be exhilarating and charged with hopeful anticipation. But, so long as the institutions of modernity endure, we shall never be able to control completely either the path or the pace of the journey. In turn, we shall never be able to feel entirely secure, because the terrain across which it runs is fraught with risks of high consequence'* (Giddens 1990: 139).

Like writers before him, Giddens identifies three key elements in globalisation:

- The *economic* – the growth of global markets and the rise to power of the modern multinational such as Sony or Ford with markets and factories throughout the world;
- The *cultural* – the growth of global ideas, images and identities created by the mass media and satellite broadcasting;
- The *political* – the shift to international diplomacy, the rise of supranational and world government agencies and networks from the European Union and the United Nations Organisation through to the Association of South-East Asian Nations (ASEAN).

In Giddens' view we now live in a global world in which every aspect of life and even personal identity is subject to global influences, if not forces. Globalisation surpasses and even on occasion supplants national boundaries and even the poorest countries in the world have not escaped the seductive consumer power of McDonald's and Coca-Cola. Unchecked now by the alternative ideology of communism, Western capitalism appeared to rule the world of the late twentieth century; September 11th 2001 may have changed that perception. It may have signalled a new force, that of Islamic fundamentalism, challenging and confronting Western and particularly American imperialism, but that remains to be seen.

Giddens analyses globalisation in terms of five key dimensions:

- Capitalism, its growth and economic dominance of the world economy on the basis of the private ownership of capital, commodity production, 'propertyless' wage labour and an associated class system.

- Industrialism and the spread of modern technology and modern industrial methods – the 'world factory' and production lines that stretch from Britain and Europe to Asia and the Third World.

- Surveillance systems and the capacity of modern governments and organisations to survey and supervise their citizens and workers through information technology.

- The interstate system of international networking and co-operation that still at present leaves the 'nation state' as the principal actor in the world order of international events and international decisions.

- Militarism and the growth of 'world' wars, world power and international struggles in various and varying parts of the world, be they Bosnia, Afghanistan or the Middle East.

Giddens sees all five factors as being interrelated but equally separate. Moreover, while they are all aspects of modern capitalism, they may be used to oppose Western imperialism as much as reinforce it. The Asia nations of South Korea, Hong Kong and Singapore, for example, have adopted and adapted Western industrial technology and used it to create multinationals of their own capable of competing with the West. Terrorist groups equally have used modern tele-communications and weapons of war to attack America and all she stands for.

While appreciating and recognising the negative aspects of globalisation, not least its threat to national cultures and identities and its impact on the environment, Giddens himself takes a relatively optimistic view of the future provided it is managed constructively and with humanity. In *The Third Way* (1998) he argues for cosmopolitanism, a common humanity that embraces and encourages cultural diversity within a common framework of tolerance and human rights. For Giddens, the three key aspects of globalisation are:

- *Time-space distanciation* – time, space and distance are no longer major factors in separating out the modern world. Rather, through modern communications and transport systems, the world is a smaller place and we can communicate across the globe in seconds and travel across it in hours. Such shrinkage, however, also makes global control easier and control from distant and impersonal corporations or governments more possible and more likely.

- *Dismembering* – the destruction of local community, cultures and structures by distant far-off forces such as the international banks and corporations, making decisions elsewhere that undermine or destroy local or even national identities and their sense of control. The debate in Britain over the euro and the implications of the loss of the pound to national identity is but one example.

- *Reflexivity* – man's capacity to reflect on and consciously control his actions is at the heart of Giddens' optimism about the future. Amid the global struggles for power and domination and despite the potential for globalisation to lead to the destruction of our planet, Giddens believes that ultimately globalisation will lead man to reflect and to act to make the world a better place, free of disease, famine and war. Like Ulrich Beck, however, Giddens is sensitive to the fact that we live in a 'risk society' and that man is as capable of making foolish or even evil decisions, many of which will have unintended consequences, as he is of making wise and humane ones.

Giddens' theory of globalisation is therefore a multidimensional, pluralistic one, sensitive to the huge variety of conflicting forces acting on the post-modern world but equally hopeful that wisdom and humanity will prevail. He fears the 'juggernaut' but has faith in man's capacity to at least steer it in the right direction and to find a balance between risk and reality, ideals and ambitions, a sort of 'utopian realism'.

The Idea in Action

Giddens' PERSPECTIVE ON GLOBALISATION IS FIRMLY ROOTED IN THE LIBERAL TRADITION of enlightenment and the hope that despite man's inclination for conflict and self-destruction, ultimately reason and wisdom will prevail and peace and harmony will overcome conflict and chaos. Writers such as Malcolm Waters (1995) and Roland Robertson (1992) are similarly hopeful. Robertson, for example, sees globalisation as predating the growth of capitalism in the nineteenth century and dates it back to the Renaissance and world exploration of the fifteenth and sixteenth centuries. He puts his faith in the development of a 'global consciousness' based on human rights and a sense of common humanity. Malcolm Waters focuses more on the potential for global governance and international law to promote global order and resolution of conflict – while recognising the inadequacies of organisations such as the League of Nations in the 1930s and the UN today.

Marxist writers, however, fundamentally disagree with such liberal aspirations. For them, post-modern globalisation is the inevitable outcome of modern capitalism and its relentless pursuit of profit and new markets through a global economy and global consumerism. Immanuel Wallerstein (1989) sees the advent of the 'capitalist world system' in the development of the nation state and the imperial explorations of countries such as Britain, France and Spain in the sixteenth and seventeenth centuries. In contrast to Giddens and Robertson, Wallerstein and other radical writers are deeply pessimistic about the potential for change. In their view the post-modern world is one of global imperialism with the capitalist West controlling the world economy and promoting exploitation, inequality and the suppression of human rights. Such oppression may be expressed in military terms through the suppression of radical movements and the support given to pro-Western dictatorships. It may equally be economic – through the control of world markets and world prices – or cultural – through Western control of global communications and their use. Globalisation in their view involves the spread of *Western* lifestyles and consumerism to the point that national identities and cultures are rendered irrelevant. Western ways of living become 'normal' and enjoy a form of world hegemony in which 'McDonaldisation' is rife (Ritzer 1993).

Moreover, argue Marxist writers, whatever progress may have been made on human rights, the scale of inequality between the First and Third World remains as great as ever. Anti-capitalist movements have grown up even in Western countries in protest against American power and imperialism. They made their voices heard in demonstrations in Seattle in 1999 and in London in 2001. More violent protests culminated in the terrorist attacks on the World Trade Centre in New York and the Pentagon in Washington in September 2001 – two key symbols of American economic power and military might.

Globalisation is therefore a central concept in post-modern sociological debate, just as it is in international diplomacy following September 11th and the American pursuit of international terrorism. Tony Giddens, like Tony Blair, the British Prime Minister, seeks to inform this debate and to promote a rational discussion of the issues, the need for controls and for reform of the global process and the global powers of the military and the multinationals. He does not see the present world as a post-modern one but one of high or late modernity. He does, however, foresee a post-modern world, one where scarcity has been eliminated, democracy is widespread and technology has been humanised. Such idealistic hopes are just that; but in Giddens' view they are achievable where the collective will is strong and determined enough. He sees his writings and that of like-minded sociologists as a contribution to this debate, its reflection and resolution. Noreena Hertz's recent publication, *The Silent Takeover* (2002), is equally a pragmatic but passionate response to the global issues facing modern capitalism and the 2002 Earth Summit in Johannesburg. The UN, for example, estimates that 1.2 billion people live on less than £0.66 a day and 3 billion on less than £1.30; 800 million are underfed and 1 billion lack access to clean water. With the world population due to reach 9–10 billion by 2060, the crisis is growing daily – and yet getting the world powers, not least America, to agree on an action plan to tackle these needs is as far away as it was at the world summit in Rio ten years ago. While Giddens and Hertz hope that pragmatism, common sense and even self-interest will prevail, at present the evidence for a co-ordinated response to the global crisis is scarce. Nevertheless, Giddens' contribution to the debates on globalisation have gained him an international reputation and as Mike O'Donnell (2001) has commented, '*It is arguable that (Anthony) Giddens has explained or attempted to explain more about social life on planet earth in "late modernity" than any other sociologist.*'

 See Also

- **DEPENDENCY THEORY** (p. 92) and **MODERNISATION THEORY** (p. 146) for earlier ideas on world society and global development.
- **INFORMATION(AL) SOCIETY** (p. 220) and **RISK SOCIETY** (p. 255) as contemporary ideas on society in the future.

Suggested Reading

AN excellent, up-to-date and very readable introduction to globalisation today is Noreena Hertz's recent analysis, *The Silent Takeover: Global Capitalism and the Death of Democracy*, 2nd edn, Arrow Books, 2002.

Further Reading

MOST of Anthony Giddens' writings are more for the advanced or undergraduate reader and are listed below alongside commentaries on his work. However, his textbook *Sociology* is accessible as an introduction to his ideas including those on globalisation, while *The Third Way* is quite readable and valuable for those interested in the politics of New Labour.

GIDDENS, A. (1990) *The Consequences of Modernity*, Polity Press, Cambridge.

GIDDENS, A. (1991) *Modernity and Self Identity: Self and Society in the Late Modern Age*, Polity Press, Cambridge.

GIDDENS, A. (1997) *Sociology*, Polity Press, Cambridge.

GIDDENS, A. (1998) *The Third Way: The Renewal of Social Democracy*, Polity Press, Cambridge.

MCLOHAN, M. (1964) *Understanding Media: The Extensions of Man*, New American Library.

RITZER, G. (1993) *The McDonaldization of Society*, Pine Forge Press, Thousand Oaks, CA.

ROBERTSON, R. (1992) *Globalisation*, Sage.

WALLERSTEIN, I. (1989) *The Modern World System III: The Second Era of Great Expansion of the Capitalist World Economy 1730–1840*, Academic Press, New York.

WATERS, M. (1995) *Globalisation*, Routledge.

Information(al)
Society

Manuel Castells

The Idea

W E ALL NOW LIVE IN AN INFORMATION AGE; WE ARE ALL PART OF AN INFORMATIONAL society. Information is the new source of wealth and power, and information technology (IT) is the new *means of production*. Assessing the impact of IT on a global society and a world economy, however, has challenged writers and world leaders for the past decade or more. One of the leading writers in this field is Manuel Castells, a Spanish sociologist and radical theorist who has written widely on urban sociology, the modern city and more recently, global capitalism. For Castells, the defining characteristics of post-modern society are information technology, the Internet and the *informational* society that is being created all round us, a scenario that he has sought to outline in detail in his monumental three-volume work, *The Information Age* (1996–1998).

Information and communication have been central to all previous societies and they have been critical to their economic, social and political development. In the ancient and mediaeval worlds, travel and communication were restricted and even the state had only limited information about its people. The Industrial Revolution, however, revolutionised transport and communication. Through the advent of the railways, steamships, cars and eventually the aeroplane, the world became a smaller place and transnational communication mushroomed through the development of the telephone, the telegram, radio and television. The late twentieth century has seen a Communications Revolution not only in terms of mass communication through satellite technology but also through personal communication and access to information. The personal computer, the mobile phone and access to the Internet are transforming information societies – societies where information is important and widely used – to *informational* societies – societies where information technology is a way of life, an essential feature of the home as much as the workplace, societies that are part of a global network of communication and economic activity. And, at the heart of the Information Revolution is the Internet, the queen of all networks and the subject of none.

The Internet itself originated in a daring scheme dreamt up by the US Defence Department's Advanced Research Projects Agency (DARPA) in the 1960s as a way of combating the possible threat of a Soviet take-over or the destruction of the American communication system through nuclear war. The beauty of the Internet is that it has no centre, no command point that would enable the enemy to knock out the whole system in one blow. Rather, it is a true network linking up thousands of individual and autonomous computers that talk to each other without any central control. Today, over 400 million users are linked up worldwide from major corporations, banks and shops through to students and housewives, protest groups and (ironically) terrorists. It truly is the 'people's network' and the central symbol of the power, breadth and depth of a worldwide computer network to create a global informational society if societies worldwide adopt and integrate it into their lifestyles and workstyles. Castells cites as an example the failure of the USSR to embrace information technology as a major reason why it imploded in on itself in the 1980s while the other great statist, or centrally planned economy, China, has exploited the new technology, become more flexible and decentralised and so survived even in a world now dominated by global capitalism.

If worldwide and individual networking is one of the key features of the Internet, the other is its speed – its speed of response and its speed of development and expansion. Anyone with access to a PC and modem can link up to anywhere in the world and anyone, whatever their age, can try out their entrepreneurial skills by setting up an online business that requires no offices, no shops, no specialist marketing. This freewheeling, carefree experimentation and risk taking was just what got the Information Revolution going in the 1970s as the young, ex-hippies of the west coast of America played around with the new technology and used it to challenge the major corporations of the east coast and those in authority and in government.

Although initially a threat, the new technology quickly became the means and the opportunity for Western capitalism, argues Castells, to restructure and rejuvenate itself after the oil crises and economic depressions of the 1970s. Moreover, through its speed and its access to individual homes and businesses worldwide, it gave the opportunity to expand into a global economy with access to markets, resources and finance across the First, Second and Third Worlds. It offered and has now created in Castells' view a new form of modern capitalism, informational capitalism. While post-war capitalism was based on the Keynesian model of economic growth and on industrial production – a model that collapsed in on itself amid the rampant inflation of the 1970s – informational capitalism is based on networking, technological innovation and the rapid and relentless accumulation and transmission of knowledge, information and finances across the world in the pursuit of new markets, new profits and new sources of capital. Modern or post-modern capitalism is thus fundamentally different to the forms of capitalism that emerged with the Industrial Revolution and after World War II. It is based not on industrial production but on global networks that facilitate the flow of global finance in a sort of worldwide casino or fruit machine. These funds are generated by groups as disparate as major corporations, banks and governments through to individual investors, the Mafia and terrorist groups all seeking to invest in new markets and to find new profits at minimum risk. The production of goods and services is simply a source of investment and profit, be it in the First World or the Third. And the essence of the new system is speed and effective networking to provide instant information and the rapid redeployment of funds from one market, one company to another in a way and at a speed even the modern stock markets and money markets have trouble coping with. The new technologies have therefore created a new form of capitalism, a new capitalist system, a new capitalist class linked not by social background or any other identifiable feature but by their use and control of the global networks in 'an endless search for money by money'. It is almost pure capitalism, a capitalism based almost solely on the inner logic, ebbs and flows of the global economy and though there are monopolies and oligopolies controlling specific markets (e.g. oil) no class or group is predominant over worldwide capitalism. It is a worldwide capitalist network driven by the pursuit of profit and restricted by neither time nor space, country nor continent.

'While capitalism still rules, capitalists are still randomly incarnated and the capitalist classes are restricted to specific areas of the world where they prosper as appendixes to a mighty whirlwind which manifests its will by spread points and futures options ratings in the global flashes of computer screens' (Castells 1996: 505).

However, while capital and management in the new economy operate at a global and centralised level, labour is local and decentralised, fragmented and individualised. While capital is timeless and spaceless 'operating by a small brains trust inhabiting the virtual palaces of global networks' (Castells 1996: 506), even the trade union – that most effective and collective form of worker power – is helpless to respond against a system that is faceless, countryless and beyond control. 'At its core capital is global. As a rule, labor is local' (ibid.).

Capitalists and workers may live in the same countries but they live very different lifestyles and inhabit different spaces and times; they live in different worlds. The old Marxist concept of a class struggle no longer holds; rather 'the struggle between diverse capitalists and miscellaneous working classes is subsumed into the more fundamental opposition between the bare logic of capital flows and the cultural values of human experience'. 'Here may lie the roots of the "class" conflict of the future,' argues Castells (1996) 'between the logic of the market and the search for identity and meaning by the individual, the group or the country.' The protests of environmental groups or consumers against monopoly capitalism, be it the oil industry or the car manufacturers may be but one example of this underlying conflict; the rise of religious and nationalist fundamentalists another. Both fear the power of the new system and its effect on national, cultural and individual identities. Both ironically have quickly learnt how to use the new technologies, not only to communicate and organise worldwide, but in the case of terrorism, how to hit at the City – in this case New York – the very heart of informational capitalism and its financial networks, as September 11th 2001 so vividly illustrated.

But the Informational Revolution is not, argues Castells, simply an economic phenomena. It is potentially leading to a new type of social order, a new type of informational or networked society. Informational societies are not just societies where information is important, but where information networks permeate and underpin the life of that society and facilitate, even motivate, all forms of social and individual activity from work and leisure through to voting and shopping. They are supported and promoted by the media and the new technologies but increasingly through the computer and mobile phone they have ironically become interactive and interpersonal. Networking and information flows are not only part of the culture of the informational society, they are the culture. Distance and time disappear in an informational age networked across the world.

We are entering a new age, a new social order, argues Castells. While different societies are at different stages of development, different levels of networking and integration into the global economy and World Wide Web, ultimately all will be drawn in over time by the logic of the market (or implode and collapse in on themselves like the Soviet Union) and become internally and culturally networked as well as externally connected. While in the history of man, ancient societies survived nature and modern man conquered and industrialised it, post-modern man is entering a new age, the information age in which *culture*, not nature, is in the ascendancy. We now have the capacity to *'live in a predominantly social world – but this is not necessarily an exhilarating moment. Because alone at last in our human world, we shall have to look at ourselves in the mirror of historical reality'* (Castells 1996) and we may not like what we see.

The Idea in Action

IN *THE INFORMATION AGE* (1996–1998) MANUEL CASTELLS HAS SET OUT TO IDENTIFY, describe and analyse what he considers to be the key features of post-modern society and economy. He seeks to do so in three volumes. Volume 1 (1996) focuses in on the Internet and the economic implications of the 'network society'. Volume 2 (1997) focuses in on the implications for the self, for personal and communal identity in a networked age when the traditional sources of identity, the family and the nation-state no longer seem relevant. Volume 3 (1998) seeks to draw all these strands and trends together, combining theory and observation into overall conclusions about the nature and shape of society in the future.

It is a massive enterprise and one that clearly focuses on the essential features and developments today, the new technologies, the Internet, the global economy and the apparent loss of personal, cultural and national identity that the new networked world seems to bring. Certainly, in his conclusion to Volume 1, Castells is fearful that the new global economy, however perfect it may be in theory in connecting markets and facilitating the flow of information and money, is becoming an automaton, a monster with a mind of its own, a relentless logic that no-one, no government, no corporation, no organisation seems able to control. As he puts it later *'humankind's nightmare of seeing our machines taking control of our world seems on the edge of becoming reality – not in the form of robots that eliminate jobs or government computers that police our lives, but as an electronically based system of financial transactions'* (1996: 56) that leaves everyone helpless in the face of the global market.

His fears about the collapse of traditional social structures and loss of identity in a social world that man can no longer shape as he wishes, are equally profound and pessimistic.

However, according to *The Rise of Network Society* (1996), the Information Age also offers new hopes.

- A free flowing networked world economy is as open to individual enterprise as it is to the big corporation in a way that the industrial economies of the past were not.

- A World Wide Web is as open to individuals and to small groups or communities to use as it is to the major networks and to the multinational corporations. It can break down barriers, facilitate worldwide communication on a level previously undreamed of. It can be used to challenge those in power, through alternative information or group collaboration, just as much as it can be to create new communities, clubs or societies. Personal identity is now a much more open matter. It is no longer so dependent on birth, origin, family or nation. It is no longer restricted by traditional roles or identities. Men and women, children and the old are now able to create their own identities and less likely to have them imposed upon them.

We can, in Castells' view, regain control of our lives and use the new technologies to challenge those in power, either through international regulation of global capitalism or through deregulation, local empowerment and community renewal. As an example, he cites Finland, the most developed information society in the world where all schools have Internet access and most of the population is computer literate. At the same time it has an effective welfare state and a well-run economy. The message is where there is a will, the people have the means to gain control and to use the Information Revolution to their advantage and their benefit. The alternative scenario of a world controlled by capitalist networks pursuing profit at any price in an impersonal world of artificial identities, alienation and political conflict is equally plausible and equally likely. The Net, argues Castells, gives us the choice but the choice is down to us – and given the speed of change, time is running out.

 **See Also**

- **POST-INDUSTRIAL SOCIETY** (p. 239) for one of the original ideas on future society.
- **RISK SOCIETY** (p. 255) and **SIMULATIONS** (p. 260) for contemporary ideas on the world tomorrow.

Suggested and Further Reading

WHILE the three volume 'The Information Age' is an awesome read, even volume by volume, it is readable for the more advanced student keen to extend his or her ideas about the global impact of information technology.

CASTELLS, M. (1996) *The Information Age: Economy, Society and Culture*. Vol. 1: *The Rise of Network Society*, Blackwell, Oxford.

CASTELLS, M. (1997) *The Information Age: Economy, Society and Culture*. Vol. 2: *The Power of Identity*, Blackwell, Oxford.

CASTELLS, M. (1998) *The Information Age: Economy, Society and Culture*. Vol. 3: *End of Millennium*, Blackwell, Oxford.

CASTELLS, M. (2002) *Information Society and the Welfare State*, Open University Press, Milton Keynes.

Legitimation Crisis

Jürgen Habermas

T HE CONCEPT OF LEGITIMATION CRISES HAS BEEN DEVELOPED BY THE GERMAN PHILOSO-
pher and sociologist, Jürgen Habermas as part of a much bigger and grander
project and as a newer and more up-to-date version of critical theory, the theory
initially developed by his colleagues at the Frankfurt School of Sociology (see p. 84).

The term 'legitimation' refers to the way a government or social system attempts to
justify its existence and its power. All governments need to legitimise their rule, to
justify their right to power, to promote their authority as a means to gaining popular
support, or at least, acquiescence, without which they are likely to collapse and fall
from power. Traditional societies used myth, magic or the authority of God to legitimise their rule; modern governments use the notion of democracy to justify their
power and authority. They claim to represent the 'will of the people' as reflected in the
public elections and written constitutions. The term 'crisis' refers to the situation
whereby the strains within society have reached such a point that the whole social
system cannot cope and is in imminent danger of collapse. The term *legitimation crisis*
therefore refers to the point where the legitimacy of modern governments is under so
much stress and attack that the government collapses into anarchy and chaos.

The aim of Habermas's book *Legitimation Crisis* published in 1973 was to try and
identify the crisis points within advanced capitalist societies and how the modern state
continues both to manage such crises and maintain the legitimacy of the capitalist
system. He sought to take account of contemporary developments, not least the
growth in state power and the decline of class conflict and class consciousness,
especially among the working class. He sought to explain that although advanced
capitalism seems stronger than ever, it is in fact undergoing constant crises that
ultimately will threaten the legitimacy of the system, and so cause its collapse.
Classical Marxism, with its overriding emphasis on economic factors, can only offer
a limited explanation of contemporary developments. Habermas, by emphasising

cultural and ideological factors as well, sought to update and reconstruct both modern Marxism and modern critical theory.

In *Legitimation Crisis* (1973) Habermas analyses late capitalist societies in terms of three key sub-systems – the economic, political and socio-cultural. For society to be stable all three sub-systems must be in balance and closely interrelated. Advanced capitalism, for example, requires the state to manage the economy as a way of overcoming the instabilities and conflicts of market forces and to alleviate the inequalities created by exploitation and the pursuit of profit. Hence the growth of state planning and regulation of the economy and the expansion of the welfare state to combat poverty, ill-health and industrial pollution. However, the state in turn must maintain popular support and mass loyalty. Therefore it must tax private enterprise to pay for educational and welfare services, never appear to be biased solely towards big business, and develop techniques, both ideological and physical, for securing mass conformity and control. The socio-cultural system must create the correct ideological climate and social consensus to support capitalism and motivate its members into the 'enterprise culture'. If any one of these sub-systems fails to function effectively in balancing the social system then a crisis will occur.

Habermas identified four possible crisis tendencies within the modern capitalist system, each of which might trigger off a chain of crises elsewhere – economic crises and crises of rationality, legitimation and motivation. The whole capitalist system is riddled with inherent contradictions created by the very nature of it being an irrational system designed to promote inequality and exploitation rather than a just distribution of wealth and power. It is in a permanent state of crisis management and is only kept in balance by one sub-system compensating for the deficiencies of another. For example, an economic crisis caused by a decline in profits may be offset by state hand-outs to 'lame duck' industries. However, this may in turn generate a rationality crisis, may bring to the surface what Marxists call the irrationality or anarchy of a market economy in which there is no rational planning according to human need, but only the unstable forces of supply and demand, underpinned by the motivation of private profit and personal gain. Thus, government hand-outs to ailing private enterprises may in turn produce inflation and a financial crisis as the government has to borrow the money involved. This, in turn, generates a *legitimation crisis* as the state is seen to be favouring business against labour, or industry against finance, especially if it attempts to manage this financial crisis by cutting welfare spending. It will be seen as politically biased, lose popular support and have its legitimacy as representative of the people questioned. This may lead to a motivation crisis, to people questioning why they should work for the 'system', why they should support or vote for it. With the spread of monopoly capital, the welfare state and affluence, there is a general decline in people's motivation to work. The work ethic and spur of competition are no longer so strong, while the growth of bureaucracy increases people's sense of alienation. Increasingly unable to participate in formal politics, disillusioned with decision-making by faceless bureaucrats and planners, more and more people stop voting or participating, or they turn to extra-parliamentary movements such as Women's Liberation or environmental groups as a way of challenging the 'system'.

A full-blown legitimation crisis would threaten the whole state apparatus with disintegration and produce either a radical change in the social structure or a spate of authoritarian repression as the state sought to reassert its authority and control by force. Consider as an example of such a cycle of crises the state of British capitalism in the 1970s and 1980s as it went through a downswing in the business cycle. The economic crisis of low productivity and rising inflation led to the attempts in the 1970s by both Conservative and Labour governments to manage the crisis by state subsidies and wage restraint. These irrational policies led to crises of legitimation and motivation as even Labour's own supporters, the trade unions and working class, went on strike against the 'system' and helped bring down their 'own' government in 1979. The election of Mrs Thatcher saw an attempt to reassert the power of the state, re-establish the legitimacy of pure capitalism and remotivate the British people by liberating market forces and reviving the nineteenth-century ideologies of self-help and individual enterprise. The application of monetarism and market forces to all walks of life led to conflicts with the unions, increased economic and social inequality and ultimately to Black Wednesday and the downfall of the Tory adminis-tration of Mrs Thatcher and her successor, John Major. While New Labour under Tony Blair has sought to find a Third Way to manage modern capitalism, a mixture of private enterprise and public expenditure, he too is facing challenges to the legitimacy and competence of his government, challenges reflected in public criticism of his handling of the welfare state and a collapsing transport system, challenges reflected in the lowest voter turnout in the 2001 General Election since 1960, challenges reflected in the instabilities of the current stock market and the collapse of major corporations such as Enron.

Legitimation in late capitalist societies is thus primarily based on ideological control, on the ability of the state and cultural apparatus (media, etc.) to convince the mass of the people that the existing system is just, fair, rational, and so, legitimate. Like Weber, Habermas sees the essence of modern legitimacy – whether in organised capitalist societies or bureaucratic socialist ones – as rationality, the logic of reason and debate. This principle underlies the social, political and ideological structures of modern societies. It is reflected in the spread of bureaucracy, technology and economic planning. Today we judge the rationale of all proposals, decisions and plans in terms of their merits by reasoned discussion and debate. Such logical thought is most clearly reflected in modern science and its techniques of experimentation and constant testing. It is through reason that modern civilisation with all its benefits of mass educa-tion, mass democracy and mass prosperity has emerged.

However, like his mentors of the Frankfurt School, Habermas sees rationality today as a distortion of pure reason, as a form of 'instrumental' reason, as a form used to promote and justify the capitalist system rather than to identify the real needs and purposes of mankind at large. While in the past reason has been a progressive force, liberating human thought from the tyrannies of myth, superstition and arbitrary power, helping man escape the oppressions of poverty and ill-health, today it is being used to make an inherently irrational system – late capitalism – appear rational, just and legitimate. Science and technology are now being used as instruments for increasing exploitation of both man and nature as a means to promoting the profits of monopoly capital and increasing social control. Through new technologies, workers have been deskilled or eliminated, consumers and voters mass-manipulated and the planet raped and polluted. Modern bureaucracy and technical experts have taken over all forms of planning and decision-making, leaving the individual today feeling trapped, isolated and frustrated in an 'iron cage', powerless against an impersonal system that, while apparently rational, is equally faceless and oppressive. Yet the power of science and technology, the new ideology that Habermas calls 'technocratic consciousness', seems irresistible and all-pervasive. Who can challenge such apparently progressive forces as automation, nuclear power, genetic engineering or the space race? Certainly scientists and technologists appear to rarely question the ethics or use of biotechnology or new chemicals, rarely consider their value to mankind at large as compared to their contribution to the profits of the corporations they work for. Rationality today serves the 'system' rather than, as in the past, challenging it; it legitimises and reinforces capitalist domination and so helps perpetuate and reproduce capitalism rather than seeking to discover more sane, humane and just ways of organising social life.

This is how, argues Habermas, modern capitalism has advanced, has overcome its inherent crises, retained its legitimacy and ideological control and subdued both the class struggle and class consciousness. As Michael Pusey (1987) argues, 'Revolution conceived in the classical way after the French and the Russian experience as the forcible seizure of power no longer makes sense in the context of late capitalist society.'

Habermas, however, is far more optimistic than his forefathers in the original Frankfurt School. He still believes that pure reason can be liberated to provide the basis for both collapsing capitalism and for creating a truly free and rational society. This is because legitimation, when based on irrationality, is ultimately limited. It is limited by:

- The ability of the state to continue managing crisis situations and the ability of the sub-systems to compensate for each other.

- The general consensus that holds society together, the normative value systems underlying our legal, political and other social systems that set limits on oppressive behaviour by the state or its agents.

- The inherent logic of rationality by which, even in the most oppressive social systems, rational debate must occur, and ultimately this will lead to critical reflection and questioning of irrationality. This is especially so in Western democracies where public debate, limited though it may be, has to take place as part of our political system. Ultimately Habermas therefore hopes that the 'inherent' irrationality of the capitalist system and 'technocratic consciousness' will come to light, so creating a legitimation crisis which, in turn, will set off crises elsewhere in the system. Further, the spread of post-industrial society will break down traditional social institutions and sources of legitimation (the break-up of local communities and family life, for example) and increase the extent of bureaucratic administration and planning, leaving the masses alienated, rootless and increasingly dependent on a state which can no longer balance their increasing demands for welfare with capital's demand for reduced taxation and state spending. The very forces of instrumental rationality which are at present upholding late capitalism ultimately contain the seeds of its own destruction and the collapse of its legitimacy. The whole system would collapse in a chain-like reaction, set off by popular discontent and the inner logic of rationality, that would ultimately unmask the underlying irrationality of advanced capitalism and reveal its true nature. According to Habermas, the alternative to this liberation of reason from service to the 'totally administered society' is that we continue on our present course and ultimately destroy ourselves in one of a number of ways, be it by nuclear war or global pollution.

The Idea in Action

HABERMAS'S CONCEPT OF LEGITIMATION CRISIS FORMS PART OF HIS MORE GENERAL political sociology and theory of historical materialism. His overall aim has been to try to combine philosophy and sociology as the basis of a revived critical theory based on analysing the process and progress of rationalisation within modern societies. He has sought to revive and reconstruct both critical theory and modern Marxism. In contrast to classical Marxism which emphasised the primacy of the economic substructure in historical materialism, Habermas has argued that political and cultural factors do have an independent force, even an inner logic of their own – as highlighted in his thesis of *legitimation crisis*. While economic factors may have been the determining influence in early capitalism, they alone cannot explain developments in late capitalism where ideological forces are also obviously of considerable importance. While Marx's economism is still pre-eminent in Habermas's theory of historical materialism, he has also added the ideas of Hegel, Parsons, Freud and, in particular, Weber's analysis of rationality and the development of reason in human history. His ideas have stimulated other colleagues at both the Frankfurt Institute and the Max Planck Institute. Claus Offe, for example, has undertaken research into the corporate power of the state in late capitalism and into the achievement principle as a major legitimating principle in advanced capitalist societies.

The notion of legitimation crises arises in Habermas's work from the notion that the growth of scientific and technical knowledge, the rationalisation of society through state planning and control is counterproductive; it generates ever-increasing expectations (e.g. of health and wealth) that it cannot satisfy. This undermines public faith and creates a crisis of legitimation, a disillusion with the false promises of capitalism to produce a better life. In contrast, improved forms of communication, forms improved ironically by the progress of rationality and technology, enable the masses to criticise the state and to mobilise a critical and rational debate on the issues involved. Rationality, therefore, in Habermas's view is a contradiction for modern capitalism. It increases controls on work and the economic aspects of life, but also offers greater opportunities for free speech and open debate. The growth of bureaucracy, of technological specialists and planners remote from everyday life has led to a highly impersonal and soul-less world, a *colonisation*, as Habermas calls it, of the 'lifeworld'. However, through modern communication new social movements are able to arise, communicate and protest, be it about nuclear weapons or the rape of the countryside. They demand debate, question the official perspective and offer an alternative ideology or lifestyle based on an alternative, non-capitalist set of values. The legitimacy of capitalism, its claims to offer the ultimate society, a utopia of consumerism, is therefore under continual challenge and subject to ongoing debate. Its domination at the ideological level, its 'colonisation of the lifeworld' is therefore never complete. It is constantly in crisis and its legitimation under challenge. Habermas's faith in reason as the primary source of progress and liberation is firmly rooted in the tradition of Western Enlightenment.

Habermas followed in the footsteps of the original Frankfurt School in seeking to revive the humanist and subjective elements of Marx's early work. However, like

Parsons before him he also sought to combine this actor and action perspective with a structural analysis that not only embraced traditional Marxism but also the sustainable elements of non-Marxist theories as disparate as structural functionalism, Weberianism and phenomenology as well as the approaches of other social sciences, notably psychology – a mammoth and encyclopaedic project. For Habermas the Frankfurt School's approach had been too narrow, too focused on the cultural superstructure ignoring both the economic substructure and the struggles and realities of everyday life. Habermas argued for Marxism to be reformulated by integrating the systems theory of Talcott Parsons with the action theories of Weber, Mead and Schutz, the philosophy of Hegel with the psychology of Freud, and so link 'system' integration with social integration', the social system with its underlying 'lifeworlds', society at large and the members within it. There is in his view a constant tension between these two levels as the system seeks to overpower and 'colonise' everyday life while within 'the lifeworld' individuals struggle against big government and big business to reassert their individuality and freedom.

For Habermas the key is 'communicative interaction', the constant and ongoing debate about consensus in modern society. The essence of Habermas's theory, therefore, is *language communication* and the nature of the discourse or debate by which a consensus is negotiated and maintained and the truth resolved. Here he draws extensively on phenomenology and Alfred Schutz's notion of lifeworld and shared meaning. While the lifeworld functions through communicative action, the social and economic systems function through purposive, instrumental and strategic action in achieving specified goals and outcomes, be it the production of goods or the maximisation of profit. Through public discussion and public opinion, however, a debate takes place in the public sphere approving or challenging the actions, strategies and values of those running the political or economic systems in terms of the impact of their actions on everyday life and on the quality of life. The very force that has created major advances in modern communication has also created its own critic, and enabled the individual and a plethora of protest groups to voice their opinions and to criticise the government or big business. It is thus in Habermas's view the 'lifeworld' within which the inherent contradictions of modern capitalism are revealed, rationalised and challenged; here that social conflict is most apparent as the systems of capitalism seek to pursue the underlying logic of its own rationality (i.e. the maximisation of profit).

'At the heart of Habermas's Critical Theory is a contradiction between a deterministic systems theory and a voluntaristic action theory' (Swinglewood 2000: 207). It is within the lifeworld through open and rational discourse, argues Habermas, that the emancipation will come and capitalism will be subordinated to the will of the people rather than to the self-interest of its masters.

In contrast to the Frankfurt School, Habermas advances the proposition that the primary inheritance from the Enlightenment – rationality and the power of reason – is not only the source of man's subservience under capitalism but also the source of his liberation. In contrast to his predecessors, Habermas sees reason as the ultimate arbiter of truth and rationality, the ultimate criteria for communicating and evaluating argument. He therefore rejects the one-sided and narrow conception of both Weber and the Frankfurt theorists of *reason* being used solely to improving the control and efficiency of modern capitalism and bureaucracy, so enslaving the modern masses in the interests of the ruling classes. Rather, in his view, reason is an end in itself and operating at the everyday level of public debate it has the potential within a free and undistorted discussion to allow the truth to emerge and criticisms to be voiced. Capitalism is therefore open to challenge by the very means it introduced and developed to exploit modern mass markets. Mass communication systems such as the Internet ironically give the consumer and the individual the power and the means to challenge and confront the power of those in charge, and to question capitalist values and standards head on – be they Third World Debt, car safety or the price of petrol.

In *The Theory of Communicative Action* (1982), Habermas analyses the ongoing crises inherent in modern capitalism which undermine its legitimacy and right to act. Habermas sees the solution in terms of open debate in the public sphere as the way in which modern capitalism will be transformed and reformed in the public interest based on a new consensus, a new and open moral order underpinned by rationality, an order that in an age of global markets may be applicable in any society and across nations.

Criticisms of Habermas's work, including his concept of legitimation crisis, however, have been as extensive as its praise – they have even been encouraged by Habermas as part of his 'critical' debate.

Marxist criticisms

MARXIST writers criticise his work, like that of the original Frankfurt School, for over-concentrating on modern society, for over-emphasising ideological forces and for failing to provide a detailed analysis of historical change and, in particular, of the economic organisation of advanced capitalism. In their view he over-emphasises the cultural forces in late capitalism and underestimates the power of an economic crisis alone to bring down capitalism. In particular, they claim he underplays, though does not ignore, the power of class conflict as the key dynamic in social change, emphasising instead the power of reason and the inherent contradictions of the capitalist system. However, though Habermas's concept of legitimation sees class as a latent rather than an active force in modern politics, his thesis does take much better account than traditional Marxism of such new sources of extra-parliamentary political action such as the Peace Movement and Women's Liberation as both protests against the 'system' and calls for a more rational society: '*the new conflicts are not sparked by problems of distribution but concern the grammar of forms of life*'.

Post-modern criticisms

POST-MODERNISTS like Jean François Lyotard criticise Habermas's view of modern society as a highly European one, one that fails to recognise the multicultural variety of the modern world. Moreover his whole idea of a rational consensus seems to neglect the multiplicity and incompatibility of conflicting values and life forms. The notion of a universal morality based on a rational consensus is hotly disputed.

Analytical criticisms

HABERMAS'S theory of legitimation crisis fails to outline in detail the mechanisms by which the different sub-systems are interrelated or the means by which, for example, an economic crisis becomes a rationality or legitimation crisis. The very generalised nature of Habermas's analysis, which is a deliberate rejection of determinist-type claims to cause and effect, also leaves many readers feeling frustrated because he refuses to predict in detail the 'chain of reaction' by which crises in capitalist societies will ultimately lead to the collapse of capitalism itself. He hopes for radical change, hopes that critical reflection will release 'repressed traces of reason' but, equally, accepts the ability of the system to continue managing crises and regress deeper into irrationality. He is opposed to social engineering of the type seen in Eastern Europe as merely creating a new form of domination and irrationality imposed from above. His ultimate faith is in pure democracy, free communication, critical reflection and rational discourse.

Since the publication of *Legitimation Crisis* (1973), Habermas has continued his life time ambition of developing a comprehensive theory of the development of modern society. Habermas's overall theoretical framework is one of the most all-embracing of the twentieth century, one that seeks to draw on all major previous theories, from Durkheim to Parsons, from Marx and Weber and to embrace rational critiques of his own ideas. His framework operates at both the microlevel of the 'lifeworld' and the macrolevel of 'the system'; it combines voluntarism and determinism within the notion that under certain conditions people are able to act freely as well as be controlled. His is a more optimistic perception of future society than the Frankfurt theorists and he sees in contrast to his predecessors the Enlightenment and the advance of reason and rationality as forces for good and for liberation as much as sources of domination and oppression.

Habermas's political sociology, his thesis of legitimation crisis, his analysis of historical materialism and his theory of communicative action have stimulated extensive discussion throughout the social sciences, inspiring major debates on the modern state, the nature of modern communication, modernity and even art. His prime aim is to inspire *critical reflection* as the mechanism to releasing popular understanding about the true nature of modern society and its underlying irrationality, and so stimulating a rational debate about a more just and free society. The influence of critical theory and of Habermas's work in particular has been and continues to be immense. It has even generated a third generation of critical theorists such as Thomas McCarthy, Clause Offe and Klaus Eder. Habermas himself is as active as ever and in the process of developing his ideas on globalisation and the modern state.

As Michael Pusey (1987) concludes, '*Scarcely anyone would now challenge [the view that Habermas] is one of the most important figures in German intellectual life today and perhaps the most important sociologist since Max Weber.*'

 See Also

- **ALIENATION** (p. 14).
- **HISTORICAL MATERIALISM** (p. 43), **HEGEMONY** (p. 121), **CRITICAL THEORY** (p. 84), **STRUCTURAL MARXISM** (p. 265) and **RELATIVE AUTONOMY** (p. 250) as background ideas in the ongoing debate on the changing nature of the power and role of the state in advanced capitalist societies.

Suggested Reading

PUSEY, M. (1987) *Jürgen Habermas,* Tavistock, London – the best short introduction to Habermas's ideas.

Further Reading

ANDERSEN, H. (2000) Jürgen Habermas, Ch. 21 Part II in Andersen, H. and Kaspersen, L.B. (eds.), *Classical and Modern Social Theory*, Blackwell, London.

BAERT, P. (2001) Jürgen Habermas, Ch. 7 in Elliott, A. and Turner, B.S. (eds.), *Profiles in Contemporary Social Theory*, Sage, London.

OUTHWAITE, W. (1996) *Habermas: A Critical Introduction*, Polity Press, Cambridge.

OUTHWAITE, W. (1998) Jürgen Habermas, Ch. 15, Part II in Stones, R. (ed.), *Key Sociological Thinkers*, Macmillan, Basingstoke.

Post-Fordism

Michael Piore

T HE CONCEPT OF POST-FORDISM CANNOT BE ATTRIBUTED TO ANY ONE AUTHOR. Rather, it is a concept that has arisen from a variety of writers seeking to identify the distinctive features of modern industrial organisation and its methods of production, and to distinguish them from those employed at an earlier stage in industrial history; post-Fordist writers believe that industrial production today is so distinctive that it constitutes a whole new workstyle, a whole new post-modern way of working life.

One of the earliest uses of the term 'post-Fordism' can be found in the writings of Michael Piore and C. Sabel (1984) and their description of the new flexible styles of manufacturing and networking they found in Northern Italy in the 1980s. This term, however, has been equally used by Marxist writers such as Bob Jessop (1994), Lash and Urry (1987) to characterise post-modern capitalism and by Robin Murray (1989) to tease out the characteristics of the ideal type of 'flexible firm'.

The term post-Fordism, however, has gained wider currency and it has equally been employed as an analytical tool for describing the service sector, public services and even post-modern industrial society itself.

'Post-Fordism here signals the rise of a new mode of social organisation generally; it marks the maturation of new forms of 'post-industrial' labour (primarily service and white-collar work), whilst marking the beginning of the end for the traditional blue-collar workforce and the older class system to which it was wedded. At the core of these changes lie quite massive technological innovations to the production processes. These not only transform the nature of modern working practices and industrial relations, but also mark the onset of new forms in the construction, surveillance and interpretation of markets and consumption (and all of the social, cultural and aesthetic implications that these changes entail)' (Lee 1993: 110).

Post-Fordism is in effect a whole new economic era distinct from the mass production methods of the past. Post-Fordism is associated with the rise of information technology, flexible production methods, the rise of the multinationals and the globalisation of financial markets (Lee 1993).

Post-Fordism is best understood by contrasting it with Fordism, with the mass production methods adopted and promoted by Henry Ford in the early part of the twentieth century and which became the model for all industrial production until the post-war period in America, Europe and even among the Soviet states of the USSR until the 1970s and 80s.

The key characteristics of Fordism can be summarised as follows:

- large-scale factories using mass production methods and moving assembly lines with workers, mainly male, performing routine, repetitive and unskilled or semi-skilled tasks that eventually were taken over by robots;
- standardised production methods that dramatically reduced costs through huge economies of scale;
- bureaucratic hierarchical management structures based on a rigid division of labour, power and responsibility between management and workers.

The 'scientific' ideas and techniques of consultants such as F.W. Taylor (see Scientific Management, p. 175) turned Fordism into a fine art and made it both cost effective and very efficient. However, while society at large enjoyed the huge benefits of mass production, industrial workforces across the world became increasingly dissatisfied, deskilled and alienated and industrial conflict became a key feature of post-war industrial relations in the way so vividly described by Harry Braverman (p. 98).

Post-Fordism in contrast seems to be characterised by:

- Flexible production methods capable of short-term customised production runs catering for a diverse and specialist range of customers and employing the latest technologies and highly skilled workforces in meeting new and ever-changing market demands.
- Flexible and fluid management structures that seek to empower workers, decentralise control and enable production teams to respond rapidly and independently to changing market needs. Demarcation lines notably between managers and workers have all but disappeared and workers now enjoy high rewards, high status, high job satisfaction – and even on occasion a place on the Board. Industrial harmony seems to have replaced industrial conflict.
- Focused attention on quality and customer need as the modern consumer demands high standards, style and immediate response. Even such well-established companies as Marks & Spencer can no longer rely on customer loyalty alone.

The new technologies – the micro chip, the computer and the intelligent robot – have freed man from the drudgery and discipline of Fordism and allowed the modern worker in the factory, office or public service to regain control of the fruits of his/her labour and to enjoy the fruits of high rewards and individual lifestyles. Small-scale specialist companies compete with the major corporations by specialising in high quality 'niche' markets or working in networks or partnerships with others, within nations and across the globe. A new international division of labour seems to be emerging as new markets, new technologies and new resources arise across the world to meet post-modern consumer demands.

Writers such as John Atkinson (1985) have gone further as they seek to develop the concept of an 'ideal-type' flexible firm, one that employs a core or central workforce directed at the company's primary market(s) but flexible enough to diversify into newer secondary markets as the opportunity arises. Such firms engage or dismiss secondary labour as the need arises, so keeping costs at a minimum and response rates very high. However, while the core workers enjoy job security, high rewards and high levels of training, the secondary workers are often subcontracted on temporary contracts with low pay and semi-skills and often living in the ghetto areas of inner cities or in the Third World. High profile, high style companies in the fashion or sports-wear world such as Nike, Adidas and GAP are classic examples of such 'rapid response' taskforces, operating on a global basis to meet ever-changing customer demand in the East as well as in the West.

The Idea in Action

POST-FORDISM THUS SEEMS TO BE THE NEW AGE OF INDUSTRIAL PRODUCTION AND industrial relations; the flexible firm has become the 'flexible friend' serving the needs of both the modern worker and the modern consumer. Harmony has replaced conflict as workers and managers work together in the pursuit of quality and customer need. The revolutionary ideas of the Japanese, the Swedes and the Germans have replaced the mass production practices of Henry Ford and modern capitalism has come to terms with itself as such international giants as BMW, Toshiba and Coca-Cola seek to serve the needs of consumers across the globe.

Post-Fordism, however, has not been without its critics both as a concept and as a defence of post-modern global capitalism.

First, as a concept, as an analytical tool, it fails to distinguish as clearly as some of its defenders claim between modern and post-modern capitalism. Certainly it does not, say its critics, distinguish post-modern society and industry from the past sufficiently well enough to claim that industry today has entered a new post-industrial age completely different from anything in the past. Rather, argue writers like Anna Pollert (1988), many key features of industrial practice today existed back in the heyday of Fordism in the 1920s and 1950s, notably in the small-scale production techniques of the food, drinks and toy industries of that era.

Secondly the post-modern production techniques lauded by post-Fordian writers are very expensive and require the sort of massive restructuring that only the larger corporations – or the newer, young firms – could afford or dare attempt to introduce. Not all firms today have discarded traditional methods in favour of new technologies and new dynamics. Many prefer evolution to revolution.

Thirdly the use of contract labour on short-term contracts is nothing new. Henry Ford and his contemporaries always kept a 'reserve army' of male or female labour at hand for times of boom and many traditional industries such as the docks relied heavily on casual labour.

Finally the post-modern, post-industrial landscape is probably as varied and competitive, as ruthless and relentless as any period of industrial capitalism. The 'flexible firm' may represent a feature of industrial development today but it is but one 'ideal type' among many. As writers as diverse as Dex and McCullock (1997) and Paul Thompson (1993) conclude, the case for flexible working with all its acclaimed benefits has probably been exaggerated. The trend back to full-time employment and to central control is evident even among the most advanced of firms. Rather than any one industrial type emerging, researchers such as Amin (1994) and Kelly (1989) argue that the post-Fordian era is as rich and diverse, as flexible and fluid as consumers today demand. Modern capitalism may have become more consumer friendly, more quality conscious, but has it really changed its 'genetic spots'? It may have changed its methods, adapting to changing needs and adopting new technologies, but ultimately, argue radical writers, the end remains the same – the relentless pursuit of profit across a global economy in which national boundaries are no obstacle to opening up new market opportunities, new frontiers and new profits.

As Paul Thompson (1993) points out, the post-modern multinational will adapt its organisational style and technique to suit the country it is in and its level of economic and cultural development. While post-Fordian techniques may suit the workstyles of the sophisticated West, traditional Fordism, its factories and assembly lines may prove as effective as ever in the low cost economies of the Third World. From this perspective, post-Fordism is but one new strategy, one new approach to managing labour. Ultimately control remains at the centre as multinationals today flex their muscles as well as their methods in pursuing new markets and new profits. The spirit and character of modern capitalism may, argues Mike O'Donnell (2001), be better captured in such concepts as 'global' or 'informational' capitalism than in the restricted notion of post-Fordism. George Ritzer (1996) has gone further and advanced the thesis that it is the philosophy and practices of the fast food chain, McDonald's, that characterises post-industrial society rather than those of post-Fordism:

'Even if we are willing to acknowledge that elements of post-Fordism have emerged in the modern world, it is equally clear that elements of Fordism persist and show no signs of disappearing. For example, something we might call "McDonaldism", a phenomenon that has many things in common with Fordism, is growing at an astounding pace in contemporary society. On the basis of the model of the fast food restaurant, more and more sectors of society are coming to utilize the principles of McDonaldism (Ritzer 1993). McDonaldism shares many characteristics with Fordism – homogeneous products, rigid technologies, standardized work routines, deskilling, homogenization of labor (and customer), the mass worker, homogenization of consumption, and so on. Thus, Fordism is alive and well in the modern world, although it has been transmogrified into McDonaldism. Furthermore, classic Fordism – for example, in the form of the assembly line – remains a significant presence in the American economy.'

Whatever its weaknesses, however exaggerated its use, the notion of post-Fordism has contributed not only to the debates about the nature and character of post-industrial society, but to those on the nature of post-modern social and cultural life and to the debates about the extent to which society today is radically and fundamentally different from the model that dominated most of the twentieth century. It has inspired debate between those who see modern capitalism as being humanised and those that perceive it to be 'disorganised', between those that apply it to industrial life and to those seeking to apply its techniques to public service, to managing education, welfare services and modern government at large.

The notion of post-Fordism may well represent an extension to the debate generated by Daniel Bell and others about the nature of post-industrial society in the 1950s and 60s (see p. 239). It may have a contribution to make about the character of post-modern society and modernity. It may equally be oversimplistic and exaggerated. Nevertheless, as even its fiercest critic, Alex Callinicos acknowledges, *'it at least has the merit of seeking to show how systematic changes in the capitalist economy justify us in speaking of a distinctively postmodern era; furthermore, these accounts are supported empirically, at least to the extent that they refer to transformations which have actually occurred. The difficulty is that they grossly exaggerate the extent of the changes involved, and fail to theorize them properly'* (Callinicos 1989: 135).

 See Also

- **POST-INDUSTRIAL SOCIETY** (p. 239) as an earlier view on the nature of industrial society.
- **DESKILLING** (p. 98), **HUMAN RELATIONS THEORY** (p. 127) and **SCIENTIFIC MANAGEMENT** (p. 175) as ideas of the 'modern period' about industrial organisation and labour practices.

Suggested Reading

DEX, S. AND McCULLOCK, A. (1997) *Flexible Employment: The Future of Britain's Jobs*, Macmillan.

PIORE, M. AND SABEL, C. (1984) *The Second Industrial Divide*, Basic Books, New York.

RITZER, G. (1993) *The McDonaldization of Society*, Thousand Oaks, CA.

Further Reading

AMIN, A. (ED.) (1994) *Post-Fordism: A Reader*, Blackwell, Oxford.

LASH, S. AND URRY, J. (1987) *The End of Organised Capitalism*, Polity Press, Cambridge.

Post-industrial Society

Daniel Bell

The Idea

THE CONCEPT OF A POST-INDUSTRIAL SOCIETY, OF A SOCIETY AFTER THE FIRST AND second Industrial Revolutions of the nineteenth and twentieth centuries, has fascinated sociologists ever since the Second World War. A multitude of writers have sought to predict the future and this was particularly so when, as the Cold War emerged, the world seemed to be faced by two very stark alternatives – the liberal capitalism propounded by the USA, or the utopia of state socialist and ultimately communism promised by the USSR and the emerging socialist states of Asia and China. Was the world tearing itself into two or was there a 'Third Way', one that ultimately would overcome such ideological divisions and lead all of us into a new prosperous and harmonious society of the future?

While the concept of a post-industrial society has been the subject of debate as far back as William Morris in the 1890s, it is Daniel Bell, Professor of Sociology at Harvard University and contributor to the Presidential Commissions on Technology, Automation and the Year 2000, who is generally seen as the leading exponent and the first person to coin the phrase of this thesis. In *The End of Ideology* (1960) Bell predicted that the Cold War ideological differences would gradually dissolve and that a new post-industrial structure would emerge. In *The Coming of Post-Industrial Society* (1974) Bell set out the key features of such a society:

- *Industrially* – the shift from manufacturing to a service economy.

- *Occupationally* – the shift from blue-collar industrial occupations to white-collar professional and technical positions, from a predominately working-class society to a more middle-class one.

- *Politically* – the creation of a new *knowledge class*, a new power-elite whose specialist knowledge and skills would challenge and subvert the traditional political and economic power of businessmen and politicians.

- *Culturally* – the pre-eminence of theoretical knowledge in driving innovation and new policies.
- *Ideologically* – a 'future orientation', an attitude and aspiration by all in society to look to the future and to use new technologies to forecast, plan and even attempt to control it.

While stressing that these components were only the key features of some abstract notion or ideal type of what a post-industrial society might look like, he did predict that by the year 2000 many of today's advanced industrial societies, including Japan, USSR and Western Europe, would be entering a post-industrial phase and he cited America as the leading example: *'the first and simplest characteristic of a post-industrial society is that the majority of the labour force is no longer engaged in agriculture or manufacturing but in services, which are defined, residually, as trade, finance, transport, health, recreation, research, education and government'* (Bell 1974).

While the growth of the service sector, and with it the rise in the proportion of professional and technical occupations, is a significant feature of a post-industrial society, the decisive characteristic is the growth of a new intelligentsia centred on the expansion of the universities, professions and government; a new 'knowledge class'.

The life-blood of a post-industrial society is not money but knowledge, in particular theoretical, or as Bell called it, 'codified' knowledge. Such knowledge is fundamentally different in nature and type from that 'discovered' by such 'leading lights' of the Industrial Revolution as Watt and Edison. Post-industrial knowledge is not generated by personal experience but by massive research programmes funded by the government or major corporations and conducted in the research laboratories of big business or the major universities. Science and technology, he argued, are increasingly interrelated with abstract theory increasingly directing practical application, and with decision-making, whether industrial or political, dependent on computer-based simulations. At the heart of this explosion in knowledge use is the modern university. Hence the rise in status and resources of universities such as Massachusetts Institute of Technology in America and of Bath and Salford in the UK.

The rise of this new knowledge class has a fundamental effect on the traditional balances of power and privilege. The new professional and technical classes represent a new form of power, that based on knowledge and expertise rather than wealth or property. Such a shift in social stratification raises the possibility of the knowledge class becoming a new ruling class, leading the post-industrial society towards a more rational, harmonious future, free of ideology and political conflict. While Bell considers this a possibility he finally rejects it. While the new intelligentsia may work with, even compete with, politicians for control of decision-making, ultimately *'the relationship of knowledge to power is essentially a subservient one'* (Bell 1974). Nevertheless he did predict a 'managerial revolution' as the owners of capital sought to employ a new managerial class to run their businesses. This separation of ownership and control creates a new managerial technostructure, one that reflects the interlocking directorships of top businessmen with the spread of shareholding among the general public.

The rise in a service economy and the rise of a new knowledge class are likely to produce a significant shift in the dominant values, norms, and culture of a post-industrial society. The traditional work ethic is likely to be superseded by a greater emphasis on individual freedom and pleasure-seeking; market forces and the profit motive are likely to be controlled or at least subdued by the increased stress on social, economic and welfare planning. Issues such as the environment, health education and even leisure may well rate higher on the political agenda than the traditional class-based conflicts over the distribution of wealth and property.

THE IDEA OF A POST-INDUSTRIAL SOCIETY HAS HAD A MAJOR IMPACT ON POST-WAR sociology. While writers like Alaine Touraine (1971) and Krishan Kumar (1978) proposed their own versions of this concept, Daniel Bell's probably has had the greatest influence. He offered an ideal type of future society, which like Weber's notion of bureaucracy contained the key features of modern development without actually depicting all known societies. It was designed as a 'logical construct', a skeleton outline of post-industrial society to stimulate debate and research, not a picture of a specific or concrete society. It was a paradigm or social framework that identified new axes of social organisation and new axes of social stratification in advanced Western society. Social structures do not, however, change overnight, and it may often take a century for a complete revolution to take place from one ideal type to another. It was not an attempt to describe in detail all advanced industrial societies, though that is how some readers have perceived it.

Inevitably such an attempt at futurology inspired much comment and much criticism. First, Bell's economic and industrial analysis has been challenged in a variety of ways:

- The view that the post-industrial order is a social and economic structure radically different from that in the past has been severely criticised by writers such as Kumar (1978) and Williams (1985). They claim that the shift towards a service-based economy is not a new order but merely the extension of an existing trend that dates back to the beginning of industrialism itself. As Anthony Giddens (1989) explains: *'from the early 1800s onwards manufacture and services BOTH expanded at the expense of agriculture, with the service sector consistently showing a faster rate of increase than manufacture . . . Easily the most important change has not been from industrial to service work, but from farm employment to all other types of occupation.'*

- The notion of a service sector equally needs more careful and detailed analysis. It is a very heterogeneous occupational sector, covering an enormous range of jobs and occupations, some of which might be classified as white-collar (finance officers, economists and scientists) while others are essentially manual and even unskilled (e.g. petrol station attendants). Even among those service occupations that are white collar, most involve little specialised knowledge and many are increasingly subject to mechanisation. This is evident in most lower level office work involving secretarial or clerical duties. As Jonathan Gershuny (1978) argued, more than half the existing service occupations are in fact part of, or at least contribute to, the manufacturing process. The engineer, technician or computer programmer working for an industrial concern is in fact part of the manufacturing sector, not a member of a distinct and separate occupational class.

- No-one can be certain of the long-term impact and use of the new technologies, in particular microprocessing and electronic communications systems. At present they are part of modern manufacturing rather than displacing it and creating a new form of production. The decline in the proportion of production workers and the proportionate rise in service occupations may not therefore represent a decline of the manufacturing sector but simply its restructuring. Manufacturers are replacing industrial workers with automation and new technologies, transferring production to the Third World where labour is cheap and creating a wide variety of new white-collar occupations to 'service' – not replace – the manufacturing process.

Secondly, Bell's thesis of the pre-eminence of theoretical knowledge has been questioned. The notion of codified knowledge and the idea that information is becoming the main basis of the economic system are highly debatable. As huge multi-nationals have increasingly dominated the world economy so the growth in theoretical knowledge, in research and development, has reflected the changing nature of big business and world markets. Radical writers see the growth in collaboration between universities and big business not as a Brave New World where rational thought and intellectual harmony will reign supreme, but as an extension of the traditional pursuits of profit and power. New knowledge can be used to develop new products and new markets and even the increase in government spending on research is primarily in the fields of defence and space rather than in health, education or welfare. Neither big business nor government, they claim, aims to create knowledge for knowledge's sake; neither has any intention of allowing society to be run by the planners or technocrats. Rather, both intend to use such experts to pursue new markets and new profits, to perpetuate the existing industrial and political order, not to overthrow it.

Thirdly, Bell portrayed the United States as a key example of a post-industrial society, but as Anthony Giddens (1989) argued, it may well be that America is the exception rather than the rule. *'The American economy has long been different from that of other industrialised countries; throughout this century, a higher relative proportion of workers has been in service occupations in the United States . . . it is not clear that other countries will ever become as service-based as the U.S.A.'* America may not therefore be the best basis for generalising about society at large.

Fourthly, Marxists in particular have criticised Bell's optimistic prediction that the exploitative features of capitalist societies would disappear in favour of a post-industrial society orientated to the public interest and based on co-operation and planning rather than profit seeking and private wealth. As Bob Jessop (1998) has argued, this is a key prediction that Bell seems to have got wrong. Modern corporations may be more organised, more global and more knowledge-based but they are still inherently capitalist in nature. They are still driven by the search for profit and capital accumulation. As multinational corporations they may operate on a grander, global scale, they may employ more scientists and technologists; they may have adopted strategies that are less overtly exploitative and show more concern for their workers, for Third World countries and for the environment, but they are still capitalist at heart, still exploitative by nature and by intent. The new information or knowledge society, Bell predicts, is but a further phase in the development of capitalism, and far from such knowledge becoming public property the major corporations are fighting tooth and nail to copyright, control and license the new technologies in their own interests and as new sources of profit. Note the billions of dollars spent by the major companies on buying up the rights to own and control the airwaves for television and for mobile phones, and for purchasing the genetic maps underpinning DNA as a way of marketing genetic materials in the future.

Finally, Bell's thesis is often associated with convergence theory and as such is criticised for exaggerating the importance of economic factors in producing social change. This represents a distorted view of his writings. He in fact rejected the idea that all advanced industrial societies are 'converging' towards some common social, economic and political system ('As a social system, post-industrial society does not "succeed" capitalism or socialism but, like bureaucratization, cuts across both') and dismissed any idea that the post-industrial society was some sort of 'sub-structure initiating changes in a superstructure'. Post-industrialism, he argued, is but one (important) 'dimension of a society whose changes pose management problems for the political system' to resolve. Daniel Bell's vision of a post-industrial society may therefore represent a continuation of existing social, economic and political tendencies rather than a radical new social order.

In The Coming of Post-Industrial Society (1973) Bell presented an optimistic vision of a future society free of social tensions and conflicts. By 1976, however, 'the cultural contradictions of capitalism' had become more evident and Bell himself sought to identify the new and unresolved tensions between the three 'axial' principles of modern society:

- techno-economic efficiency and the pursuit of rational, technical and scientific solutions to societies' problems;
- universal citizenship, political equality and entitlements to social welfare;
- individual expression and self-gratification.

This mixture of optimism and pessimism about the future of industrial society has pervaded the literature about industrialisation ever since and informs much common discussion today about society now and in the future.

Despite such criticisms, Bell's analysis of America in the 1960s and 70s was analytically and statistically sound and the main aspects of America's experience of post-industrial society are now reflected in industrial societies throughout the Western world:

- the growth of white collar, service economies;
- the growth in power and use of the new technologies at home and in the workplace, not least the computer, the Internet, global communication and biotechnology;
- the growth in power and flexibility of the multinational corporation and their ability to organise mass production on a global scale using the latest technologies;
- the growth in diversity of lifestyles with the individual consumer holding greater influence and self-conscious power in the face of the multifarious pressures and strains, challenges and opportunities of modern life.

Bell correctly identified many of the trends and strains evident in the 1970s as America moved towards some form of post-industrial society. Many of his predictions still hold true and the notion of a 'post-industrial society' still informs much economic and social debate concerning the nature of society today and in the future. It is an attractive concept and one that needs reviving as we enter the twenty-first century; a century in which the speed of change already threatens to outpace the most able and outlandish of futurologists and forward thinkers. Given what we know today and given what little was evident in the 1970s when Daniel Bell was first writing, he has rightly been acclaimed by many as the 'world's greatest living sociologist' (New Society, 18 December 1987).

See Also

- **GLOBALISATION** (p. 214) and **INFORMATION(AL) SOCIETY** (p. 220) as late modern views on the development of post-industrial society.
- **POST-FORDISM** (p. 234).

Suggested Reading

BELL, D. (1987) Future Society, *New Society*, 18 December – reflects his recent thinking on industrial and social trends.

SCHUMACHER, E.E. (1973) *Small is Beautiful*, Abacus Books, London.

Further Reading

BELL, D. (ED.) (1969) *Towards the Year 2000*, Houghton Mifflin, Boston.

BELL, D. (1974) *The Coming of the Post-Industrial Society*, Heinemann, London.

BELL, D. (1995) *Communitarianism and its Critics*, Clarendon Press, Oxford.

Post-modernism/
Post-modernity

Jean-François Lyotard

![The Idea]

T HE TERM 'MODERN' IS A TERM WE ARE ALL QUITE FAMILIAR WITH AND COMFORTABLE in using. It describes the world we live in, the lifestyle of society today and the sense of difference and change we feel that distinguishes life today from societies in the past. *Post-modern* is a phrase used to describe life and society in the future, in the period after modern society and in the ways that life today and in the future are distinctly different from Western society after World War II. Post-modernism, therefore, is a term used to embrace a rich and diverse array of philosophers and writers who have deliberately sought to offer a very different and quite radical view of post-modern society, of society in the 1980s, 1990s and particularly in the new millennium, from that proposed by traditional and even modern sociology. They believe that the post-modern world will be a very different place, a radical change from the industrial societies of the twentieth century, and from the modern societies of the post-war era.

Writers such as Jean François Lyotard and Jean Baudrillard (whose ideas on Simulation are described on p. 260) have sought to establish post-modernism as a distinct and fresh perspective on the society we live in, a perspective that on the one hand rejects the classical and modern theories of sociology to date and on the other hand seeks to develop a valid and accurate theoretical framework for describing the new type of society they believed was emerging at the end of the twentieth century, a 'post-modern world', a world that is distinctly new and fundamentally different from which has gone before.

Post-modernists reject traditional sociology wholesale. They reject even the possibility of a comprehensive and all-embracing sociological theory capable of analysing the whole of society, its past, its present and its future. They reject the notion that over time society is progressing either by evolution or revolution towards a better future, towards a more humane, civilised and rational stage of development. They reject scientific method and the potential power of reason and objectivity to discover the truth about society and the underlying laws of historical development.

In essence they reject modern sociology as it has developed to date. Modern sociology emerged as a distinct and distinguished academic discipline through the application by the founding fathers, Marx Weber and Durkheim, of scientific method to the study of society and its historical development. Their ideas gave birth to the sociological tradition and their ideas were fuelled by the Age of Reason, the period of Enlightenment born from the Intellectual, Scientific and Political Revolutions of the seventeenth and eighteenth centuries and the Industrial and Technological Revolutions of the last two centuries. This Enlightenment project and its faith in man's progress through reason, was best captured in Karl Marx's belief in a communist utopia. In its place, post-modernists have adopted a much more relativist, subjective approach that recognises and accepts that there is no one absolute and all-encompassing truth but rather a rich diversity of beliefs and perspectives. The role of sociology is not to explain away such truths and realities but to acknowledge, appreciate and celebrate them.

Jean François Lyotard's particular contribution to the development of post-modernism has been two-fold:

1. In the 1970s he launched a devastating attack on modern intellectual thought and development. He abandoned Marxism and embarked on a powerful and passionate critique of the grand theories of classical sociology and in particular on Marxism and liberal capitalism, the two dominant ideologies of the post-war world. His fury was particularly directed against modern science and technology and their arrogant claims that through new technologies they are masterminding human progress and saving the world. In Lyotard's view, technoscientific development is the cause of man's malaise, not its salvation. Rather than enriching and enlightening man, scientific progress is dividing the rich from the poor and encouraging exploitation of the Third World by the First. It has created a poverty of intellectual ideas by sweeping aside emotional intelligence and creating a world that is clinically efficient but emotionally bankrupt, an alienating world where human experience and emotion have no place. This is most evident, argues Lyotard, in modern art and architecture where few people today can empathise or even understand abstract art or futuristic buildings that seem devoid of human warmth or feeling. The totalitarianism of science and technology may rule the modern world but beneath the surface, argues Lyotard, an alienation, a dissatisfaction and resentment is growing that will challenge and overthrow the power of reason and the power of the scientist/technologist.

2. Lyotard has sought to sketch out a new alternative vision of society based on plurality and diversity. In writings such as the *Post Modern Condition* (1979) and *The Differend: Phases in Dispute* (1983), he argues that post-modern society has its roots in developments in the 1950s and is particularly evident in changes in language.

Using the concept of *language games*, Lyotard has argued that social life and social power are essentially organised around the power of certain social groups to control debate and discussion, and to impose their version of the truth on society at large. In pre-industrial societies, myths and legends were the principal language game and such tales not only gave tribal societies the means to make sense of their being and their environment, but also determined and legitimised the power of the elders and the witchdoctors in controlling decision making, wealth and authority. They alone spoke to God and in return the spirits spoke to them alone.

Through the Enlightenment and the Scientific Revolution, modern Western society has moved from the language games of mediaeval Europe, the Church and Christian beliefs to the reasoning and objectivity of scientific method. Ignorance and superstition have been swept away; reason has been liberated and celebrated as the dominant language game or 'narrative' as he calls it. In fact, in his view, modern science constitutes a 'metanarrative', a sort of supernarrative capable of explaining all other narratives, capable of producing new discoveries and insights into nature and the universe, whether it be Einstein's theory of relativity, Darwin's of evolution or Marx's of historical materialism.

Lyotard, however, rejects such grand theorising and believes that people have lost faith in technological perfection. Rather, post-modern man displays '*an incredulity towards metanarratives*' and is critically aware that every major scientific advance brings in its wake the potential seeds of man's destruction – nuclear power and nuclear destruction, fossil fuels and global warming, wonder drugs and superbugs, sexual liberation and AIDS, communism and totalitarianism. For him the two key characteristics of post-modern society are:

- an abandonment of the search for one absolute truth, one overriding denotative language game, one metanarrative in favour of a diversity of wide ranging theories and perspectives;
- the replacement of all-embracing denotative narratives by specialist technical language games designed not for primary research but for making practical every day judgements about the potential use and efficiency of the mass of new products and new ideas now on the market.

For Lyotard the principal 'force of production' is the modern computer. It is at the forefront today of scientific and technological development. All knowledge is increasingly computerised and modern social life, let alone economic life, increasingly revolves around IT and home computers. Control over information technology is now one of the primary battlegrounds for control over the modern world and companies like Microsoft, BT and Vodafone lead the way in seeking to control and exploit the world's networks. For Lyotard, the production, exchange and use of knowledge is at the heart of post-modern society. It is bought, sold and marketed and it defines and determines modern social and economic relationships. The search for marketable knowledge has replaced the search for truth as the driving force of modern science. It has become a source of technological dominance that threatens to enslave the human spirit and dampen human creativity. He is not totally pessimistic, however. While modern technology has given us '*as much terror as we can take*', the very diversity of post-modern society and the power of the new technologies holds out some hope of greater tolerance and communication between nations as individual people use IT and the Internet to communicate across national boundaries and outside of the traditional structures of power.

Jean François Lyotard therefore rejected the absolutism of grand theory for the relativism involved in competing paradigms, narratives or language games, each of which have their own set of intellectual assumptions and beliefs, each their own '*discourse*', each their own claim to truth. From this perspective there is no one truth, only 'power struggles' for intellectual dominance. In his view, all 'discourses' are equally valid and even modern science has no more claim to the truth than any other ideology. All that has happened is that the language game of modern science has reigned supreme longer than most. It ruled the 'modern post-industrial world' but now it is under attack on a variety of fronts as knowledge becomes more diverse and decentralised and as more and more people challenge scientific 'truths' and the right of technology to rule our lives.

Lyotard therefore seeks to encourage and legitimise the quest for *paralogy*, for endless debate informed by access to all sources of modern knowledge so that even the least powerful, the least literate, can contribute to and take part in the language games of the future. The global corporations may control the technologies of the future but the Internet gives people across the world access to that information and the means to discuss it.

The Idea in Action

LYOTARD'S CRITIQUE OF GRAND THEORY AND OF THE SCIENTIFIC TRADITION HAS struck a central chord in the post-modern psyche. People today are increasingly concerned, if not fearful, about modern technological developments. They are increasingly aware of its excesses and its impact on our environment. Modern technology seems to be out of control, seems to be serving the needs of faceless corporations and invisible bureaucracies rather than serving the needs of mankind. The excesses and exploitation by Western capitalism are as evident as the failures of world ideologies such as communism. Though global capitalism now seems all powerful in the wake of the collapse of the Berlin Wall (1989) and the demise of the USSR, it too has had to become more diverse, pluralistic and sensitive to human rights and equality of opportunity. Such developments, however, have undermined Lyotard's thesis as much as supported it. While the diversity and humanism he advocated may seem to be more evident, the moral relativism he argued for has not replaced the search for underlying or fundamental truth. The September 11th attack on New York was as much an attack on American and capitalist immorality as it was on its economic and military power; as much a protest on behalf of religious truths as an attack on the American way of life.

Lyotard's attack on modern science and his claim that it lacks either objectivity or ethical integrity has provoked a stinging response from the scientific community. By lampooning Lyotard and other post-modern writers, Sokal and Bricmont (1997) have sought to show just how shallow and invalid post-modern descriptions of scientific method really are. Others have made similar criticisms. While his generalisations may enjoy emotional appeal, they are often exaggerated, unsubstantiated and lack intellectual depth. Lyotard's lack of an ethical stance or moral standard in particular have left him vulnerable to the criticism that his relativist perspective can be used to justify, even apologise for modern capitalism as much as challenge it. Thus the diversity of post-modern theory, its rejection of grand narratives and its celebration of different points of view has been both its strength and its weakness. For some it is a carnival, a new fad in the cycle of cultural fashion; for others its impact on social theory has been so great that it cannot be ignored. The very term 'post-modern' has defied definition and re-emerged as 'post-modernism and post-modernity'. It has no single intellectual niche or discipline but has pervaded, if not invaded, the full gamut of the arts, sciences and social sciences. Its high priests and founding fathers come primarily from non-sociological disciplines and only recently has it gained real acceptance within sociology itself. As George Ritzer (1996: 607) concludes, '*the simple fact is that post modernism can no longer be ignored by sociological theorists*'. Some like Baudrillard have sought to reanalyse social theory as a whole; others like Weinstein and Weinstein (1993) have sought to resurrect past figures such as Georg Simmel as a post-modernist before his time. C. Wright Mills has been subject to similar re-evaluation and resurrection.

Whatever the outcome of such debates, whatever the final place of post-modernism in the history of sociology, it has made a profound impact and forced writers in this field to re-evaluate the worth and validity of the sociological tradition and its founding fathers. It has provoked a major debate on the nature of post-modern society and challenged the whole of the social sciences, the arts and the sciences, to critically review – and in some cases revise – their traditional ways of thinking and theorising.

 See Also

- INFORMATION(AL) SOCIETY (p. 220), RISK SOCIETY (p. 255), DISCOURSE (p. 208) and SIMULATIONS (p. 260) as alternative perspectives on the nature and character of late modern/post-modern society today.

Suggested and Further Reading

Jean-François Lyotard's writings are not easy, even for advanced students of sociology and certainly not for 'A' level students.

Mike O'Donnell (2001) and the relevant chapters in recent textbooks such as Haralambos and Holborn (2000) may help introduce readers to the complex but provocative writings of post-modernists.

Below are Lyotard's key works in this field and some critical commentaries.

LYOTARD, J.F. (1979) *The Post Modern Condition*, Manchester University Press, Manchester.

LYOTARD, J.F. (1983) *The Differend: Phases in Dispute* (trans. G. Van den Abeele), Manchester University Press, Manchester.

LYOTARD, J.F. (1992) *The Postmodern Explained to Children*, Turnaround, London.

LYOTARD, J.F. (1995) *Toward the Postmodern*, New Jersey Humanities Press.

SOKAL, A. AND BRICMONT, J. (1997) *Intellectual Impostures: Post Modern Philosophers' Abuse of Science*, Profile Books, London.

WEINSTEIN, D. AND WEINSTEIN, M.A. (1993) *Postmodern(ised) Simmel*, Routledge.

Relative Autonomy

Nicos Poulantzas

The Idea

A KEY DEBATE WITHIN POLITICAL SOCIOLOGY HAS BEEN OVER THE ROLE OF THE STATE in advanced capitalist societies. Is the state – the government, the civil service, the police and the military – representative of and responsible to the people in the true sense of democracy? Or is it an instrument of class control, a means by which the ruling capitalist class – either by propaganda or by force – imposes its will on the people and preserves and protects its powers and privileges? While this overall debate between liberal and more radical writers has been part of the pluralist-elitist debate (see Power Elite, p. 171), the debate within Marxist circles has not been about *whether* the modern state is an instrument of class control – that is taken for granted in Marxist writings – but *how* it rules and how such class control is exercised. Traditionally Marxist writers have argued that even today the state is primarily controlled by the capitalist class simply because members of their class – drawn from upper middle class backgrounds and educated at public schools and Oxbridge – hold most of the top positions in the government, civil service, judiciary and army and operate according to a common code and culture that protects their class interests. Good examples of this form of analysis include the works of Sam Aaronovitch (1961) and Ralph Miliband (1969).

Nicos Poulantzas, a Greek academic and lawyer and a leading Marxist intellectual during the 1970s developed a very different thesis about ruling class methods and tactics, one based on *relative autonomy* rather than direct class control. In a famous and long-running debate with Ralph Miliband, Poulantzas proposed a more structural analysis of capitalist societies that does not depend on either the individuals nor the parties in power. Whoever in his view rules in a capitalist society they will have to run it in the interests of capitalism.

In an attempt to draw up an ideal model of the capitalist system and capitalist state, Poulantzas argues that the capitalist mode of production comprises three key levels or sub-systems – the economic, political and ideological – which, though inter-related, also have some measure of autonomy or independence. Thus, while the economic system significantly influences the political and ideological, it is equally possible for political and ideological events to influence the economy and/or develop a momentum of their own.

Amid this complex interaction, the role of the modern capitalist state is to regulate the system as a whole, protect the long-term interests of capitalism, maintain bourgeois rule and healthy profits and keep the proletariat under control – by force if necessary, by ideology if possible. In particular, it has to regulate the class struggle, an underlying antagonism between capital and labour that cannot be eliminated but which can be controlled to prevent actual class revolution breaking out. And the way to do this in an age of mass democracy and liberal freedoms is not by direct suppression, but by indirect control, by the state having 'relative autonomy' from the ruling class. In this way the government, police and judiciary can 'appear' to be independent of any one class and so gain the support and consent of all classes in society. Moreover, an 'independent' state can better protect the long-term interests of the capitalist system than can the capitalist class itself, which is highly fragmented and divided into a variety of 'factions' or competing interests which range from large landowners and big business to high finance and the multinationals. By having relative autonomy, the government can mediate between the various factions of the capitalist class and between the bourgeoisie and the proletariat, thus giving the ruling class vital unity and leadership and preventing outright class conflict. Such autonomy allows the government to grant short-term concessions to the working class, such as increased welfare provisions, and even allows it to introduce restrictions against capitalist 'factions' or groups such as speculators, whose greed threatens to upset the whole system or the reputation of capitalism. The capitalist state is thus able to discipline the ruling class and fragment the working class, protect the long-term interests of capitalism and preserve its appearance of neutrality. Such neutrality is a vital element in modern class control. By 'appearing' to represent all the people and all social classes, the modern state can rule by consent rather than by force as in the past. Such ideological control is far more effective than coercion, than military might and direct suppression. Poulantzas, therefore, distinguished between the repressive and the ideological state apparatus; the instruments of coercive control (the police, army and government) and those of ideological control such as the church, schools and even the family.

But how is such a delicate balancing act achieved? How does the state know when or how to respond to the ever-changing balance of power between capital and labour? For Poulantzas the key mechanism is the 'class struggle' which at all times is reflected in the state apparatus – in parliament, government, the civil service, etc. – as a balance of power between workers and capitalists, one that ebbs and flows as each side grows in strength or weakens. When, for example, the unions are strong, as in the early 1970s in Britain, the government will grant concessions in the form of wage rises, welfare benefits or new laws against landlords or employers. When the working class is weak or disunited, or when key interests of capitalism are threatened, then the government will stamp down on the unions, restrain wages, cut taxes and boost profits rather than jobs, as in the Britain of the 1980s. And it does not really matter which party is in power. Both monetarism and trade union restrictions, key aspects of the Conservative Government of Mrs Thatcher, were originally initiated by Labour governments in the late 1960s and 1970s and have been continued by New Labour ever since.

For Poulantzas, the class background of top politicians, judges and civil servants, is irrelevant. What is crucial is the fact that the structure of capitalist society forces the state to act in the long-term interests of capitalism, whoever occupies the seats of power. Its autonomy, however, is always relative and limited. The state could never be used to destroy or undermine capitalism, so severely restricting the potential for a socialist party in Western capitalist society to democratically achieve power and effect a peaceful transition to socialism. The form that this class control takes, be it military rule, fascism or liberal democracy, will depend on particular national political developments.

The role of the state in capitalist society, therefore, is to maintain stability and to create the conditions for capitalism to flourish. It is part of the capitalist superstructure and so operates ultimately in the interests of the ruling class, irrespective of whether members of the ruling class occupy top positions in the state. In fact, the freer the state seems to be from the ruling class, the better, in both representing all factions and interests among the bourgeoisie and in maintaining the myth of independence needed to legitimise its rule and attract public consent. It must disguise its real role as representing the interests of capitalism. The more disguised that rule, the better.

'The capitalist state best serves the interests of the capitalist class only when members of this class do not participate directly in the state apparatus, that is to say when the Ruling Class is not the politically governing class' (Poulantzas 1973).

The Idea in Action

ACCORDING TO POULANTZAS' BIOGRAPHER, BOB JESSOP (1985), *'IT IS NO EXAGGERATION to claim that Poulantzas remains the single most important and influential Marxist theorist of the state and politics in the post-war period'*. His ideas have had influence as far afield as Latin America and Scandinavia and his concept of relative autonomy continues to be a major contribution to both the theory and practice of the modern capitalist state, of how the ruling class continues to rule, and of strategies by which that rule might be undermined by stimulating struggles between the various factions of the capitalist class *within* the state as well as by encouraging revolution outside by the working class.

However, the concept of relative autonomy has also been subject to serious criticism over both its vagueness and the difficulty of finding evidence of it at work. Exactly how relative is relative autonomy? How autonomous and constrained is the state? Dearlove and Saunders (1984) have identified four particular weaknesses of Poulantzas' theory:

- It is circular. The only way to gauge the strength or weakness of the working class is by the amount of concessions it is granted. However, it could equally be argued that even when the working class is weak it may gain state benefits, especially if the Labour party is in power.
- It is tautologous. The idea of relative autonomy is untestable. It can be used to explain everything and nothing because Poulantzas fails to provide any criteria for

testing it empirically. The notion of relative autonomy is almost impossible to prove or disprove. Any action the state takes can be interpreted as either benefiting the ruling class or being a concession to the proletariat. There is therefore no basis for evaluating or critically examining this concept.

- It is too narrow. It only includes the class struggle, so ignoring the rise of many other groups and interests in post-war society which cut across class lines – feminism, blacks, gays, environmental groups, etc. Poulantzas' attempts to subsume all such pressure groups under a class analysis is inadequate.

- It is incomplete. It ignores the influence of individual personalities, groups and factions, offering only a mechanical analysis which implies that it makes no real difference whether Margaret Thatcher or Tony Benn, the National Front or Militant Tendency are in power.

This is the essence of the alternative Marxist view of the workings of the modern capitalist state proposed by writers like Ralph Miliband (1969) in his long-running debate with Poulantzas. Miliband argued that members of the capitalist class actually staff the modern state, steering it through the periodic crises that are endemic to capitalism and using it to suppress the class struggle. Miliband accused Poulantzas of 'superstructure determinism' and of a lack of detailed evidence to support his claim that the state always acts in the interests of capitalism. He questions the idea that institutions such as the family constitute part of the state apparatus. Miliband's approach in contrast is more flexible and less deterministic than Poulantzas', dependent more on people and personalities than the underlying structure and logic of the system, but it, too, suffers from problems of actually measuring such a balance of power, and of proving that a concession was a concession, not a reform. Neither approach clearly answers the key practical question of whether a socialist or labour party can transform capitalism and convert it into socialism – though neither is optimistic.

In his final work (*State, Power and Socialism*, 1978) and in research notes published after his death, Poulantzas himself was moving away from the idea of relative autonomy. Nevertheless, it has stimulated a major debate within modern Marxism and brought to the forefront of sociological theory, the role and functioning of the modern state.

 See Also

- **HEGEMONY** (p. 121) and **STRUCTURAL MARXISM** (p. 265) as the parent theories for this idea, albeit from different theoretical bases.
- **LEGITIMATION CRISIS** (p. 225) as Jürgen Habermas's theory of the role and power of the state in late-modern capitalist societies.
- **DISCOURSE** (p. 208) as a post-modern/post-structuralist view of power and the state today.

Suggested Reading

JESSOP, B. (1985) *Nicos Poulantzas,* Macmillan, London – as an overview of Poulantzas' life and work.

URRY, J. AND WAKEFORD, J. (EDS.) (1973) *Power in Britain,* Heinemann, London – summarises the Miliband–Poulantzas debate.

Further Reading

MILIBAND, R. (1969) *The State in Capitalist Society,* Weidenfeld & Nicolson, London – a relatively easy read of an alternative view of the structure of the modern state although now rather dated.

POULANTZAS, N. (1978) *State, Power, Socialism*, New Left Books, New York.

Risk Society

Ulrich Beck

The Idea

MODERN SOCIETIES ARE FULL OF RISKS. WE LIVE IN A *RISK SOCIETY* WHERE EVERY DAY we face the risk of accidents, illness and major disasters on a scale that is far greater than those faced by societies in the past – AIDS, nuclear warfare, global warming and, after September 11th 2001, international terrorism that can strike down ordinary citizens just as much as they hit big business and military installations.

A variety of writers have sought to use the concept of risk as the defining characteristic of post-modern society and to build a theory of social and political change upon this framework. One of the leading figures in this field is Ulrich Beck, a German academic who has studied in London, Cardiff and Berlin, and who has served on the German government's Future Commission. Beck's most famous publication, *Risk Society: Towards a New Modernity* (1992), was originally published in 1986 shortly after the Chernobyl nuclear disaster in the Soviet Union. In it, Beck laid out a new theoretical framework for understanding post-modern society, a framework that on the one hand sought to supersede neo-Marxism and the revival of liberal theories of social change, and on the other hand sought to link together a vast array of apparently disconnected and unconnected events and activities – events as far flung as Chernobyl and BSE, HIV and Third World debt – with such social and political movements as feminism, mass consumerism and the decline of class warfare.

For Ulrich Beck, risk is the defining characteristic of post-modern society. We live in a risk society. Beck (1992) defines risk as '*a systematic way of dealing with hazards and insecurities induced and introduced by Modernisation*'.

Beck thus characterises modern society in terms of risk and distinguishes it from pre-industrial and industrial society by the fact that risks today are largely man made and global. In pre-industrial society, risks and dangers were largely natural and beyond man's control – floods, famines, plagues. In industrial society, man began to systematically gain control of his own environment, began to gain control of nature. He overcame the threat of natural disasters by building flood barriers, growing his own food and by developing medicines to reduce and prevent deadly diseases. He began, however, to create new, mainly man-made dangers; dangers that threatened man's health and well-being but on a local or national scale rather than on an international one – the smog of the new industrial cities of the nineteenth century, the pollution of the new industrial factories.

Today in post-modern society, man has not only increased his power over nature, he has sought to gain *control* of nature itself and in so doing he has also put his universe at risk of total destruction. Splitting the atom gave man the power to generate nuclear energy. It also gave him the means to create weapons of mass destruction; deciphering DNA has given man not only the secret of genetic life but also the power to play God and to create human clones; fossil fuels have given mankind 200 years of global energy but man's exploitation and wasteful use of such fuels now threaten to destroy the planet through global warming. As man gains more and more control of his universe so, paradoxically, the risks to life and to the earth itself seem to become far greater and to affect all humankind, not just individual nations and communities in the East or the West, the North or the South.

This paradox is equally reflected in the social structures of societies today. As the individual becomes freer and more independent so, paradoxically, the social structures that previously protected people start to collapse. The church, the community, the family, even the class structures of modern Western societies all provided people with a sense of belonging, identity and purpose within what appeared to be a stable social order. In post-modern society the individual is increasingly on his or her own, isolated, vulnerable and without protection. 'Social' crises appear as individual crises and social problems are increasingly perceived as personal rather than collective problems; problems to be dealt with at the psychological level rather than at the social or political level by the government, the school or the family.

Beck identifies a new and fundamental shift in the relationship between society and the individual; a new mode of socialisation as society seeks to prepare its young for the risks of the future. While the aim in class-based societies was the pursuit of wealth and happiness, in a risk society the primary goal is simply to survive. The pursuit of security and stability has superseded the pursuit of profit. The ravages of risk now affect all societies, all communities, all classes. No-one can completely escape the potential risks of HIV, BSE or biological warfare. Managing risk is now as much a personal dilemma as a social one. In an age where the individual seems freer than ever before – materially, psychologically and spiritually – people ironically are more vulnerable and helpless, less in control of their lives and the world around them. To survive, people must become more 'self-reflective, more self-disciplined and self-controlled'. They have to learn to take more control of their own lives, their own lifestyles. They have to learn how to evaluate and manage risk and to take responsibility for their own actions if they are to survive and thrive. Personal decision-making thus becomes the basis of social decision-making. Politicians and those in authority can no longer tell people what to do in a modern democracy; they have to inform them of the risks ahead and encourage rather than command conformity. In the open and opportunistic societies of today it is individual decision making, decision making about lifestyle, about personal habits and personal mores that will determine the future – decisions about smoking and drug-taking; decisions about sexual habits and personal relationships that will encourage *or* eliminate, for example, the spread of cancer or HIV.

Personal decisions now have international consequences at a time when the world at large seems to be out of control and totally unpredictable. We have therefore entered, in Beck's view, not a post-modern world but a 'second modernity' in which risk and the management of risk are the defining characteristics; an age of 'reflective modernisation' in which every action at whatever level – individual, social or international – has unintended consequences on an unpredictable scale. As we know more through modern science and technology, and communicate more through the global media and Internet, so we control less. We become more fearful, more risk conscious, more security minded about the foods we eat, the drugs we take, the planes we catch. We may equally become more fatalistic, even carefree and careless. Why not live for today when who knows what tomorrow will bring?

In his more recent writings, Beck has gone on from the personal and social level to consider the nature of society at large. We live, in his view, not just in a global society but a 'world risk society', a modernity in which progress cannot be assumed and in which every advance produces its own set of risks, its dangers, its dark side. Every new medical treatment, every new technological development has its downside, its side-effects, the impact of which, like global warming and radiation, will only begin to be apparent in the years, even the generations ahead. We no longer trust the expert; we no longer defer to our politicians, our scientists, our doctors. We know risks exist in all walks of life and we now demand that they be exposed, evaluated, and that we be informed so that we can personally assess the risks for ourselves. The traditional and institutional decision makers, the traditional decision-making processes, are now more open to public scrutiny and debate. New developments lead to new debates and on occasion to struggles over the decision-making agenda; struggles reflected in the growth of mass protest movements – protests over the environment, over genetic engineering, over global capitalism; protests that reverberate around the globe aided by the mass media and the Internet. As more is known, more is feared. Nature has been politicised and the risks of tampering with it are far better understood. In Beck's view, today nature and society are intertwined; 'nature is society and society is also nature' (1992).

National governments are being by-passed by the new breed of sub-politics, protest groups who have identified new sources of risk and who are prepared to take direct action against them, be they the oil rigs of the petroleum giants or the scientific laboratories of the pharmaceutical companies.

Risk is a feature of modern life. It is generating a new breed of social citizen, aware of and capable of 'reflecting' on and assessing such risks and making individual decisions accordingly. However, while risk and class may no longer be directly related, risk and wealth do enjoy an inverse relationship. The poor and those at the bottom of the social scale are particularly vulnerable to risk; those at the top can at least 'purchase safety and freedom from risk' (Beck 1992) even if they cannot avoid it. Such a relationship, such an exposure to risk is equally applicable to the relationship between the First and the Third Worlds. While HIV, floods and disease impact on Western societies, the poorer nations of the world are devastated by them and have no defences. Yet ironically, the poor, too, are able to reflect on risk, assess its causes and mobilise to reduce or minimise its impact through international protest or, in extreme cases, through international terrorism.

The Idea in Action

ULRICH BECK'S THESIS OF RISK AND HIS BELIEF THAT POST-MODERN SOCIETY IS A RISK society has proved to be a major contribution to the debate about the nature of society today and to the culture that underpins it. His notion of risk has not only informed the development of his own writings but also influenced the ideas and theorising of writers as prominent as Anthony Giddens. The whole notion of risk as a feature of society and as a determining influence on modern man has equally risen to the forefront of popular thinking with the events of September 11th 2001 and the terrorist attacks on New York and the Pentagon. Risk consciousness and reflection on risk have risen to new heights as people throughout the world reassess their lifestyles and the risks associated with them. Security is top of the agenda as people reassess the risks of travelling, communicating and even opening their post. The 'sub-politics' described by Beck have reached new heights as the protest groups of the poor convert the technologies of travel into weapons of mass destruction. The world of today seems even riskier than that of yesterday. Nothing is sacred, nothing is secure in the emerging world of international politics. One can only assess the risks and make personal choices.

The new politics of terrorism have equally supported Beck's contention that although we are moving into a new world order, a second modernity, we have not yet reached it. We are in transition from industrial society to a risk society but many of the features of the past persist, not least the risks created by the industrial age. What a contrast then, to see America, the greatest and most modern society in the world taken on in September 2001 by terrorists claiming to represent Islam, one of the most traditional and fundamentalist of religious movements, as a way of resisting modernisation – and Western control.

The central issue in classical modernity was the creation of wealth and its distribution. The central feature of post-modern society, according to Beck, is risk, its distribution, prevention and control. Safety and security have replaced equality and freedom as primary political goals. Risk today knows no boundaries and while the poor and the people of the Third World seem more exposed to risk through what Beck calls the 'boomerang effect', the First World will ultimately be forced to face up to the hazards and dangers they have created in the past – be it the arms Western nations supplied to nations like Iraq and ironically used against them in the Gulf War, or the exploitation of Third World economies that has produced the poverty and anger that have fuelled anti-American fervour and fanaticism, or the destabilising impact on the world economy of the booms and slumps of the world's stock markets.

To survive in a chaotic world, the modern individual has to become more self-conscious, more self-reflective, more risk conscious. The modern corporation and organisation has to plan for risk and integrate risk management into its management structure. We all have to reflect more openly on our own actions and on the actions of others, to consider more carefully the potential consequences of our actions and the actions of our governments. We no longer enjoy the protection of our families, the church or authority. We have, in Beck's view, to protect ourselves – and we may all be better for doing so.

Ulrich Beck's *Key Idea* has struck a real chord in modern experience and modern imagination. The future is frightening but modern man, in his view, is capable of coping. Whether he will survive remains to be seen. Whether Beck has captured in his concept of risk the key feature and the underlying dynamic of post-modern or late modern society is equally debatable. It has nevertheless contributed to the debate as well as reflecting our own 'gut' feeling that the world today is a riskier place to live in, a world on the edge of a new social order – or on the verge of self-destruction.

 **See Also**

- **GLOBALISATION** (p. 214) and **INFORMATION(AL) SOCIETY** (p. 220) as alternative 'late' modern views of world development.
- **POST-MODERNISM** (p. 245) and **SIMULATIONS** (p. 260) as post-modern perspectives on the nature of society today.

Suggested and Further Reading

The references below are only really appropriate for the more advanced student.

BECK, U. (1985) *Ecological Politics in the Age of Risk,* Polity Press, Cambridge.

BECK, U. (1992) *Risk Society: Towards a New Modernity* [1986], Sage, London.

BECK, U. (1997) *The Reinvention of Politics: Rethinking Modernity in the Global Social Order*, Polity Press, Cambridge.

BECK, U. (1999) *World Risk Society*, Polity Press, Cambridge.

Simulations

Jean Baudrillard

THE TERM 'SIMULATION' IS USUALLY USED TO REFER TO IMITATION OR REPRESENTATION of something real. Modern computers are now at the forefront of product design in *simulating* the finished article or putting it through its paces, whether it be a new car, vacuum cleaner or motorbike. Many people enjoy the spills and thrills of flying an aircraft or spaceship simulator at a funfair or aviation display – great fun and none of the fears or dangers of flying the 'real' thing. Simulation is a pretend experience, an imitation of the real thing – often so real it is difficult to tell the difference.

The radical French philosopher, Jean Baudrillard, used this concept in his book *Simulations* in 1983 to argue that the post-modern world of today is not a real society but a simulated one, a *virtual reality* within which symbols and images have replaced the real and the tangible. Rather than exchanging goods and services we exchange symbols and images; rather than satisfying real material needs we now seek psychological satisfaction of wants and desires. The clothing industry today is a classic example of Baudrillard's argument. The need for clothing to keep people warm and dry has been replaced by the desire for the latest, high status designer labels. Such clothing has nothing to do with need and everything to do with image. Jeans and trainers from Marks & Spencer or British Home Stores would be just as good as those from Levis or Nike, but in this fashion conscious age, what teenager would be seen 'dead in them'? Gucci, Addidas and Reebok thrive on image and people today seem to judge each other more by the labels they wear than by the person they are. Image is all and the self-satisfaction it temporarily brings is used by manufacturers throughout the world to promote and sell apparently very similar products be they shoes or cars, holidays or homes.

From this basic observation, Baudrillard has sought to develop a radical theory about the nature of post-modern society, a theory based on the power of *signs*. Baudrillard argues that signs in human culture have developed in four main stages.

- The first stage involves the development of signs (words and images) as reflections of reality.
- In the second stage, signs begin to embellish, exaggerate or distort the truth but overall they still reflect and symbolise reality.
- In the third and fourth stages, signs and simulation take over from reality and ultimately replace it with a symbolic society, a society of pure 'simulacrum', where symbols and signs have no relationship to anything real and where even human relationships are purely symbolic. Thus for Baudrillard post-modern society is nothing like anything that has gone before it. It is a world of images and free floating signs, a world where the mode of production has been replaced by the code of production. And to support his argument, Baudrillard cites the examples of Las Vegas and Hollywood, the dreamworlds of Western society with Disneyland as the perfect simulacrum.

'In both Disneyland and Disney World, it is clear that everything that can be derived from the imaginary has been caught, represented, made representable, put on display, made visual. Literally putting on a show for consumption without any metaphors is obviously a radical deterrent to the imaginary. Once again, utopia becomes reality' (Baudrillard 1993: 246).

He saw America in particular as 'the finished form of the future catastrophe' (Baudrillard 1986), a society based on fiction with no history, no past reality to help make sense of the present.

Other examples he cites include the removal of the Egyptian mummy Pharaoh Rameses II from its original burial ground and its presentation through museums and mass television as a symbol of the past torn from its natural habitat and exploited commercially as a mass spectacle. Modern 'soaps' and programmes, like Big Brother or Castaway, may equally be cited as examples of pseudo reality, simulated relationships be they on television or a desert island. In Baudrillard's view we are experiencing 'the dissolution of life into TV and the dissolution of TV into life' (1983).

Baudrillard's conclusion and his image of post-modern society is both gloomy and pessimistic. It is potentially socially fatal. If it is now impossible to grasp reality, then it is impossible to change it. We live in a meaningless, unreal world, a perpetual motion picture where there is no longer any basis for judging right or wrong, no standard for distinguishing the truth from the lie. We live in a hyper-reality where the media has moved from being a mirror of reality to being reality itself. Like the film Fatal Attraction, if the audience do not like the ending, then the producers will change it.

In the field of politics, Baudrillard does not see power as evenly or unevenly distributed. Rather, he sees real power as not existing at all. It's all a giant 'playstation'. Whereas in the past, when Presidents and Prime Ministers played wargames, they played them for real using real weapons – or at least they threatened to use real weapons even if nuclear weapons could not actually be used. Now power struggles are more like Star Wars, played out on television with the good guys, the Americans, usually defeating such evil villains as Saddam Hussein or Osama Bin Laden. The harsh reality of war, the victims, the aftermath and the underlying causes of conflict are rarely shown and soon forgotten as the cameras move on to the next news story. World leaders, presidents and prime ministers are similarly pre-packaged and sold to the electorate as symbols of leadership, bought and sold at the polling booth whatever the substance under the suit. We live in a world of political images and symbols of power rather than one where the realities of power and the horrors of war are accurately portrayed. We can watch fighting in Afghanistan or the Middle East, famine and starvation in the Third World as we sit on our sofas eating TV dinners in front of the six o'clock news. It's unreal!

Post-modern man in Baudrillard's view is inactive and inert, living in a world of unreality that he is helpless to change and one he can only watch and comment on, not one he can take part in or experience. Real power lies with the media and the politicians, those who control this reality through the global networks, those who decide what, when and how we shall see, and who edit out the inconvenient or the challenging; those who create the soundbites that sell advertising space. Modern sport is a classic example of the commercial packaging of mass spectator television. It is awash with advertising and imagery. Young sports men and women are elevated to the status of young gods and goddesses, sex symbols within a game that is itself endlessly created, recreated and even redesigned through video replays, edited highlights and perpetual commentary. It is difficult to remember at times, amid the amounts of money spent, the hours that television devotes to sport and the passions that it evokes, that ultimately sport itself is not real; it is a simulated battlefield for today's young gladiators to perform on. As Boris Becker famously commented when losing at Wimbledon, 'it's only a game'.

Everything today, even the news and the weather, is a commodity to be packaged, a product to be sold using status symbols and images of a dreamlife in a dreamworld. The realities of such products – their effect on the environment, the exploitation of child labour in the Third World – is rarely mentioned.

In Baudrillard's view modern culture is undergoing a massive and catastrophic revolution. The masses are being desensitised and dehumanised, passive audiences to be manipulated and fed the 'pap' that constitutes commercial television. For Baudrillard, the revolution is dead, particularly that promised by Karl Marx and the utopia of communism and contemporary post-modern society is a 'death culture' devoid of all life and meaning, a consumer culture with no past, no future and no purpose where the masses are saturated and seduced by the symbols and signs of a good life that is unreal and unattainable. There is nothing beyond appearance because appearance is all we have.

'Life is conducted in a ceaseless circulation of signs about what is happening in the world (signs about news), about what sort of identity one wishes to project (signs about self), about one's standing (signs of status and esteem), about what purposes buildings serve (architectural signs), about aesthetic preferences (signs on walls, tables, side-boards), and so on' (Webster 1995: 177).

There is no longer any reality; there is no past – the media has even reinvented history – there is no future, there is no meaning.

The Idea in Action

BAUDRILLARD'S IMAGE OF THE 'SIMULATED SOCIETY' AND HIS CRITIQUE OF ITS VALUES and superficiality has struck a strong and powerful chord in societies where the mass media is so strong and all pervasive that it seems to be in control of all that we know and see. The power of the symbol, the power of modern advertising, permeates every aspect of our lives. Every three-year old, whether he or she lives in the jungles of Peru or the penthouses of Manhattan, recognises the signs and symbols of Coca-Cola and McDonald's.

However, in arguing his case, Baudrillard's own style and presentation have come under criticism.

- His writing and documentation are often as abstract and obscure as the society he describes. He relies on 'persuasive' examples to support his arguments rather than substantive evidence based on academic rigour. His style of writing is itself difficult to decipher and often beyond the audiences he is apparently trying to address.

- His exaggerated style reached its peak in 1995 when he claimed that the Gulf War in the Middle East against Iraq was not a real war but a 'simulated' one, one created by the military and the media for public consumption. Claims like this left his critics wondering whether he himself had lost his grip on reality and whether he was in danger of being seduced by his own propaganda.

- His attitude towards the public at large is at times contemptuous and patronising. He makes no attempt to recognise that in fact ordinary people are as capable of distinguishing fantasy from reality, are just as capable of seeing through all the hype and are as cynical and critical about modern politicians as he is. They recognise quality when they see it, whether it be in judging goods or people and ultimately they are capable of taking control either individually – by switching off the television or moving out into the country – or collectively as voters, viewers or consumers. The people have the ultimate power to control elections or demand better programmes or purchases by not voting or not buying. In the meantime they may well enjoy the delights of Disneyland or the lights of Bond Street if only to escape the harsh realities of everyday life.

His greatest fault, however, for many critics, is his attempt to deny the continuity of social and historical change. He over-emphasises the distinctive character of the present in his attempt to portray post-modern society as a distinctly different and separate stage from all that has gone before it. However, in denying history as a real and distinct influence on the present, Baudrillard is at a loss to explain how the present got here. It cannot simply have happened. It must have at least some of its roots in the past. It cannot just have arrived. Moreover, his portrayal of the future is so dreadful, so fatalistic that no-one seems able to change it. As George Ritzer (1996) pointed out, post-modernism and in particular the radical ideas of Jean Baudrillard promised a real alternative to the grand theories of the founding fathers, and in particular to those of Karl Marx; 'big ideas' capable of standing the test of time and capable of tackling the big issues of the post-modern world. Unfortunately, like Baudrillard's thesis, the reality of post-modernism has not always lived up to its promise. In rejecting grand theory and grand narratives in favour of 'fragments of ideas' without any underlying or coherent framework, post-modernists have defied judgement by normal standards of academic rigour. Their very style – which in Baudrillard's case is at times bizarre, playful, even irreverent – defies structured and ongoing debate and their vision of the future is at times so gloomy and pessimistic, so hopeless, that it is difficult to subscribe to without considering suicide or social isolation. Baudrillard's vision of the future is one of an imploding black hole, a death culture consumed by its own consumerism and search for meaning in a meaningless material world. As Kellner has summed it up:

'Acceleration of inertia, the implosion of meaning in the media, the implosion of the social in the mass, the implosion of the mass in a dark hole of nihilism and meaninglessness; such is the Baudrillardian post-modern vision' (Kellner 1989: 118).

Baudrillard has been hailed as the *'high priest of post-modernism'* (Miles 2001) and described as the most radical and outrageous of post-modernists (Ritzer 1996). However, while Baudrillard's view of society and his vision of the future may be fatalistic and pessimistic, an extreme and exaggerated portrayal of reality, while his ideas and those of his fellow writers may defy grand theory and lack theoretical structure, they have nevertheless challenged and provoked modern sociology and forced all of us to re-examine and seriously question the world we live in, its materialism, its meaning and its future.

 **See Also**

- **DISCOURSE** (p. 208) and **POST-MODERNISM** (p. 245) as alternative perspectives on the nature and character of post-modern society.

Suggested and Further Reading

EVEN a cursory review of the titles of Jean Baudrillard's books listed below is enough to whet the appetite and to convey the range and excitement of his critique of postmodern society. Unfortunately, like many post-modern writers, his books are as inaccessible as his titles are attractive, and they can only really be recommended for undergraduate students. There are equally few easy introductions so, like Jean François Lyotard, A-level students are best advised to rely on standard textbooks.

BAUDRILLARD, J. (1975) *The Mirror of Production* [1973], Telos Press.

BAUDRILLARD, J. (1983) *Simulations*, Semiotext (e).

BAUDRILLARD, J. (1986) *America*, Verso.

BAUDRILLARD, J. (1990) *Seduction*, Macmillan.

BAUDRILLARD, J. (1993) *Symbolic Exchange and Death*, Sage.

BAUDRILLARD, J. (1994a) *The Illusion of the End*, Polity Press, Cambridge.

BAUDRILLARD, J. (1994b) *Simulacra and Simulation*, University of Michigan Press.

BAUDRILLARD, J. (1995) *The Gulf War Did Not Take Place*, Power Publications.

BAUDRILLARD, J. (1997) *Fragments. Cool Memories III*, Verso.

KELLNER, D. (1989) *Jean Baudrillard: From Marxism to Post Modernism and Beyond*, Polity Press, Cambridge.

WEBSTER, F. (1995) *Theories of the Information Society*, Routledge, London.

Structural Marxism

Louis Althusser

The Idea

AFTER THE ATROCITIES COMMITTED BY JOSEPH STALIN IN SOVIET RUSSIA IN THE 1930S and the brutal dictatorships that seemed to be emerging in Eastern Europe, China and Asia under the name of communism, Western Marxism faced a fervent and philosophical dilemma. Could such brutality be defended? Did Marxism still have a future in post-war society? Could it still inspire the people to revolution or had post-war capitalism won the ideological and philosophical battle as well as the moral high ground in the era of the Cold War?

Many Marxist writers, disillusioned with Orthodox Marxism, turned back to Marx's earlier, more humanistic writings for inspiration. Others like Louis Althusser, a Professor of Sociology in Paris in the 1960s, argued instead for a more scientific or *structuralist* analysis for post-war Marxism.

For Althusser, Marxism is not just a political ideology. It is a revolutionary and scientific analysis of history and society that offers a political strategy for promoting and achieving working class revolution in a capitalist society. His aim, therefore, was nothing less than to update modern Marxism and to apply it to the complexities and conflicts of modern Western society. To do this he developed a highly *structured* and systematic version of Marxism based on five key concepts.

Social structures and social practices

HERE Althusser identified three key elements in the structure or 'formation' of society – the economic, the political and the ideological.

Relative autonomy

WHILE traditional Marxism had always emphasised the importance of economic factors in determining the shape and direction of industrial society, Althusser sought to also recognise the influence and importance of political and ideological factors in promoting revolutionary activity, not least because it was political revolution that drove change in Soviet Russia and political activity that was inspiring the students and workers in Paris at the time he was writing. He therefore developed the notion that both the political and ideological 'formations' in modern society have relative influence – or relative autonomy as he called it – though ultimately it is the economic structure that is pre-eminent 'in the last instance'.

Overdetermination

ALTHUSSER went on to recognise that not only do the economic, political and ideological structures have relative autonomy and a very complex relationship with each other, but they too have internal contradiction and conflicts. Compare, for example, the needs and interests of the landed classes with those of industrialists and financiers; or those of the petit bourgeoisie, the managers, accountants and the like who serve their capitalist masters but who equally have interests of their own. A similar analysis of the working 'classes' would equally show a high degree of internal class conflict and fragmentation among the proletariat; the conflict, for example, between skilled and unskilled workers or between those in trade unions and those outside them. Such internal conflicts, argued Althusser, meant that someone had to act as a referee or policeman, judge and jury keeping the peace and preventing open warfare, not only between the social classes but within them. That role in his view fell to the capitalist state.

Ideological state apparatus (ISA)

THE traditional Marxist view of the capitalist state was that it acted solely in the interests of capitalism, on the orders of the ruling class, using the law to protect property and profit and the police and army to suppress the masses.

Althusser argued for a more subtle interpretation of the modern state, arguing not only that the state must have some form of independence or relative autonomy from the capitalist class, but that it may have to, on occasion, act on behalf of the workers against big business in the interests of preventing class conflict and outright revolution. To rule effectively, the modern capitalist state has to maintain an 'ideological distance' if it is to remain in power, be re-elected by the masses and not have to resort to force. It cannot be perceived to be the 'mouthpiece' of capitalism or else it will lose its authority and credibility and become itself a focus for revolution and take over. For Althusser, therefore, the modern state does not rule by force – although in the last instance it may have to. It rules 'ideologically'. It rules by creating an ideological and cultural climate within which capitalism, capitalist values and a consumerist way of life are accepted as normal, natural and ultimately morally defensible; worth fighting and dying for against the threat of socialist or communist alternatives. Althusser's notion of the state, therefore, was much broader than the traditional idea of the state apparatus as the government civil service, courts, police and army. His concept included the ideological and cultural apparatus, the church, the media, the education system, the law and even the family, all the institutions that helped to communicate and propagate capitalist ideas and values.

Death of the subject

ALTHUSSER'S version of Marxism was therefore a highly sophisticated, highly structured one. It focused almost completely on the key structures of capitalist society, the relationships and conflicts between the economic, political and ideological formations and in particular on the role of the modern capitalist state in ameliorating and moderating class conflict, not only between classes but within classes. His analysis, therefore, wrote out and excluded the role of or influence of the individual. Contrary to some of Marx's early writings, Althusser was firmly committed to the view that we are all products of historical materialism. While we might think that we can change our lives, while we might believe we can change history – ultimately that is an illusion, a capitalist illusion. Rather, we are all acting out roles and responsibilities assigned to us by our class position, puppets on the strings of historical destiny. For Althusser, therefore, while he sought to encourage radical political action, particularly in France, ultimately in his view such action has only a 'relative' influence on historical change; ultimately history is a 'process without a subject'.

The Idea in Action

ALTHUSSER'S STRUCTURALIST INTERPRETATION OF MARXISM STIMULATED INTERNATIONAL recognition and widespread enthusiasm in the late 1960s and 1970s as a major challenge to both orthodox and humanist Marxism. Althusser's approach 'liberated' many Western intellectuals and especially Marxists from the rigid determinism of orthodox Marxism and legitimised their analysis of non-economic and especially political and cultural developments as part of an alternative Marxist framework. It justified and explained the outbreak in the 1960s and 70s of a plethora of protest movements from the Green Left to the feminists of the women's movement, as the grass roots of society demanded change. It inspired intellectuals and students on both sides of the Atlantic, and generated important empirical research, both within and outside the social sciences. His work attempted to tackle an inherent paradox in Marxism as to whether the ultimate driving forces in historical change are the impersonal ones of underlying economic forces or the revolutionary action of exploited and oppressed people united as social classes. Althusser's sophisticated analysis of scientific Marxism came down firmly in favour of the former view, but by allowing the political level 'dominance' in the late capitalist stage, he was able to continue encouraging contemporary political action by students, revolutionaries and the Communist party. His division of Marx's writings into 'early' and 'late' and his key concepts, particularly 'mode of production', 'ISA' and 'death of the subject', inspired intense debate and research, and structuralism spread into an international movement which included Paul Hirst and Barry Hindess in Britain and Pierre Bourdieu in France.

Althusser's central argument was that Marx's early writing on alienation and the social actor was a distinct and immature phase in the development of his ideas and that it wasn't until 1845 that Marx made his epistemological break and developed his true framework for analysing history and capitalism, a new and scientific problematic. Althusser was anti-humanist in the sense that he rejected the notion that man alone could change history; rather men are changing *within* history and the underlying forces for change in the economy and superstructure. However he rejected 'economic determinism', the notion that the economic base of society determines all else in favour of the more complex and multivariate view that the ideological, political and theoretical or scientific spheres also have a part to play. They interrelate and even have their own internal contradictions and dynamics. Marx, in his view, had not had the time to adequately develop his theory of the superstructure. That was the role of modern Marxism. Althusser was not, however, arguing that politics and ideology had equal weight with the economic foundation – only that they had 'relative autonomy' and relative weight. Ultimately the whole social structure depended on and was interrelated with the economic substructure and thus 'causal weight' ultimately lies with economic change.

Althusser's work, however, inspired as much criticism as adoration, criticism that was often quite bitter and highly personal. This was not only because his writings are quite complex and difficult to read, but because of his own arrogance and intolerance of others. He claimed not only to be reinterpreting Marx, but to be speaking for him and he was quite vitriolic about mainstream sociology and about any who dared to criticise or challenge him.

Part of the criticism against him was philosophical, part of it was ideological. At a philosophical level, while his notions of relative autonomy and class conflict offered a more sophisticated analysis of the realities of modern capitalism, it was very difficult to explain how these relationships actually work, how the economic, political and ideological structure interrelate, how class conflict actually emerges, how the individual fits in.

This criticism led on to the ideological critique that by leaving the 'subject' out, by disregarding human action, Althusser struggled to explain where the dynamic for social change comes from. If individual people promoting and pursuing change are not the primary force, what is? How can the capitalist system develop its own system dynamic if people are not involved in driving it? And this became the chief criticism of Althusser's model; it was too structural, too scientific, too mechanistic. Its notion of interlocking systems made it seem inhuman and mechanical. It lacked the human factor and so lacked the appeal of 'humanist' interpretations of Marxism.

Thus Althusser's claim of structuralism as a scientific theory of history and knowledge ended up being self-defeating. Althusser rejected the empiricist idea that the ultimate test of all theories and ideas is the real world, in favour of the claim that every theory is its own judge; every theory has its own framework of thought (what he called problematic) and so can only be judged on its own terms. While it may make sense to argue that we cannot judge all theories against facts in the so-called real world – we cannot, for example, actually see a mode of production or a social class but we can still usefully use such concepts to make sense of the world – it does not make sense to say that we have no way of judging between theories or of criticising them except in their own terms. If this were true, how could Althusser himself claim that structuralism was superior to crude Marxism or humanism? How could structuralists distinguish between scientific and non-scientific theories? Surely his writings were just as ideological as all others? Althusser sought to overcome this problem by claiming that structuralism was outside ideology, a sort of super-science. Such claims to intellectual superiority, to being above criticism, were swiftly decimated by other academics.

Althusser's theory was ultimately undermined by its lack of humanist appeal. It lacked the moral outrage felt in the West, even among left wing radicals about the atrocities committed in Eastern Europe and Soviet Russia in the name of socialism. It even seemed to be anti-human in spirit and to be advocating an even worse example of Big Brother – state socialism in which the human spirit had no place to play.

Althusser sought to revise his work in the light of such criticism and argued that far from being anti-human, he was in fact trying to rescue Marxism from the humanists and to re-establish it as a practical and scientific analysis of historical change and human liberation. Such revisions, however, undermined the originality, verve and passion of his initial thesis.

Ultimately Althusser's work is yet another example of the attempts by Western philosophers to revise and update Marxism, to make it relevant to post-war and post-modern society. Althusser's thesis was one of the most powerful and influential of such attempts and even today, 20 years later, it is still informing research across the whole spectrum of the social sciences. It anticipated many of the post-structural themes of post-modern theory today and even the collapse of communism in Eastern Europe and Soviet Russia in the 1980s and 1990s has not undermined the power and potential of Althusser's writings.

Althusser himself died in 1990 after confessing to killing his wife Hélène and being assigned to a mental institution as a manic depressive. His writings, however, inspired the radical students in France in the late 1960s and even today form part of post-modern debate in fields as disparate as sociology, anthropology and philosophy. He inspired hatred but he also inspired admiration. As Ted Benton (1998) has commented *'He was certainly the most influential Marxist thinker of his time and one of the most influential social theorists working in any tradition'.*

 See Also

- **HISTORICAL MATERIALISM** (p. 43) as an outline of what Marx and Engels actually said.
- **RELATIVE AUTONOMY** (p. 250) as an example of structural Marxism by one of Althusser's collaborators, Nicos Poulantzas.
- **CRITICAL THEORY** (p. 84) and **HEGEMONY** (p. 121) as very different *humanist* approaches to modern Marxism.
- **LEGITIMATION CRISIS** (p. 225) as Jürgen Haberman's contribution to the development of Marxism today.

Suggested Reading

CALLINICOS, A.T. (1976) *Althusser's Marxism*, Pluto Press, London.

Further Reading

BENTON, T. (1984) *The Rise and Fall of Structural Marxism*, Macmillan.

BENTON, T. (2000) Louis Althusser, Ch. 14, Part II in Andersen, H. and Kaspersen, L.B. (eds.), *Classical and Modern Social Theory*, Blackwell, Oxford.

CALLINICOS, A.T. (1999) *Social Theory: An Historical Introduction* (Ch. 11), Polity Press, Cambridge.

ELLIOT, G. (1987) *Althusser: The Detour of Theory*, Verso.

SMITH, S. (1984) *Reading Althusser*, Connell University Press.

THOMSEN, J.P.F. AND ANDERSEN, H. (2000) Neo-Marxist Theories, Ch. 11 Part II in Andersen, H. and Kaspersen, L.B. (eds.), *Classical and Modern Social Theory*, Blackwell, Oxford.

Structuration

Anthony Giddens

SOCIOLOGISTS THROUGHOUT THE AGES HAVE WRESTLED WITH THE FUNDAMENTAL question of social theory, the relationship between the individual and the society that he or she lives in. Are we the products of the society we live in or do we collectively and individually create the social world around us? Is the individual free and in control of his or her own life, or are we all merely the subjects of the society that we were born into, puppets on the strings of the rich and powerful, pawns in a giant game of chess where every move is controlled by political and sociological forces beyond our control and our understanding? Does Big Brother rule OK? This debate has provoked a veritably *Holy War* throughout the history of sociology with the deterministic views of structural functionalists and structural Marxists facing the massed ranks of phenomenology, symbolic interactionism and those who believe in the rights and freedom of the individual.

The British sociologist, Anthony Giddens, like Max Weber before him, has rejected the dogmatism of both structuralism and individualism and has proposed instead the notion of *structuration*; the notion that within the structures of society the individual has the power and freedom to express him or herself and over time to change those structures for the better. In his view, neither society nor the individual are all powerful. Rather, they are two sides of the same coin. While social structures – the family, community, work – are created by human action, so too they define and determine human behaviour and social life. *'There is no sense in which structure determines action or vice-versa'* (Giddens 1984: 219). Social structures and human action do not exist independently of each other; rather they are interdependent and intertwined. As Giddens explained in 1976, social life is the product of 'active subjects'; society is not a thing out there, outside of us controlling our every move, rather it is the product of *'skilled, knowledgeable and reflexive agents'* operating within specific contexts or structures (Swinglewood 2000). Giddens uses the example of speech and language to illustrate his argument. All languages are governed by a set of rules about how to speak, write and communicate if there is to be any common understanding or meaning. Those rules determine how language is learnt and used and no individual independently and at will can change those rules without causing immense confusion and misunderstanding. However, over time languages do change and evolve as new ideas and new concepts arise – and as the ideas and jargon of subgroups or new technologies enter the mainstream. The young in particular like inventing new 'in' words that exclude adult understanding – 'wicked' or 'fit' mean very different things to teenagers today than they did to their parents in the past and 'logging on' was not a word, let alone a verb, in the 1950s.

There is therefore, in Giddens' view, a 'duality of structure' by which social structures both constitute human agency (or action) and create it. Structure and agency are the core elements of Giddens' theory.

Social structures

SOCIAL structures centre around rules and resources. They are the basis of social order and organised human behaviour. *Rules* may be informal or formal, required behaviour or expected behaviour. Either way they expect conformity whether it is in obeying the law or queuing in the 'correct' manner. *Resources* on the other hand refer to the materials and the means used in producing goods and services (allocative resources) and to the skills and powers men and women bring to the production process.

Men and women as actors, and particularly as leaders and managers, create social, economic and political structures as a means to mobilising and organising people and materials in the service of mankind; in building and operating factories or running airlines or financial services. Man as an acting and reflexive human being is, in his view, at the centre of social life, not at its periphery as many structuralist or determinist theories argue. Nor, however, in Giddens' view, is man a totally free agent. He or she may create and reproduce social structures but the individual is also constrained by them because they have been *collectively* created and enforced, particularly by those in power. Hence the paradox of modern society where the individual appears to be free and all-powerful – as a voter or a consumer – but in practice often feels that it is society that is all powerful, is in control of his or her life and that it is he or she who is helpless, isolated and alienated.

Giddens recognises this duality and argues instead that while society may at times appear all-powerful and omnipresent, ultimately man is capable of changing society, changing its leadership and its structure if there is the collective will to do so. Even the greatest of dictators can remain in power only so long as their subjects allow them to, even if fear and fatalism are the basis of that compliance rather than joyful support.

Human agency

FOR Giddens the key to human behaviour is neither motivation nor self-interest. It is rather man's capacity to 'know how to act' in any given situation and his/her capacity to adapt their behaviour should the situation require it. Man has the unique capacity for conscious or self-conscious behaviour and Giddens identifies a hierarchy of such thinking:

- Discursive or reflective consciousness as men and women consider ways of tackling a problem or a situation and reflect on their past or future action.

- Practical consciousness, the practical often taken for granted or sub-conscious knowledge we all have of how to act in any given situation.
- Unconscious consciousness, the underlying motivation and needs we all have for security and survival that drive our behaviour, particularly in emergency situations when normal social structures have collapsed as in a fire or a disaster such as the Twin Towers in New York.

Social structures and human agency are therefore intimately bound together in an ongoing process of 'structuration' or structured action by which human action creates social structures, while social structures, once created, sustain and control human behaviour until the point when through evolution or revolution those structures are amended or overturned by collective human action. Daily social life relies on a mass of unspoken, taken for granted rules and routines, assumptions and expectations, laws and legislation to give it a sense of order and predictability. Take those away and chaos will reign, be it in the queues in shops, the traffic on the roads, or obedience to the law. Imagine the chaos if cars in Britain suddenly began to drive on the right-hand side of the road instead of the left or if shoppers refused to pay for their goods and simply walked off with them.

Human beings are not robots, however, controlled from on high. They are creative and conscious beings capable of generating, even controlling, change through reflexive thought and collective action. Every day people reflect on the society around them and adapt accordingly, whether it is a change from travelling to work by car rather than train due to a rail strike, or taking to the streets in defiance of an oppressive government. Giddens, therefore, has a very optimistic and positive view of human behaviour and this is reflected in his use of the term 'human agency'. Men are free but only within the rules and structures they have created. Only in exceptional circumstances are men either totally free or totally constrained. There is always choice, albeit often constrained choice, and behind that constraint is power; the capacity and ability of some individuals to change or transform society, a social structure or a social system in the name of or at least with the support of others. However powerful modern governments or modern corporations may appear to be, ultimately they too are constrained and dependent on the support of the people they rule, be they voters, consumers or citizens; ultimately even they are subject to the law, be they the international company Enron or its firm of auditors, Arthur Andersen, both of whom were originally highly respected but later accused in 2002 of massive financial fraud.

Giddens' theory of structuration is therefore a very practical thesis. It seeks to integrate rather than segregate sociological theories and it seeks to understand the relationship between the individual and society as a means for informing public policies designed to improve society in the future. Both individual creativity and social order are essential elements of the modern world and modern life. Change and with it unforeseen consequences are at the heart of life today, and while at times it appears that society is out of control, man in Giddens' view has the capacity through *reflective* thought and *collective* action to control and redirect it – but only if he or she chooses to do so!

The Idea in Action

THE THEORY OF STRUCTURATION APPEARS TO OFFER A VERY REAL AND A VERY PRACTICAL way of reconciling and resolving the age old tension between conflicting views of structure and action, between macro and micro sociology, between determinist and voluntarist views of man and society. In its depth and its breadth, Giddens' thesis has *'captured the imagination of the social scientific community'* (May 1996: 118).

The theory of structuration predated Giddens' later works on modernity and globalisation but the concepts of human agency, social structure and reflexivity are as evident as ever. They draw together the minutiae of everyday life and order with the grand sweep of human history and in particular Giddens' theory highlights the importance of power in social relations and in social order. While structuration theory identifies the interrelationship between those in political power and their subjects, it is equally applicable to analysing gender or ethnic relationships and the way that over time such 'power' relationships change through human agency. Consider, for example, the way equal opportunities legislation and the Human Rights Act are fundamentally changing social relations between men and women, majority and minority ethnic groups and are promoting a more egalitarian social order and social culture. As Giddens argued in 1981, *'the weak . . . always have some capabilities of turning resources back against the strong'* – in this case minority groups have used the law to reform society and improve their position and their opportunity for a better lifestyle and standard of living.

The theory of structuration inevitably – particularly in sociology – has attracted its critics; any thesis that has sought to combine sociological theories that were apparently irreconcilable is particularly vulnerable to attack.

Margaret Archer (1982), for example, has criticised Giddens for locking agency and structure too closely together. In her view they are two essentially different concepts that are not easy to reconcile. How can man enjoy free will and yet choose to be constrained; how much freedom do men really have to change society? Man's ability to change society is, in her view, very constrained. True social revolution is a rare occurrence. Moreover, Archer feels that Giddens has failed to fully explain the relationship between social change and social order and how this operates in a particular situation. This argument is reinforced by the attempt by Layder et al. (1991) to use structuration theory to study the transition from school to work. While he and his co-researchers supported Giddens' theory in general, they too concluded that structure and agency are at least *'partly autonomous and separate domains'* (p. 461). In Derek Layder's view (1997) while the concepts of agency and structure overlap, they do need separate and specific analysis for the full force of both elements to be fully appreciated. Thompson (1984) and Livesay (1989) have extended this point and criticised Giddens for over-emphasising the power and potential of the individual actor and for underestimating the constraints they face.

Ian Craib (1992a), one of Giddens' biographers, has gone further and criticised Giddens' work for lacking ontological depth, for being oversimplistic and for failing to reflect the messy complexity of modern social life. In particular, Craib argues that

Giddens' thesis fails to fully exploit the insights of such grand social theory as structural functionalism. Structuration theory is at such a high level of generalisation that on the one hand it is saying the obvious, and on the other it is hard to refute because it lacks detailed explanation and evidence. This may, however, be one of its great strengths. While modern social theory had become so complex and obtuse, it has taken a thinker of Giddens' power and persuasion to redirect sociological debate back onto real social life as ordinary people rather than academics experience it.

Giddens has rejected many of these criticisms. He rarely concedes points to his critics and in his more recent writings he has argued that structuration theory has the scope and power to inform a very broad range of social issues, from public policy and politics through to sexuality and intimacy. The great strength of Giddens' work is on the one hand the sheer breadth and power of his sociological analysis, and on the other, his refusal to be dogmatic and his determination to be open-minded and pragmatic. He is committed to using sociological theory to help to improve society and to promoting liberal-democratic values. He is not an armchair critic and his contributions to the policies of the New Labour government have been openly acknowledged by the British Prime Minister, Tony Blair. The very notion of the *Third Way*, the concept developed by Anthony Giddens and adopted by New Labour, reflects the essential ideas of structuration theory. Tony Blair has sought to promote New Labour as a Third Way between the extremes of Old Labour's socialism and Mrs Thatcher's radical New Right, as an alternative to the political dogmatism of these two approaches, one that reflects a commitment to social reform and equality of opportunity, but one that is pragmatic rather than dogmatic in its approach. As Anthony Elliott concludes (2001) Giddens' work has provided '*a comprehensive social theory for the analysis of social reproduction and political domination, a powerful interpretation of the complex ways in which action and structure intersect*'.

 **See Also**

- **STRUCTURAL FUNCTIONALISM** (p. 190) as a positivist (see p. 56) approach to integrating social structure and individual action.
- **ETHNOMETHODOLOGY** (p. 104) and **SYMBOLIC INTERACTIONSIM** (p. 195) as attempts to combine individual action and social structure from a phenomenological (see p. 165) perspective.

Suggested Reading

GIDDENS, A. (1984) *The Constitution of Society: Outline of the Theory of Structuration*, Polity Press, Cambridge.

GIDDENS, A. (1998) *The Third Way: The Renewal of Social Democracy*, Polity Press, Cambridge.

GIDDENS, A. (2000) *The Third Way and its Critics*, Polity Press, Cambridge.

Further Reading

CRAIB, I. (1992a) *Anthony Giddens*, Routledge.

CRAIB, I. (1992b) *Modern Social Theory from Parsons to Habermas*, Harvester Wheatsheaf, Brighton.

GIDDENS, A. (1976) *New Rules of Sociological Method*, Polity Press, Cambridge.

LIVESAY, J. (1989) Structuration Theory and the Unacknowledged Conditions of Action Theory, *Culture and Society* 6, 263–92.

Bibliography

AARONOVITCH, S. (1961) *The Ruling Class*, Lawrence & Wishart, London.

ABBOT P. AND WALLACE C. (1997) *An Introduction to Sociology: Feminist Perspectives*, Routledge.

ABRAMS, P. (1968) *The Origins of British Sociology, 1834–1914*, University of Chicago Press, Chicago.

ADORNO, T.W. *ET AL.* (1950) *The Authoritarian Personality*, Harper, New York.

ALEXANDER, J.C. (ED.) (1985) *Neo Functionalism*, Sage.

ALTHUSSER, L. (1965a) *For Marx*, Penguin, Harmondsworth.

ALTHUSSER, L. (1965b) *Reading Capital*, New Left Books, London.

ALTHUSSER, L. (1969) *Lenin and Philosophy*, New Left Books, London.

ALTHUSSER, L. (1976) *Essays in Self-Criticism*, New Left Books, London.

ALTHUSSER, L. (1990) *Philosophy and the Spontaneous*, Verso.

ALTHUSSER, L. (1993) *The Future Lasts a Long Time*, Chatto & Windus.

AMIN A. (ED.) (1994) *Post-Fordism: A Reader*, Blackwell, Oxford.

AMIN, S. (1976) *Unequal Development*, Harvester, London.

ANDERSEN, H. AND KASPERSEN, L.B. (EDS.) (2000) *Classical and Modern Social Theory*, Blackwell, Oxford.

ARCHER, M. (1982) Morphogenesis vs Structuration, *British Journal of Sociology*, 33, 455–83.

ARONSON, R. (1995) *After Marxism*, Guildford Press.

ATKINSON, J. (1985) The Changing Corporation, in Clutterbuck, D. (ed.), *New Patterns of Work*, Gower.

ATKINSON, J.M. AND HERITAGE, J. (EDS.) (1984) *Structures of Social Action*, Cambridge University Press, Cambridge.

ATKINSON, M. (1971) Societal Reactions to Suicide: The Role of Coroners, in Cohen, S. (ed.), *Images of Deviance*, Penguin, Harmondsworth.

ATKINSON, P. (1988) Ethnomethodology: A Critical Review, *Annual Review of Sociology*, 14, 441–65.

BACHRACH, P. AND BARAZ, M.S. (1962) The Two Faces of Power, in Stanworth, M. and Giddens, A. (eds.), *Elites and Power in British Society*, Cambridge University Press, Cambridge.

BAERT, P. (2001) Jürgen Habermas, Ch. 7 in Elliott and Turner (eds.) (2001).

BALDWIN, J. (1986) *G.H. Mead: A Unifying Theory of Sociology*, Sage.

BARNES, B. (1982) *T.S. Kuhn and the Social Sciences*, Macmillan, London.

BARNET, F.J. AND MÜLLER, R.E. (1975) *Global Reach*, Jonathan Cape, London.

BARRATT, M. (1980) *Women's Oppression Today*, New Left Books, London.

BARRET, M. AND PHILLIPS, A (EDS.) (1992) *Destabilizing Theory: Contemporary Feminist Debates*, Polity Press, Cambridge.

BAUDRILLARD, J. (1975) *The Mirror of Production* [1973], Telos Press.

BAUDRILLARD, J. (1983) *Simulations*, Semiotext (e).

BAUDRILLARD, J. (1986) *America*, Verso.

BAUDRILLARD, J. (1990) *Seduction*, Macmillan.

BAUDRILLARD, J. (1993) *Symbolic Exchange and Death*, Sage.

BAUDRILLARD, J. (1994a) *The Illusion of the End*, Polity Press, Cambridge.

BAUDRILLARD, J. (1994b) *Simulacra and Simulation*, University of Michigan Press.

BAUDRILLARD, J. (1995) *The Gulf War Did Not Take Place*, Power Publications.

BAUDRILLARD, J. (1997) *Fragments: Cool Memories III*, Verso.

BECK, U. (1985) *Ecological Politics in the Age of Risk,* Polity Press, Cambridge.

BECK, U. (1992) *Risk Society: Towards a New Modernity*, Sage, London.

BECK, U. (1997) *The Reinvention of Politics: Rethinking Modernity in the Global Social Order*, Polity Press, Cambridge.

BECK, U. (1999) *World Risk Society,* Polity Press, Cambridge.

BECKER, H.S. (1963) *Outsiders,* Free Press, New York.

BECKER, H. (1974) Labelling Theory Reconsidered, in Rock, P. and McIntosh, M. (eds.), *Deviance and Social Control*, Tavistock, London.

BEECHEY, V. (1986) Women and Employment in Contemporary Britain, in Beechey, V. and Whiteley, E. (eds.), *Women in Britain Today*, Open University Press, Milton Keynes.

BEECHEY, V. AND DONALD, J. (EDS.) (1985) *Subjectivity and Social Relations,* Open University Press, Milton Keynes.

BELL, D. (1960) *The End of Ideology,* Free Press, New York.

BELL, D. (1974) *The Coming of Post Industrial Society,* Heinemann, London.

BELL, D. (1979) *The Cultural Contradictions of Capitalism*, Heinemann, London.

BELL, D. (1981) *The Crisis in Economic Theory,* Basic Books, New York.

BELL, D. (1987) Future Society, *New Society* 18 December.

BELL, D. (1995) *Communitarianism and its Critics,* Clarendon Press, Oxford.

BELL, D. (ED.) (1969) *Towards the Year 2000,* Houghton Mifflin, Boston.

BENNETT, A. (1999) Sub-cultures or Neo Tribes? Rethinking the Relationship between Youth, Style and Musical Taste, *Sociology*, 33(3).

BENNETT, J. AND GEORGE, S. (1987) *The Hunger Machine,* Polity Press, Cambridge.

BENSON, D. AND HUGHES, J. (1983) *The Perspective of Ethnomethodology,* Longman, London.

BENTON, T. (1984) *The Rise and Fall of Structural Marxism*, Macmillan.

BENTON, T. (1998) Louis Althusser, Ch. 14 in Stones (ed.) (1998).

BENTON, T. (2000) Louis Althusser, Ch. 14, Part II in Andersen and Kaspersen (eds.) (2000).

BERGER, P. AND LUCKMAN, T. (1969) The Sociology of Religion and Sociology of Knowledge, in Robertson R. (ed.), *The Sociology of Religion*, Penguin, Harmondsworth.

BERNSTEIN, B.B. (1961) Social Class and Linguistic Development – A Theory of Social Learning, in Halsey, A.H, Floud, J. and Anderson, C.A. (eds.), *Education, Economy and Society,* Free Press, New York.

BERNSTEIN, B.B. (1970) 'A Sociolinguistic Approach to Social Learning', in Worsley, P. (ed.), *Modern Sociology Introductory Readings,* Penguin, Harmondsworth.

BERNSTEIN, B. (1971) Education Cannot Compensate for Society, in Dogin, B.R., Dale, I.R., Esland, G.M. and Swift, D.F. (eds.), *School and Society*, Routledge & Kegan Paul, London.

BERNSTEIN, B.B. (1971–90) *Class, Codes and Control,* Vols 1–4, Routledge & Kegan Paul, London.

BERNSTEIN, J. (1994) *The Frankfurt School Critical Assessments*, Routledge.

BETTERTON, R. (1987) *Looking On*, Pandora, London.

BIRKE, L. (1986) *Women, Feminism and Biology,* Wheatsheaf, Brighton.

BLAU, P.M. (1963) *The Dynamics of Bureaucracy,* University of Chicago Press, Chicago.

BLAUNER, R. (1964) *Alienation and Freedom,* University of Chicago Press, Chicago.

BOCOCK, R. (1986) *Hegemony,* Tavistock, London.

BODEN, D. (1990) People are Talking: Conversational Analysis and Symbolic Interaction, in Becker, H. and McCall, M. (eds.), *Symbolic Interactionism and Cultural Studies*, Chicago University Press, Chicago.

BODEN, D. AND ZIMMERMAN, D. (EDS.) (1991) *Talk and Social Structure: Studies in Ethnomethodology and Conversation Analysis*, Polity Press, Cambridge.

BOTTOMORE, T.B. (1965) *Classes in Modern Society,* Penguin, Harmondsworth.

BOTTOMORE, T.B. (1984) *The Frankfurt School,* Tavistock, London.

BOTTOMORE, T. AND BRYM, R. (EDS.) (1989) *The Capitalist Class*, Wheatsheaf.

BOTTOMORE, T.B. AND RUBEL, M. (EDS.) (1961) *Karl Marx: Selected Writings,* Penguin, Harmondsworth.

BOUCHIER, D. (1983) *The Feminist Challenge,* Macmillan.

BRADLEY, D. AND WILKIE, R. (1974) *The Concept of Organisations,* Blackie & Sons Ltd, Glasgow.

BRANDT, W. ET AL. (1980) *North–South: A Programme For Survival,* Pan, London.

BRAVERMAN, H. (1974) *Labor and Monopoly Capital,* Monthly Review Press, New York.

BRIERLEY, P. (1991) *'Christian' England,* MARCEurope, London.

BRIERLY, P. AND LONGLEY, D. (EDS.) (1991) *UK Christian Handbook 1992/1993 edition,* Marc.

BRONNER, S.E. (1996) *Of Critical Theory and its Theorists,* Blackwell, Oxford.

BRUCE, S. (1995) *Religion in Modern Britain,* Oxford University Press, Oxford.

BRYANT, C. (1986) What is Positivism, *Social Studies Review,* January.

BURNS, T. (1986) *Erving Goffman,* Tavistock, London.

BURNS, T. AND STALKER, G.M. (1966) *The Management of Innovation,* Tavistock, London.

BUTLER, D. AND KAVANAGH, D. (1997) *The British General Election of 1997*, Macmillan, Basingstoke.

CALLINICOS, A. (1983) *The Revolutionary Ideas of Karl Marx,* Pluto Press, London.

CALLINICOS, A. (1989) Introduction: Analytical Marxism, in Callinicos, A. (ed.), *Marxist Theory*, Oxford University Press, Oxford.

CALLINICOS, A. (1999) *Social Theory: A Historical Introduction*, Polity Press, Cambridge.

CAREW HUNT, R.N. (1950) *The Theory and Practice of Communism,* Penguin, Harmondsworth.

CARRIGAN, T., CONNELL, B. AND LEE, J. (1985) Towards a New Sociology of Masculinity, *Theory and Society,* 14, 551–604.

CARVER, T. (1981) *Engels,* Oxford University Press, Oxford.

CASANOVA, J. (1994) *Public Religions in the Modern World*, University of Chicago Press, Chicago.

CASTELLS, M. (1996) *The Information Age: Economy, Society and Culture.* Vol. I: *The Rise of Network Society*, Blackwell, Oxford; 2nd edn, 2000.

CASTELLS, M. (1997) *The Information Age: Economy, Society and Culture.* Vol. II: *The Power of Identity*, Blackwell, Oxford.

CASTELLS, M. (1998) *The Information Age: Economy, Society and Culture.* Vol. III: *End of Millennium*, Blackwell, Oxford.

CASTELLS, M. (2002) *Information Society and Welfare State*, Open University Press, Milton Keynes.

CHALMERS, A.F. (1982) *What is This Thing Called Science?,* Open University Press, Milton Keynes.

CHARVER, J. (1982) *Feminism,* J.M. Dent, London.

CHRYSSIDES, G. (1994) Britain's Changing Faiths: Adaptation in a New Environment, in Parsons, G. (ed.), *The Growth of Religious Diversity in Britain from 1945,* Routledge, London.

CICOUREL, A. (1964) *Method and Measurement in Sociology,* Free Press, New York.

CICOUREL, A. (1976) *The Social Organisation of Juvenile Justice,* Heinemann, London.

CIXOUS, C. (1981) The Laugh of the Medusa, in Marks, E. and De Courtivron, I. (eds.), *New French Feminisms,* Schocken Books, New York.

CLARKE, E. AND LAWSON, T. (1985) *Gender: An Introduction,* University Tutorial Press, Slough.

CLAYMAN, S.E. (1993) Booing: The Anatomy of a Disaffiliative Response, *American Sociological Review*, 58, 110–50.

COHEN, S. (ED.) (1971) *Images of Deviance,* Penguin, Harmondsworth.

COMTE, A. (1877) *Cours de Philosophie Positive* [1830–42], Balière & Sons, Paris.

COMTE, A. (1975–77) *Système de Politique Positive* [1848–54], Longmans, Green & Co, London.

CONNELL, R. (1995) *Masculinities,* Polity Press, Cambridge.

COOK, G. (1993) *George Herbert Mead: The Making of a Social Pragmatist,* University of Illinois Press.

COSER, L. (1956) *The Functions of Social Conflict,* Free Press, New York.

CRAIB, I. (1992a) *Anthony Giddens,* Routledge.

CRAIB, I. (1992b) *Modern Social Theory from Parsons to Habermas,* Harvester Wheatsheaf, Brighton.

CROMPTON, R. AND JONES, G. (1984) *White Collar Proletariat,* Macmillan, London.

CROSSMAN, R. (1977) *The Diaries of a Cabinet Minister*, Hamish Hamilton and Jonathan Cape, London.

CROZIER, M. (1964) *The Bureaucratic Phenomenon,* Tavistock, London.

CUFF, E.C., SHARROCK, W.W. AND FRANCIS, D.W. (1998) *Perspectives in Sociology,* 4th edn, Routledge.

DAHL, R.A. (1961) *Who Governs?,* Yale University Press, New Haven.

DAHRENDORF, R. (1959) *Class and Class Conflict in an Industrial Society,* Routledge & Kegan Paul, London.

DAHRENDORF, R. (1967) *Society and Democracy in Germany,* Weidenfeld & Nicolson, London.

DAHRENDORF, R. (1975) *The New Liberty,* Routledge & Kegan Paul, London.

DAHRENDORF, R. (1979) *Life Chances,* Routledge & Kegan Paul, London.

DAVIS, K. AND MOORE, W.E. (1967) Some Principles of Stratification, in Bendix, R. and Lipsett, S.M. (eds.), *Class Status and Power,* Routledge & Kegan Paul, London.

DEARLOVE, J. AND SAUNDERS, P. (1984) *Introduction to British Politics,* Polity Press, Cambridge.

DENZIN, N. (1992) *Symbolic Interactionism and Cultural Studies: The Politics of Interpretation*, Blackwell, Oxford.

DEX, S. AND McCULLOCK, A. (1997) *Flexible Employment: The Future of Britain's Jobs*, Macmillan.

DJILAS, M. (1957) *The New Class,* Thames & Hudson, London.

DOUGLAS, J.D. (1967) *The Social Meanings of Suicide,* Princeton University Press, Princeton.

DURKHEIM, E. (1951) *Suicide: A Study in Sociology* [1897], Free Press, Glencoe.

DURKHEIM, E. (1954) *The Elementary Forms of Religious Life* [1912], Allen & Unwin, London.

DURKHEIM, E. (1958) *The Rules of Sociological Method* [1895], Free Press, Glencoe.

DURKHEIM, E. (1960) *The Division of Labour in Society* [1893], Free Press, Glencoe.

DYE, T.R. (1979) *Who's Running America?,* Prentice Hall, Englewood Cliffs.

ELDRIDGE, J. (1983) *C. Wright Mills,* Tavistock, London.

ELLIOT, G. (1987) *Althusser: The Detour of Theory*, Verso.

ELLIOTT, A. (2001) Anthony Giddens, Ch. 26 in Elliott and Turner (eds.) (2001).

ELLIOTT, A. AND TURNER, B.S. (EDS.) (2001) *Profiles in Contemporary Social Theory,* Sage, London.

ENGELS, F. (1845) *The Condition of the Working Class in England,* Blackwell, Oxford.

ENGELS, F. (1959) *Anti Dühring,* Foreign Languages Publishing House, Moscow [1877/78].

ENGELS, F. (1942) *The Origins of the Family, Private Property and the State,* International Publishers, New York [1884].

ETZIONI, A. (1964) *Modern Organisations,* Prentice-Hall, Englewood Cliffs.

FALK, W. AND ZHAO, S. (1990) Paradigms, Theories and Methods in Contemporary Rural Sociology: A Partial Replication, *Rural Sociology,* 54, 587–600.

FALUDI, S. (1992) *Backlash: The Undeclared War against Women,* Chatto & Windus.

FEYERABEND, P. (1975) *Against Method,* New Left Books, London.

FILDES, S. (1985) Women and Society, in Haralambos, M. (ed.) *Developments in Sociology,* Vol. I, pp. 109–39, Causeway Press, Ormskirk.

FILDES, S. (1988) Gender, in Haralambos, M. (ed.), *Developments in Sociology,* Vol. 4 pp. 111–36, Causeway Press, Ormskirk.

FILLINGHAM, L.A. (1993) *Foucault for Beginners,* Writers & Readers.

. FINE, G.A. (1992) Agency, Structure and Comparative Contexts: Towards a Synthetic Interactionism, *Symbolic Interaction,* 15, 87–107.

FINE, G.A. (1993) The Sad Demise, Mysterious Disappearance and Glorious Triumph of Symbolic Interactionism, *Annual Review of Sociology,* 19, 61–87.

FIRESTONE, S. (1972) *The Dialectic of Sex,* Paladin, London.

FOSTER-CARTER, A. (1985) *The Sociology of Development,* Causeway Press, Ormskirk.

FOUCAULT, M. (1965) *Madness and Civilization: A History of Insanity in the Age of Reason* [1961], Pantheon Books, New York.

FOUCAULT, M. (1971) *The Order of Things: An Archaeology of the Human Sciences* [1966], Pantheon Books, New York.

FOUCAULT, M. (1972) *The Archaeology of Knowledge* [1969], Pantheon Books, New York.

FOUCAULT, M. (1973) *The Birth of the Clinic: An Archaeology of Medical Perception* [1963], Pantheon Books, New York.

FOUCAULT, M. (1977a) *Discipline and Punish: The Birth of the Prison* [1975], Pantheon Books, New York.

FOUCAULT, M. (1977b) *Language, Counter-Memory, Practice: Selected Essays and Interviews by Michel Foucault.* (Ed. D.F. Bouchard), Cornell University Press.

FOUCAULT, M. (1978) *The History of Sexuality.* Vol. I: *An Introduction* [1976], Pantheon Books, New York.

FOUCAULT, M. (1980) *Power/Knowledge: Selected Interviews and Other Writings 1972–1977* (Gordon, C. ed.), Pantheon Books, New York.

FOUCAULT, M. (1989) *Foucault Live (Interviews 1966–1984)* (Lotringer, S. ed.) Semoiotext(e), New York.

FRANK, A.G. (1969a) *Latin America: Underdevelopment or Revolution?,* Monthly Review Press, New York.

FRANK, A.G. (1969b) *Capitalism and Underdevelopment in Latin America*, Monthly Review Press, New York.

FRANK, A.G. (1971) *Sociology of Development and Underdevelopment*, Monthly Review Press, New York.

FRANK, A. (1980) *Crisis in the World Economy*, Heinemann, London.

FRANK, A.G. (1981) *Crisis in the Third World*, Heinemann, London.

FRIEDEN, B. (1963) *Feminine Mystique*, W.W. Norton.

FRIEDRICHS, R. (1970) *A Sociology of Sociology*, Free Press, New York.

FRISBY, D. (1984) *Georg Simmel*, Tavistock, London.

FRISBY, D. (1994) *Georg Simmel: Critical Assessments*, Routledge.

GANS, H. (1962) *The Urban Villagers*, Free Press, Illinois.

GANS, H. (1968) Urbanism and Suburbanism as Ways of Life, in Pahl, R.E. (ed.), *Readings in Urban Sociology*, Pergamon Press, Oxford.

GARFINKEL, H. (1967) *Studies in Ethnomethodology*, Prentice Hall, Englewood Cliffs.

GARRETT, S. (1987) *Gender*, Tavistock, London.

GAVRON, H. (1966) *The Captive Wife*, Routledge & Kegan Paul, London.

GERSHUNY, J. (1978) *After Industrial Society*, Macmillan, London.

GIBBONS, D.C. AND JONES, J.K. (1975) *The Study of Deviance*, Prentice Hall, Englewood Cliffs, NJ.

GIDDENS, A. (1976) *New Rules of Sociological Method*, Polity Press, Cambridge.

GIDDENS, A. (1978) *Durkheim*, Fontana, Glasgow.

GIDDENS, A. (1981) *Contemporary Critique of Historical Materialism*, Macmillan, London.

GIDDENS, A. (1984) *The Constitution of Society: Outline of the Theory of Structuration*, Polity Press, Cambridge.

GIDDENS, A. (1989) *Sociology*, Polity Press, Cambridge.

GIDDENS, A. (1990) *The Consequences of Modernity*, Polity Press, Cambridge and Stanford University Press, Palo Alto.

GIDDENS, A. (1992) *The Transformation of Intimacy, Sexuality, Love and Eroticism in Modern Society*, Polity Press, Cambridge.

GIDDENS, A. (1997) *Sociology*, Polity Press, Cambridge.

GIDDENS, A. (1998) *The Third Way: The Renewal of Social Democracy*, Polity Press, Cambridge.

GIDDENS, A. (2000) *The Third Way and its Critics*, Polity Press, Cambridge.

GIDDENS, A. ET AL. (EDS.) (1994) *The Polity Reader in Gender Studies*, Polity Press, Cambridge.

GILMORE, D.D. (1990) *Manhood in the Making: Cultural Concepts of Masculinity*, Yale University Press, New Haven.

GLOCK, C.Y. AND STARK, R. (1965) *Religion and Society in Tension*, Rand McNally, Chicago.

GOFFMAN, E. (1956) *The Presentation of Self in Everyday Life*, Penguin, Harmondsworth.

GOFFMAN, E. (1961a) *Asylums*, Penguin, Harmondsworth.

GOFFMAN, E. (1961b) *Encounters*, Penguin, Harmondsworth.

GOFFMAN, E. (1963), *Behaviour in Public Places*.

GOFFMAN, E. (1968) *Stigma* [1961], Penguin, Harmondsworth.

GOFFMAN, E. (1970) *Strategic Interaction*, Blackwell, Oxford.

GOFFMAN, E. (1974) *Frame Analysis*, Harper, New York.

GOFFMAN, E. (1979) *Gender Advertisements*, Macmillan, London.

GOFFMAN, E. (1981) *Forms of Talk*, University of Pennsylvania Press, Philadelphia.

GOLDBERG, S. (1977) *The Inevitability of Patriarchy,* Temple Smith, London.

GOLDTHORPE, J.H., LOCKWOOD, D., BECHHOFER, E. AND PLATT, J. (1968) *The Affluent Worker,* Cambridge University Press, Cambridge.

GOLDTHORPE, J.H., LLEWELLYN, C. AND PAYNE, C. (1980) *Social Mobility and Class Structure in Modern Britain,* Clarendon Press, Oxford.

GOULDNER, A.W. (1954) *Patterns of Industrial Bureaucracy,* Free Press, Glencoe.

GRAMSCI, A. (1971) *Selections from the Prison Notebooks,* New Left Books, New York.

GRAY, T. (1992) *Men are from Mars, Women are from Venus,* Thorsons.

GRAY, T. (1996) *The Political Philosophy of Herbert Spencer: Individualism and Organicism,* Avebury, Brookfield, VT.

GREER, G. (1971) *The Female Eunuch,* Paladin, London.

GREER, G. (2000) *The Whole Woman,* Anchor.

HABERMAS, J. (1963) *Theory and Practice,* Heinemann, London.

HABERMAS, J. (1968) *Knowledge and Human Interest,* Heinemann, London.

HABERMAS, J. (1970) *Towards a Rational Society,* Heinemann, London.

HABERMAS, J. (1973) *Legitimation Crisis,* Heinemann, London.

HABERMAS, J. (1979) *Communication and the Evolution of Society,* Heinemann, London.

HABERMAS, J. (1982) *The Theory of Communicative Action,* Suhrkamp, Frankfurt.

HABERMAS, J. (1997) *Between Facts and Norms; Contributions to a Discourse Theory of Law and Democracy,* Polity Press, Cambridge.

HALL, S. (ED.) (1997) *Representation; Cultural Representations and Signifying Practices,* Sage, London.

HALL, S., CRITCHER, C., JEFFERSON, T., CLARKE, J. AND ROBERS, B. (1978) *Policing the Crisis, Mugging the State and Law and Order,* Macmillan, London.

HALL, S. AND DU GAY, P. (EDS) (1996) *Questions of Cultural Identity,* Sage, London.

HALL, S. AND JEFFERSON, T. (EDS.) (1976) *Resistance through Rituals: Youth Cultures in Modern Britain,* Hutchinson, London.

HALL, S. ET AL. (1982) *The Empire Strikes Back,* Hutchinson, London.

HAMILTON, P. (1983) *Talcott Parsons,* Tavistock, London.

HAMILTON, P. (1992) *George Herbert Mead: Critical Assessments,* Routledge.

HARALAMBOS, M. AND HOLBORN, M. (2000) *Sociology Themes and Perspectives,* 5th edn, Causeway Press, Ormskirk.

HARGREAVES, D.H. ET AL. (1975) *Deviance in Classrooms,* Routledge & Kegan Paul, London.

HARRISON, P. (1981) *Inside the Third World,* Penguin, Harmondsworth.

HASTE, H. (1993) *The Sexual Metaphor,* Harvester Wheatsheaf, Hemel Hempstead.

HAYTER, T. (1981) *The Creation of World Poverty,* Pluto, London.

HAYTER, T. (1985) *Aid: Rhetoric and Reality,* Pluto, London.

HERBERG, W. (1960) *Protestant–Catholic–Jew,* Anchor Books, New York.

HERITAGE, J. AND GREATBATCH, D. (1986) Generating Applause: A Study of Rhetoric and Response in Party Political Conferences, *American Journal of Sociology,* 92, 110–57.

HERTZ, N. (2002) *The Silent Takeover: Global Capitalism and the Death of Democracy,* Arrow Books.

HEWITT, C.J. (1974) Elites and the Distribution of Power in British Society, in Stanworth, P. and Giddens, A. (eds.), *Elites and Power in British Society,* Cambridge University Press, Cambridge.

HILBERT, R.A. (1990) Ethnomethodology and the Micro Macro Order, *American Sociological Review,* 55, 794–808.

HOLLINGER, D. (1980) T.S. Kuhn's Theory of Science and Its Implications for History, in Gutting, G. (ed.), *Paradigms and Revolutions*, Notre Dame University Press, Notre Dame.

HORKHEIMER, M. (1937) *Traditional and Critical Theory*, Fischer, Frankfurt.

HORKHEIMER, M. (1972) *Traditional and Critical Theory,* Herder & Herder, New York.

HUSSERL, E. (1901) *Logical Investigations,* Routledge & Kegan Paul, London [1970].

HUSSERL, E. (1913) *Ideas for a Pure Phenomenology and Phenomenological Philosophy*, Macmillan, New York.

HUSSERL, E. (1936) *The Crisis of the European Sciences and Transcendental Phenomenology*, N.W. University Press, Illinois.

JEFFERSON, G. (1984) On the Organization of Laughter in Talk about Troubles, in Atkinson, J.M. and Heritage, J. (eds.), *Structures of Social Action*, Cambridge University Press, Cambridge.

JESSOP, B. (1985) *Nicos Poulantzas,* Macmillan, London.

JESSOP, B. (1994) The Transition to Post Fordism and the Schumpeterian Welfare State, in Burrows, R. and Looder, B. (eds.), *Towards a Post Fordist Welfare State*, Routledge.

JESSOP, B. (1998) Karl Marx, Ch. 1 in Stones (ed.) (1998).

JOLL, J. (1977) *Antonio Gramsci,* Fontana, London.

KARABEL, J. AND HALSEY, A.H. (EDS.) (1977) *Power and Ideology in Education,* Oxford University Press, New York.

KEDDIE, N. (1973) *Tinker Tailor – The Myth of Cultural Deprivation,* Penguin, Harmondsworth.

KELLNER, D. (1989) *Jean Baudrillard: From Marxism to Post Modernism and Beyond*, Polity Press, Cambridge.

KELLNER, P. AND CROWTHER HUNT, LORD (1980) *The Civil Servants: An Inquiry into Britain's Ruling Class,* Macdonald, London.

KELLY, M.R. (1989) Alternative Forms of Work Automation under Programmable Automation, in Wood S. (ed.), *The Transformation of Work*, Unwin Hyman.

KEPEL, G. (1994) *The Revenge of God: The Resurgence of Islam, Christianity and Judaism in the Modern World*, Polity Press, Cambridge.

KETTLER, D. (1986) *Karl Mannheim,* Tavistock, London.

KNIGHTS, D. *ET AL.* (EDS) (1985) *Job Redesign,* cited in *Society Today/New Society,* 8 November.

KRAMARAE, C. AND TREICHLER, P. (1985) *A Feminist Dictionary,* Pandora, London.

KUHN, T.S. (1957) *The Copernican Revolution,* Harvard University Press, Cambridge.

KUHN, T.S. (1962/1970) *The Structure of Scientific Revolutions,* Chicago University Press, Chicago.

KUHN, T.S. (1977) *The Essential Tension,* University of Chicago Press, Chicago.

KUHN, T.S. (1978) *Black Body Theory and the Quantum Discontinuity,* Oxford University Press, New York.

KUMAR, K. (1978) *Prophecy and Progress: The Sociology of Industrial and Post Industrial Society*, Penguin, Harmondsworth.

LABOR, W. (1973) The Logic of Non-Standard English, in Kellie, N. (ed.), Classroom Knowledge, in Young, M. (ed.), *Tinker, Tailor: The Myth of Cultural Deprivation*, Penguin, Harmondsworth.

LACLAU, E. (1977) *Politics and Ideology in Marxist Theory,* New Left Books, London.

LANE, D. (1970) *Politics and Society in the USSR,* Weidenfeld & Nicolson, London.

LASH, S. AND URRY, J. (1987) *The End of Organised Capitalism*, Polity Press, Cambridge.

LAYDER, D. (1997) *Modern Social Theory, Key Debates and New Directions*, UCL Press.

LAYDER, D., ASTON, D. AND SUNG, J. (1991) The Empirical Correlates of Action and Structure: The Transition from School to Work, *Sociology* 25, 447–64.

LEE, M. (1993) *Consumer Culture Reborn*, Routledge.

LEMANN, H. AND ROTH, G. (1993) *Weber's Protestant Ethic: Origins, Evidence, Context*, German Historical Institute.

LEWIS, O. (1951) *Life in a Mexican Village: Tepotzlan Restudied*, University of Illinois Press, Urbana.

LIPSET, S.M., TROW, M. AND COLEMAN, J. (1956) *Union Democracy*, Free Press, Glencoe.

LIVESAY, J. (1989) Structuration Theory and the Unacknowledged Conditions of Action Theory, *Culture and Society* 6, 263–92.

LLOYD, B. AND ARCHER, J. (1982) *Sex and Gender*, Penguin, Harmondsworth.

LOADER, C. (1985) *The Intellectual Development of Karl Mannheim*, Cambridge University Press, Cambridge.

LUKES, S. (1972) *Emile Durkheim, His Life and Work*, Allen & Unwin, London.

LUKES, S. (1974) *Power: A Radical View*, Macmillan, London.

LYOTARD, J.F. (1979) *The Post Modern Condition*, Manchester University Press, Manchester.

LYOTARD, J.F. (1983) *The Differend: Phases in Dispute* (trans. G. Van den Abeele), Manchester University Press, Manchester.

LYOTARD, J.F. (1992) *The Postmodern Explained to Children*, Turnaround, London.

LYOTARD, J.F. (1995) *Toward the Postmodern*, New Jersey Humanities Press.

MACCOBY, E.E. AND JACKLIN, C.N. (1974) *The Psychology of Sex Differences*, Stanford University Press.

MacRAE, D. (1974) *Weber*, Fontana, London.

MAGEE, B. (1973) *Karl Popper*, Fontana, London.

MAINES, D.R. AND MORRIONE, T.J. (1990) On the Breadth and Relevance of Blumer's Perspective: Introduction to his Analysis and Industrialization, in Blumer, H. (ed.), *Industrialization as an Agent of Social Change: A Critical Analysis*, Aldine de Gruyter, New York.

MANN, P. (1965) *An Approach to Urban Sociology*, Routledge & Kegan Paul, London.

MANNHEIM, K. (1929) *Ideology and Utopia*, Routledge & Kegan Paul, London [1960].

MANNING, P. (1992) *Erving Goffman and Modern Sociology*, Polity Press, Cambridge.

MARCUSE, H. (1954) *Reason and Revolution*, Humanities Press, New York.

MARCUSE, H. (1955) *Eros and Civilisation*, Beacon Press, Boston.

MARCUSE, H. (1964) *One Dimensional Man*, Routledge & Kegan Paul, London.

MARTIN, D. (1969a) *The Religious and the Secular*, Routledge & Kegan Paul, London.

MARTIN, D. (1969b), *A Sociology of English Religion*, Heinemann

MARTIN, D. (1978) *A General Theory of Secularisation*, Blackwell, Oxford.

MARTIN, D. (1991) The Secularisation Issue: Prospect and Retrospect, *British Journal of Sociology*, 42 (3).

MARX, K. (1961) *Paris Manuscripts*, quoted in Bottomore and Rubel (eds.) (1961).

MARX, K. (1963) *Economic and Philosophical Manuscripts* [1843–44], Lawrence & Wishart, London.

MARX, K. (1964–72) *Theories of Surplus Value*, Vol. 2, Lawrence & Wishart, London.

MARX, K. The Eighteenth Brumaire of Louis Bonaparte, in Tucker, R. (ed.), *The Marx–Engels Reader*, Norton, New York.

MARX, K. (1965) *The German Ideology*, Lawrence & Wishart, London.

MARX, K. (1968) The Communist Manifesto, in *Selected Works*, Lawrence & Wishart, London.

MARX, K. (1970) *Das Kapital*, Lawrence & Wishart, London.

MARX, K. (1971) *A Critique of Political Economy,* Lawrence & Wishart, London.

MARX, K. (1973) *Gründrisse,* Penguin, Harmondsworth.

MARX, K. AND ENGELS, F. (1948) *Manifesto of the Communist Party* [1848], International Publishers, New York.

MARX, K. AND ENGELS, F. (1956) *The Holy Family,* Foreign Languages Publishers, Moscow.

MARX, K. AND ENGELS, F. (1967) Manifesto of the Communist Party, Taylor, A.J.P. (ed.), Penguin, Harmondsworth.

MAY, T. (1996) *Situating Social Theory,* Oxford University Press, Oxford.

MAYO, E. (1932) *Human Problems of an Industrial Civilization,* Macmillan, London.

MAYO, E. (1949) *Social Problems of an Industrial Civilization,* Routledge & Kegan Paul, London.

MCCLELLAND, D. (1961) *The Achieving Society,* Van Nostrand, Princeton.

MCCLELLAN, D. (1973) *Karl Marx: His Life and Thought,* Macmillan, London.

MCCLELLAN, D. (1975) *Marx,* Fontana, London.

MCCLELLAN, D. (1977) *Engels,* Fontana, Glasgow.

MCHUGH, P. (1974) On the Failure of Positive, in Douglas, J.D. (ed.), *Understanding Everyday Life: Towards the Reconstruction of Sociiological Knowledge*, Routledge & Kegan Paul, London.

MCINTYRE, (1970) *Marcuse,* Fontana.

MCKENZIE, R. (1964) *British Political Parties,* Mercury Books, London.

MCLOHAN, M. (1964) *Understanding Media: The Extensions of Man*, New American Library.

MCROBBIE, A. (1994) *Post-Modernism and Popular Culture*, Routledge, London.

MCROBBIE, A. (1996) Different Youthful Subjectivities, in Chambers, I. and Curtis, L. (eds.), *The Post Colonial Question: Common Skies, Divided Horizons*, Routledge.

MEAD, G.H. (1934) *Mind, Self and Society,* Chicago University Press, Chicago.

MEAD, G.H. (1938) *The Philosophy of the Act,* Chicago University Press, Chicago.

MEAD, M. (1950) *Male and Female,* Penguin, Harmondsworth.

MEAD, G.H. (1959) *The Philosophy of the Present,* Chicago University Press, Chicago.

MELTZER, B., PETRAS, J. AND REYNOLDS, L. (1975) *Symbolic Interactionism: Genesis, Varieties and Criticisms*, Routledge & Kegan Paul, London.

MERTON, R.K. (1957) Bureaucratic Structure and Personality, in *Social Theory and Social Structure*, 2nd edn.

MEYER, A.G. (1965) *The Soviet Political System,* Random House, New York.

MICHELS, R. (1911) *Political Parties,* Free Press, New York.

MILES, S. (2001) *Social Theory in the Real World,* Sage, London.

MILIBAND, R. (1969) *The State in Capitalist Society,* Weidenfeld & Nicolson, London.

MILLER, D.L. (1973) *George Herbert Mead,* University of Texas Press, Austin.

MILLETT, K. (1971) *Sexual Politics,* Abacus Books, London.

MILLS, C.W. (1951) *White Collar,* Oxford University Press, Oxford.

MILLS, C.W. (1956) *The Power Elite,* Oxford University Press, Oxford.

MILLS, C.W. (1958) *The Causes of World War III,* Simon & Schuster, New York.

MILLS, C.W. (1959) *The Sociological Imagination,* Oxford University Press, New York.

MILLS, C.W. (1960) *Listen Yankee: The Revolution in Cuba,* McGraw-Hill, New York.

MILLS, C.W. (1962) *The Marxists,* Dell, New York.

MINTZ, S.W. (1985) *Sweetness and Power: The Place of Sugar in Modern History*, Viking.

MITCHELL, J. AND OAKLEY, A. (EDS.) (1976) *The Rights and Wrongs of Women*, Penguin, Harmondsworth.

MITZMAN, A. (1969) *The Iron Cage: An Historical Interpretation of Max Weber*, Gnosset & Dunlop, New York.

MOMMSEN, W. (1974) *The Age of Bureaucracy: Perspectives on the Political Sociology of Max Weber*, Blackwell, Oxford.

MORGAN, D.H. (1986) Gender, in Burgess, R. (ed.), *Key Variables in Social Investigation*, Routledge & Kegan Paul, London.

MORRIS, J. (1974) *Conundrum*, Faber, London.

MORRIS, M.B. (1977) *An Excursion into Creative Sociology*, Columbia University Press, New York.

MURRAY, R. (1989) Fordism and Post-Fordism, in Hall, S. and Jacques, M. (eds.), *New Times and the Changing Face of Politics in the 1990s*, Lawrence & Wishart, London.

NELSON, D. (1980) *F.W. Taylor and the Rise of Scientific Management*, University of Wisconsin Press, Madison, WI.

NISBET, R.A. (1966) *The Sociological Tradition*, Heinemann, London.

O'DONNELL, M. (2001) *Classical and Contemporary Sociology: Theory and Issues*, Hodder & Stoughton, London.

OAKLEY, A. (1972) *Sex, Gender and Society*, Sun Books, Melbourne.

OAKLEY, A. (1981) *Subject Women*, Penguin, Harmondsworth.

ØRNSTRUP, H. (2000) George Simmel, in Andersen and Kaspersen (eds.), (2000).

OUTHWAITE, W. (1996) *Habermas: A Critical Introduction*, Polity Press, Cambridge.

OUTHWAITE, W. (1998) *Jürgen Habermas*, Ch. 15, Part II in Stones (ed.) (1998).

PAHL, R.E. (1965) *Urbs in Rure*, Weidenfeld & Nicolson, London.

PAMPEL, F.C. (2000) *Sociological Lives and Ideas: An Introduction to the Classical Theorists*, Macmillan, Basingstoke.

PARKIN, F. (1982) *Max Weber*, Tavistock, London.

PARKIN, F. (1992) *Durkheim*, Oxford University Press, Oxford.

PARSONS, G. (ED.) (1994) *The Growth of Religious Diversity in Britain from 1945*, Routledge.

PARSONS, T. (1939) *The Structure of Social Action*, McGraw-Hill, New York.

PARSONS, T. (1951) *The Social System*, Free Press, New York.

PARSONS, T. (1978) *Action Theory and the Human Condition*, Free Press, New York.

PARSONS, T. AND SHILS, E.A. (EDS.) (1951) *Towards a General Theory of Action*, Harvard University Press, Cambridge, MA.

PARSONS, T. AND SHILS, E.A. (EDS.) (1964) *Social Structure and Personality*, Free Press, New York.

PARSONS, T. AND SHILS, E.A. (EDS.) (1967) *Sociological Theory and Modern Society*, Free Press, New York.

PARSONS, T. AND SHILS, E.A. (EDS)(1971) *The System of Modern Societies*, Free Press, New York.

PARSONS, T. AND SHILS, E.A. (EDS.) (1977) *The Evolution of Societies*, Prentice Hall, Englewood Cliffs, NJ.

PEEL, J.D.Y. (1971) *Herbert Spencer: The Evolution of a Sociologist*, Heinemann, London.

PICKERING, M. (1993) *Auguste Comte: An Intellectual Biography*, Cambridge University Press, Cambridge.

PIORE, M. (1986) Perspectives on Labour Market Flexibility, *Industrial Relations*, 45 (2).

PIORE, M. AND SABEL, C. (1984) *The Second Industrial Divide*, Basic Books.

PIVCEVIC, E. (1970) *Husserl and Phenomenology*, Hutchinson, London.

PLUMMER, K. (1975) *Sexual Stigma*, Routledge & Kegan Paul, London.

POLLERT, A. (1988) Dismantling Flexibility, *Capital & Class* No.34.

POLLNER, M. (1991) Left of Ethnomethodology: The Rise and Decline of Radical Reflexivity, *American Sociological Review*, 56, 376–80.

PONTING, C. (1986) *Whitehall Tragedy and Farce: The Inside Story of How Whitehall Really Works*, Sphere Books.

POPPER, K. (1934) *The Logic of Scientific Discovery*, Hutchinson, London.

POPPER, K. (1945) *The Open Society and its Enemies*, Routledge & Kegan Paul, London.

POPPER, K. (1963) *Conjectures and Refutations, The Growth of Scientific Knowledge*, Routledge & Kegan Paul, London.

POPPER, K. (1972) *Objective Knowledge: An Evolutionary Approach*, Clarendon Press, Oxford.

POULANTZAS, N. (1973) *Political Power and Social Classes*, New Left Books, New York.

POULANTZAS, N. (1974) *Fascism and Dictatorship*, New Left Books, New York.

POULANTZAS, N. (1975a) *Classes in Contemporary Capitalism*, New Left Books, New York.

POULANTZAS, N. (1975b) *The Crisis of Dictatorships*, New Left Books, New York.

POULANTZAS, N. (1978) *State, Power and Socialism*, New Left Books, New York.

PUSEY, M. (1987) *Jürgen Habermas*, Tavistock, London.

RAY, L. AND REED, M. (1994) *Organizing Modernity: New Weberian Perspectives on Work Organization and Society*, Routledge, London.

REDFIELD, R. (1930) *Tepotzlan, a Mexican Village: A Study of Folk Life*, University of Chicago Press, Chicago.

REDHEAD, S. (1990) *The End of the Century Party; Youth and Pop Towards 2000*, Manchester University Press, Manchester.

REYNAUD, E. (1981) *La Sainte Virilité*, quoted in *Achilles Heel*, Nos 6 and 7, p. 62.

RITZER, G. (1993) *The McDonaldization of Society*, Pine Forge Press, Thousand Oaks, CA.

RITZER, G. (1996) *Sociological Theory*, 4th edn, McGraw-Hill, New York.

ROBERTSON, R. (1992) *Globalisation*, Sage.

ROBERTSON, R. AND TURNER, B.S. (EDS.) (1991) *Talcott Parsons: Theorist of Modernity*, Sage.

ROCK, P. (1979) *The Making of Symbolic Interactionism*, Macmillan, London.

ROETHLISBERGER, F.J., DICKSON, W.J. AND WRIGHT, H.A. (1939) *Management and the Worker*, Harvard University Press, Cambridge, MA.

ROOF, W.C. AND MCKINNAY, W. (1987) *American Mainline Religion*, Rutgers University Press, New Brunswick.

ROSE, A. (1967) *The Power Structure*, Oxford University Press, New York.

ROSE, D. AND MARSHALL, G. (1988) in Haralambos, M. (ed.) *Developments in Sociology*, Vol. 4, Causeway Press, Ormskirk.

ROSENFELD, E. (1974) Social Stratification in a Classless Society, in Lopreato, J. and Lewis, L.S. (eds.), *Social Stratification: A Reader*, Harper & Row, New York.

ROSENTHAL, R. AND JACOBSON, L. (1968) *Pygmalion in the Classroom*, Holt, Rinehart & Winston, New York.

ROSTOW, W.W. (1960) *The Stages of Economic Growth: A Non-Communist Manifesto*, Cambridge University Press, Cambridge.

ROWBOTHAM, S. (1979) The Trouble with Patriarchy, *New Statesman*.

RUIS (1986) *Marx for Beginners*, Unwin Paperbacks, London.

SACKS, H. (1965) Sociological Description, *Berkeley Journal of Sociology*, 8, 1–16.

SALAMAN, G. (1986) *Work*, Tavistock, London.

SCHEFF, T.J. (1984) *Being Mentally Ill: A Sociological Theory*, Aldine.

SCHMITT, R. (1997) *Introduction to Marx and Engels: A Critical Reconstruction*, Westview Press.

SCHUMACHER, E.E. (1973) *Small is Beautiful,* Abacus Books, London.

SCHUTZ, A. (1972) *The Phenomenology of the Social World,* Heinemann, London.

SCHUTZ, A. AND LUCKMANN, T. (1974) *The Structures of the Lifeworld,* Heinemann, London.

SCOTT, J. (1991) *Who Rules Britain,* Polity Press, Cambridge.

SEEMAN, M. (1959) On the Meaning of Alienation, *American Sociology Review,* 33, 46–62.

SEGEL, L. (1981) *Is the Future Female?* Virago, London.

SEIDLER, V.J. (1994) *Unreasonable Men: Masculinity and Social Theory*, Routledge, London.

SEIDMAN, S. (1996) *Queer Theory*, Blackwell, Oxford.

SEIDMAN, S. AND ALEXANDER, J.C. (EDS.) (2001) *The New Social Theory Reader: Contemporary Debates,* Routledge.

SELZNICK, P. (1966) *TVA and the Grassroots,* Harper, New York.

SERLE, J. (1972) Chomsky's Revolution in Linguistics, *New York Review of Books,* 18, 16–24.

SHARPE, R. (1980) *Knowledge, Ideology and the Politics of Schooling,* Routledge & Kegan Paul, London.

SHARROCK, W.W. AND ANDERSON, R. (1986) *The Ethnomethodologists,* Tavistock, London.

SIMMEL, G. (1971) The Metropolis and Mental Life, in Levine, D. (ed.), *Georg Simmel* [1903], Chicago University Press, Chicago.

SLATTERY, M. (1985) *Urban Sociology,* Causeway Press, Ormskirk.

SMITH, A. (1976) *The Body,* Penguin, Harmondsworth.

SMITH, D.E. (1993) *Texts, Facts and Feminity: Exploring the Relations of Ruling,* Routledge, London.

SMITH, G. (1988) The Sociology of Erving Goffman, *Social Studies Review*, January.

SMITH, S. (1984) *Reading Althusser*, Connell University Press.

SOKAL, A. AND BRICMONT, J. (1997) *Intellectual Impostures: Post Modern Philosophers' Abuse of Science*, Profile Books, London.

SPENCER, H. (1873) *The Study of Sociology*, King, London.

SPENCER, H. (1893–96) *The Principles of Sociology*, Vol. 1, Williams & Norgate, London.

STANFIELD, R. (1974) Kuhnian Scientific Revolutions and the Keynesian Revolution, *Journal of Economic Issues,* 8, 97–109.

STEGER, M.B. AND CARVER, T. (EDS.) (1999) *Engels after Marx*, Manchester University Press, Manchester.

STONES, R. (ED.) (1998) *Key Sociological Thinkers,* Macmillan, Basingstoke.

STRYKER, S. (1980) *Symbolic Interactionism: A Social Structural Version*, Benjamin/Cummings, Menlo Park, CA.

SWINGLEWOOD, A. (2000) *A Short History of Sociological Thought,* 3rd edn, Macmillan, Basingstoke.

TAYLOR, F.W. (1964) *Principles of Scientific Management* [1911], Harper, New York.

TAYLOR, J. (1979) *From Modernisation to Modes of Production*, Macmillan, Basingstoke.

THOMPSON, J.B. (1984) The Theory of Structuration: An Assessment of the Contribution of Anthony Giddens, in Thompson, J.B., *Studies in the Theory of Ideology*, Polity Press, Cambridge.

THOMPSON, K. (1982) *Emile Durkheim,* Tavistock, London.

THOMSEN, J.P.F. AND ANDERSEN, H. (2000) Neo-Marxist Theories, Ch. 11 Part II in Andersen and Kaspersen (eds.) (2000).

TIGER, L. AND FOX, R. (1972) *The Imperial Kingdom,* Secker & Warburg, London.

TOLSON, A. (1977) *The Limits of Masculinity,* Tavistock, London.

TÖNNIES, F. (1951) *Community and Society* [1887], Harper Row, New York.

TOURAINE, A. (1971) *The Post Industrial Society,* Random House, New York.

TURNER, B.S. (1985) Georg Simmel, in *Thinkers of the Twentieth Century,* Firethorn Press, London.

TURNER, B.S. (1992), *Max Weber: From History to Modernity,* Routledge.

TURNER, R. (ED.) *Ethnomethodology,* Penguin, Harmondsworth.

URRY, J. AND WAKEFORD J. (EDS) (1973) *Power in Britain,* Heinemann, London.

WALBY, S. (1990) *Theorising Patriarchy,* Blackwell, Oxford.

WARREN, B. (1980) *Imperialism: Pioneer of Capitalism,* New Left Books, London.

WALLERSTEIN, I. (1974) *The Modern World System,* Academic Press, London.

WALLERSTEIN, I. (1989) *The Modern World System III: The Second Era of Great Expansion of the Capitalist World Economy 1730–1840,* Academic Press.

WATERS, M. (1995) *Globalisation,* Routledge.

WEBER, M. (1958) *The Protestant Ethic and the Spirit of Capitalism,* Charles Scribner's Sons, New York [1905].

WEBER, M. (1968) *Economy and Society: An Outline of Intermediate Sociology,* Bedminister Press, New York [1921].

WEBSTER, F. (1995) *Theories of the Information Society,* Routledge.

WEEKS, J. (1986) *Sexuality,* Tavistock, London.

WEINSTEIN, D. AND WEINSTEIN, M.A. (1993) *Postmodern(ised) Simmel,* Routledge.

WIGGERSHAUS, R. (1994) *The Frankfurt School: Its History Theories and Political Significance,* Polity Press, Cambridge.

WILBY, P. (1979) Habermas and the Language of the Modern State, *New Society,* 22 March.

WILLIAMS, M. (ED.) (1986) *Society Today,* Macmillan, London.

WILLIAMS, R. (1973) *The Country and the City,* Chatto & Windus, New York.

WILLIS, P. (1990) *Common Culture: Symbolic Work at Play in the Everyday Cultures of the Young,* Oxford University Press, Oxford.

WILSON, B. (1966) *Religion in a Secular Society,* Watts, London.

WINCH, G. (ED.) (1983) 'Information Technology in Manufacturing Processes', cited in *Society Today/New Society,* 8 November 1985.

WIRTH, L. (1928) *The Ghetto,* University of Chicago Press, Chicago.

WIRTH, L. (1938) Urbanism as a Way of Life, *American Journal of Sociology,* 44, 1–24.

WOLLSTONCROFT, M. (1985) *A Vindication of the Rights of Women,* Penguin, Harmondsworth.

WOOD, S. (ED.) (1982) *The Degradation of Work? Skill, Deskilling and the Labour Process,* Hutchinson, London.

WORSLEY, P. (1982) *Marx and Marxism,* Tavistock, London.

YOUNG, M. AND WILMOTT, P. (1962) *Family and Kinship in East London,* Penguin, Harmondsworth.

ZIMMERMAN, D. (1978) Ethnomethodology, *American Sociologist,* 13, 5–15.

ZIMMERMAN, D. AND WIEDER, D.L. (1970) Ethnomethodology and the Problem of Order: Comment on Denzin, in Douglas, J. (ed.), *Understanding Everyday Life,* Aldine, Chicago.

Index